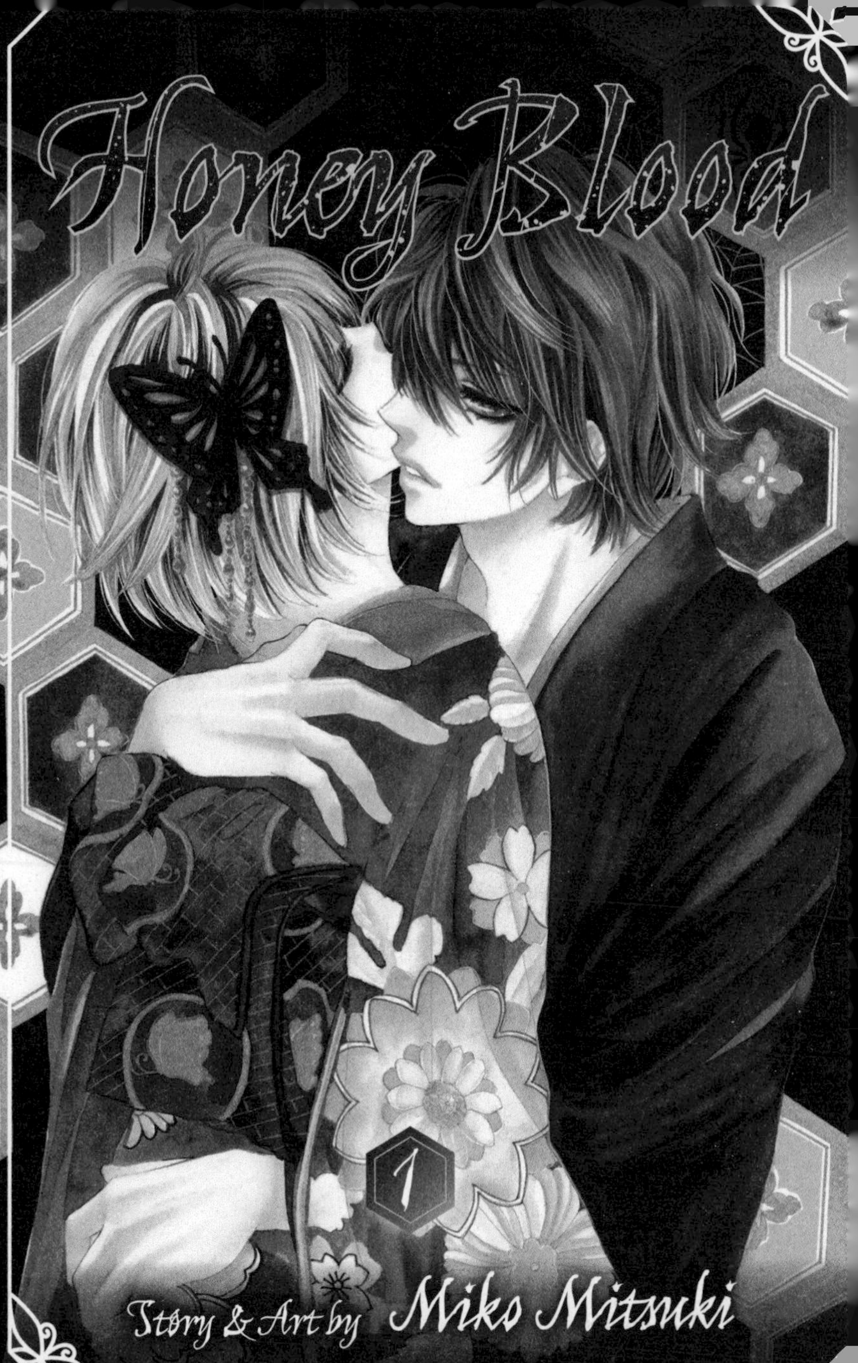
Honey Blood
1
Story & Art by Miko Mitsuki

Honey Blood

1

Contents

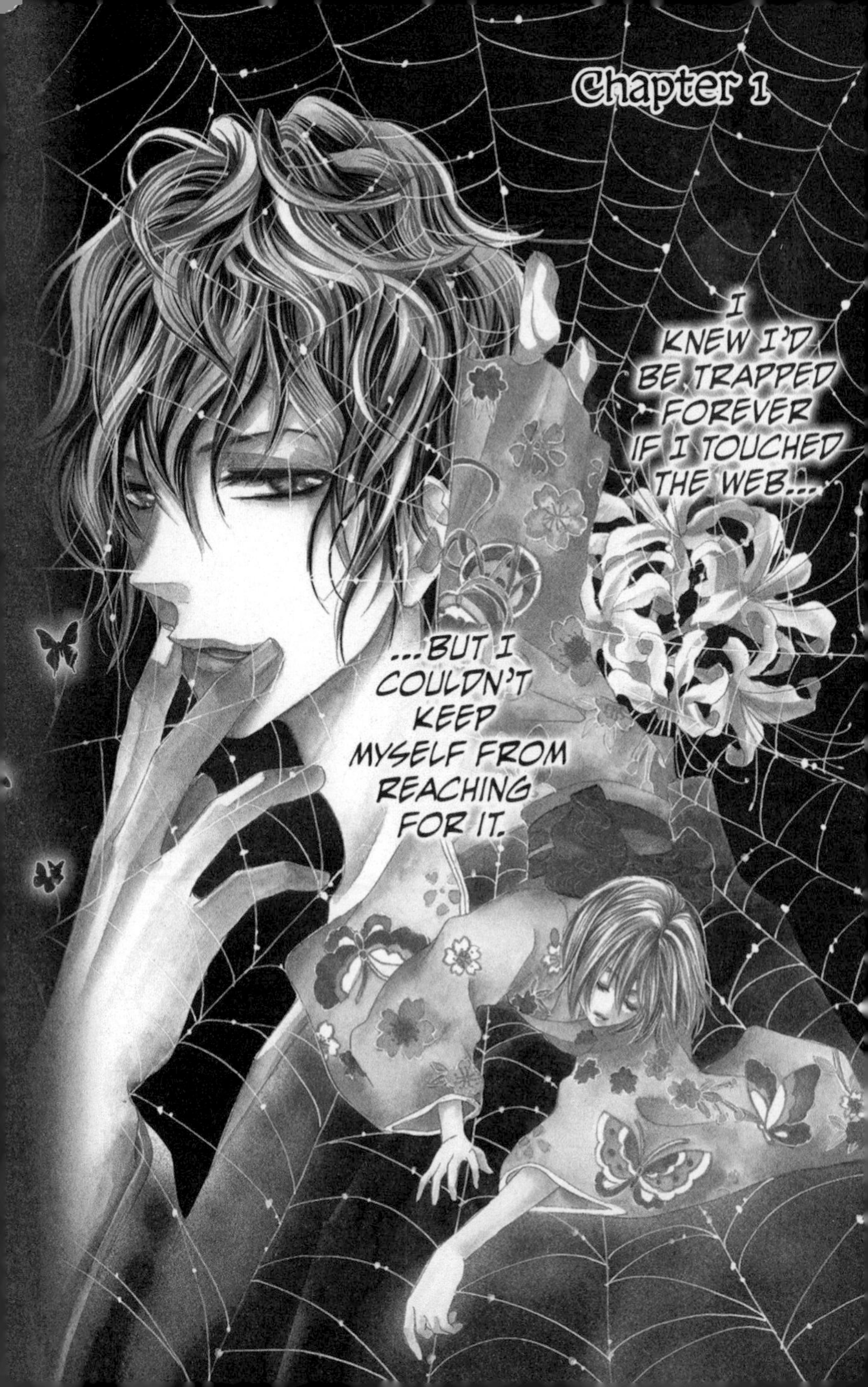
Chapter 1
I KNEW I'D BE TRAPPED FOREVER IF I TOUCHED THE WEB...
...BUT I COULDN'T KEEP MYSELF FROM REACHING FOR IT.

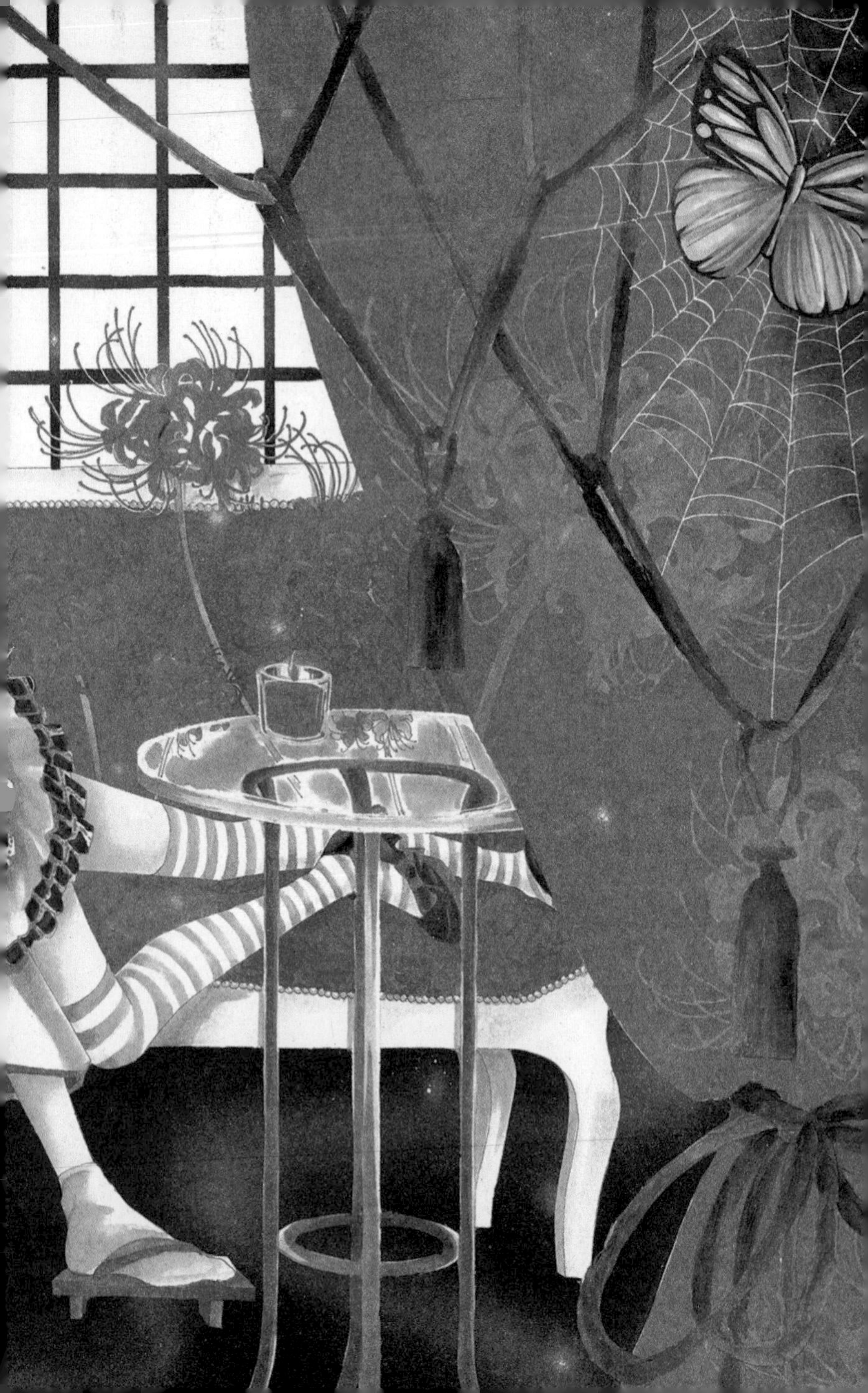

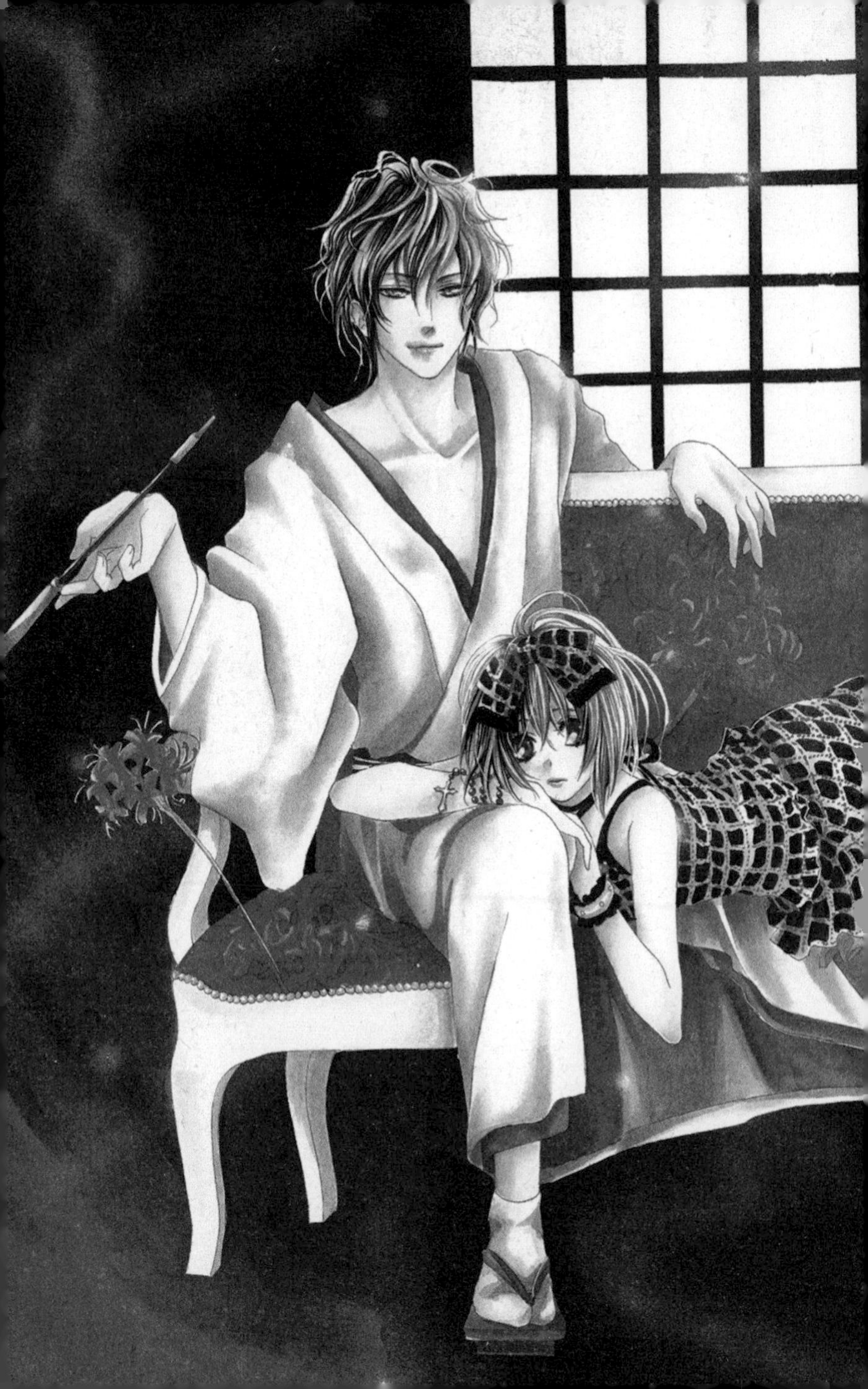

✿ Greetings! ✿

Thank you for buying this book! ♥

Welcome! Thanks for dropping in! ♥
This is my eighth book, and I'm thrilled
to meet you! I sincerely hope that you'll
enjoy this, even a little bit.

And now, on to the story!

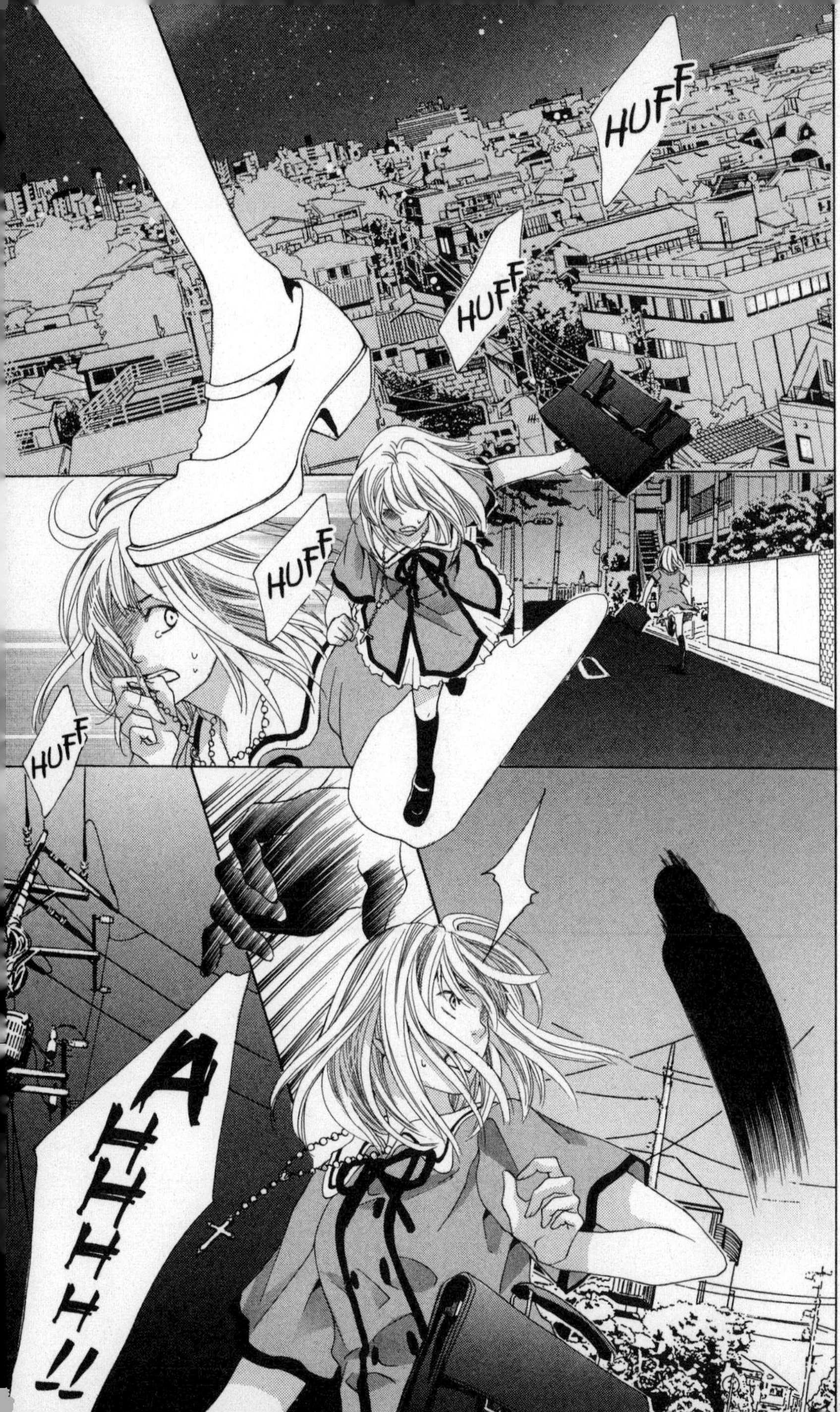
HUFF
HUFF
HUFF
HUFF
AHHHHH!!

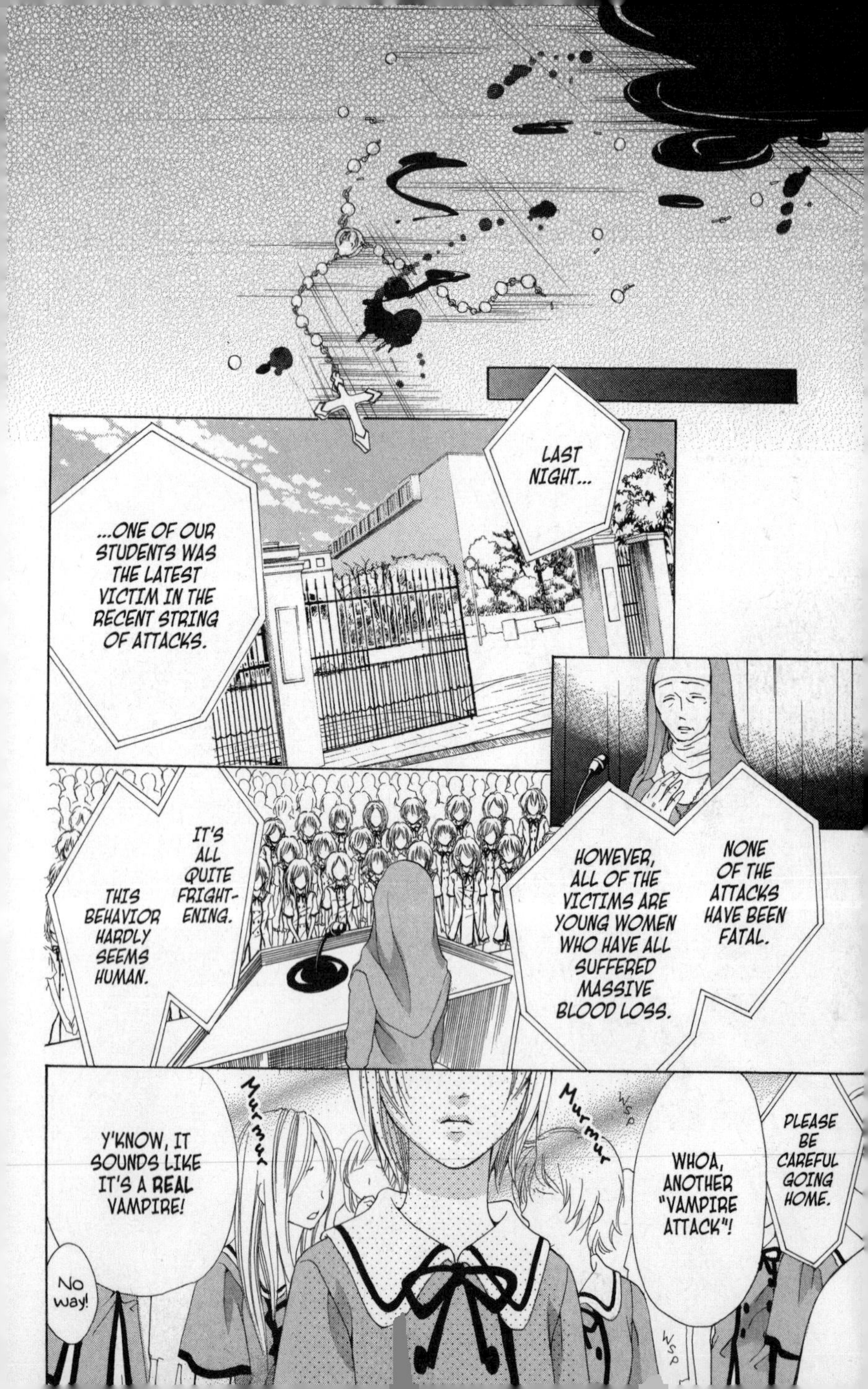
LAST NIGHT...
...ONE OF OUR STUDENTS WAS THE LATEST VICTIM IN THE RECENT STRING OF ATTACKS.
NONE OF THE ATTACKS HAVE BEEN FATAL.
HOWEVER, ALL OF THE VICTIMS ARE YOUNG WOMEN WHO HAVE ALL SUFFERED MASSIVE BLOOD LOSS.
IT'S ALL QUITE FRIGHTENING.
THIS BEHAVIOR HARDLY SEEMS HUMAN.
PLEASE BE CAREFUL GOING HOME.
WSP
WHOA, ANOTHER "VAMPIRE ATTACK"!
WSP
Murmur
Murmur
Y'KNOW, IT SOUNDS LIKE IT'S A REAL VAMPIRE!
No way!

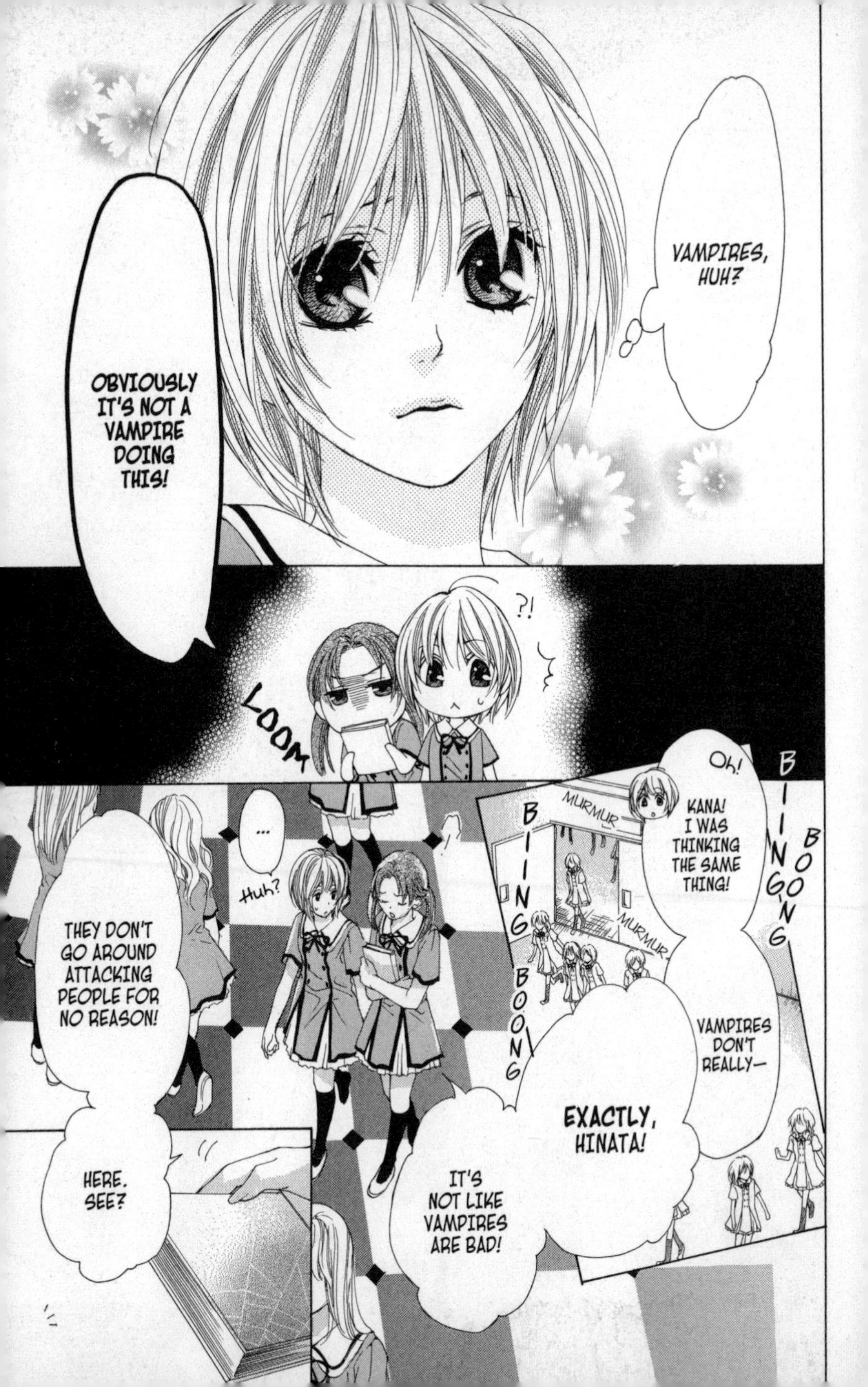
VAMPIRES, HUH?
OBVIOUSLY IT'S NOT A VAMPIRE DOING THIS!
?!
LOOM
BIING BOONG
Oh!
KANA! I WAS THINKING THE SAME THING!
MURMUR
MURMUR
BIING BOONG
VAMPIRES DON'T REALLY—
EXACTLY, HINATA!
...
Huh?
IT'S NOT LIKE VAMPIRES ARE BAD!
THEY DON'T GO AROUND ATTACKING PEOPLE FOR NO REASON!
HERE. SEE?

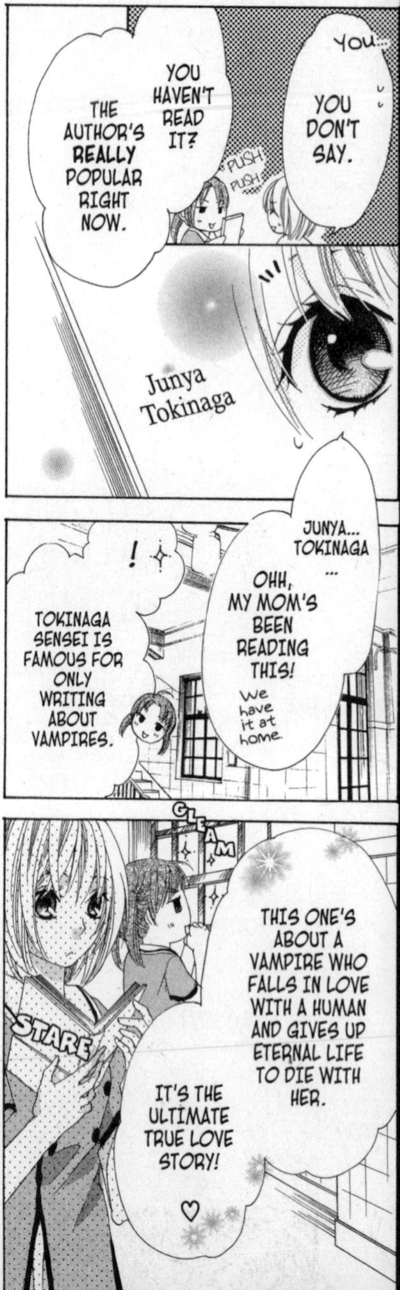
You...
YOU DON'T SAY.
PUSH PUSH
YOU HAVEN'T READ IT?
THE AUTHOR'S **REALLY** POPULAR RIGHT NOW.
Junya Tokinaga
JUNYA... TOKINAGA ...
OHH, MY MOM'S BEEN READING THIS!
We have it at home.
!
TOKINAGA SENSEI IS FAMOUS FOR ONLY WRITING ABOUT VAMPIRES.
GLEAM
THIS ONE'S ABOUT A VAMPIRE WHO FALLS IN LOVE WITH A HUMAN AND GIVES UP ETERNAL LIFE TO DIE WITH HER.
IT'S THE ULTIMATE TRUE LOVE STORY! ♡
STARE

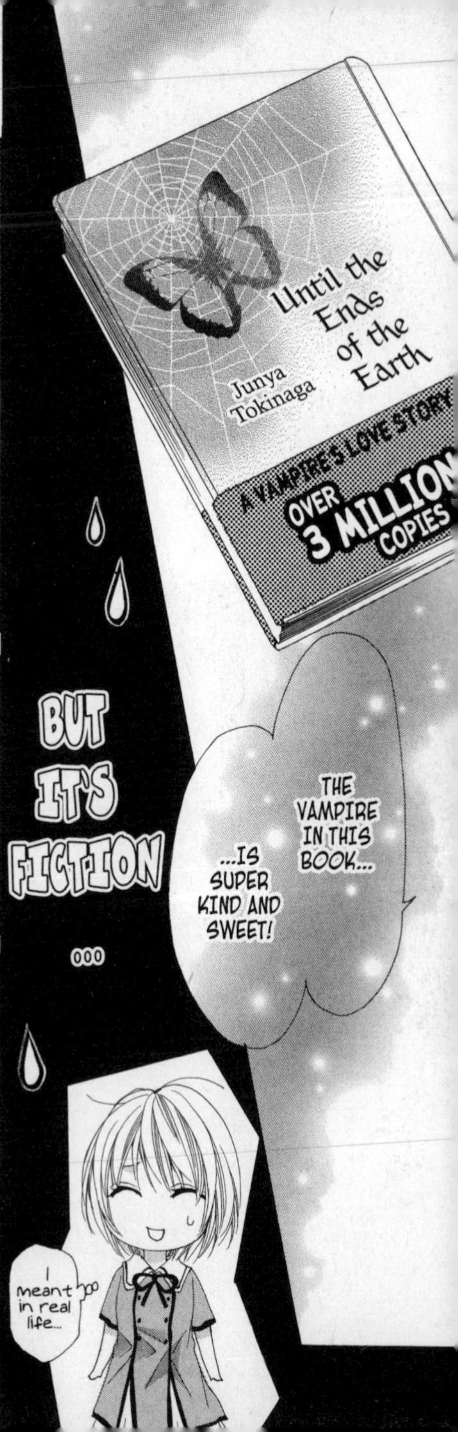
Until the Ends of the Earth
Junya Tokinaga
A VAMPIRE'S LOVE STORY
OVER 3 MILLION COPIES
THE VAMPIRE IN THIS BOOK...
...IS SUPER KIND AND SWEET!
BUT IT'S FICTION ...
I meant in real life...

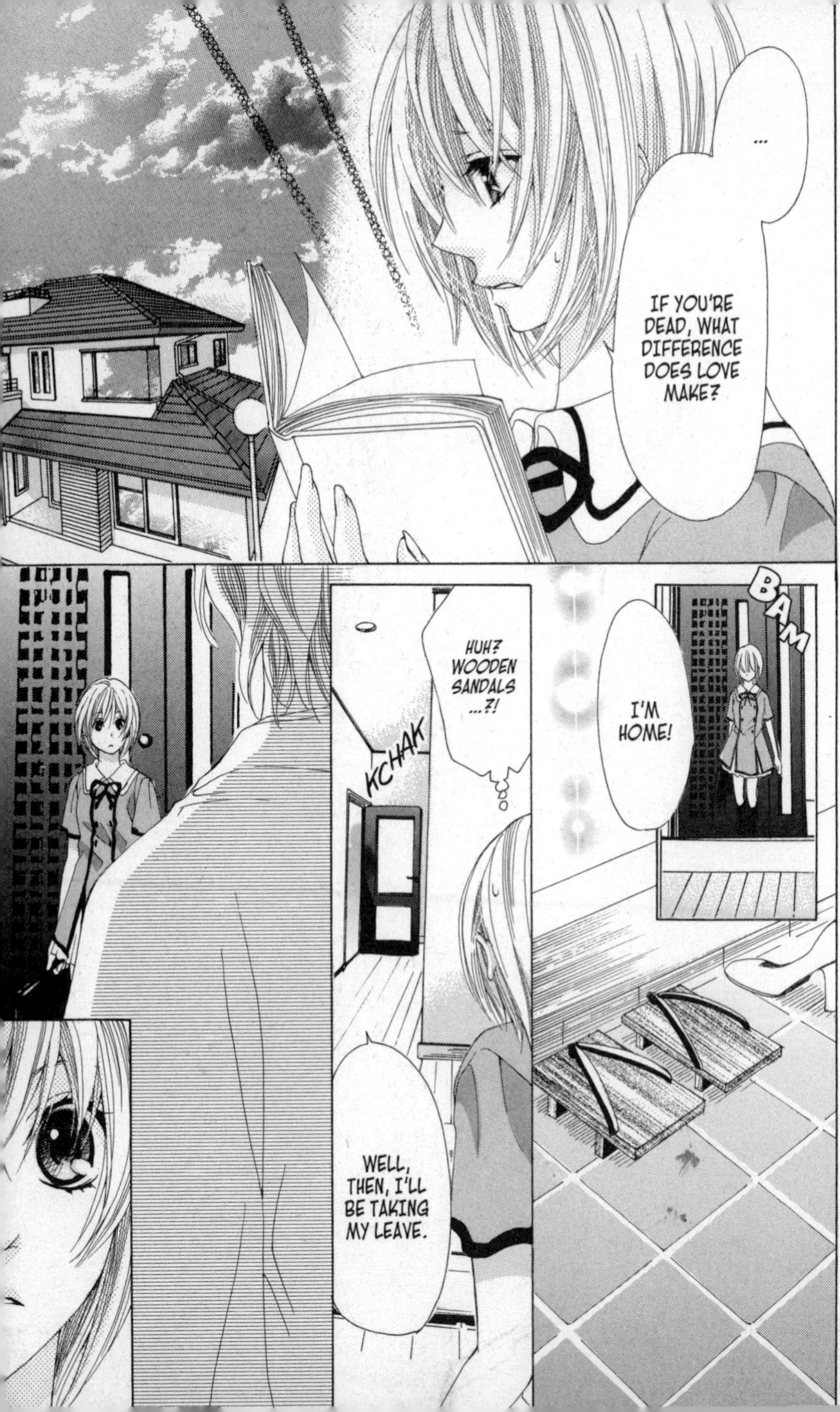
...
IF YOU'RE DEAD, WHAT DIFFERENCE DOES LOVE MAKE?
BAM
I'M HOME!
HUH? WOODEN SANDALS ...?!
KCHAK
WELL, THEN, I'LL BE TAKING MY LEAVE.

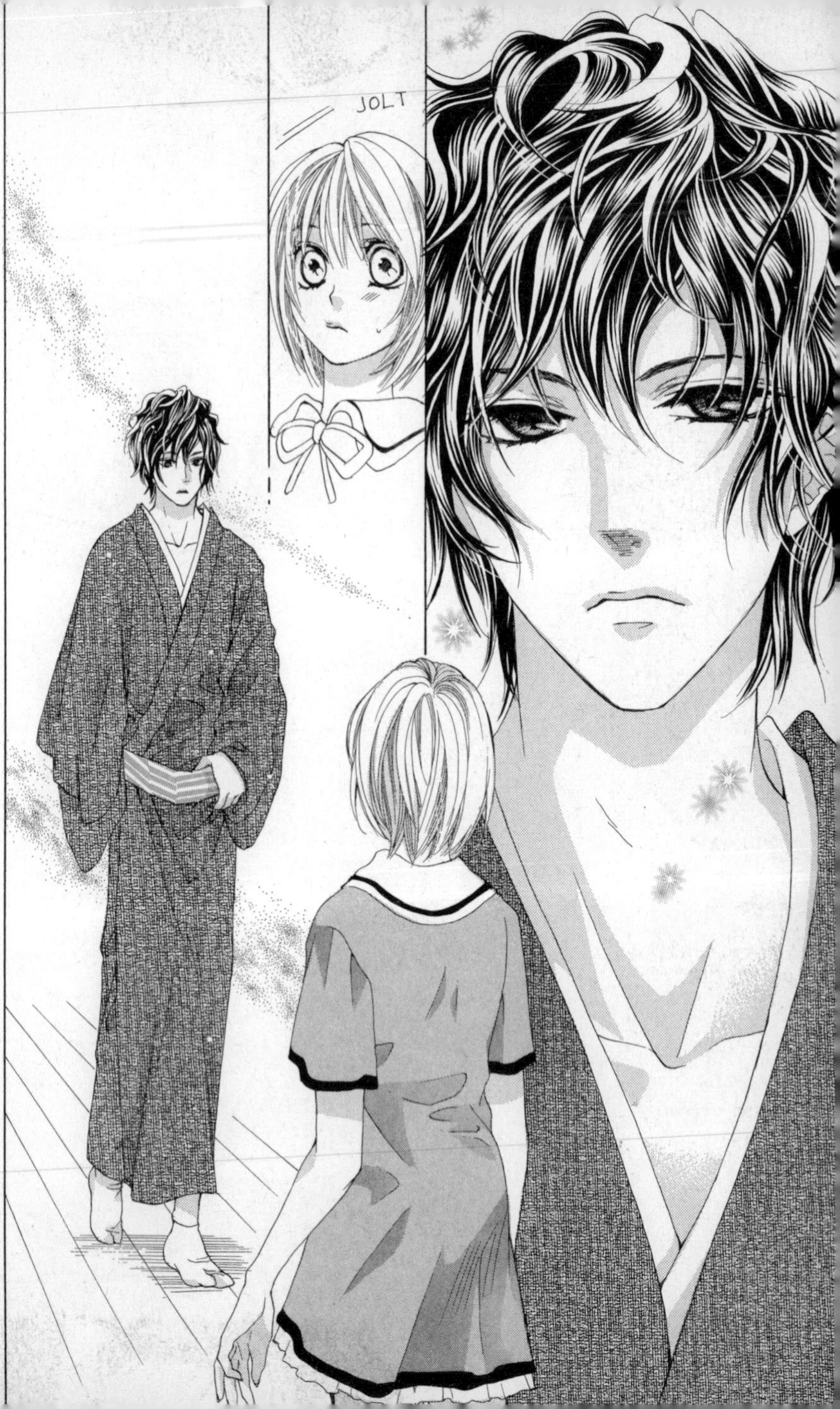
JOLT

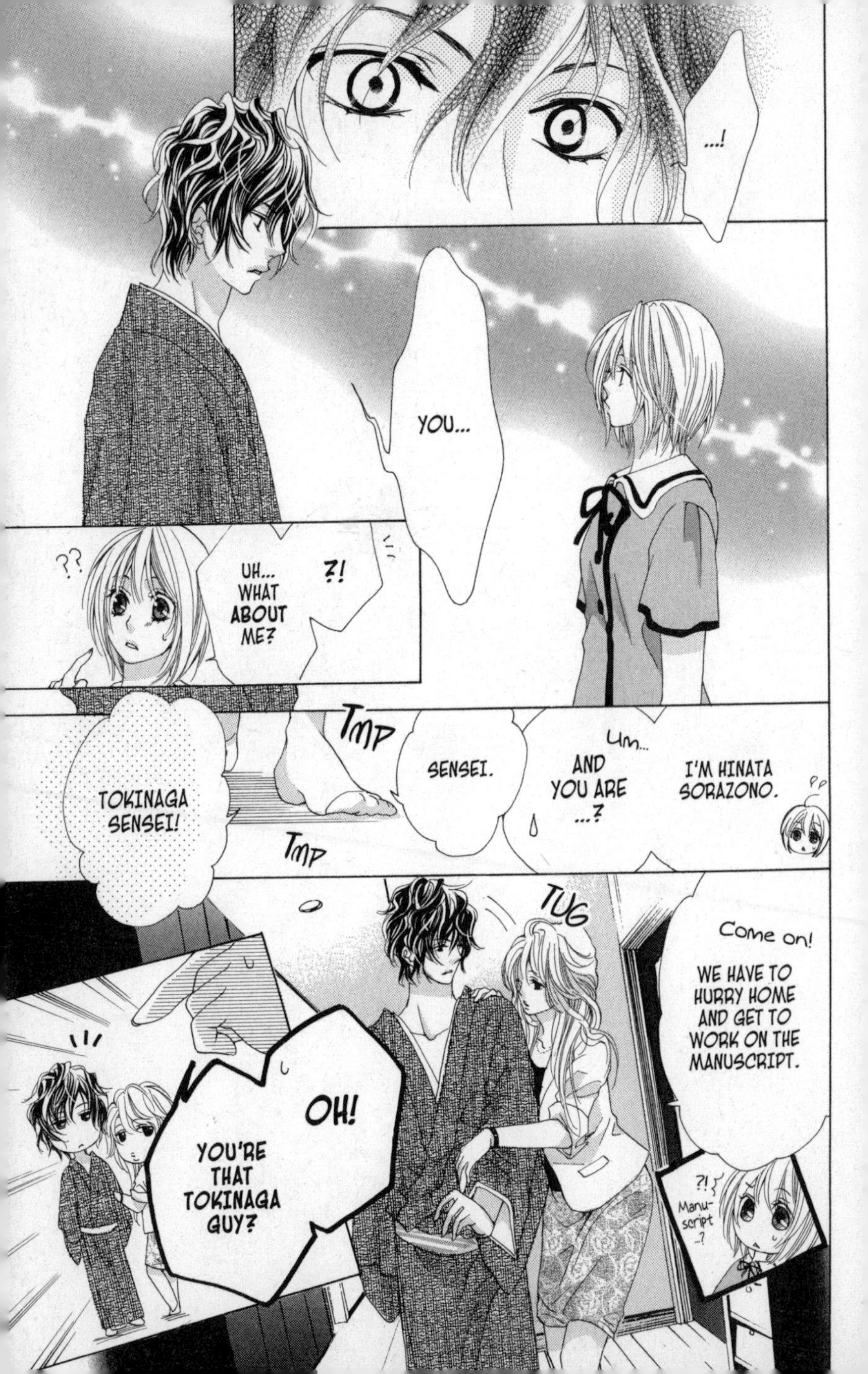
...!
YOU...
??
?!
UH... WHAT ABOUT ME?
I'M HINATA SORAZONO.
Um...
AND YOU ARE ...?
SENSEI.
TMP
TOKINAGA SENSEI!
TMP
Come on!
WE HAVE TO HURRY HOME AND GET TO WORK ON THE MANUSCRIPT.
?!
Manu-script ...?
TUG
OH!
YOU'RE THAT TOKINAGA GUY?

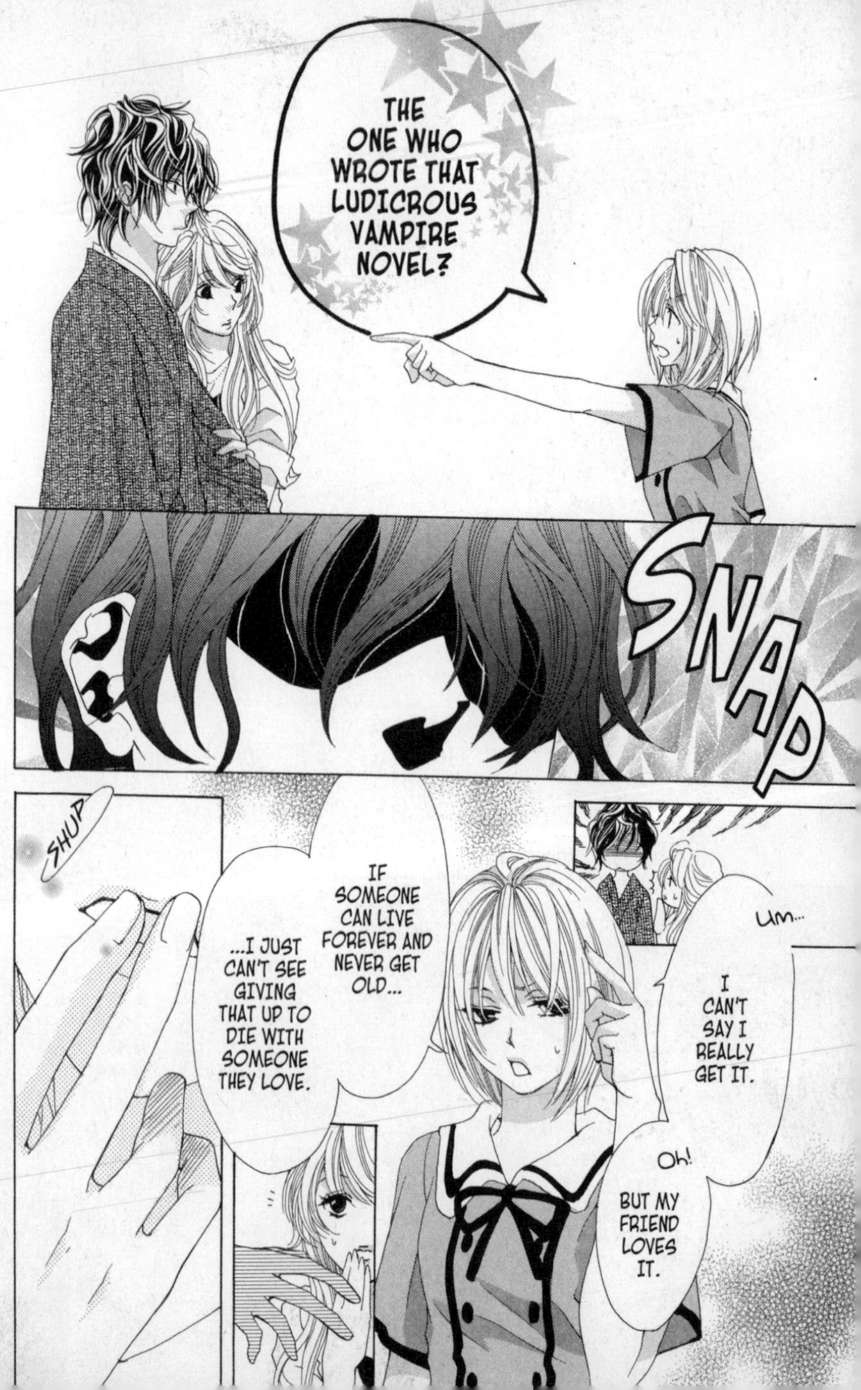
THE ONE WHO WROTE THAT LUDICROUS VAMPIRE NOVEL?
SNAP
Um...
I CAN'T SAY I REALLY GET IT.
Oh!
BUT MY FRIEND LOVES IT.
IF SOMEONE CAN LIVE FOREVER AND NEVER GET OLD...
...I JUST CAN'T SEE GIVING THAT UP TO DIE WITH SOMEONE THEY LOVE.
SHUP

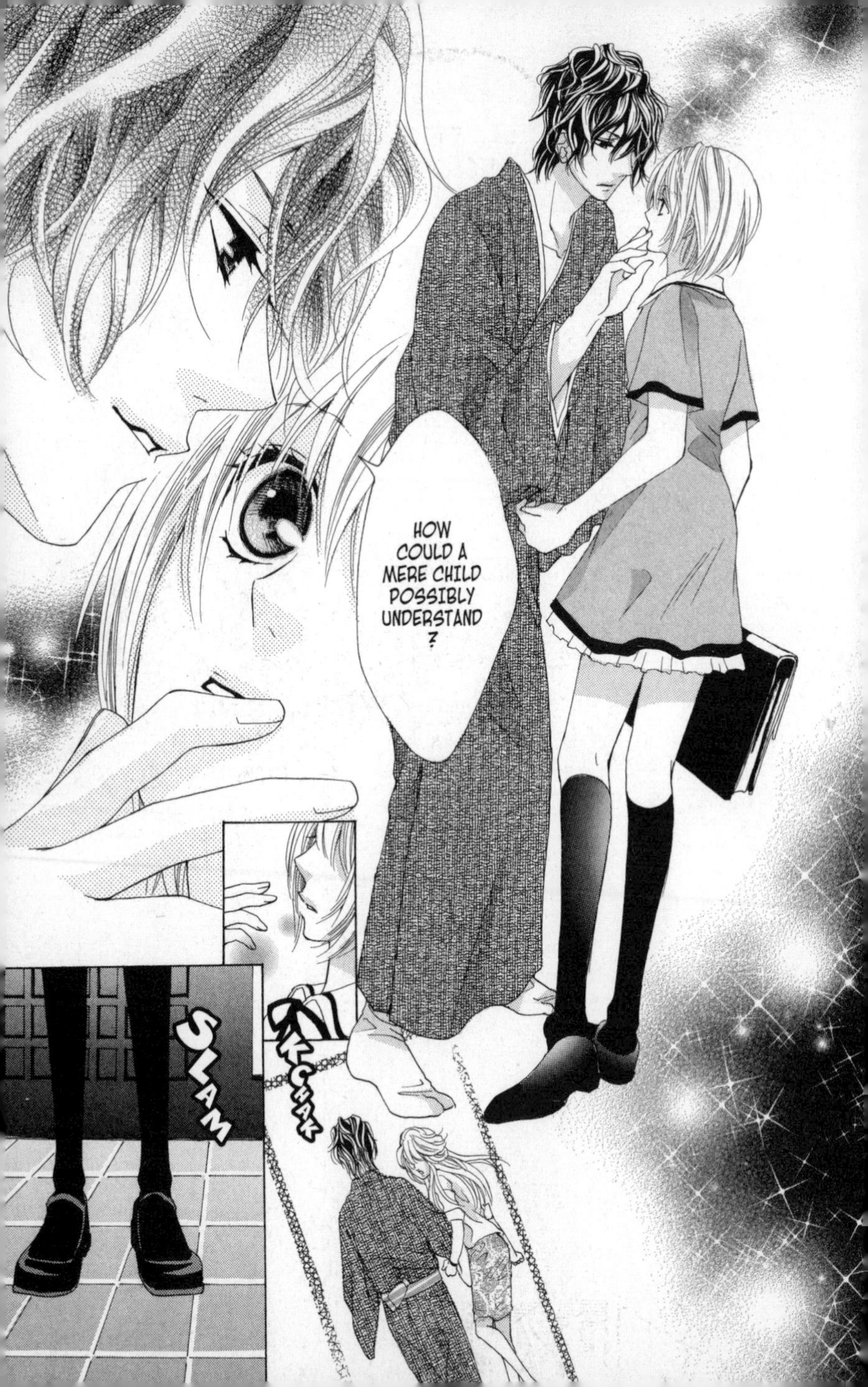
HOW COULD A MERE CHILD POSSIBLY UNDERSTAND?
KCHAK
SLAM

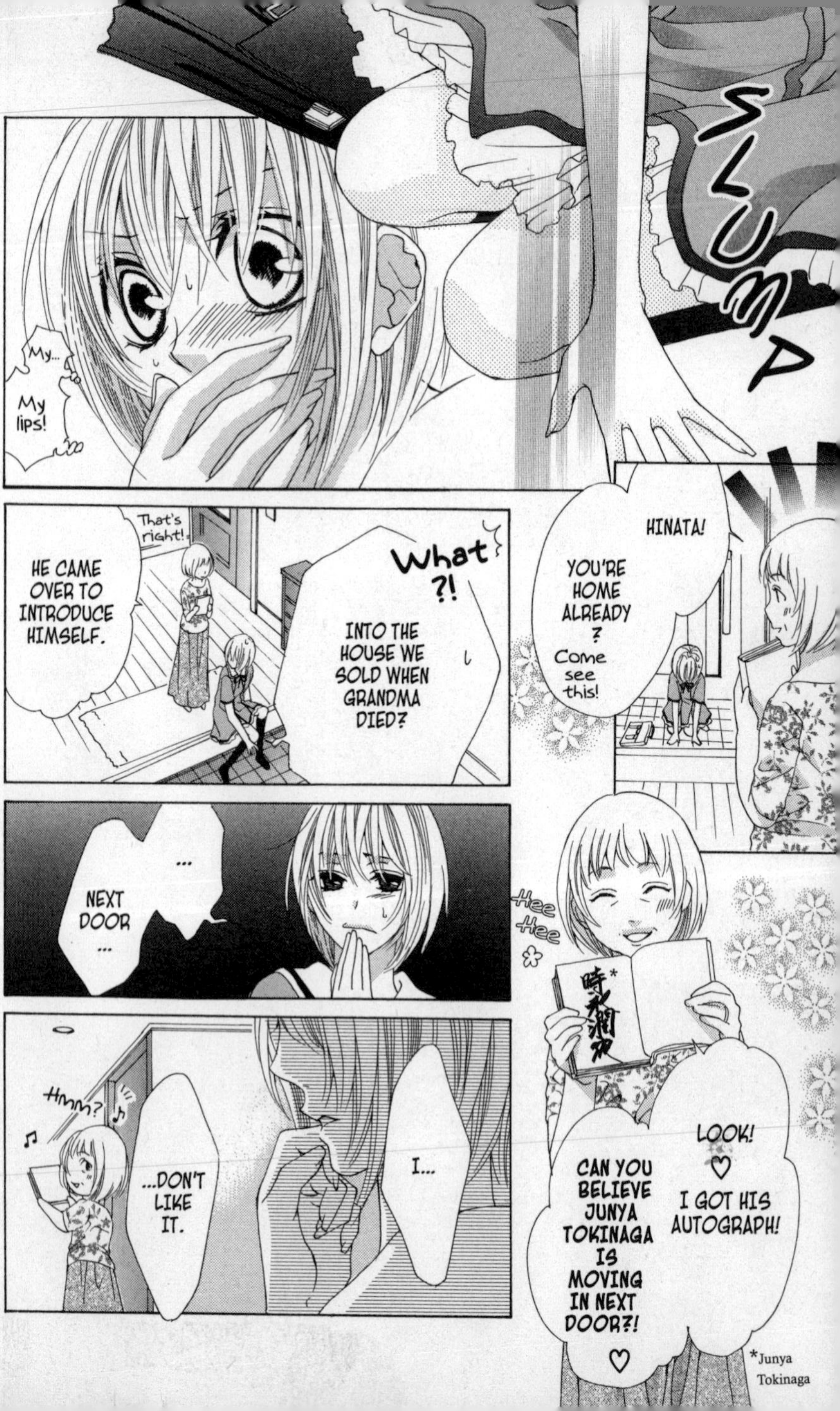
SLUMP
My...
My lips!
HINATA!
YOU'RE HOME ALREADY?
Come see this!
Hee Hee
時永潤也*
LOOK! ♡ I GOT HIS AUTOGRAPH!
CAN YOU BELIEVE JUNYA TOKINAGA IS MOVING IN NEXT DOOR?! ♡
What?!
INTO THE HOUSE WE SOLD WHEN GRANDMA DIED?
That's right!
HE CAME OVER TO INTRODUCE HIMSELF.
...
NEXT DOOR...
I...
Hmm?
...DON'T LIKE IT.
*Junya Tokinaga

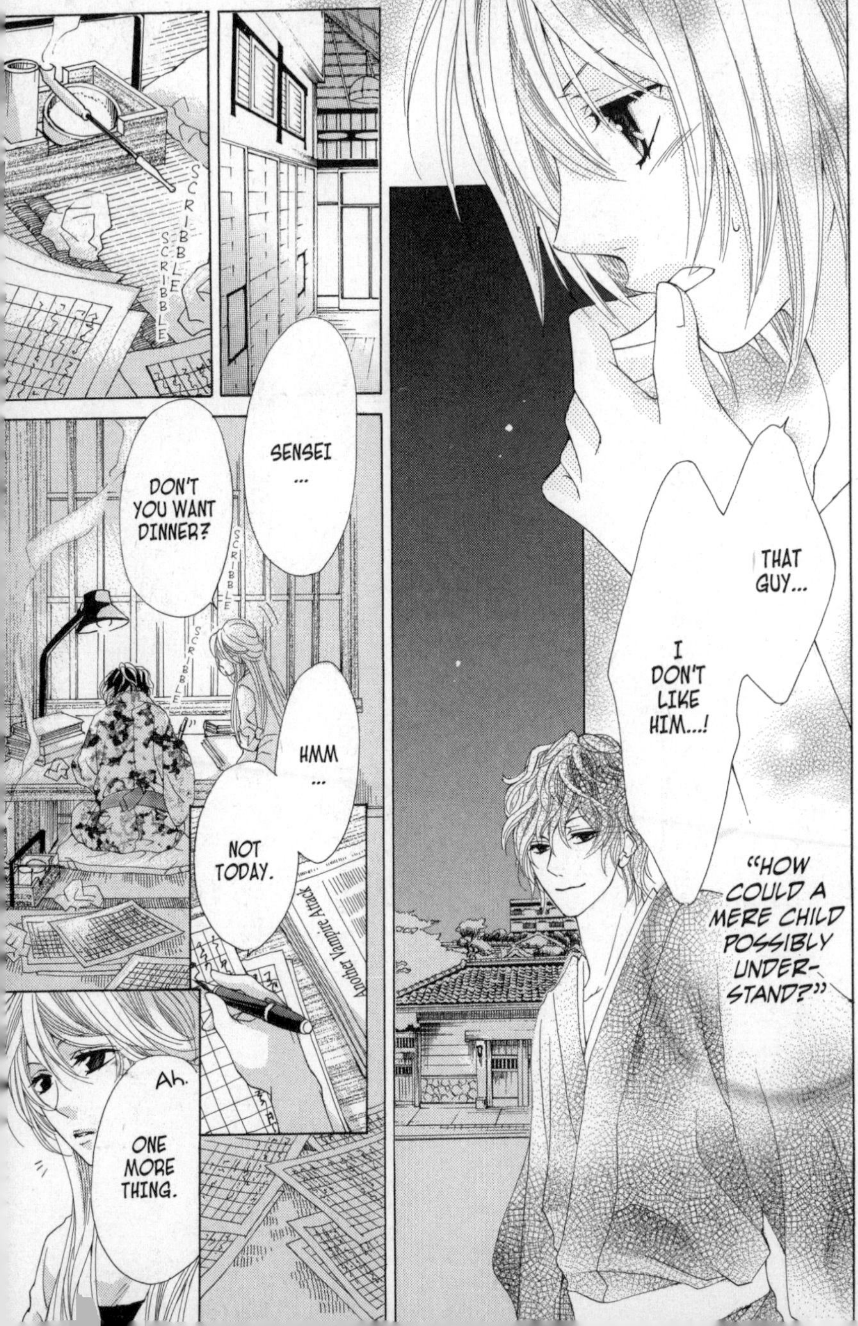
THAT GUY...
I DON'T LIKE HIM...!
"HOW COULD A MERE CHILD POSSIBLY UNDER-STAND?"
SCRIBBLE SCRIBBLE
SENSEI...
DON'T YOU WANT DINNER?
SCRIBBLE SCRIBBLE
HMM...
NOT TODAY.
Another Vampire Attack
Ah.
ONE MORE THING.

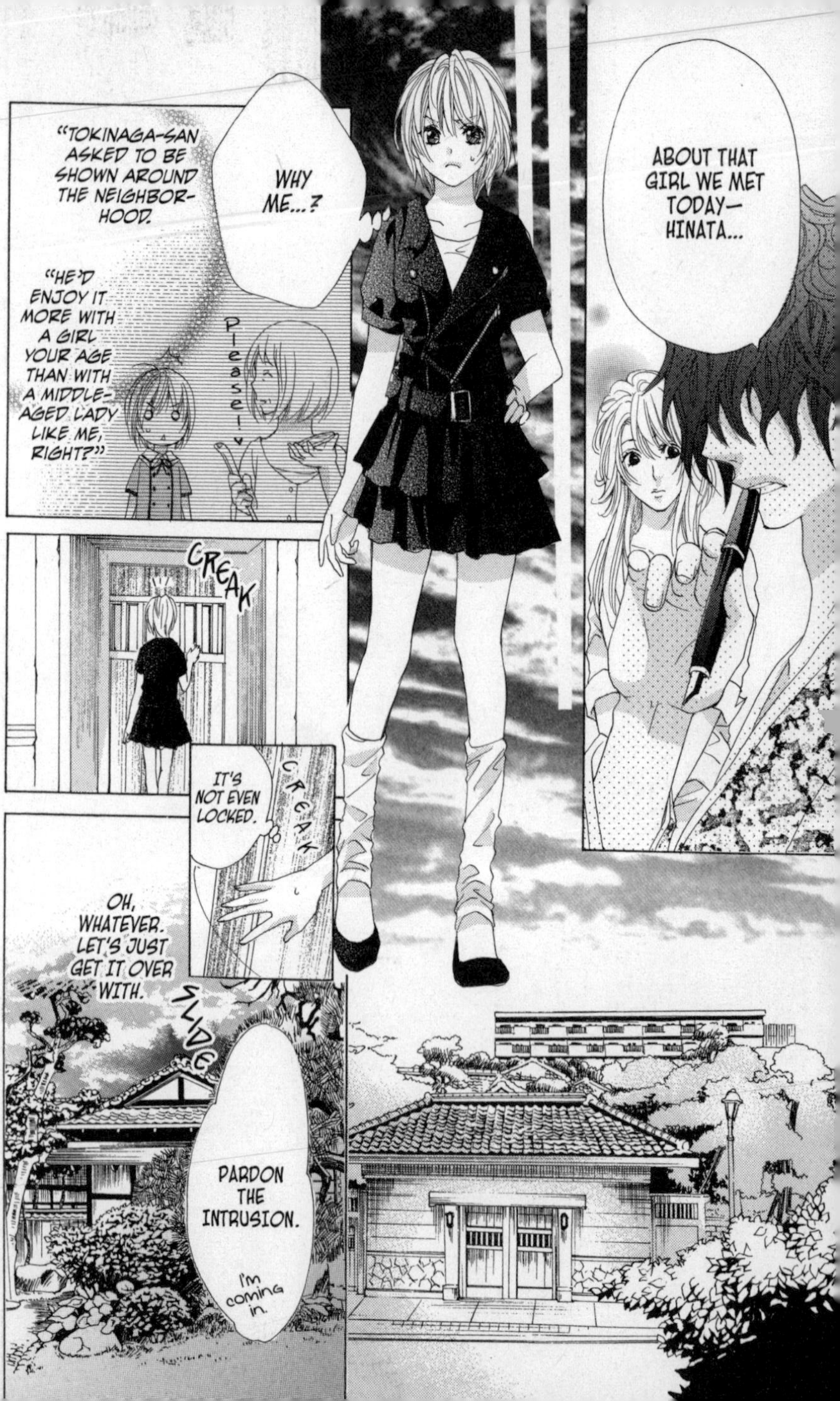
ABOUT THAT GIRL WE MET TODAY— HINATA...
WHY ME...?
"TOKINAGA-SAN ASKED TO BE SHOWN AROUND THE NEIGHBOR-HOOD.
"HE'D ENJOY IT MORE WITH A GIRL YOUR AGE THAN WITH A MIDDLE-AGED LADY LIKE ME, RIGHT?"
Please!♥
CREAK
CREAK
IT'S NOT EVEN LOCKED.
OH, WHATEVER. LET'S JUST GET IT OVER WITH.
SLIDE
PARDON THE INTRUSION.
I'm coming in.

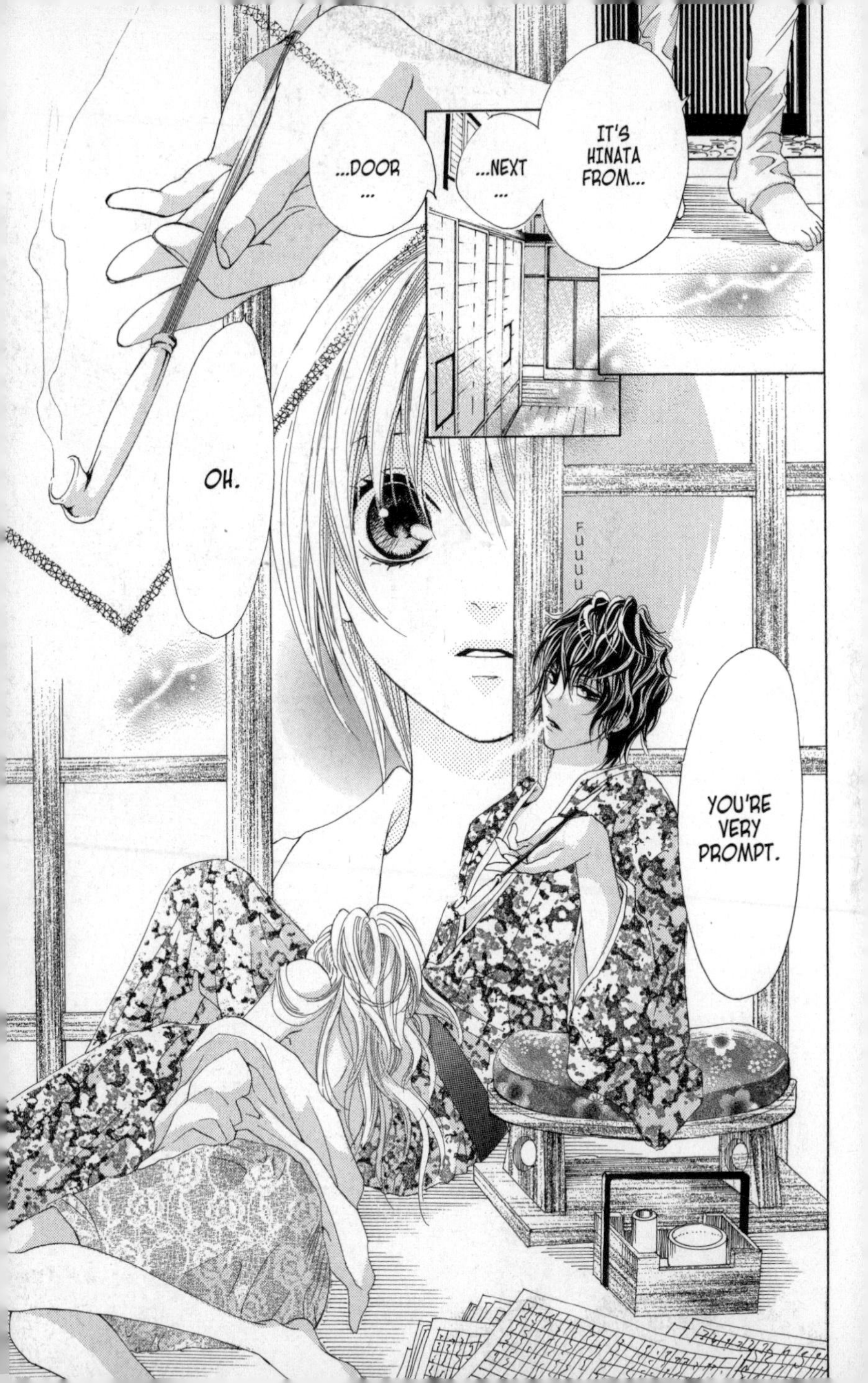
IT'S HINATA FROM...
...NEXT ...
...DOOR ...
OH.
FUUUU
YOU'RE VERY PROMPT.

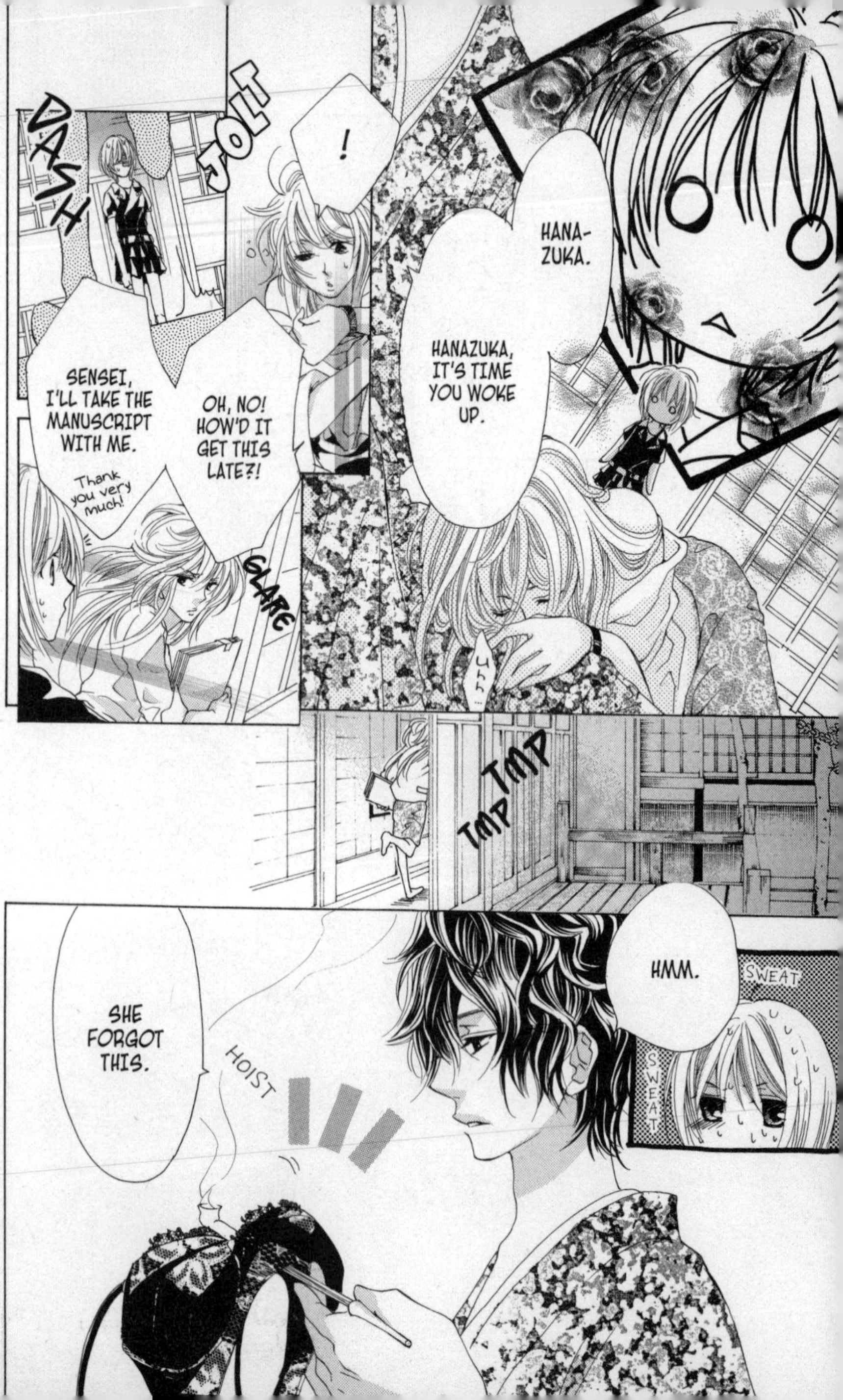
HANA-ZUKA.
HANAZUKA, IT'S TIME YOU WOKE UP.
Uhh...
!
JOLT
OH, NO! HOW'D IT GET THIS LATE?!
DASH
SENSEI, I'LL TAKE THE MANUSCRIPT WITH ME.
Thank you very much!
GLARE
TMP TMP
HMM.
SWEAT
SWEAT
SHE FORGOT THIS.
HOIST

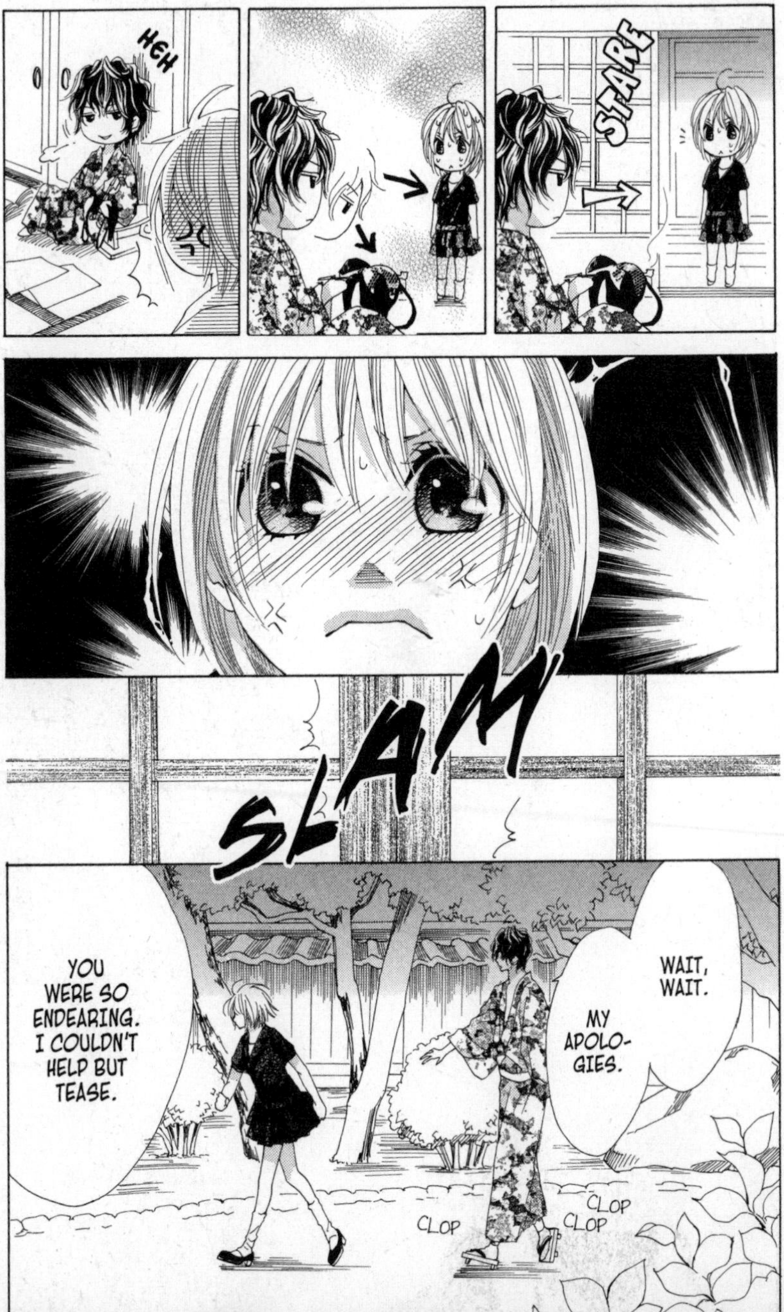
STARE
HEH
SLAM
WAIT, WAIT.
MY APOLO-GIES.
CLOP CLOP
CLOP
YOU WERE SO ENDEARING. I COULDN'T HELP BUT TEASE.

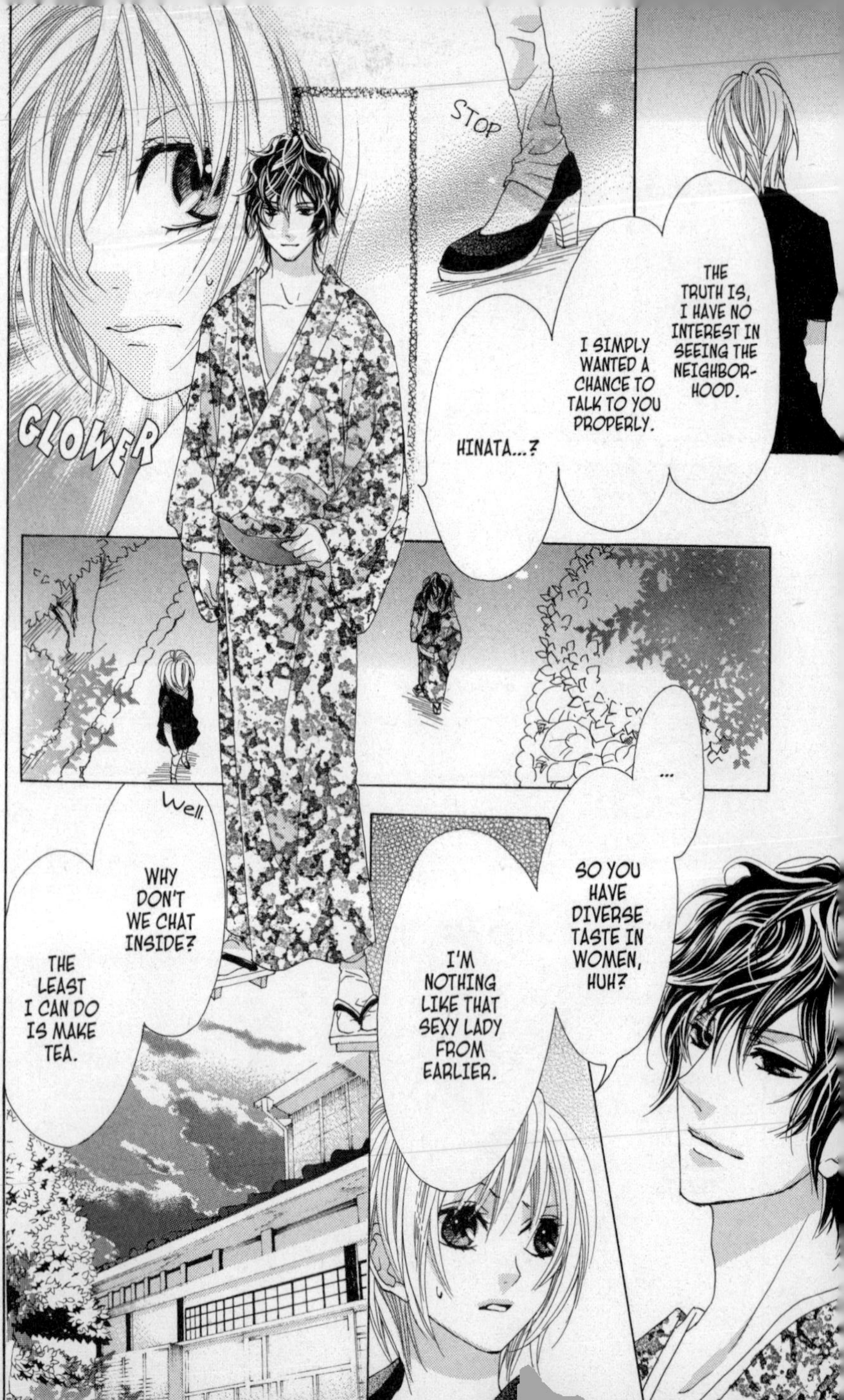
STOP
THE TRUTH IS, I HAVE NO INTEREST IN SEEING THE NEIGHBORHOOD.
I SIMPLY WANTED A CHANCE TO TALK TO YOU PROPERLY.
HINATA...?
GLOWER
...
SO YOU HAVE DIVERSE TASTE IN WOMEN, HUH?
I'M NOTHING LIKE THAT SEXY LADY FROM EARLIER.
Well.
WHY DON'T WE CHAT INSIDE?
THE LEAST I CAN DO IS MAKE TEA.

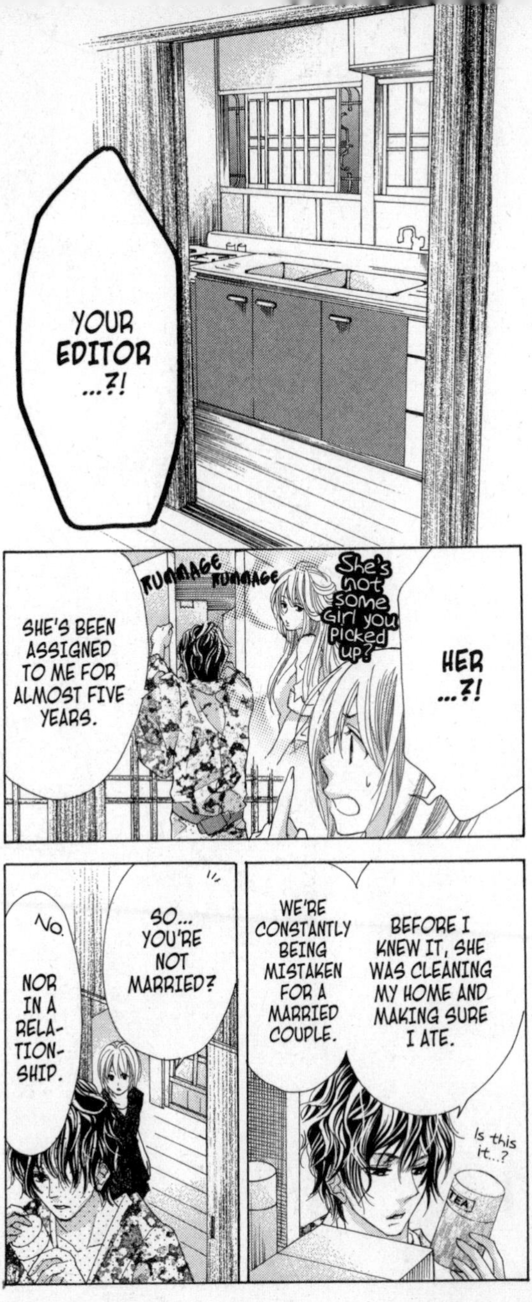
YOUR EDITOR ...?!
HER ...?!
She's not some girl you picked up?
SHE'S BEEN ASSIGNED TO ME FOR ALMOST FIVE YEARS.
RUMMAGE RUMMAGE
BEFORE I KNEW IT, SHE WAS CLEANING MY HOME AND MAKING SURE I ATE.
WE'RE CONSTANTLY BEING MISTAKEN FOR A MARRIED COUPLE.
Is this it...?
SO... YOU'RE NOT MARRIED?
No.
NOR IN A RELA-TION-SHIP.

Small Talk

①

Let me formally introduce myself! I'm Miko Mitsuki. I'm so grateful to you for buying this book and letting people see you take it to the cashier, even with an embarrassing title like *Honey Blood*.

A friend of mine said that this series doesn't fit in with the other titles that run in *Sho-Comi*, for a variety of reasons...
But I still love it.

I hope you enjoy it. I'll be so pleased if you do!

Every time I'm confronted with this empty third of a page to fill up, I find myself at a loss for words.

I don't know what readers might want to see here! Can anyone make suggestions?

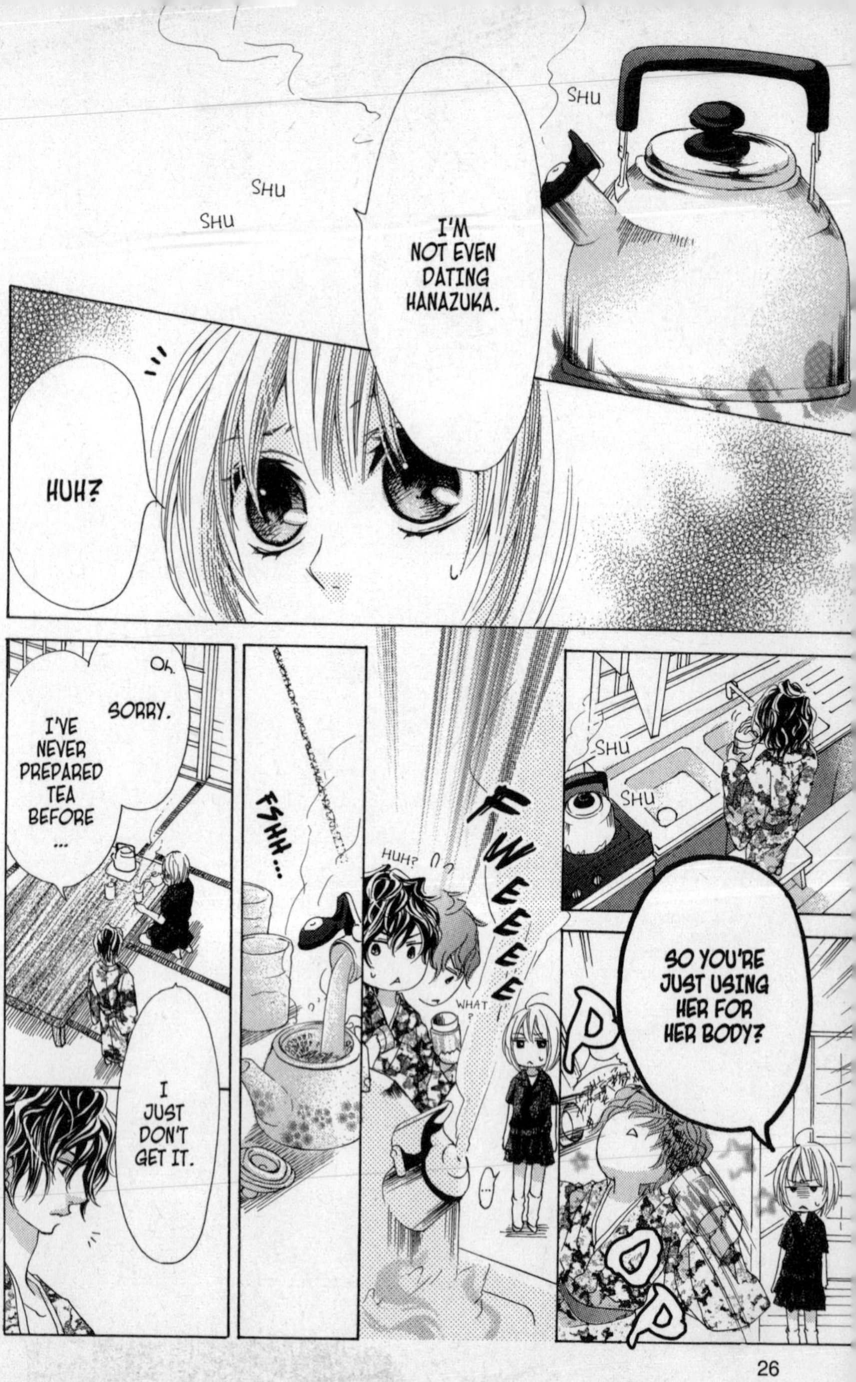
SHU
SHU
SHU
I'M NOT EVEN DATING HANAZUKA.
!!
HUH?
SHU
SHU
SO YOU'RE JUST USING HER FOR HER BODY?
POP
POP
POP
FWEEEEE
HUH?
WHAT?
...
FSHH...
Oh.
SORRY.
I'VE NEVER PREPARED TEA BEFORE...
I JUST DON'T GET IT.

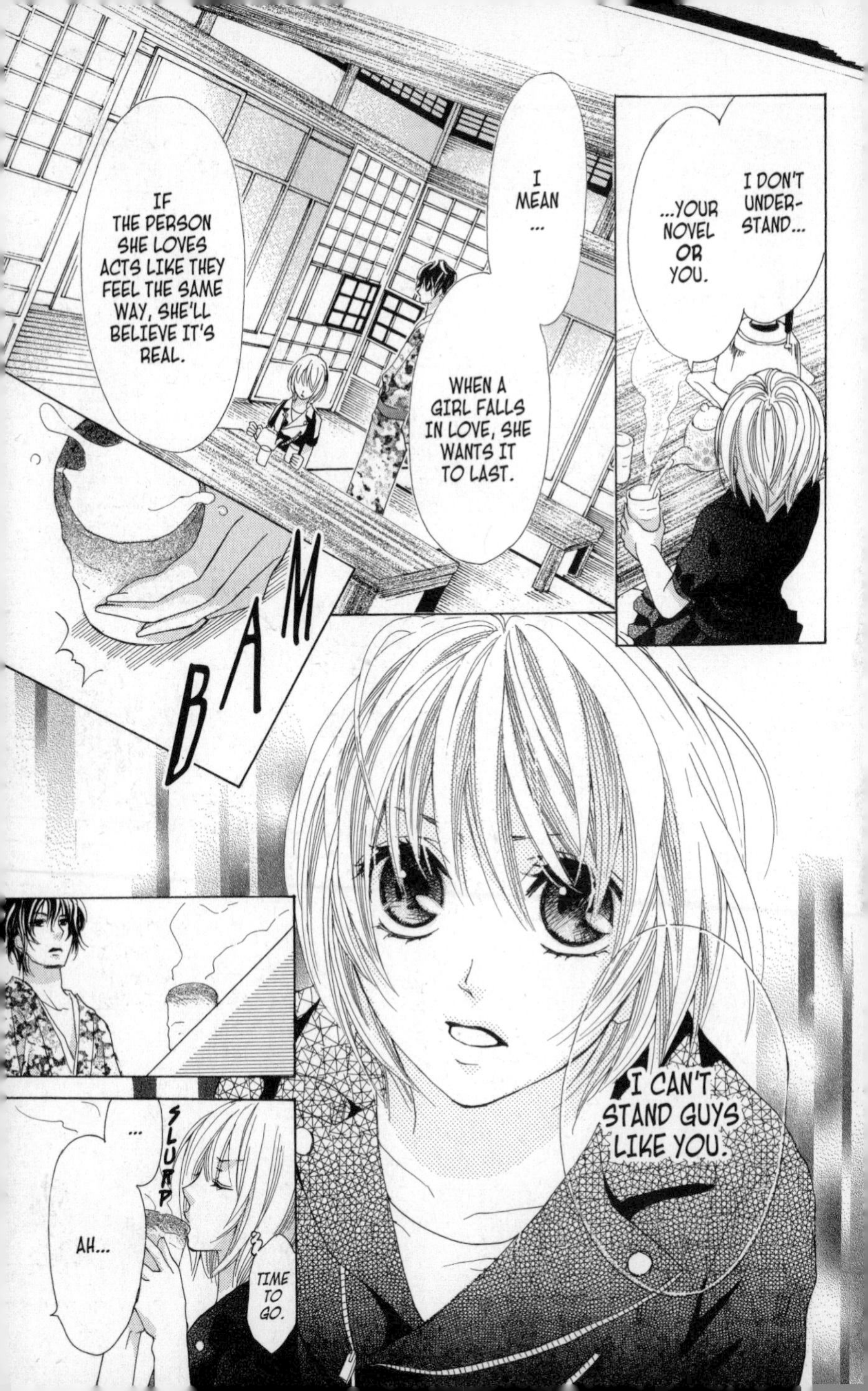
I DON'T UNDERSTAND...
...YOUR NOVEL OR YOU.
I MEAN ...
WHEN A GIRL FALLS IN LOVE, SHE WANTS IT TO LAST.
IF THE PERSON SHE LOVES ACTS LIKE THEY FEEL THE SAME WAY, SHE'LL BELIEVE IT'S REAL.
BAM
I CAN'T STAND GUYS LIKE YOU.
SLURP
...
AH...
TIME TO GO.

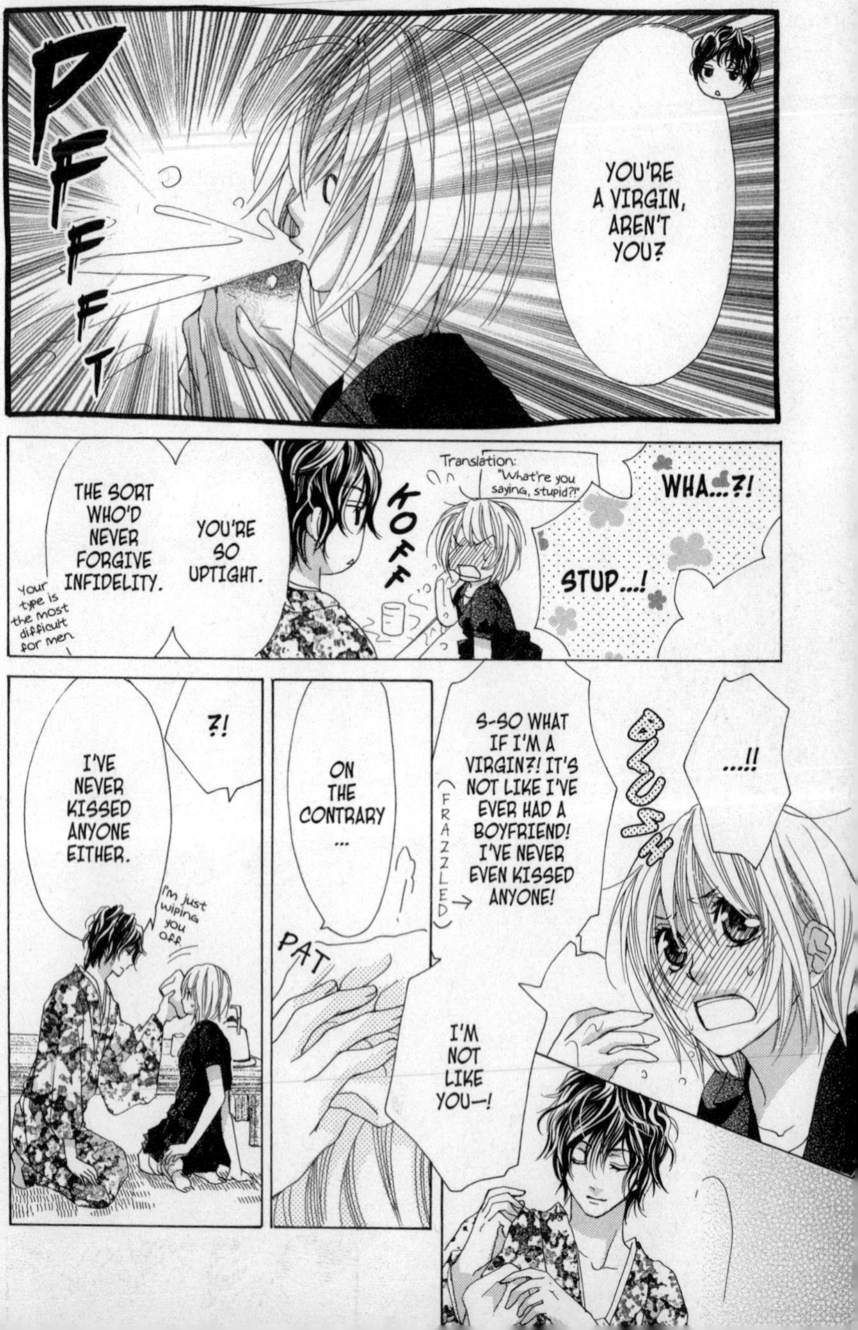

YOU'RE A VIRGIN, AREN'T YOU?
PFFFFT
WHA...?!
STUP...!
Translation: "What're you saying, stupid?!"
KOFF
YOU'RE SO UPTIGHT.
THE SORT WHO'D NEVER FORGIVE INFIDELITY.
Your type is the most difficult for men.
...!!
BLUSH
S-SO WHAT IF I'M A VIRGIN?! IT'S NOT LIKE I'VE EVER HAD A BOYFRIEND! I'VE NEVER EVEN KISSED ANYONE!
(FRAZZLED)
I'M NOT LIKE YOU—!
ON THE CONTRARY...
PAT
?!
I'VE NEVER KISSED ANYONE EITHER.
I'm just wiping you off.

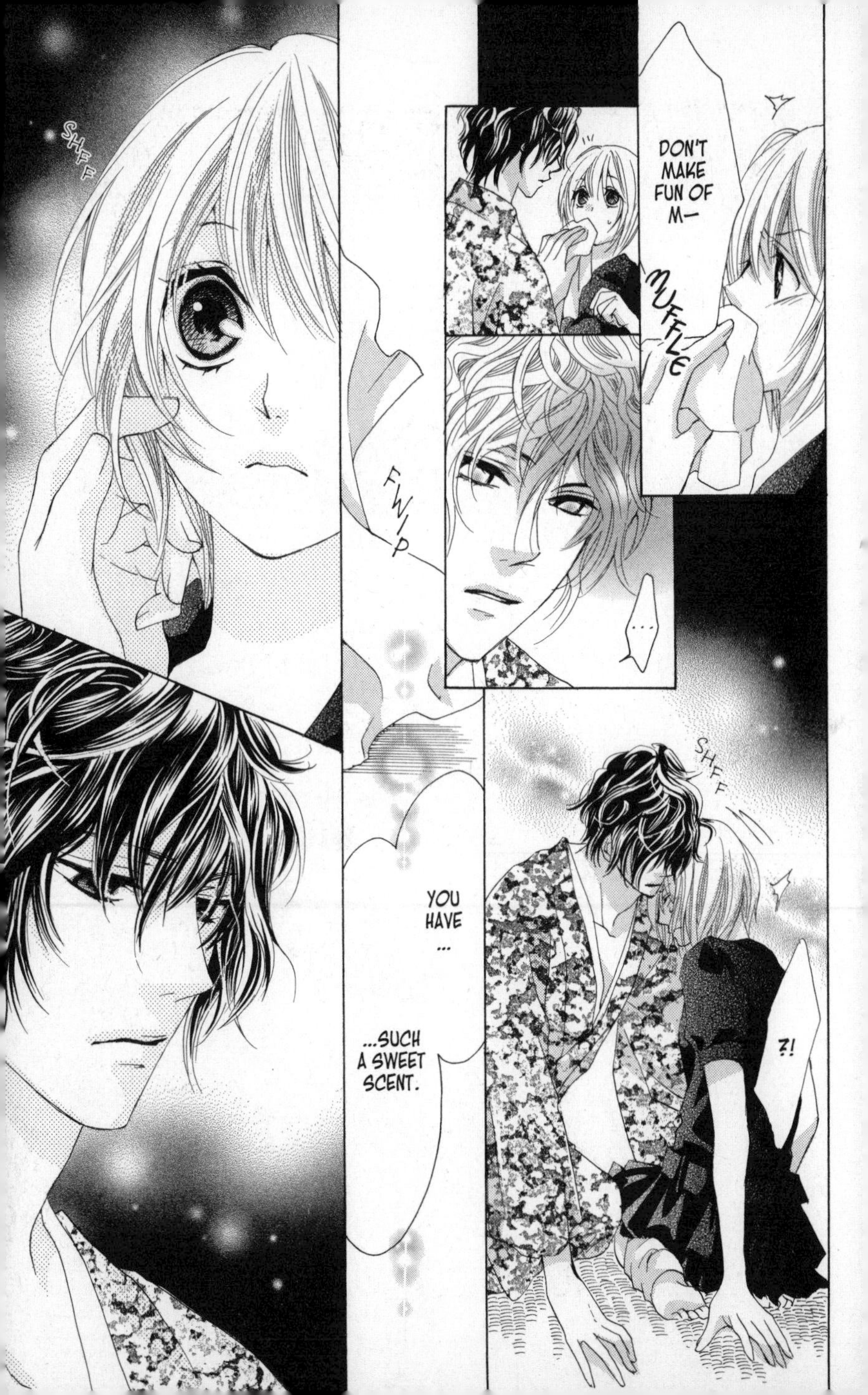
DON'T MAKE FUN OF M—
MUFFLE
FWIP
...
SHFF
?!
YOU HAVE ...
...SUCH A SWEET SCENT.
SHFF

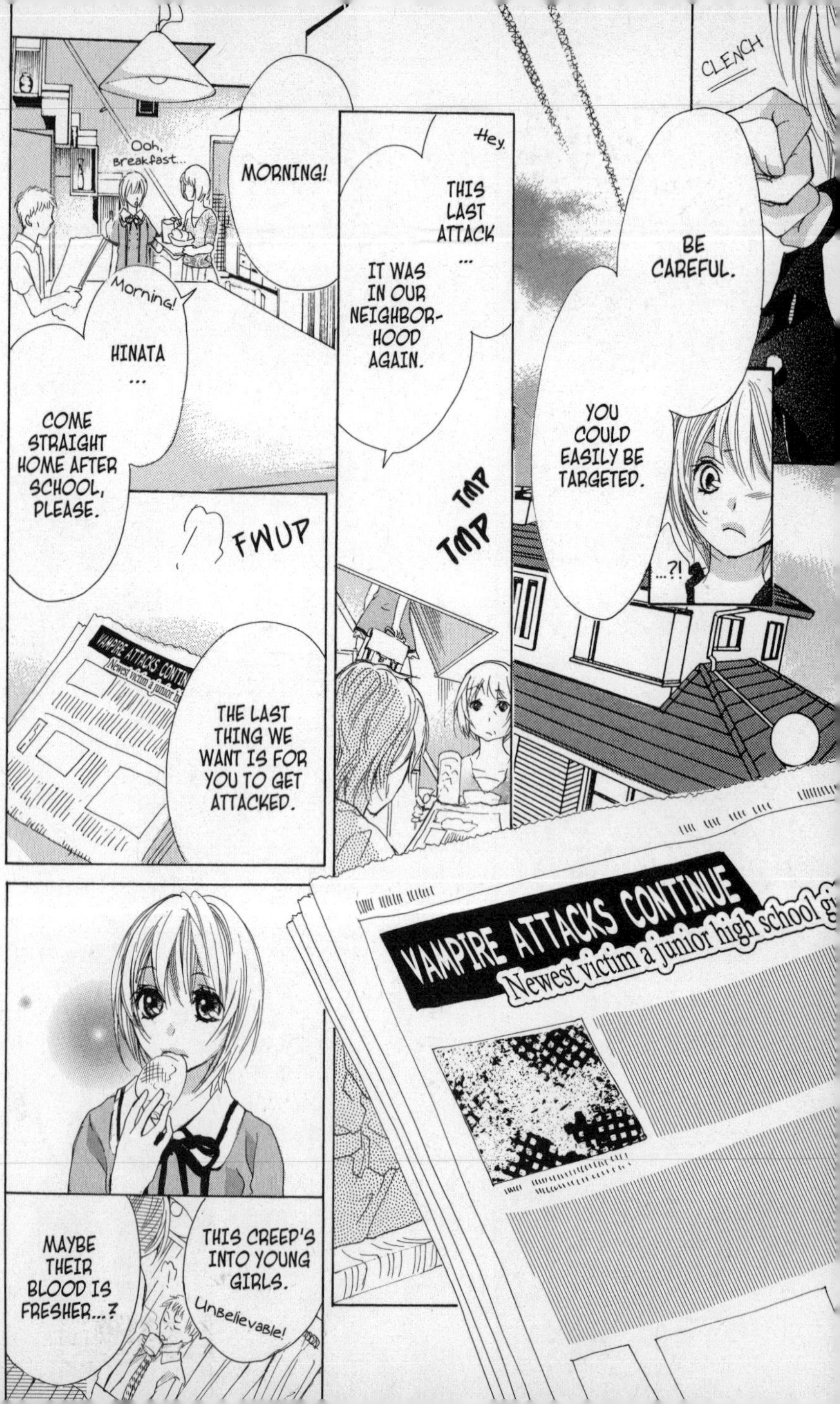

CLENCH
BE CAREFUL.
YOU COULD EASILY BE TARGETED.
...?!
Hey.
THIS LAST ATTACK...
IT WAS IN OUR NEIGHBORHOOD AGAIN.
TMP TMP
MORNING!
Ooh, breakfast...
Morning!
HINATA...
COME STRAIGHT HOME AFTER SCHOOL, PLEASE.
FWUP
VAMPIRE ATTACKS CONTINUE
THE LAST THING WE WANT IS FOR YOU TO GET ATTACKED.
VAMPIRE ATTACKS CONTINUE
Newest victim a junior high school gi
THIS CREEP'S INTO YOUNG GIRLS.
Unbelievable!
MAYBE THEIR BLOOD IS FRESHER...?

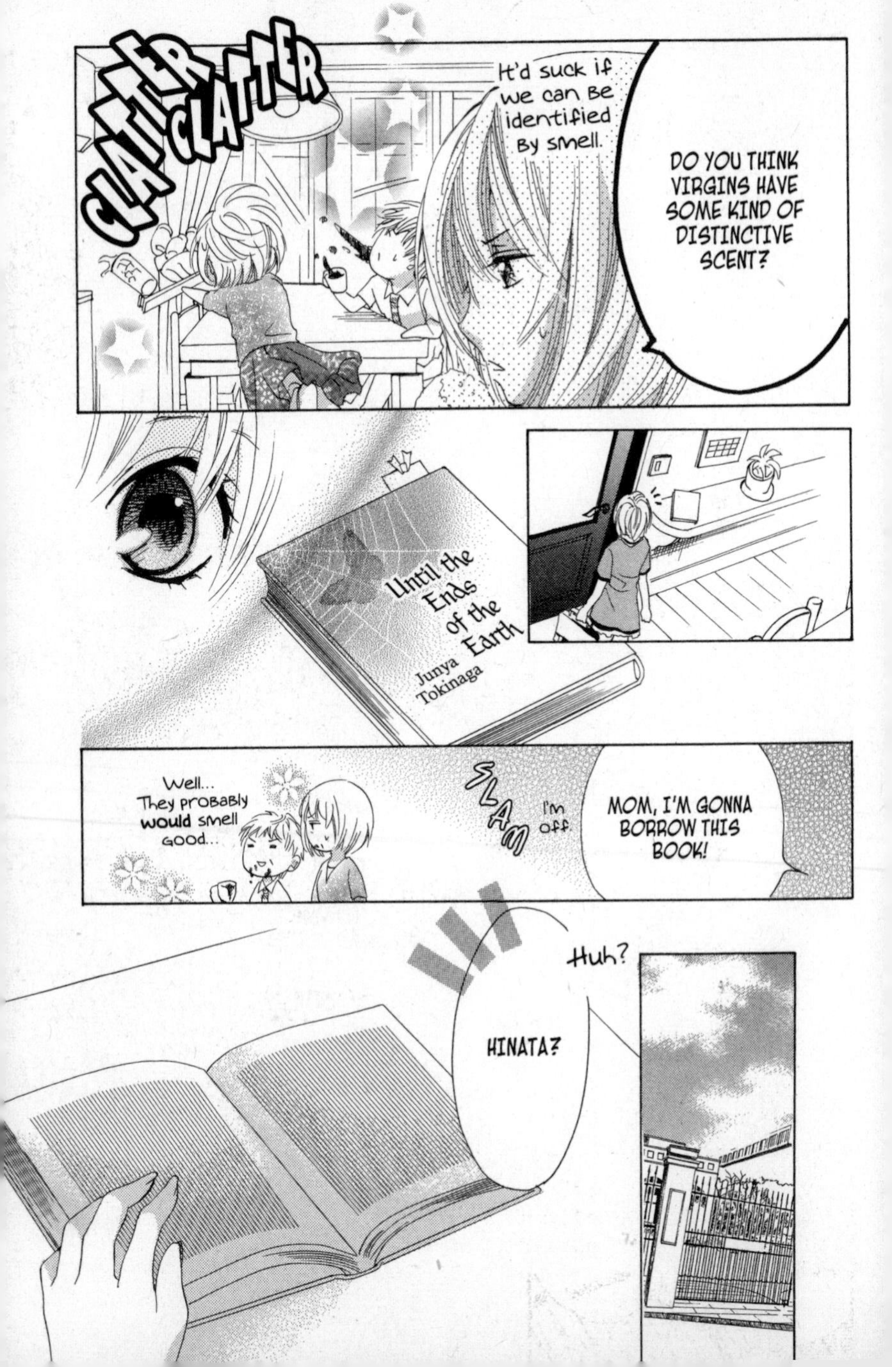
DO YOU THINK VIRGINS HAVE SOME KIND OF DISTINCTIVE SCENT?
It'd suck if we can be identified by smell.
CLATTER CLATTER
Until the Ends of the Earth
Junya Tokinaga
MOM, I'M GONNA BORROW THIS BOOK!
I'm off
SLAM
Well... They probably would smell good...
Huh?
HINATA?

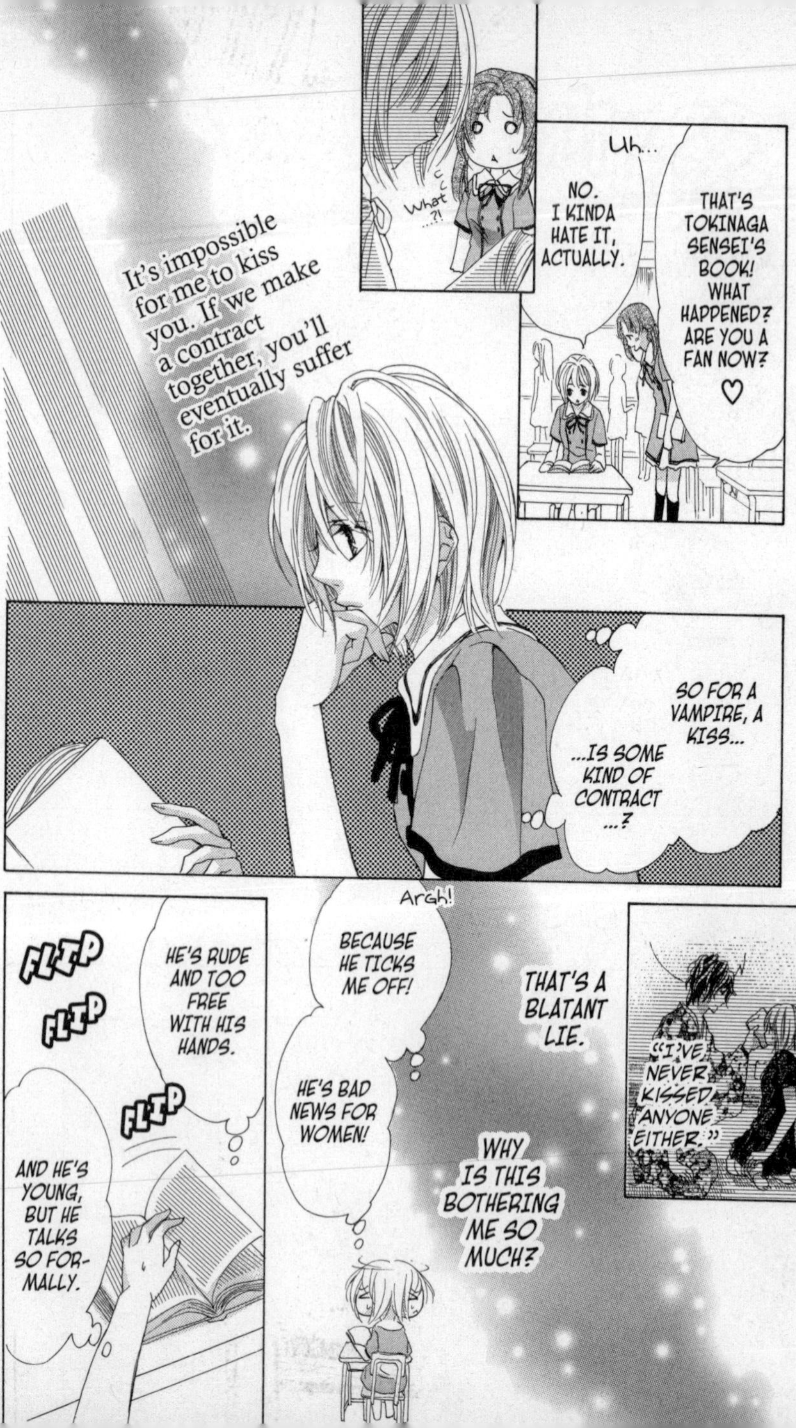
THAT'S TOKINAGA SENSEI'S BOOK! WHAT HAPPENED? ARE YOU A FAN NOW? ♡
Uh...
NO. I KINDA HATE IT, ACTUALLY.
What...?!
It's impossible for me to kiss you. If we make a contract together, you'll eventually suffer for it.
SO FOR A VAMPIRE, A KISS...
...IS SOME KIND OF CONTRACT...?
"I'VE NEVER KISSED ANYONE EITHER."
THAT'S A BLATANT LIE.
WHY IS THIS BOTHERING ME SO MUCH?
Argh!
BECAUSE HE TICKS ME OFF!
HE'S BAD NEWS FOR WOMEN!
FLIP
FLIP
HE'S RUDE AND TOO FREE WITH HIS HANDS.
FLIP
AND HE'S YOUNG, BUT HE TALKS SO FOR-MALLY.

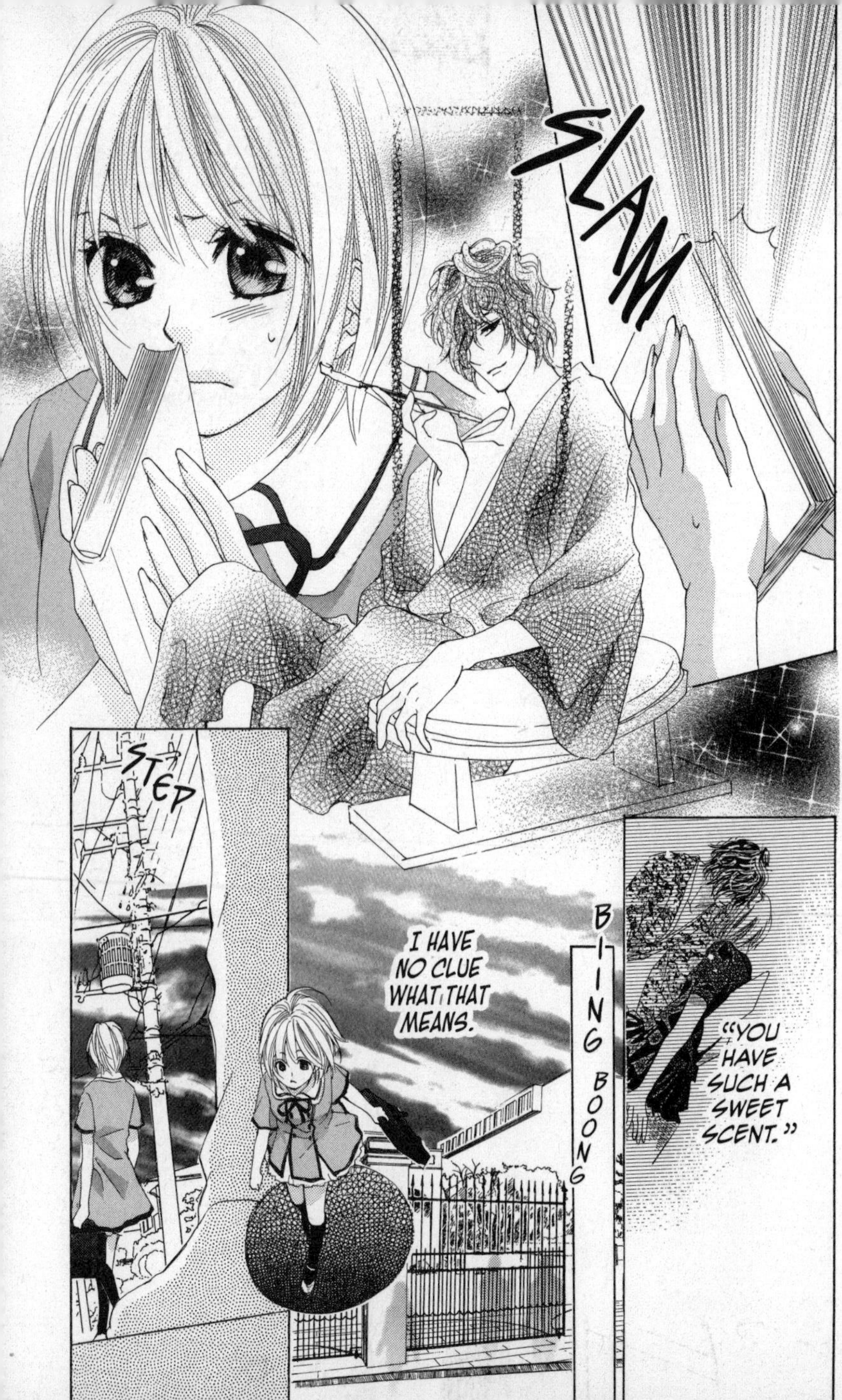
SLAM
"YOU HAVE SUCH A SWEET SCENT."
BIING BOONG
I HAVE NO CLUE WHAT THAT MEANS.
STEP

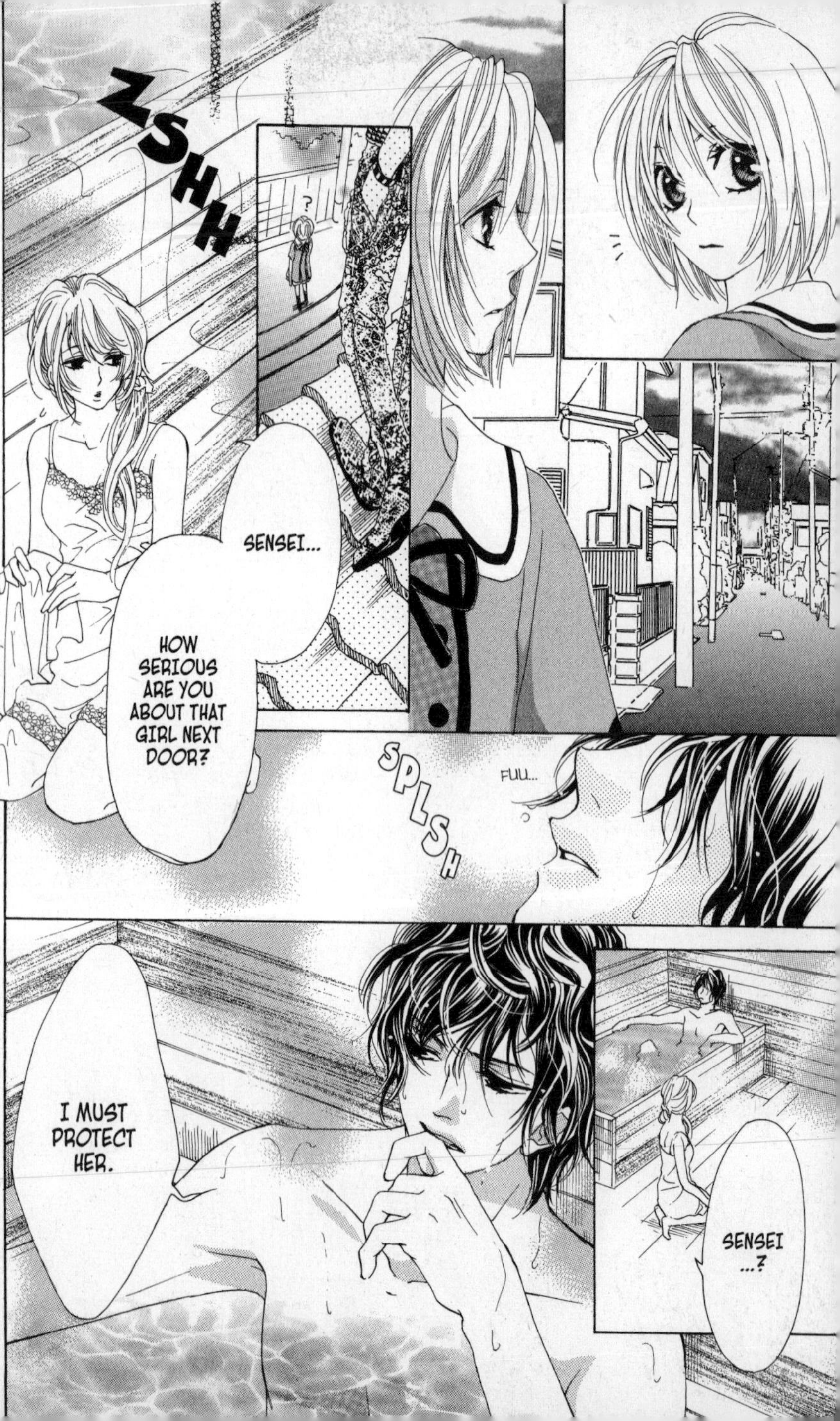
?
ZSHH
SENSEI...
HOW SERIOUS ARE YOU ABOUT THAT GIRL NEXT DOOR?
SPLSH
FUU...
SENSEI ...?
I MUST PROTECT HER.

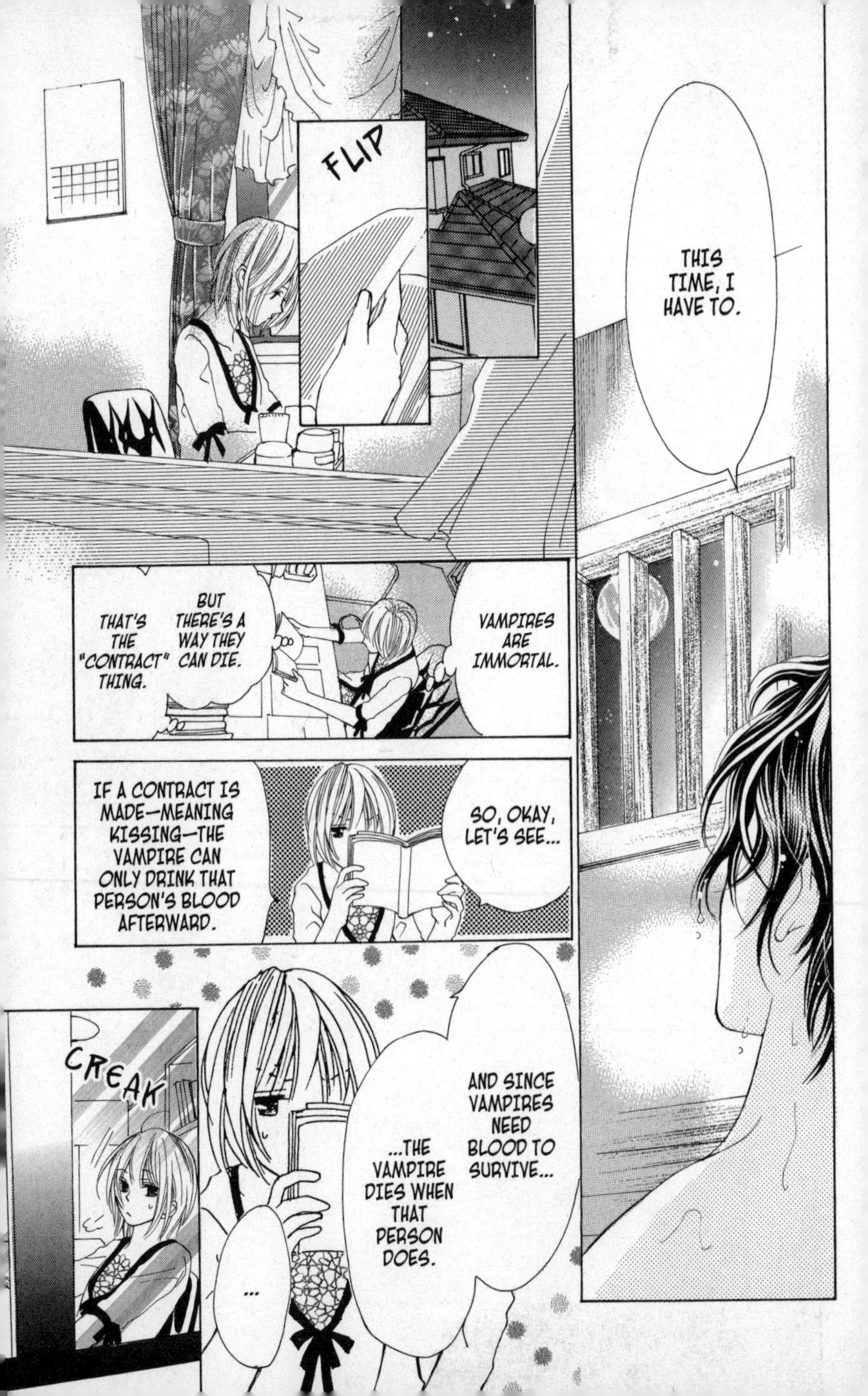
THIS TIME, I HAVE TO.
FLIP
VAMPIRES ARE IMMORTAL.
BUT THERE'S A WAY THEY CAN DIE.
THAT'S THE "CONTRACT" THING.
SO, OKAY, LET'S SEE...
IF A CONTRACT IS MADE—MEANING KISSING—THE VAMPIRE CAN ONLY DRINK THAT PERSON'S BLOOD AFTERWARD.
AND SINCE VAMPIRES NEED BLOOD TO SURVIVE...
...THE VAMPIRE DIES WHEN THAT PERSON DOES.
...
CREAK

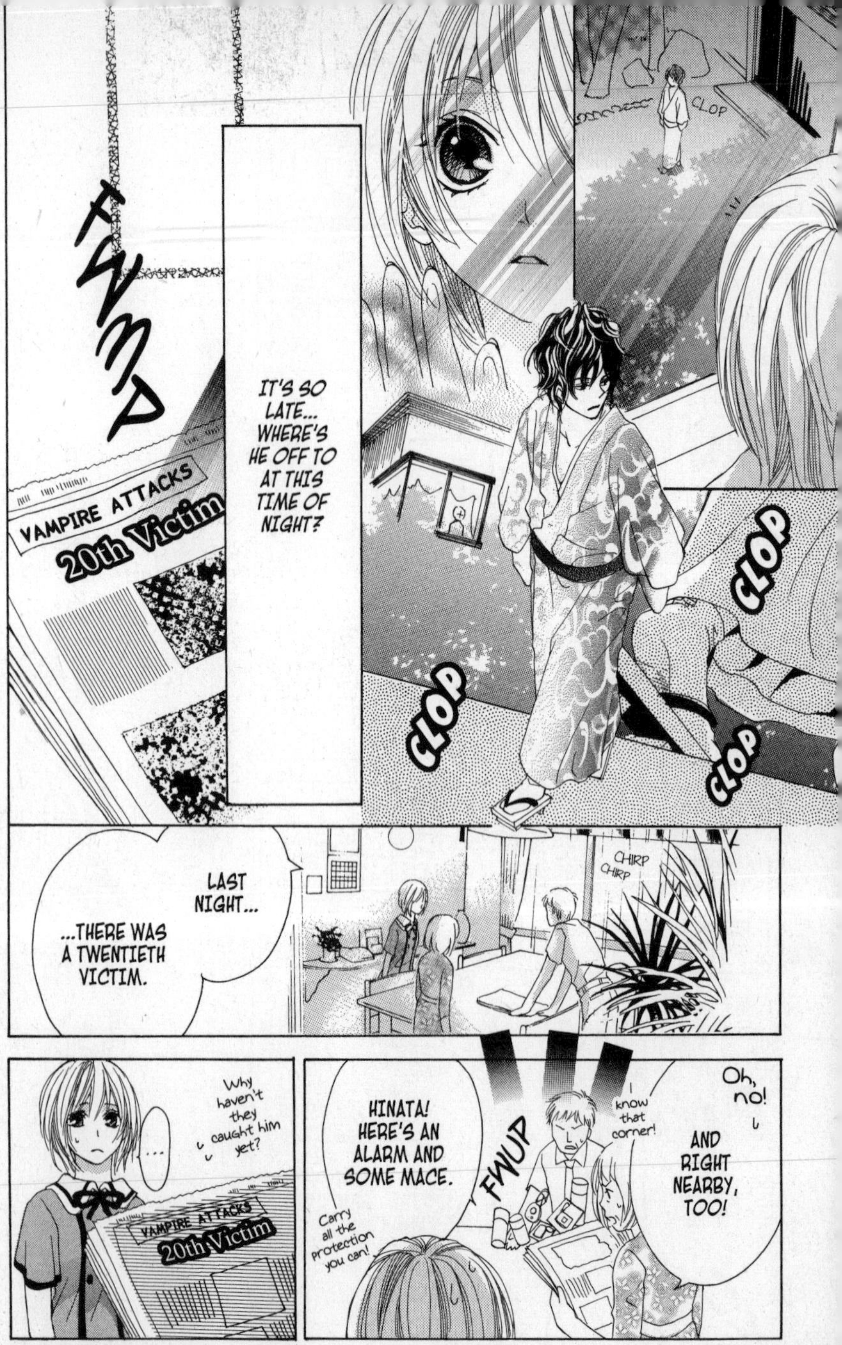
CLOP
IT'S SO LATE... WHERE'S HE OFF TO AT THIS TIME OF NIGHT?
CLOP
CLOP
CLOP
FWMP
VAMPIRE ATTACKS
20th Victim
CHIRP CHIRP
LAST NIGHT...
...THERE WAS A TWENTIETH VICTIM.
Oh, no!
AND RIGHT NEARBY, TOO!
I know that corner!
FWUP
HINATA! HERE'S AN ALARM AND SOME MACE.
Carry all the protection you can!
Why haven't they caught him yet?
...
VAMPIRE ATTACKS
20th Victim

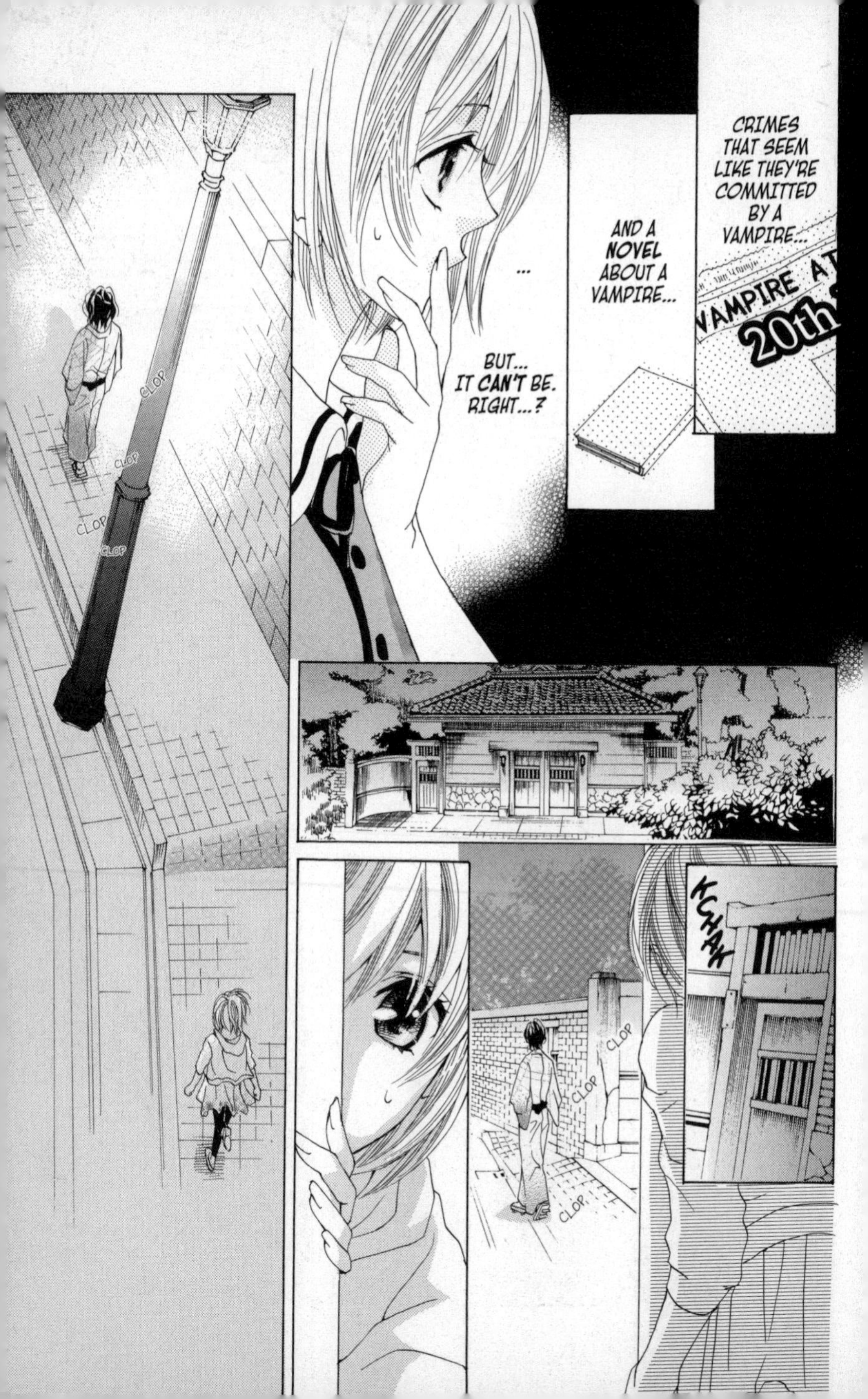
CRIMES THAT SEEM LIKE THEY'RE COMMITTED BY A VAMPIRE...
AND A NOVEL ABOUT A VAMPIRE...
...
BUT... IT CAN'T BE. RIGHT...?
KCHAK
CLOP CLOP
CLOP
CLOP
CLOP
CLOP
CLOP
CLOP

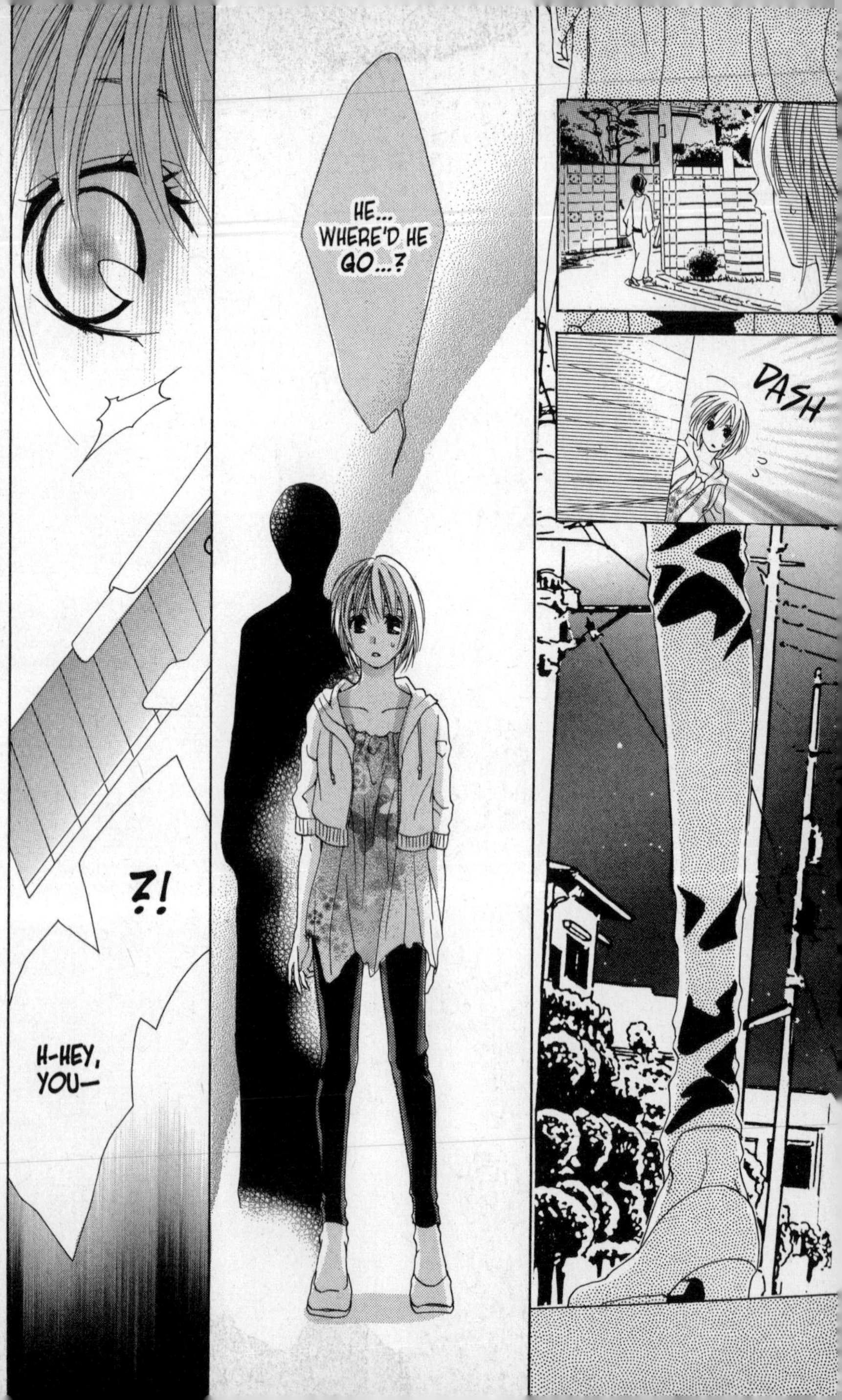
DASH
HE... WHERE'D HE GO...?
?!
H-HEY, YOU—

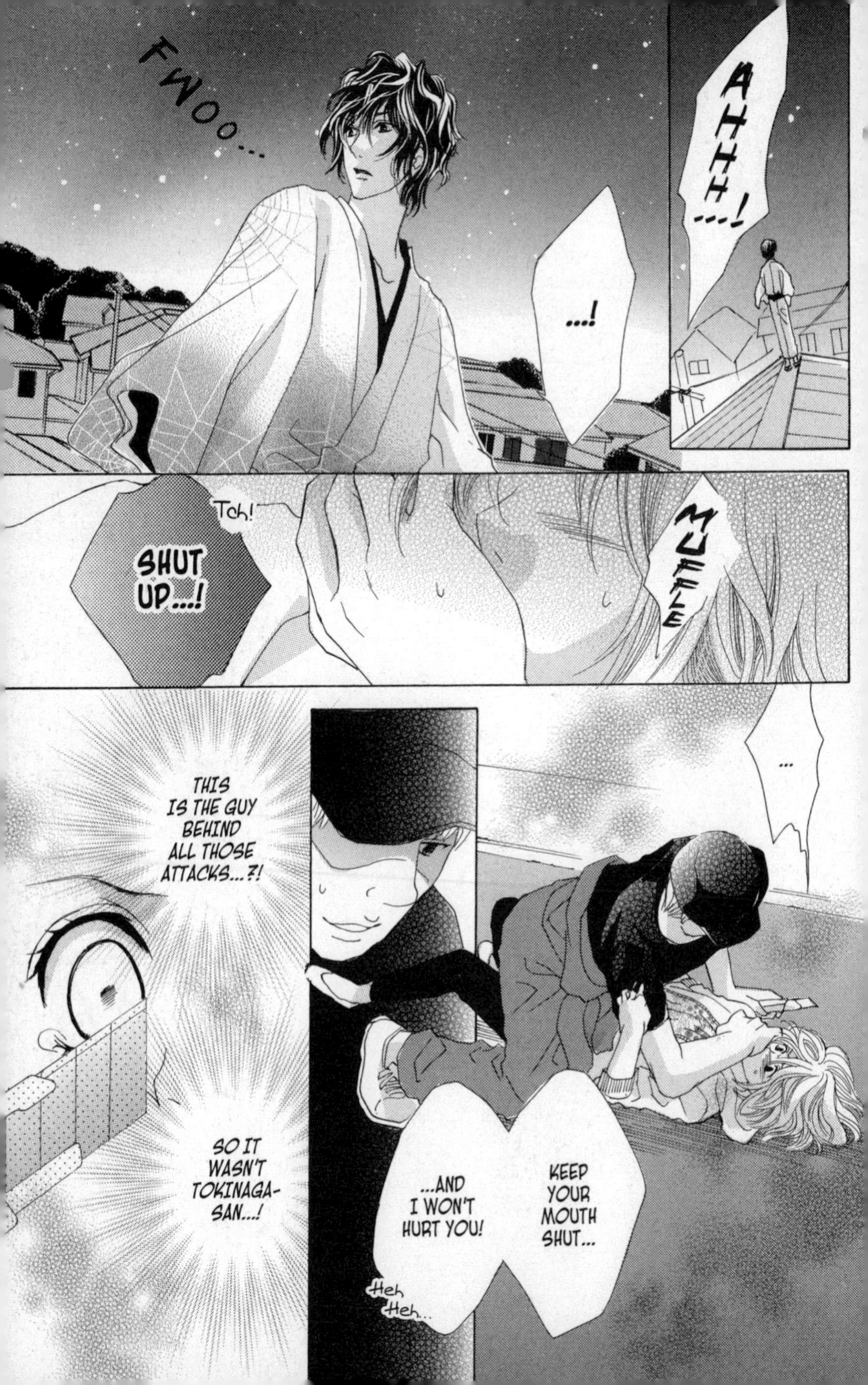
AHHH...!
...!
FWOO...
MUFFLE
Tch!
SHUT UP...!
...
KEEP YOUR MOUTH SHUT...
...AND I WON'T HURT YOU!
Heh Heh...
THIS IS THE GUY BEHIND ALL THOSE ATTACKS...?!
SO IT WASN'T TOKINAGA-SAN...!

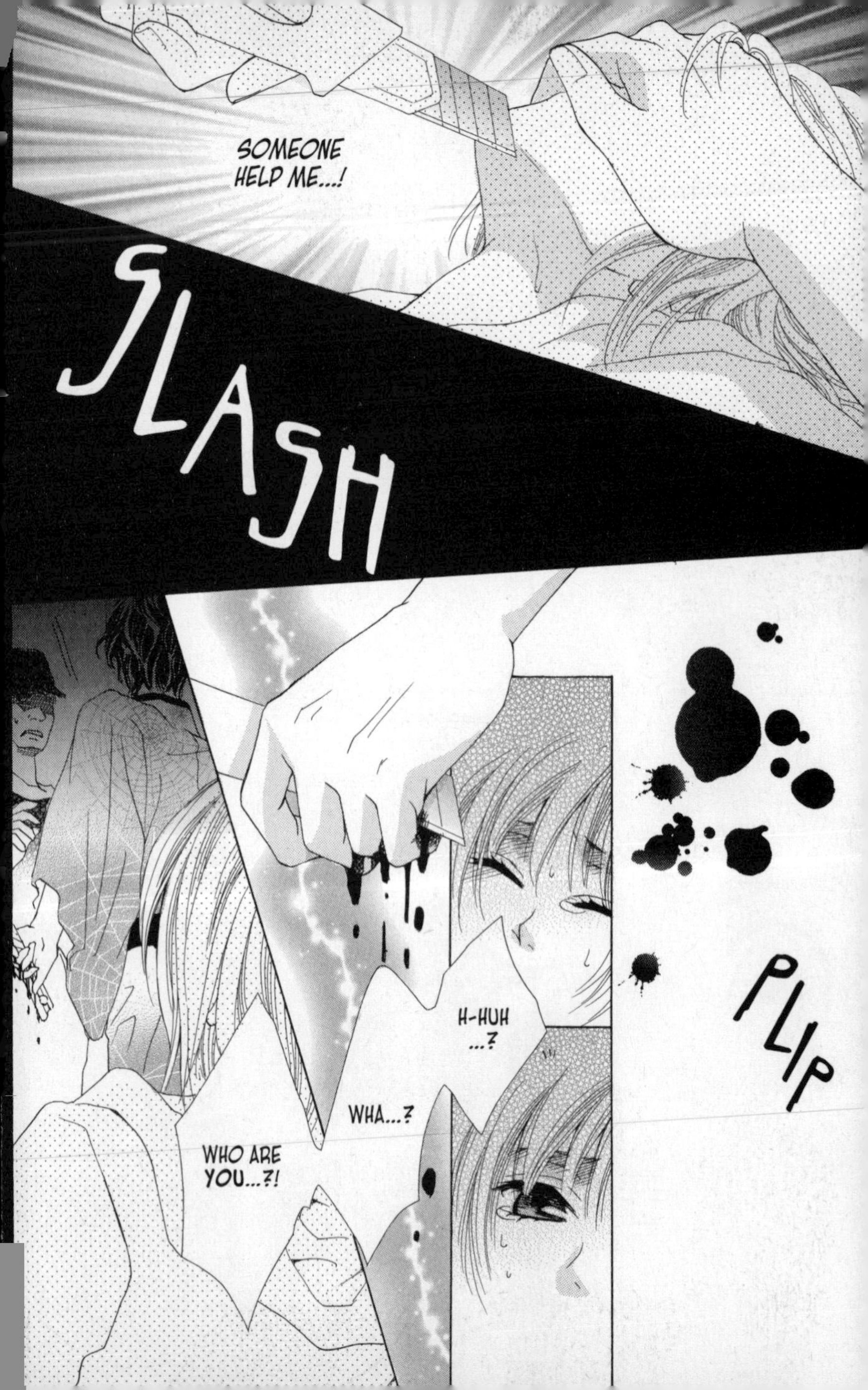
SOMEONE HELP ME...!
SLASH
PLIP
H-HUH ...?
WHA...?
WHO ARE YOU...?!

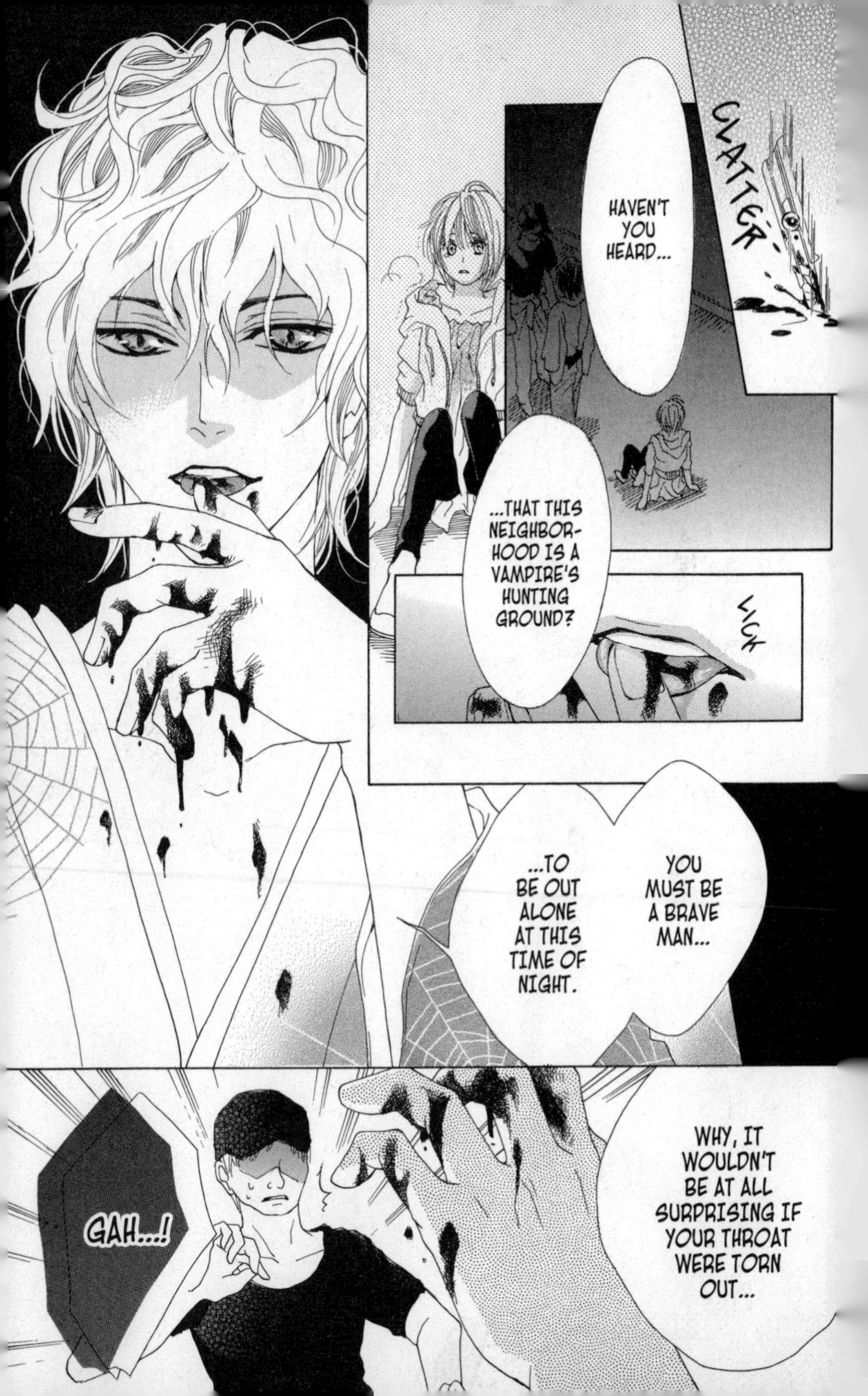
CLATTER
HAVEN'T YOU HEARD...
...THAT THIS NEIGHBOR-HOOD IS A VAMPIRE'S HUNTING GROUND?
LICK
YOU MUST BE A BRAVE MAN...
...TO BE OUT ALONE AT THIS TIME OF NIGHT.
WHY, IT WOULDN'T BE AT ALL SURPRISING IF YOUR THROAT WERE TORN OUT...
GAH...!

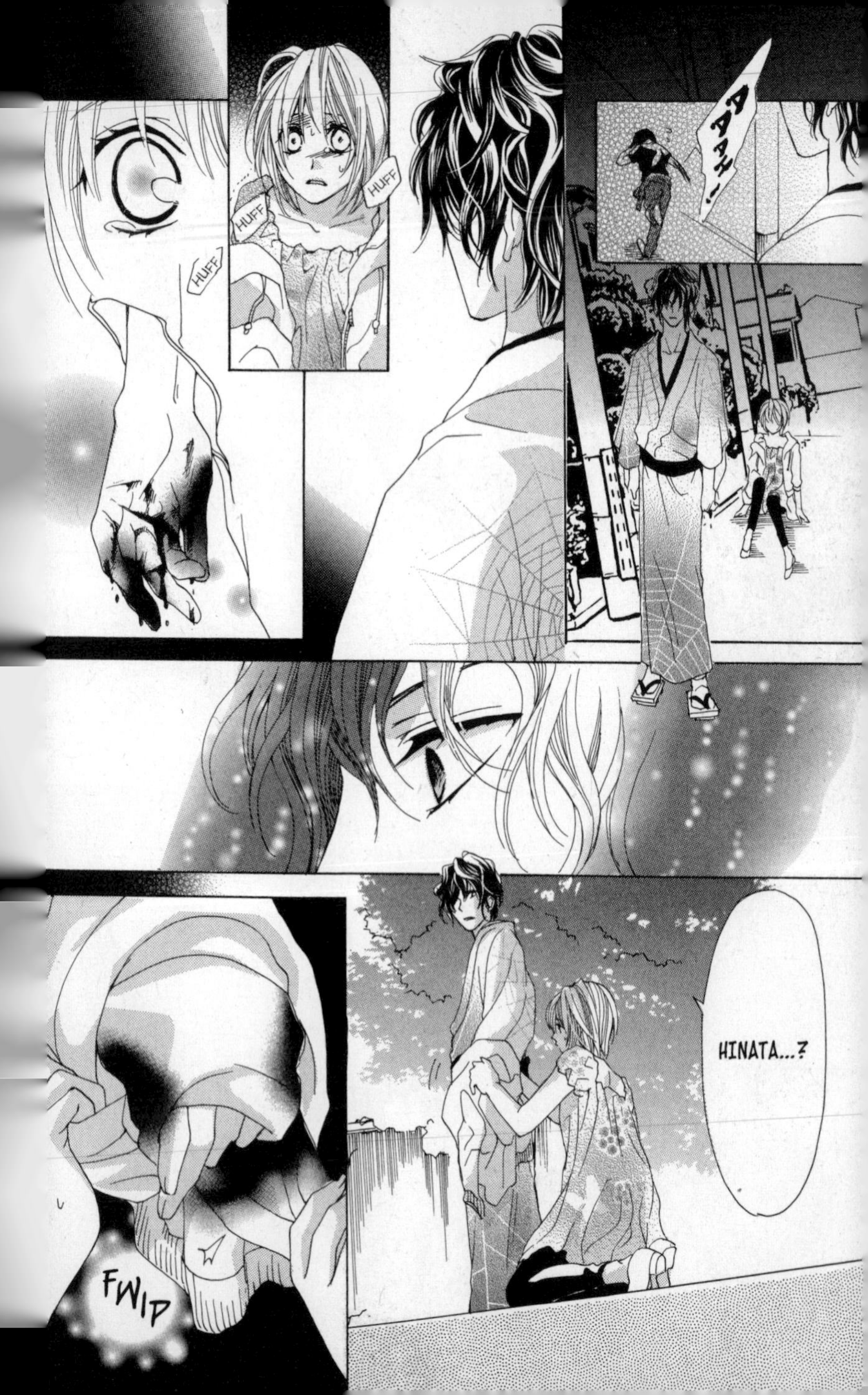
AAAH!
HUFF
HUFF
HUFF
HUFF
HINATA...?
FWIP

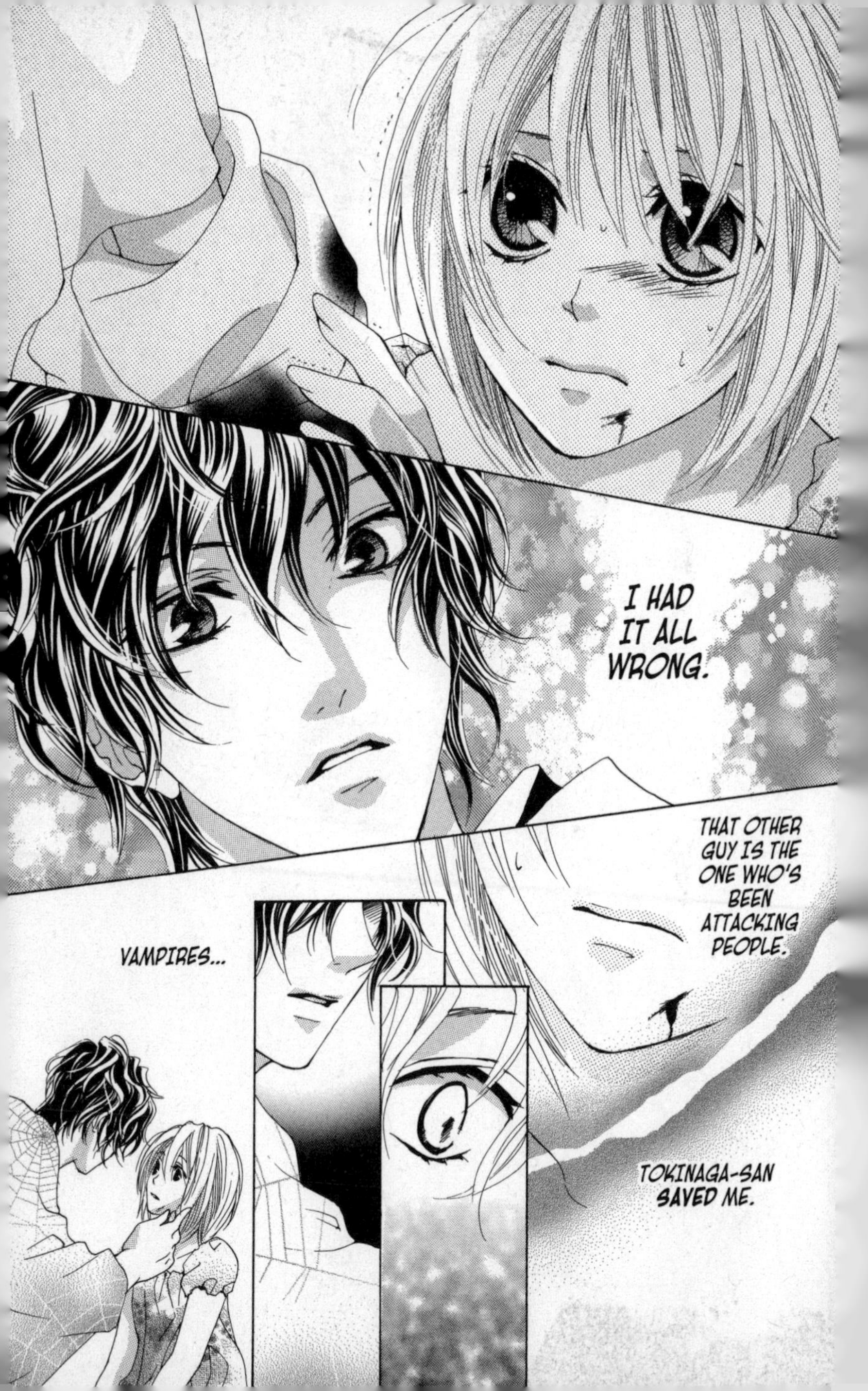
I HAD IT ALL WRONG.
THAT OTHER GUY IS THE ONE WHO'S BEEN ATTACKING PEOPLE.
VAMPIRES...
TOKINAGA-SAN SAVED ME.

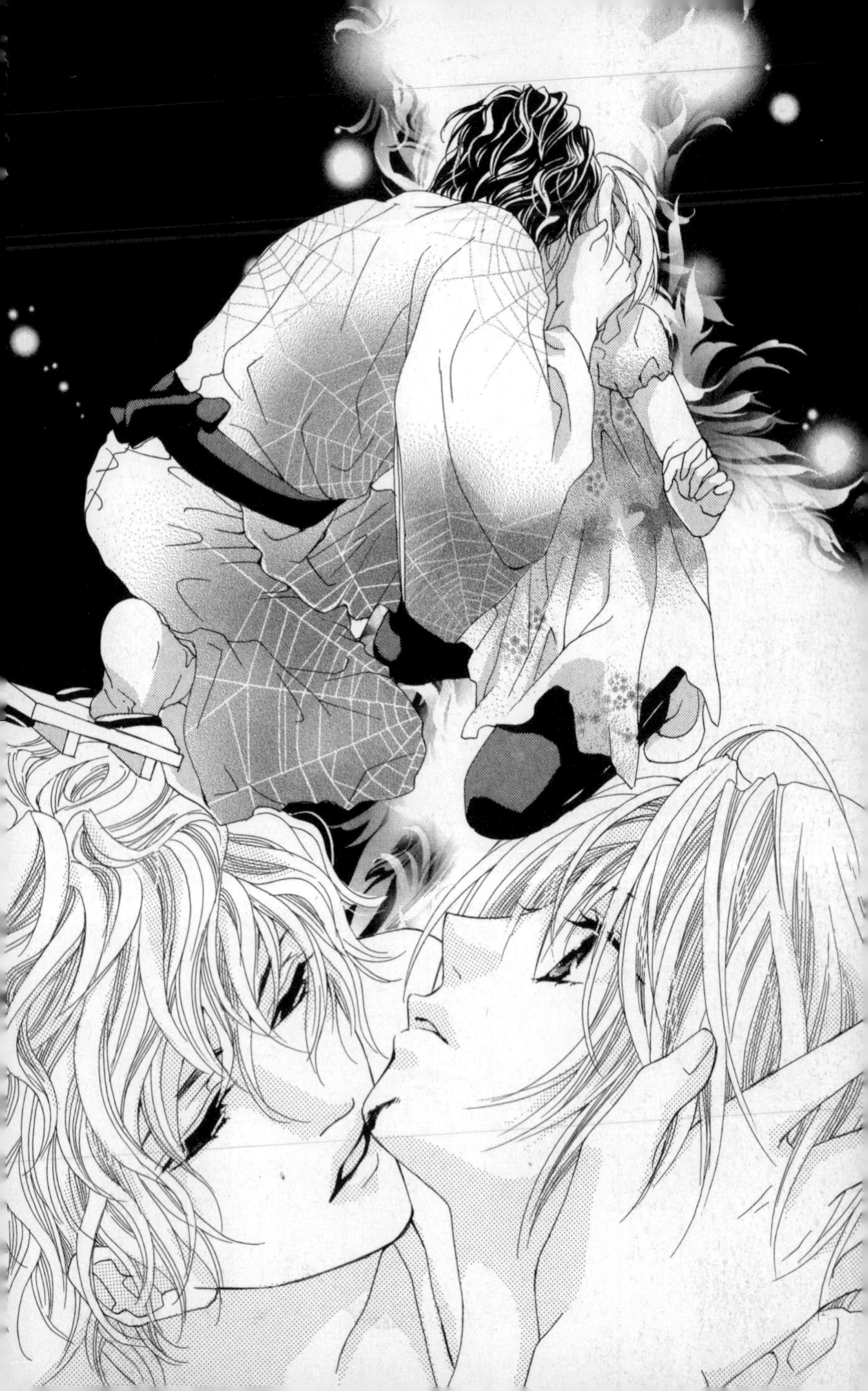

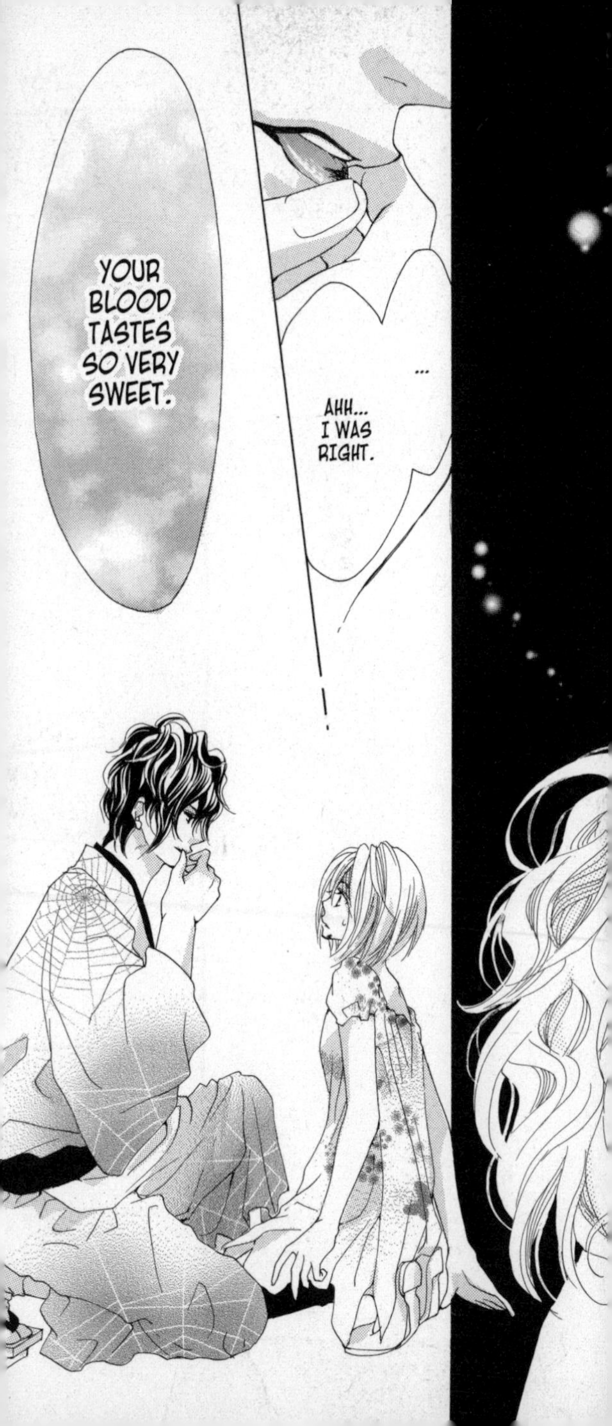
...
AHH... I WAS RIGHT.
YOUR BLOOD TASTES SO VERY SWEET.

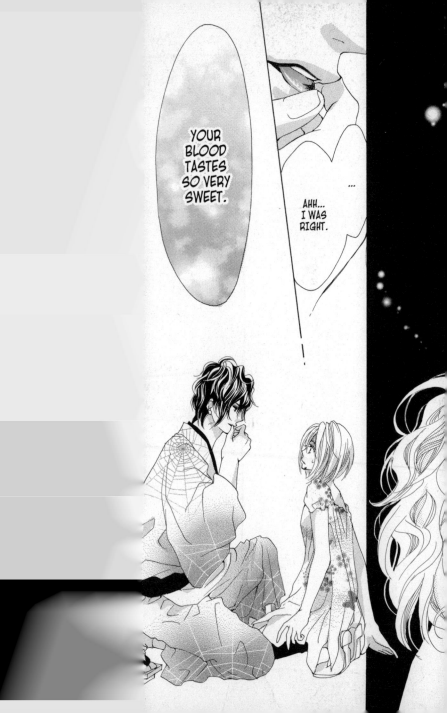

About My Editor

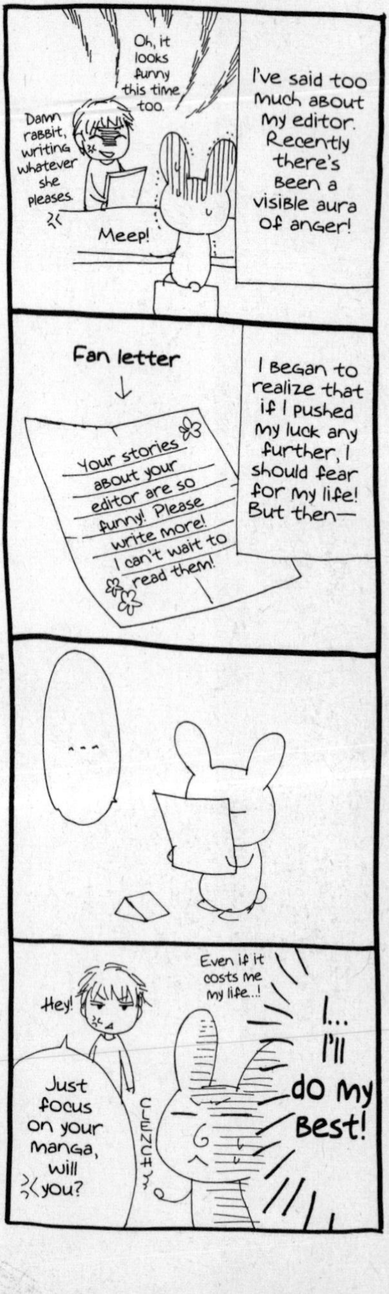
I've said too much about my editor. Recently there's been a visible aura of anger!
Oh, it looks funny this time too.
Damn rabbit, writing whatever she pleases.
Meep!
I began to realize that if I pushed my luck any further, I should fear for my life! But then—
Fan letter
Your stories about your editor are so funny! Please write more! I can't wait to read them!
...
Even if it costs me my life...!
I... I'll do my best!
Hey!
CLENCH
Just focus on your manga, will you?

Chapter 2

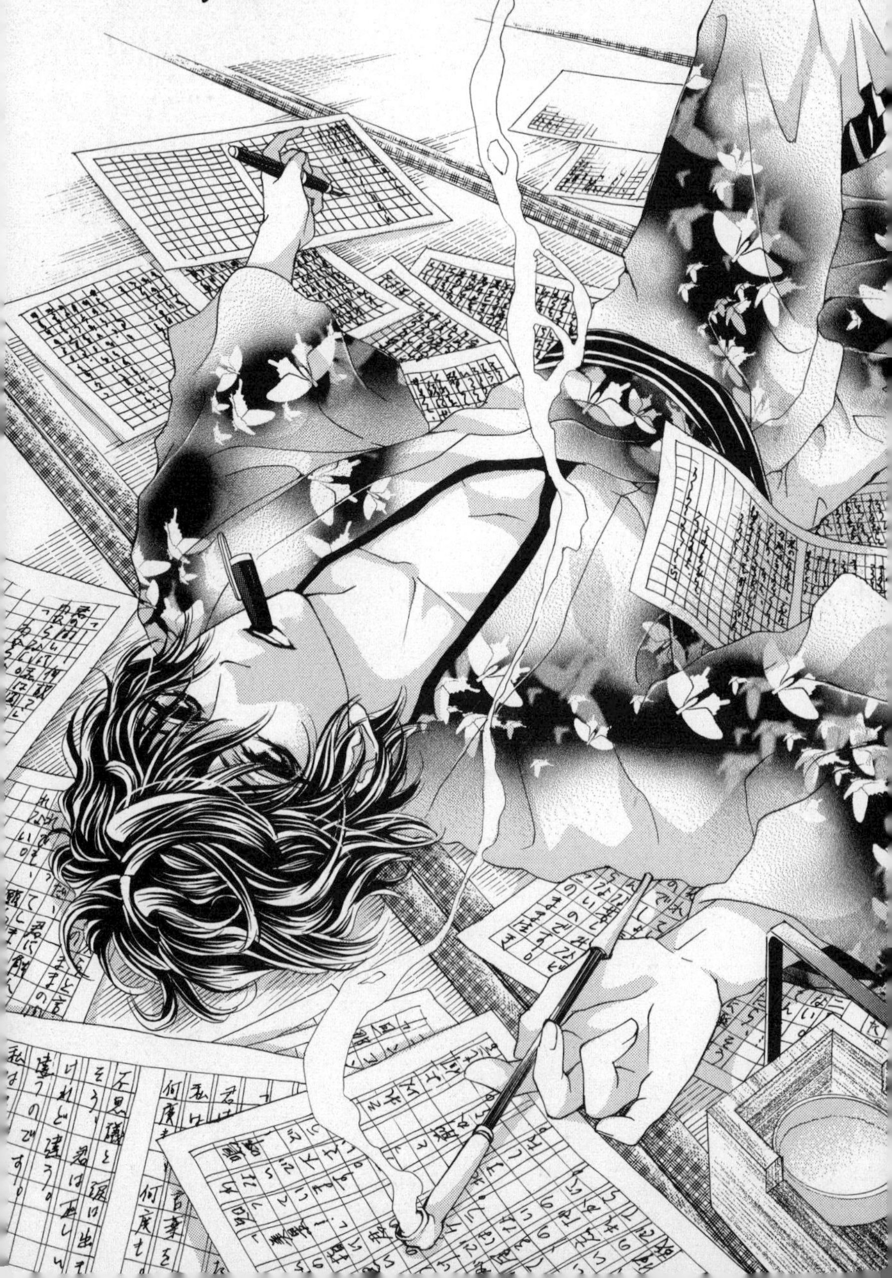

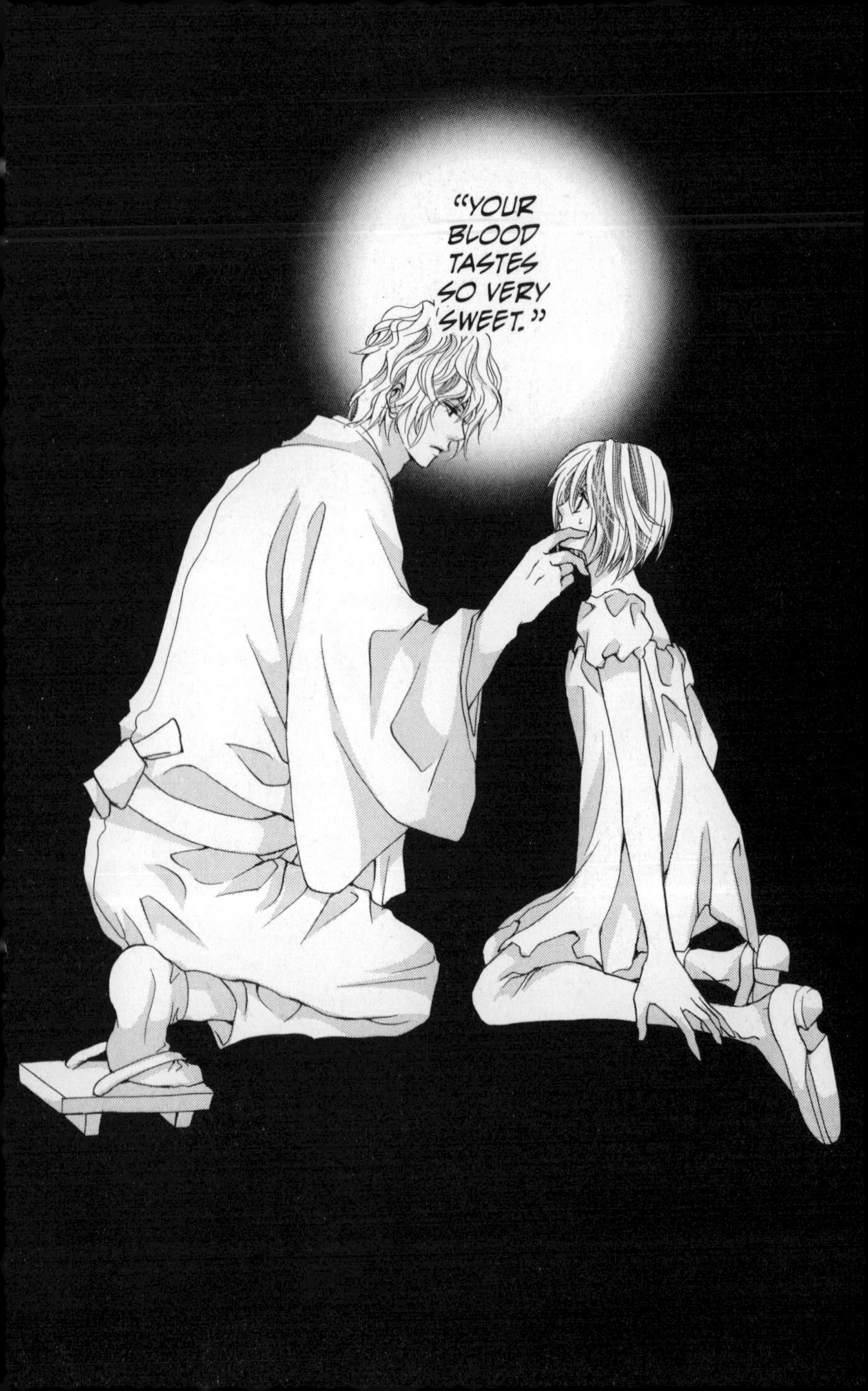
"YOUR BLOOD TASTES SO VERY SWEET."

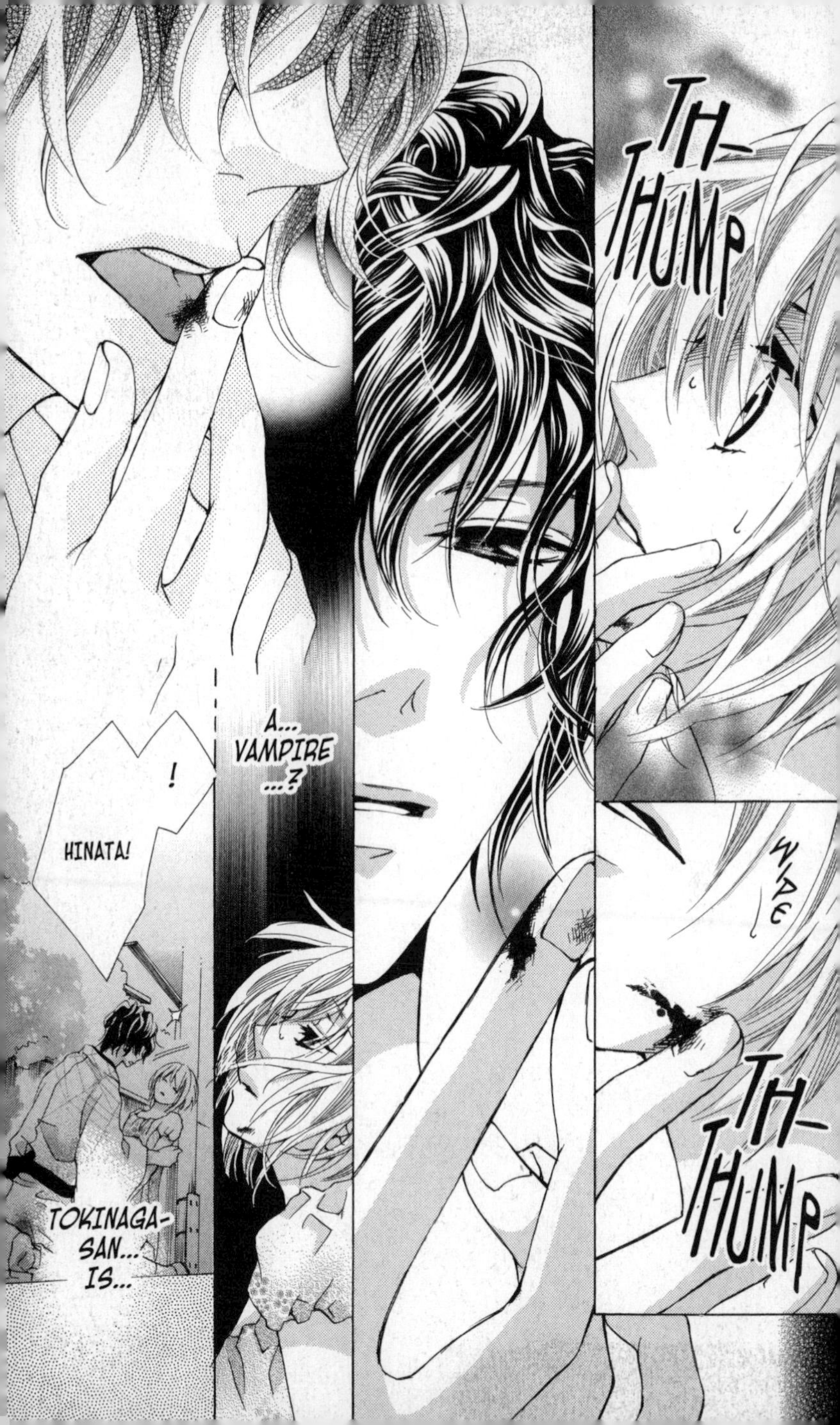
TH-THUMP
WIDE
TH-THUMP
A... VAMPIRE ...?
!
HINATA!
TOKINAGA-SAN... IS...

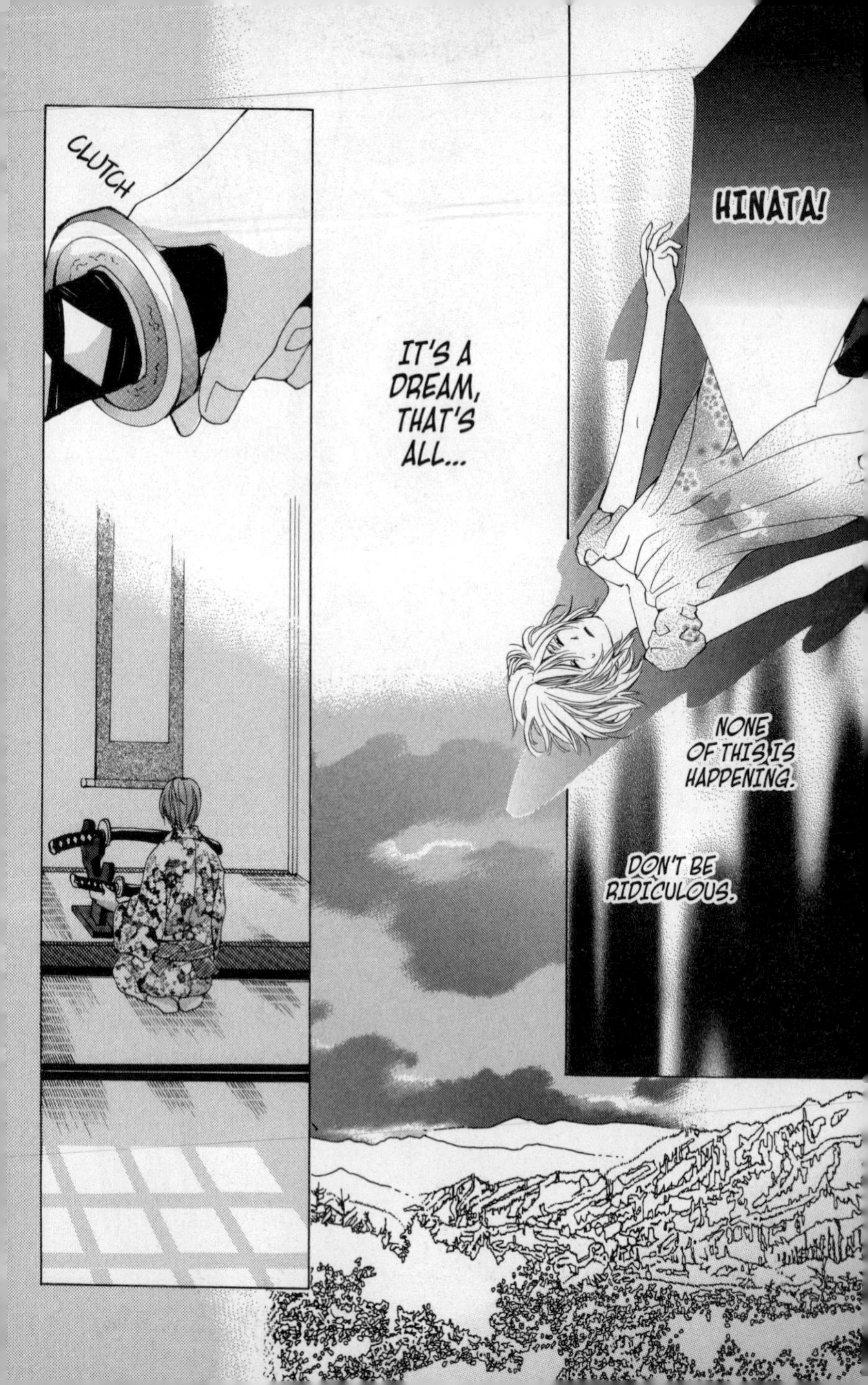
HINATA!
NONE OF THIS IS HAPPENING.
DON'T BE RIDICULOUS.
IT'S A DREAM, THAT'S ALL...
CLUTCH

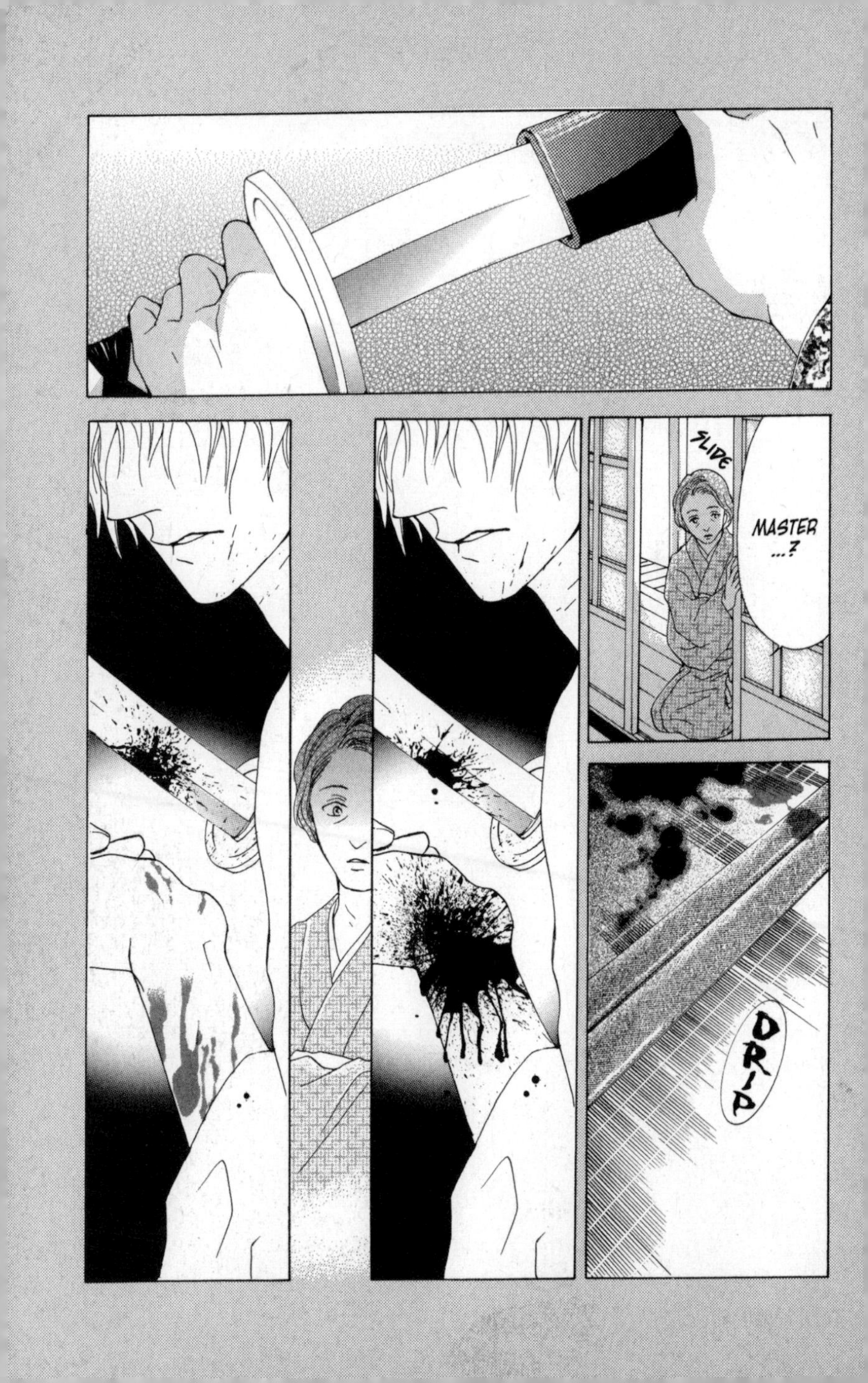
SLIDE
MASTER ...?
DRIP

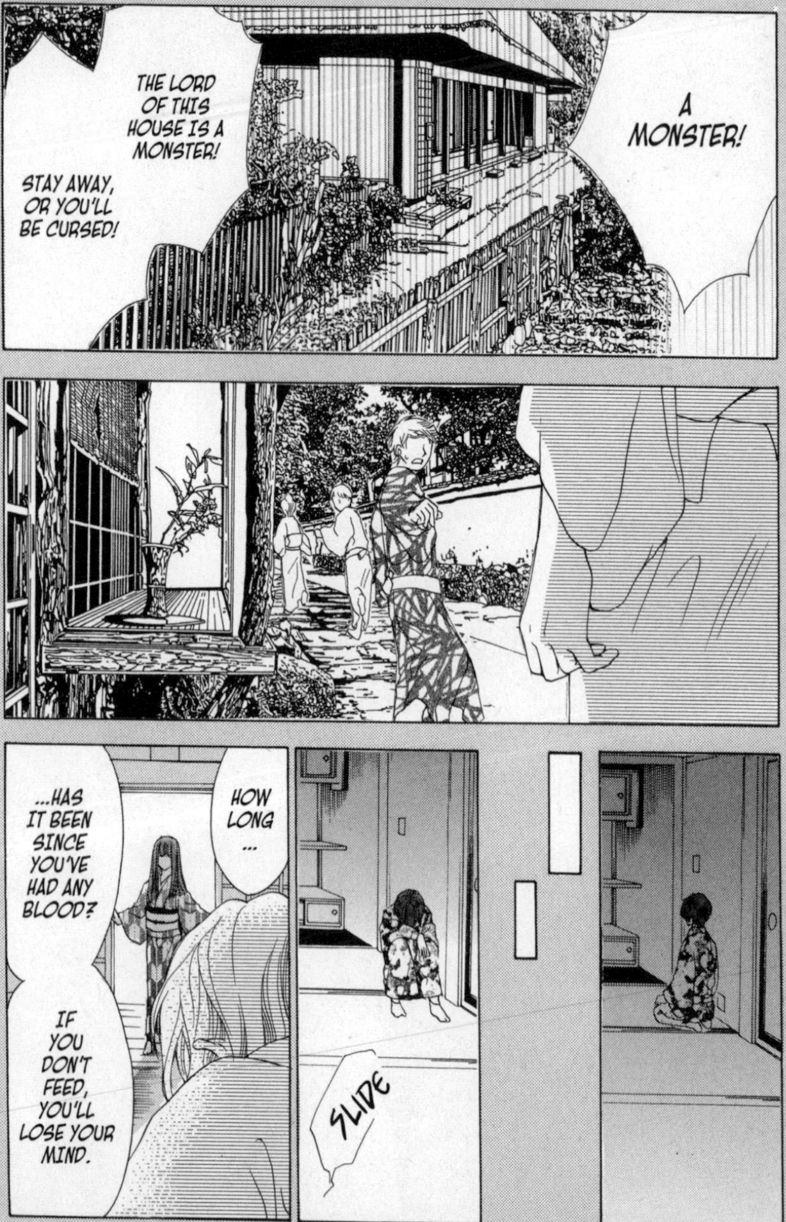
A MONSTER!
THE LORD OF THIS HOUSE IS A MONSTER!
STAY AWAY, OR YOU'LL BE CURSED!
SLIDE
HOW LONG ...
...HAS IT BEEN SINCE YOU'VE HAD ANY BLOOD?
IF YOU DON'T FEED, YOU'LL LOSE YOUR MIND.

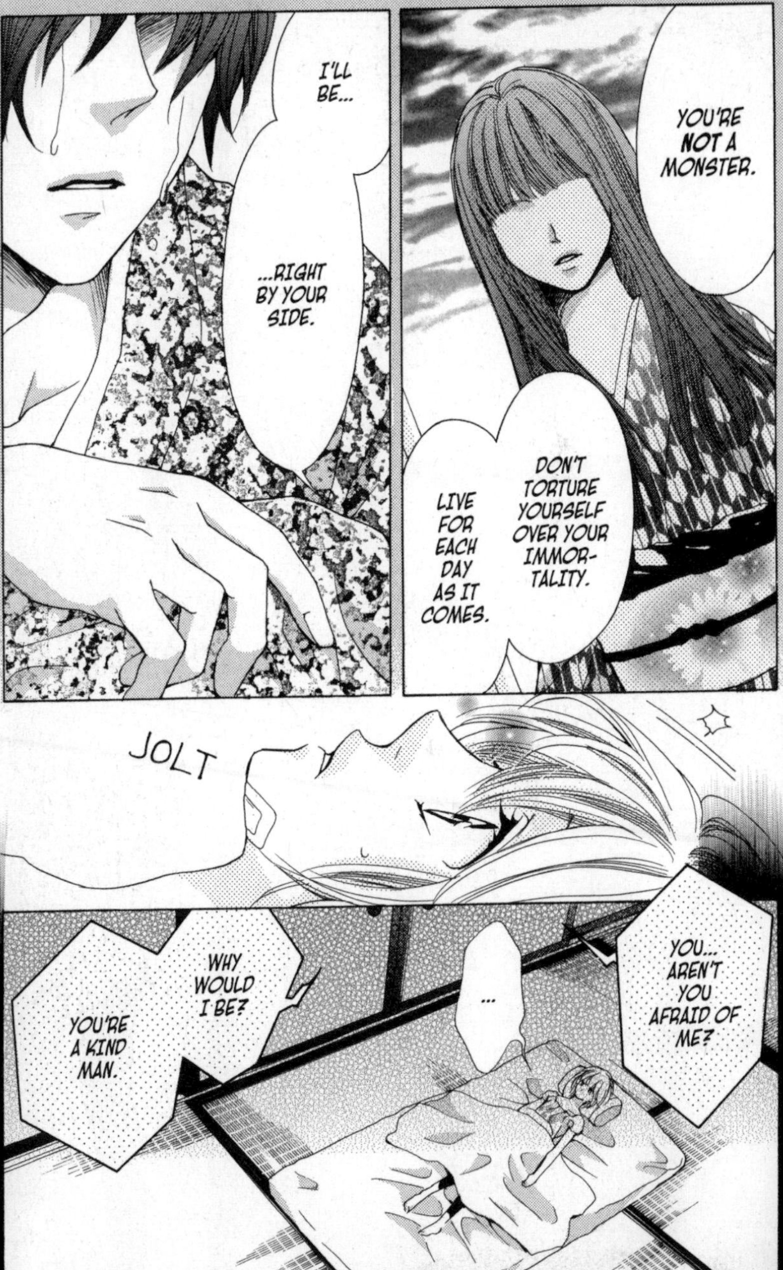
YOU'RE NOT A MONSTER.
DON'T TORTURE YOURSELF OVER YOUR IMMOR-TALITY.
LIVE FOR EACH DAY AS IT COMES.
I'LL BE...
...RIGHT BY YOUR SIDE.
JOLT
YOU... AREN'T YOU AFRAID OF ME?
...
WHY WOULD I BE?
YOU'RE A KIND MAN.

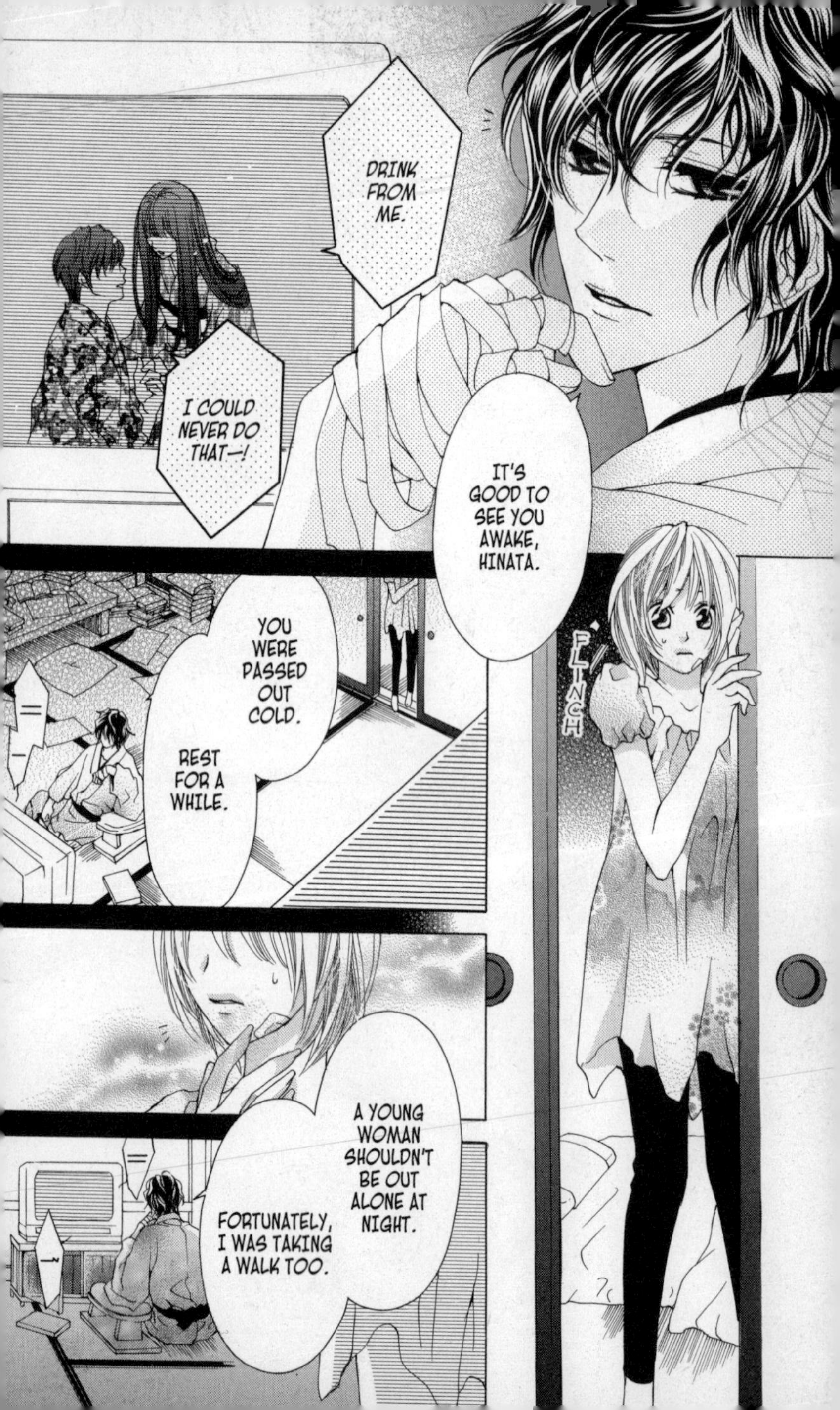
DRINK FROM ME.
I COULD NEVER DO THAT—!
IT'S GOOD TO SEE YOU AWAKE, HINATA.
FLINCH
YOU WERE PASSED OUT COLD.
REST FOR A WHILE.
A YOUNG WOMAN SHOULDN'T BE OUT ALONE AT NIGHT.
FORTUNATELY, I WAS TAKING A WALK TOO.

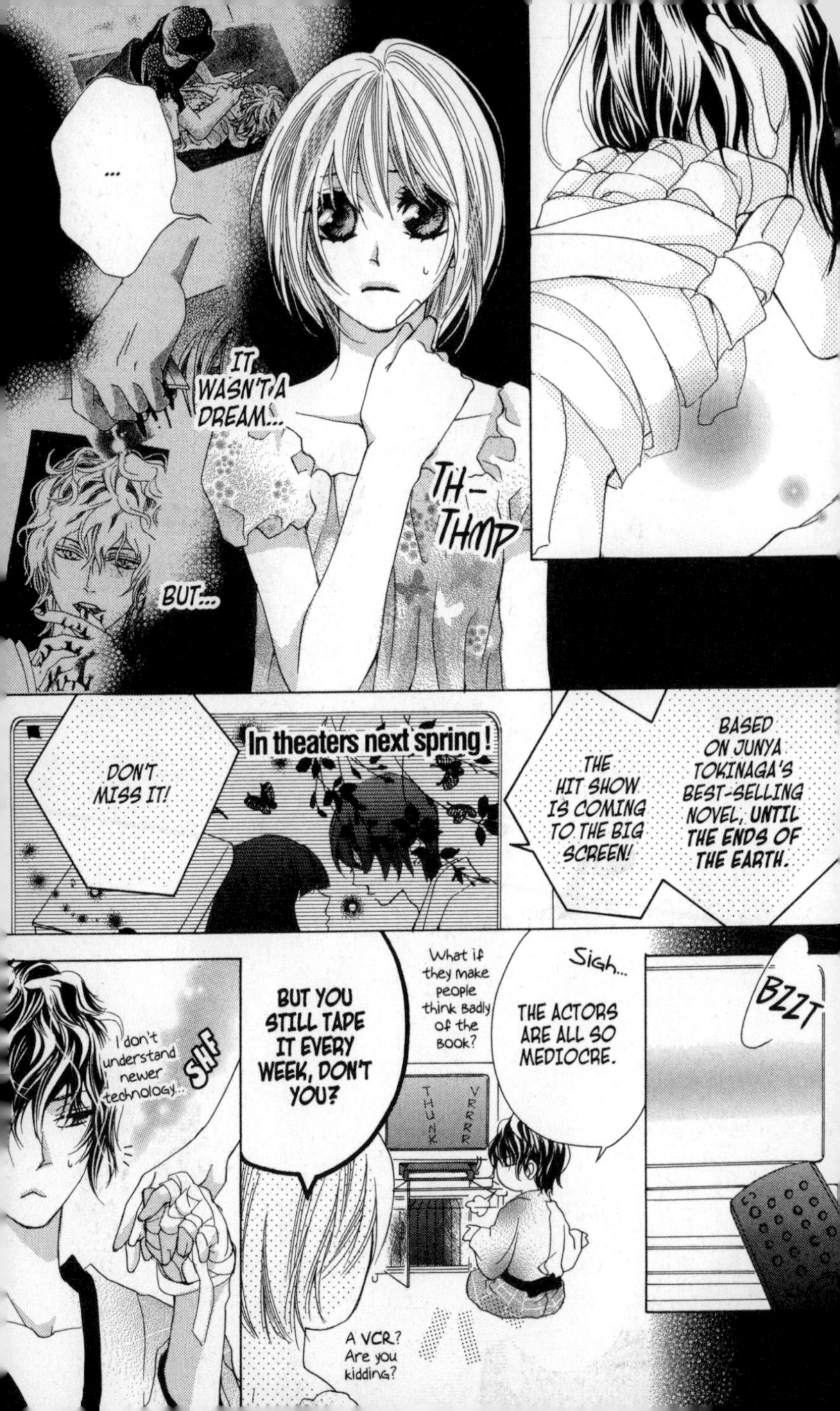
...
IT WASN'T A DREAM...
TH-THMP
BUT...
BASED ON JUNYA TOKINAGA'S BEST-SELLING NOVEL, UNTIL THE ENDS OF THE EARTH.
THE HIT SHOW IS COMING TO THE BIG SCREEN!
In theaters next spring!
DON'T MISS IT!
BZZT
Sigh...
THE ACTORS ARE ALL SO MEDIOCRE.
What if they make people think badly of the book?
VRRRP
THUNK
BUT YOU STILL TAPE IT EVERY WEEK, DON'T YOU?
A VCR? Are you kidding?
SHF
I don't understand newer technology...

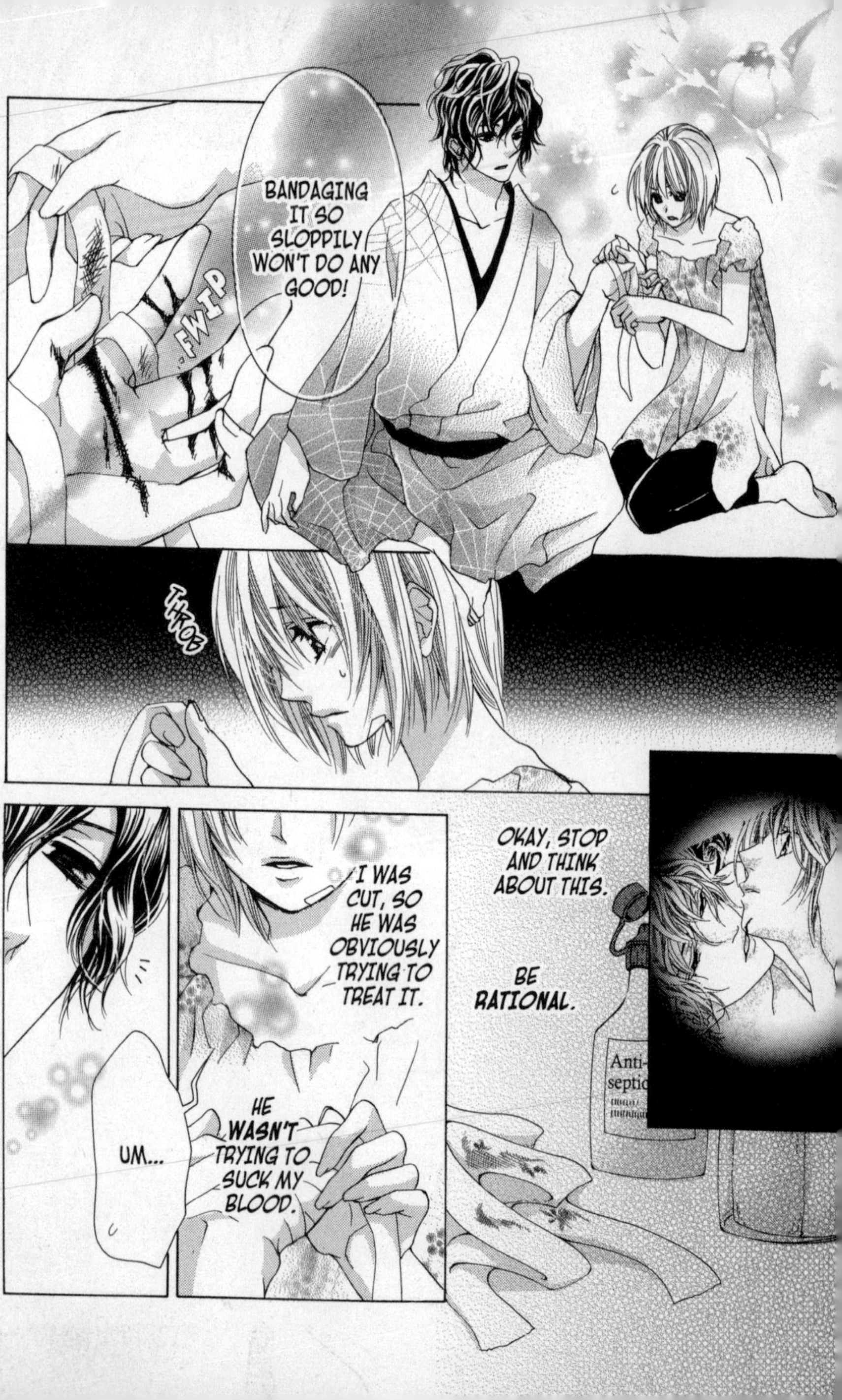
BANDAGING IT SO SLOPPILY WON'T DO ANY GOOD!
FWIP
THROB
OKAY, STOP AND THINK ABOUT THIS.
BE RATIONAL.
Anti-
I WAS CUT, SO HE WAS OBVIOUSLY TRYING TO TREAT IT.
HE WASN'T TRYING TO SUCK MY BLOOD.
UM...

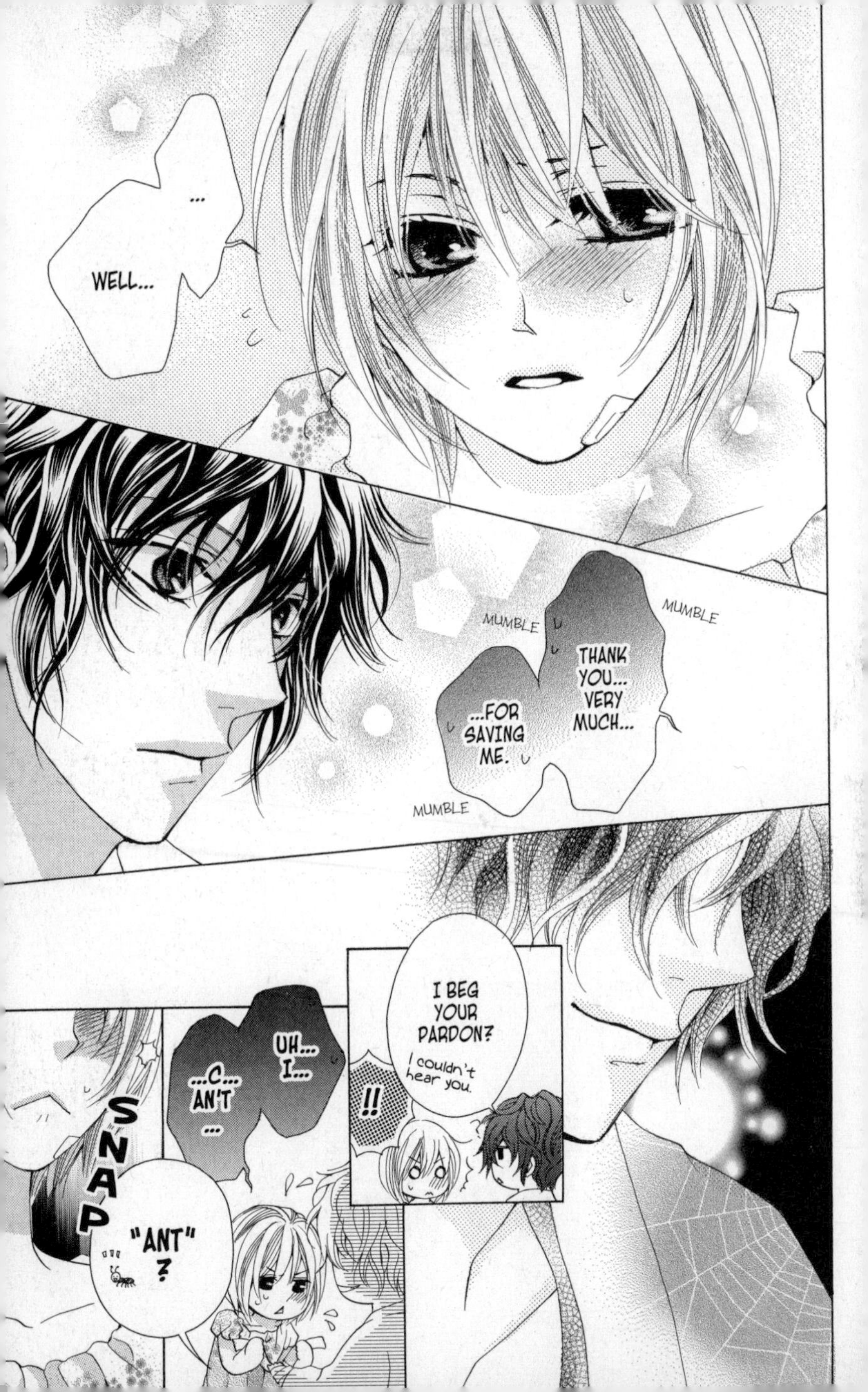
...
WELL...
MUMBLE
THANK YOU... VERY MUCH...
...FOR SAVING ME.
MUMBLE
MUMBLE
I BEG YOUR PARDON?
I couldn't hear you.
!!
UH... I...
...C... AN'T ...
SNAP
"ANT"?

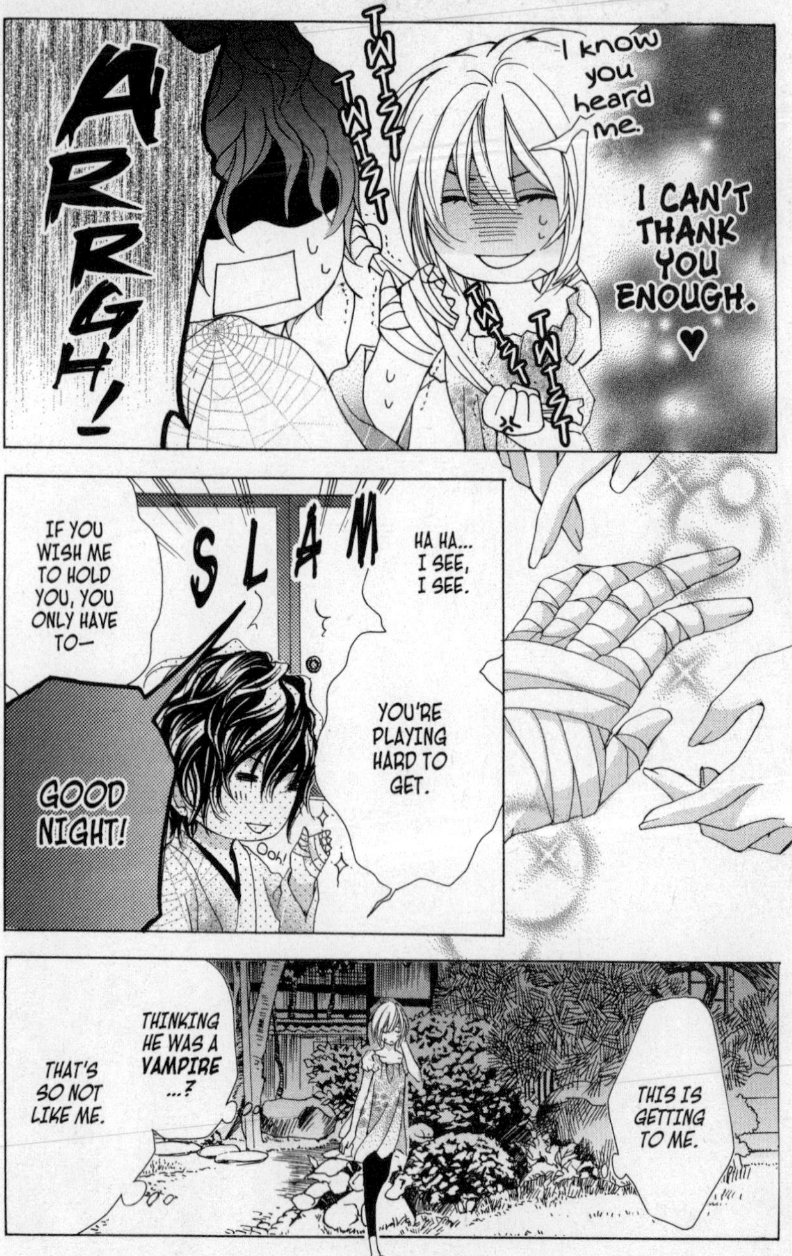
I know you heard me.
I CAN'T THANK YOU ENOUGH. ♥
TWIST TWIST
TWIST TWIST
ARRGH!
HA HA... I SEE, I SEE.
YOU'RE PLAYING HARD TO GET.
Ooh!
SLAM
IF YOU WISH ME TO HOLD YOU, YOU ONLY HAVE TO—
GOOD NIGHT!
THIS IS GETTING TO ME.
THINKING HE WAS A VAMPIRE ...?
THAT'S SO NOT LIKE ME.

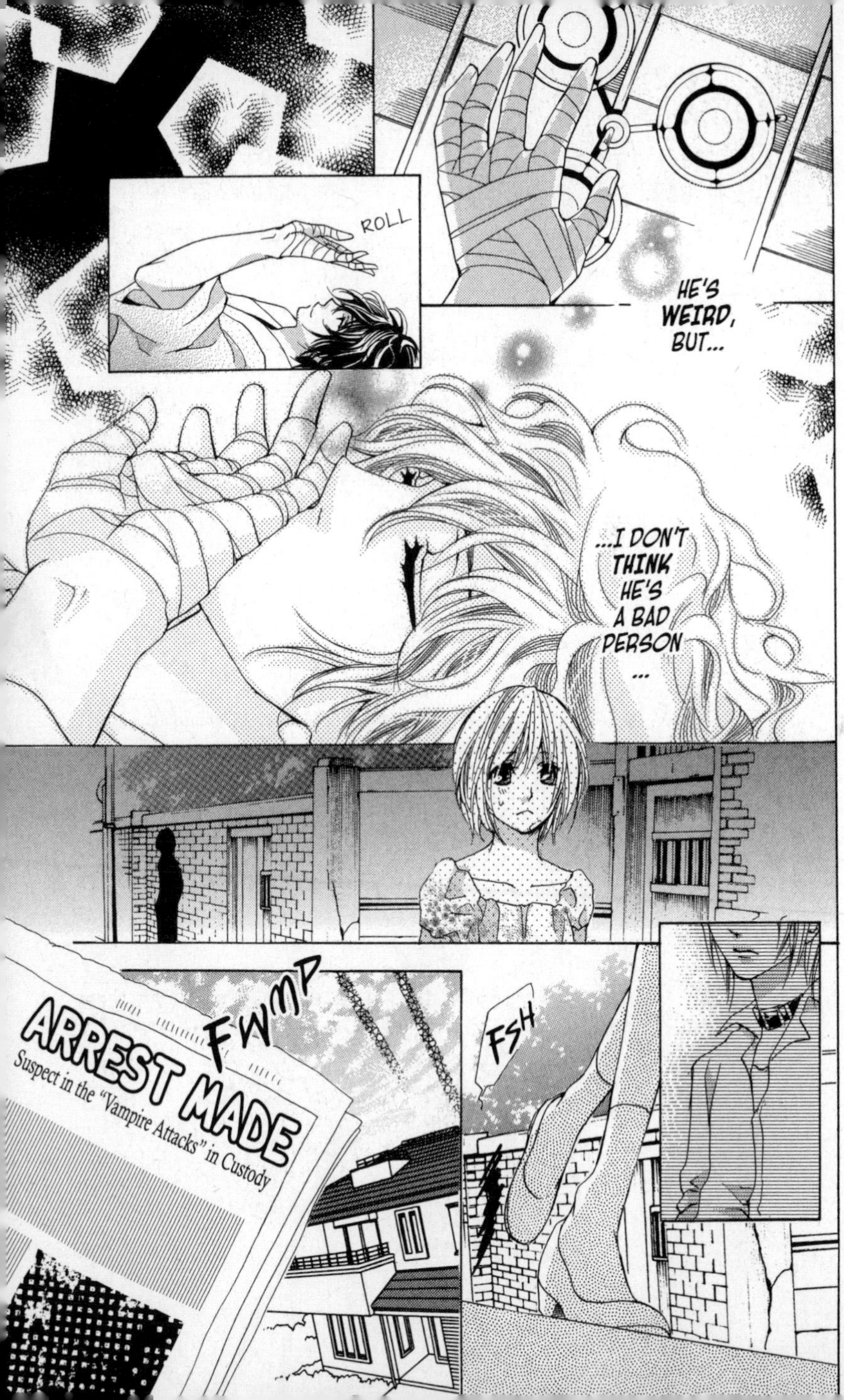
ROLL
HE'S WEIRD, BUT...
...I DON'T THINK HE'S A BAD PERSON...
FSH
FWMP
ARREST MADE
Suspect in the "Vampire Attacks" in Custody

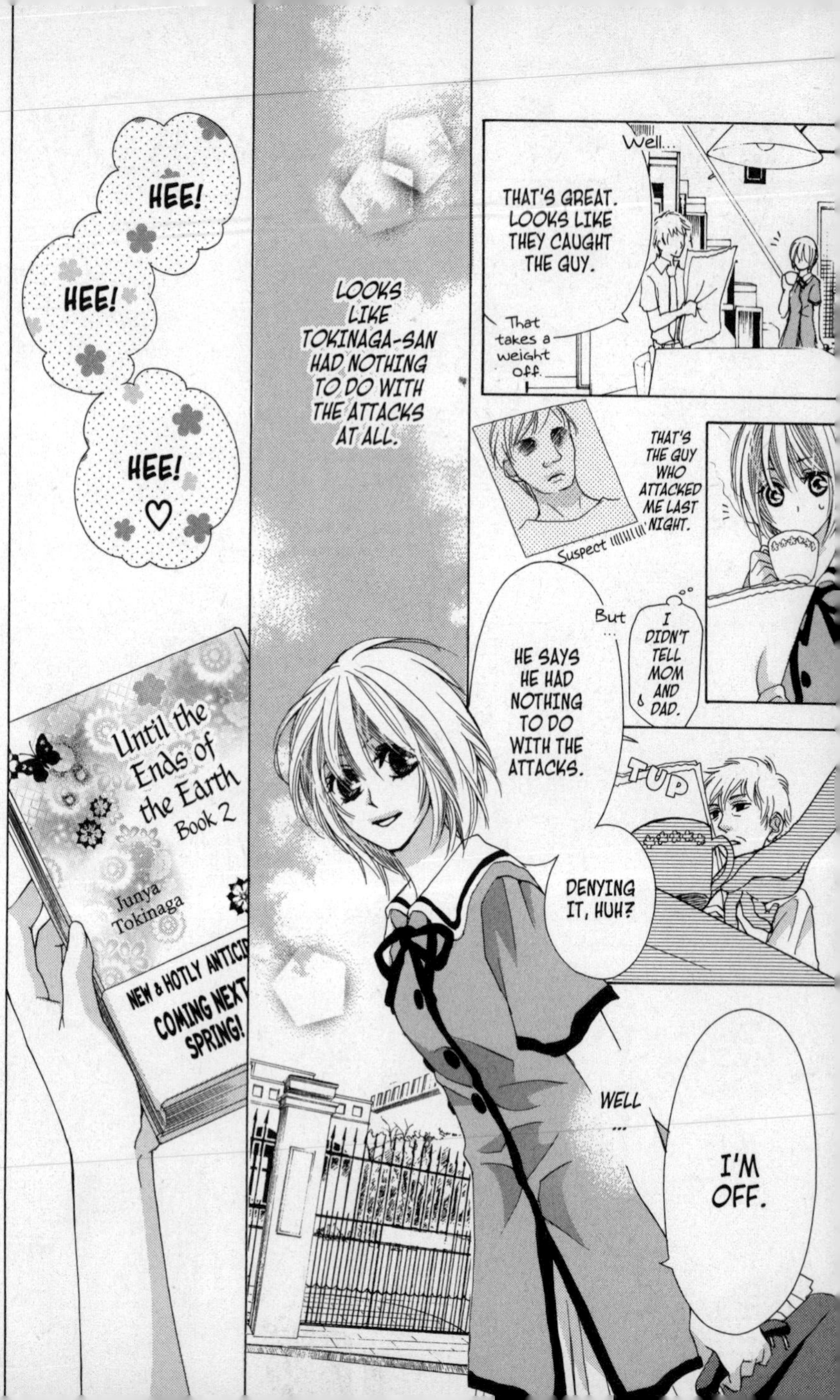
Well...
THAT'S GREAT. LOOKS LIKE THEY CAUGHT THE GUY.
That takes a weight off.
THAT'S THE GUY WHO ATTACKED ME LAST NIGHT.
Suspect
I DIDN'T TELL MOM AND DAD.
But ...
HE SAYS HE HAD NOTHING TO DO WITH THE ATTACKS.
TUP
DENYING IT, HUH?
WELL ...
I'M OFF.
LOOKS LIKE TOKINAGA-SAN HAD NOTHING TO DO WITH THE ATTACKS AT ALL.
HEE!
HEE!
HEE! ♡
Until the Ends of the Earth Book 2
Junya Tokinaga
NEW & HOTLY
COMING NEXT SPRING!

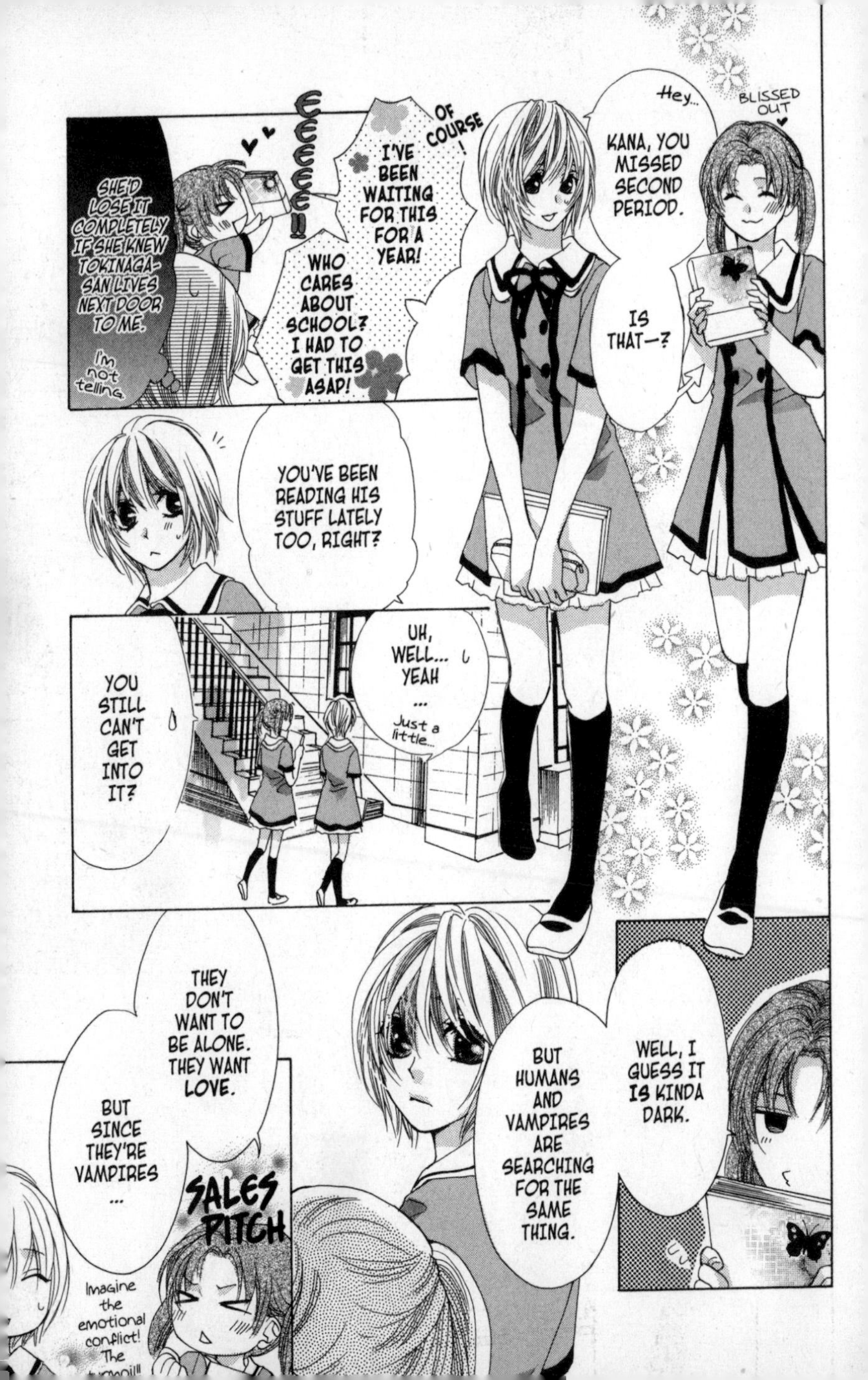
Hey...
BLISSED OUT ♥
KANA, YOU MISSED SECOND PERIOD.
IS THAT—?
OF COURSE!
I'VE BEEN WAITING FOR THIS FOR A YEAR!
EEEEEE!!
WHO CARES ABOUT SCHOOL? I HAD TO GET THIS ASAP!
SHE'D LOSE IT COMPLETELY IF SHE KNEW TOKINAGA-SAN LIVES NEXT DOOR TO ME.
I'm not telling.
YOU'VE BEEN READING HIS STUFF LATELY TOO, RIGHT?
UH, WELL... YEAH ...
Just a little...
YOU STILL CAN'T GET INTO IT?
WELL, I GUESS IT IS KINDA DARK.
BUT HUMANS AND VAMPIRES ARE SEARCHING FOR THE SAME THING.
THEY DON'T WANT TO BE ALONE. THEY WANT LOVE.
BUT SINCE THEY'RE VAMPIRES ...
SALES PITCH
Imagine the emotional conflict! The

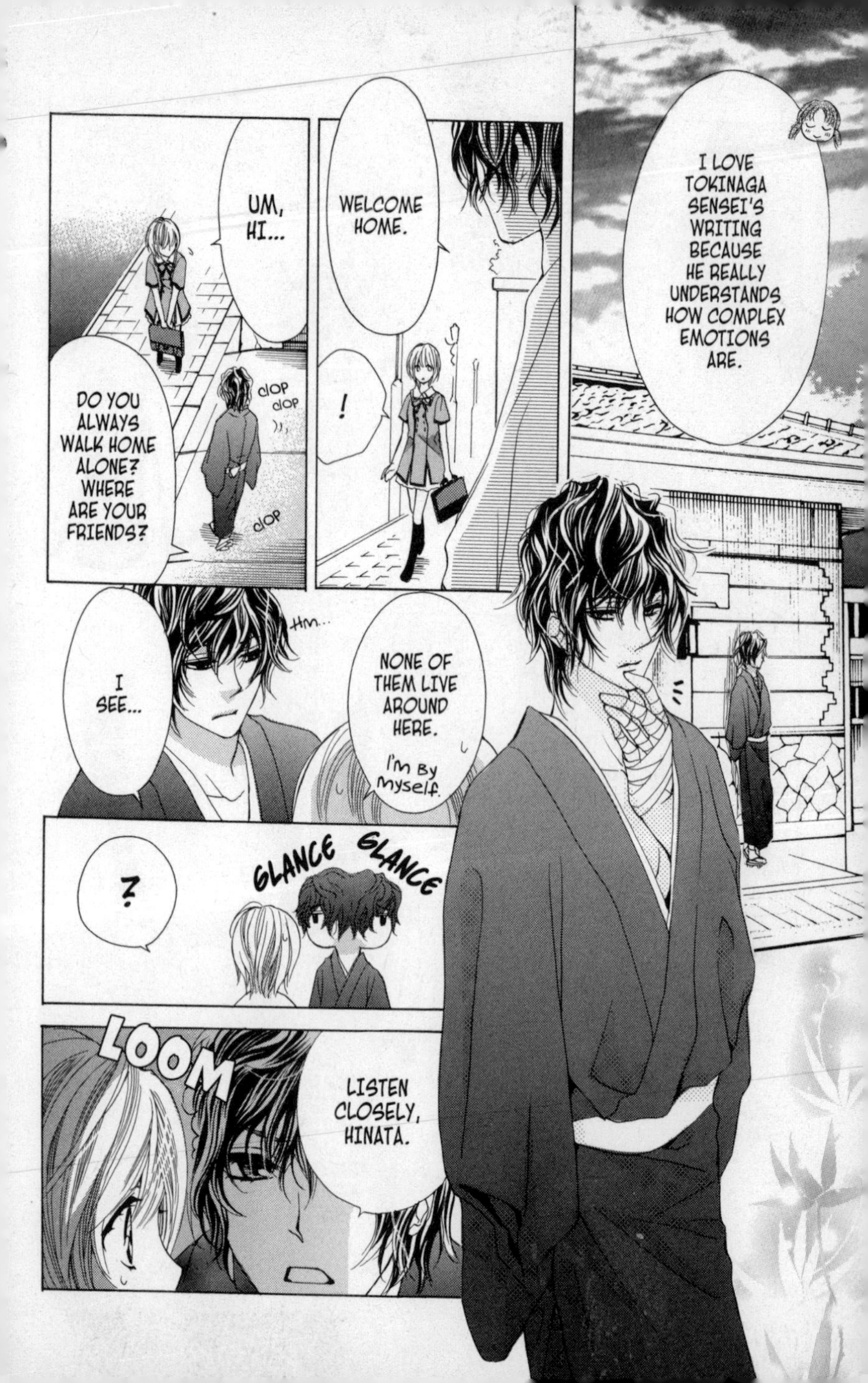
I LOVE TOKINAGA SENSEI'S WRITING BECAUSE HE REALLY UNDERSTANDS HOW COMPLEX EMOTIONS ARE.
WELCOME HOME.
!
UM, HI...
clop clop
DO YOU ALWAYS WALK HOME ALONE? WHERE ARE YOUR FRIENDS?
clop
Hm...
NONE OF THEM LIVE AROUND HERE.
I'm By myself.
I SEE...
GLANCE GLANCE
?
LOOM
LISTEN CLOSELY, HINATA.

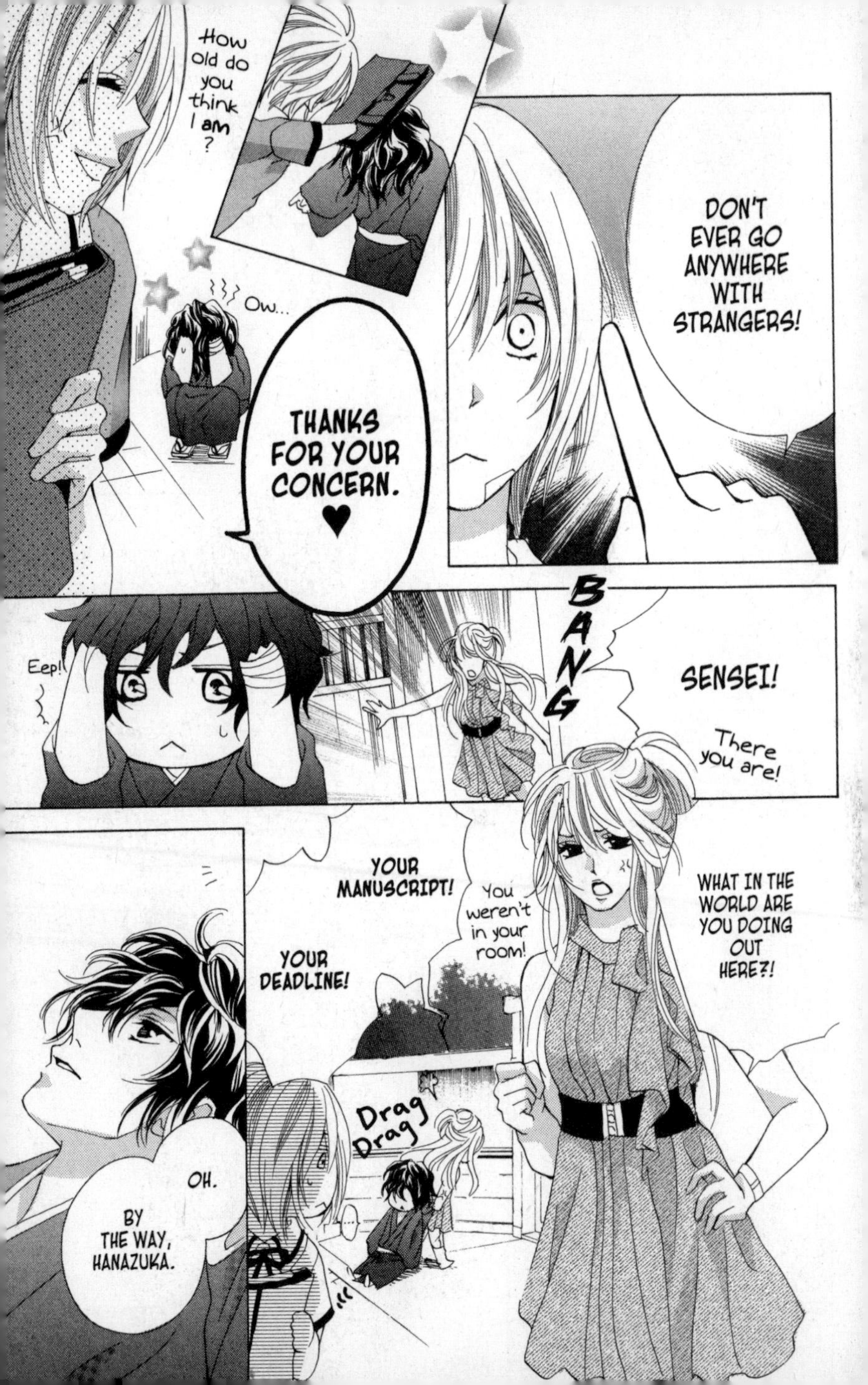

DON'T EVER GO ANYWHERE WITH STRANGERS!
How old do you think I am?
Ow...
THANKS FOR YOUR CONCERN. ♥
BANG
SENSEI!
There you are!
Eep!
WHAT IN THE WORLD ARE YOU DOING OUT HERE?!
You weren't in your room!
YOUR MANUSCRIPT!
YOUR DEADLINE!
Drag Drag
...
OH.
BY THE WAY, HANAZUKA.

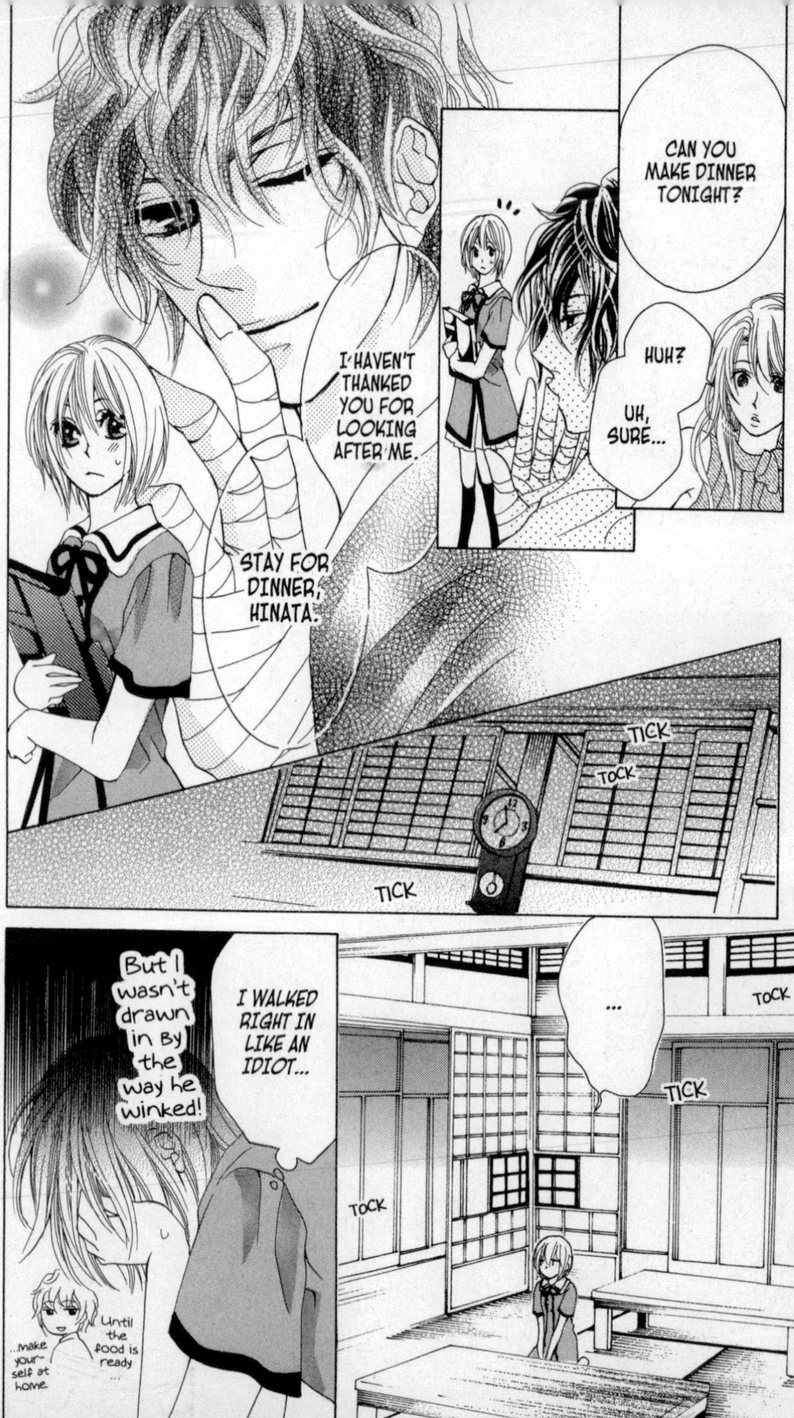
CAN YOU MAKE DINNER TONIGHT?
HUH?
UH, SURE...
I HAVEN'T THANKED YOU FOR LOOKING AFTER ME.
STAY FOR DINNER, HINATA.
TICK
TOCK
TICK
...
TOCK
TICK
TOCK
I WALKED RIGHT IN LIKE AN IDIOT...
But I wasn't drawn in by the way he winked!
Until the food is ready...
...make yourself at home

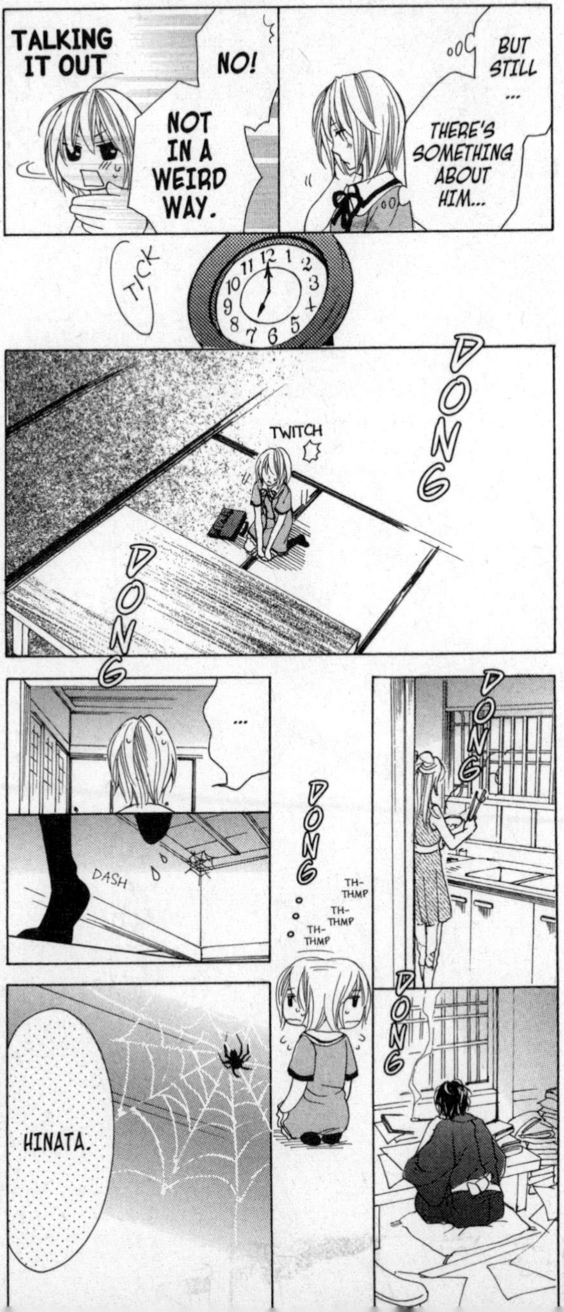
BUT STILL...
THERE'S SOMETHING ABOUT HIM...
TALKING IT OUT
NO!
NOT IN A WEIRD WAY.
TICK
TWITCH
DONG
DONG
DONG
...
DASH
DONG
TH-THMP
TH-THMP
TH-THMP
DONG
HINATA.

Small Talk

②

Lately it seems like there's a constant parade of weddings!

Back in my hometown, I have five good friends whom I've known since middle school (some of them from elementary school, even). I'll probably be good friends with them forever. They're my precious, precious friends.

S was the first in the group to get married. ♥ At the end of September I attended her wedding. I had just finished a manuscript, so I was exhausted. But when I saw S walk in at the church with her (younger!) groom, she was sooo beautiful. The joy on her face made me so happy that it blew all my tiredness away.

The hotel in Kagoshima was located in an elevated area. We were looking at Sakurajima, off in the distance, when S tossed her bridal bouquet. I-chan (another of my five friends) caught it as easily as if it had been thrown right to her.

← Continued in ③

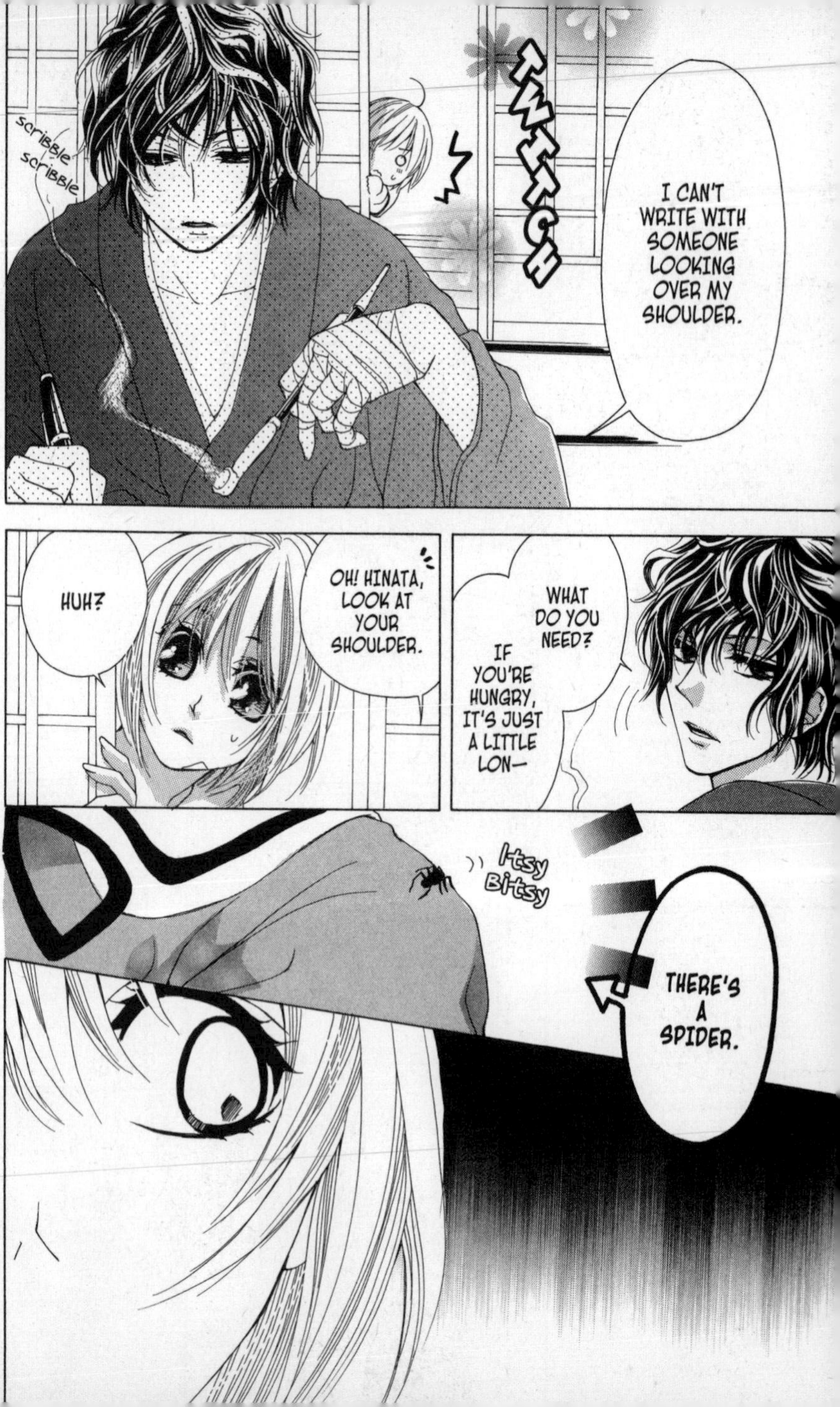
I CAN'T WRITE WITH SOMEONE LOOKING OVER MY SHOULDER.
TWITCH
scribble scribble
WHAT DO YOU NEED?
IF YOU'RE HUNGRY, IT'S JUST A LITTLE LON—
OH! HINATA, LOOK AT YOUR SHOULDER.
HUH?
Itsy Bitsy
THERE'S A SPIDER.

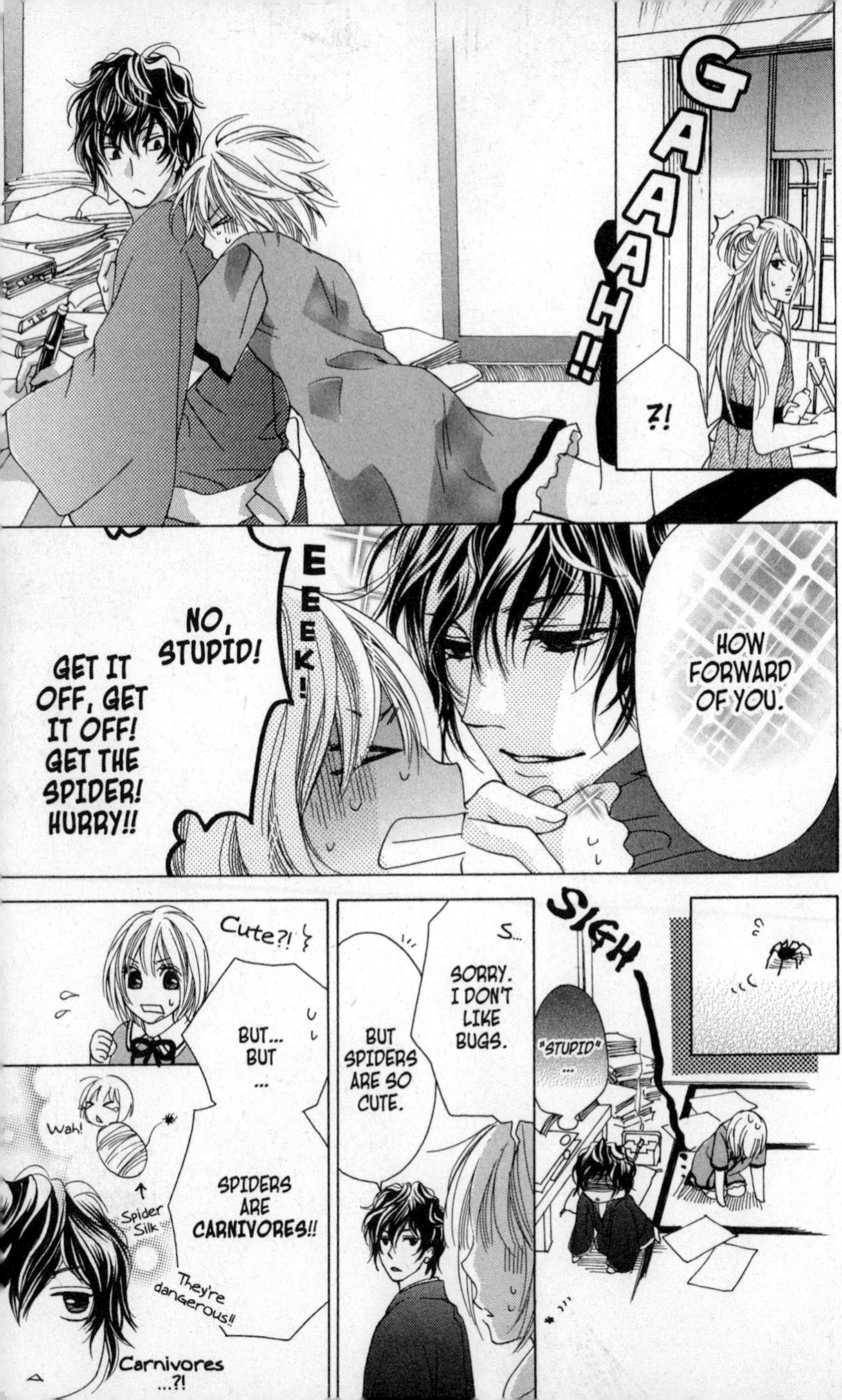
GAAAAH!!
?!
HOW FORWARD OF YOU.
EEEK!
NO, STUPID!
GET IT OFF, GET IT OFF! GET THE SPIDER! HURRY!!
SIGH
"STUPID" ...
S... SORRY. I DON'T LIKE BUGS.
BUT SPIDERS ARE SO CUTE.
Cute?!
BUT... BUT ...
SPIDERS ARE CARNIVORES!!
Wah!
Spider Silk
They're dangerous!!
Carnivores ...?!

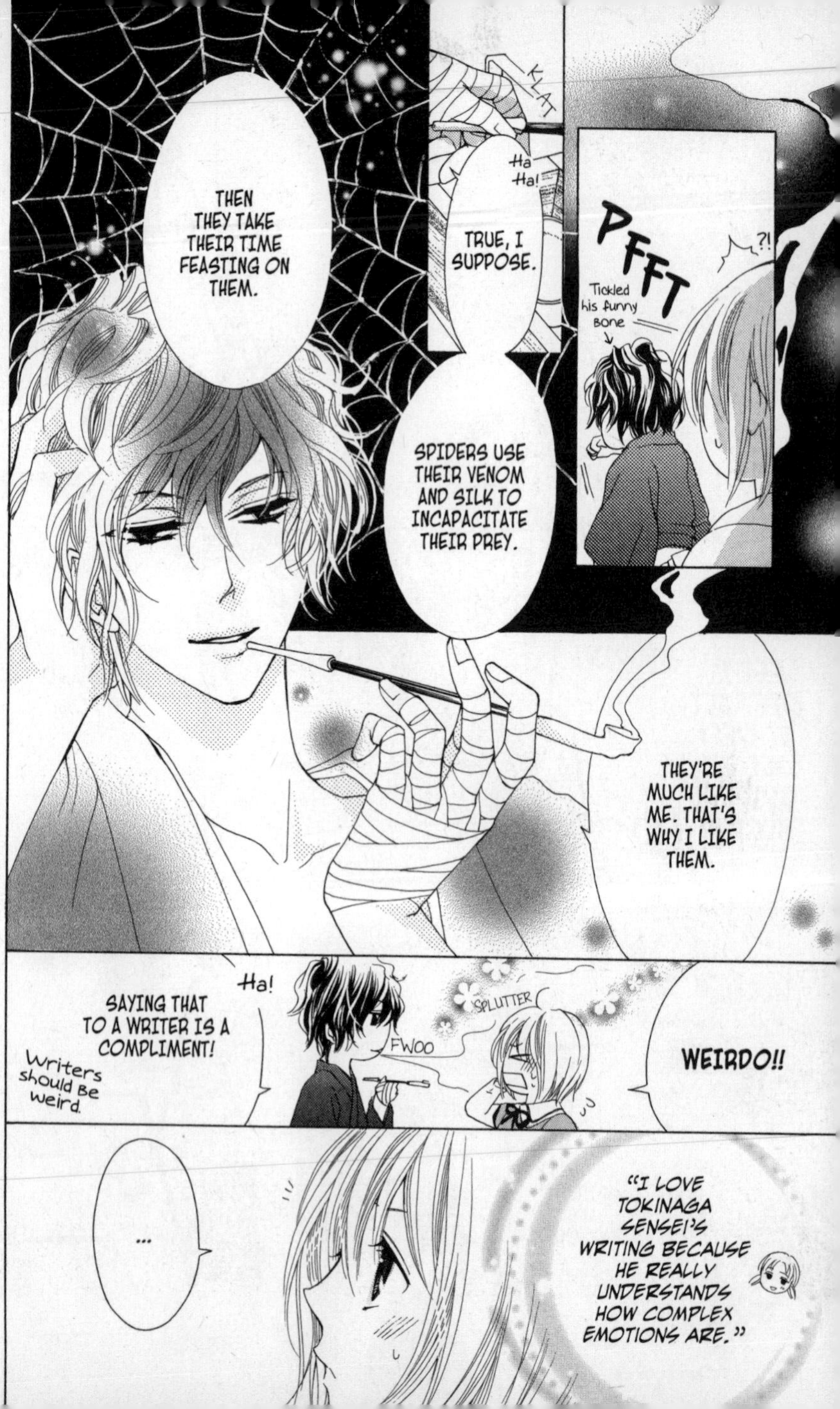
PFFT
?!
Tickled his funny bone
KLAT
Ha Ha!
TRUE, I SUPPOSE.
THEN THEY TAKE THEIR TIME FEASTING ON THEM.
SPIDERS USE THEIR VENOM AND SILK TO INCAPACITATE THEIR PREY.
THEY'RE MUCH LIKE ME. THAT'S WHY I LIKE THEM.
WEIRDO!!
SPLUTTER
FWOO
Ha!
SAYING THAT TO A WRITER IS A COMPLIMENT!
Writers should be weird.
"I LOVE TOKINAGA SENSEI'S WRITING BECAUSE HE REALLY UNDERSTANDS HOW COMPLEX EMOTIONS ARE."
...

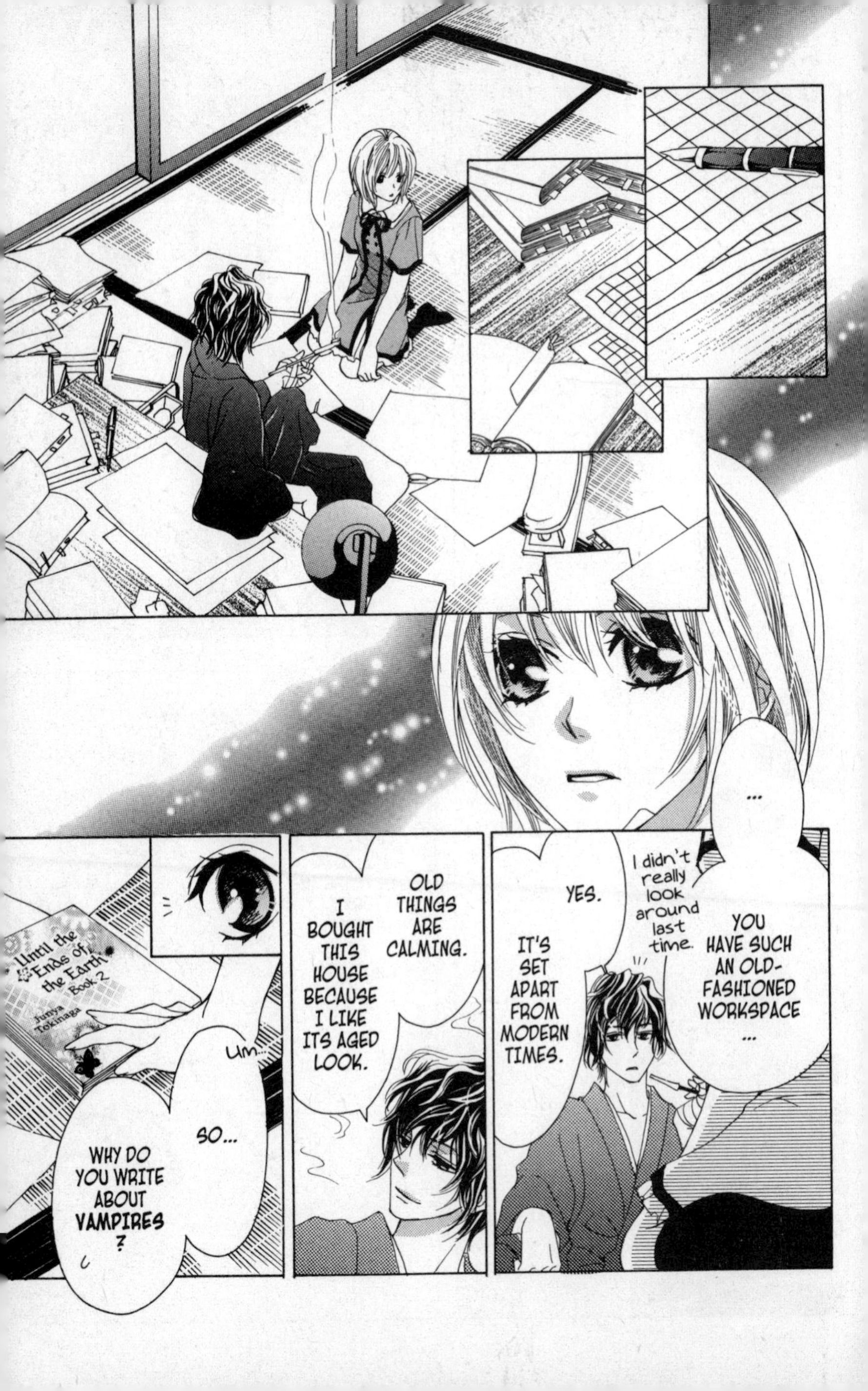
...
YOU HAVE SUCH AN OLD-FASHIONED WORKSPACE ...
I didn't really look around last time.
YES.
IT'S SET APART FROM MODERN TIMES.
OLD THINGS ARE CALMING.
I BOUGHT THIS HOUSE BECAUSE I LIKE ITS AGED LOOK.
Until the Ends of the Earth Book 2
Junya Tokinaga
Um...
SO...
WHY DO YOU WRITE ABOUT VAMPIRES?

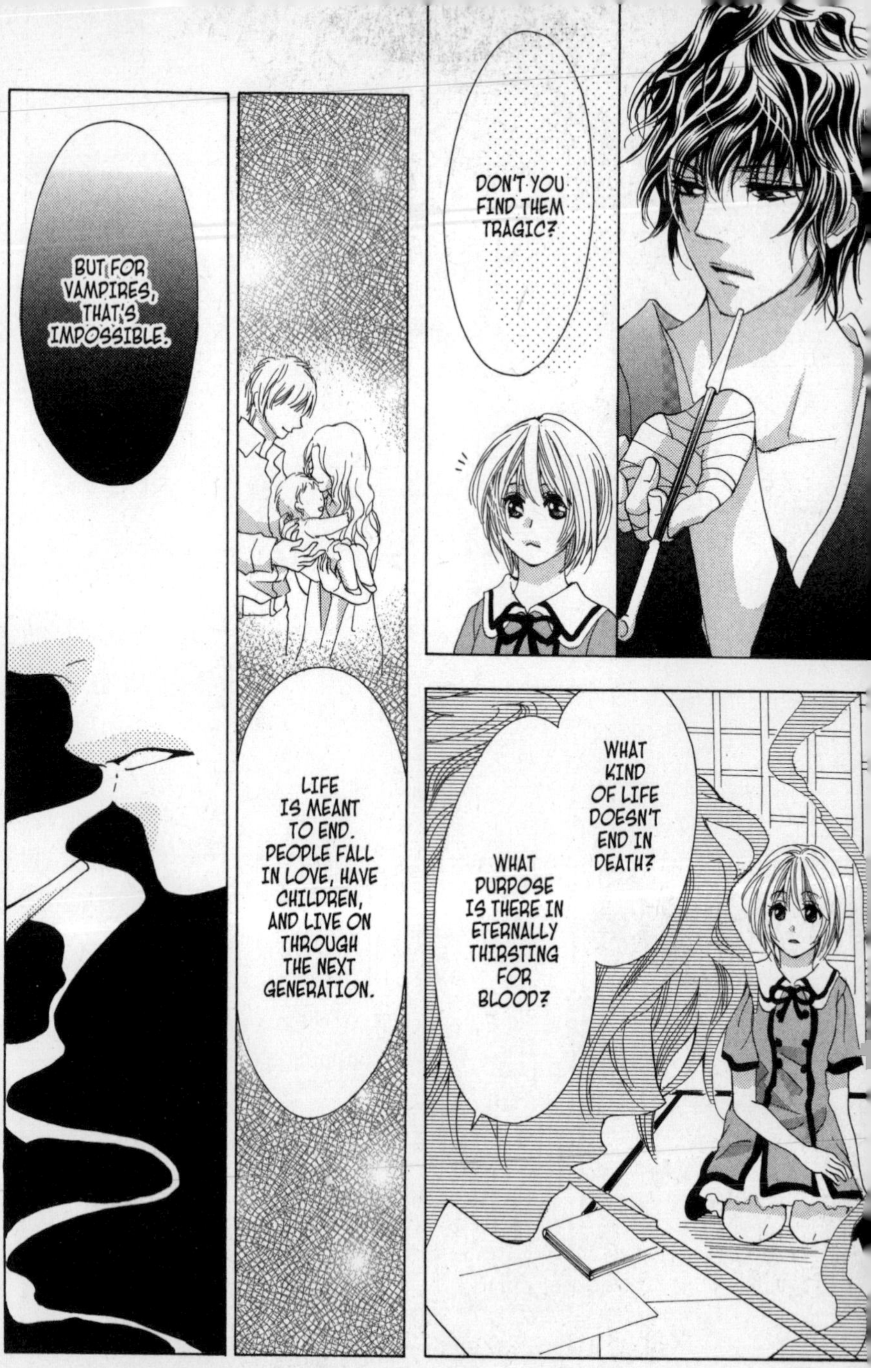
DON'T YOU FIND THEM TRAGIC?
WHAT KIND OF LIFE DOESN'T END IN DEATH?
WHAT PURPOSE IS THERE IN ETERNALLY THIRSTING FOR BLOOD?
LIFE IS MEANT TO END. PEOPLE FALL IN LOVE, HAVE CHILDREN, AND LIVE ON THROUGH THE NEXT GENERATION.
BUT FOR VAMPIRES, THAT'S IMPOSSIBLE.

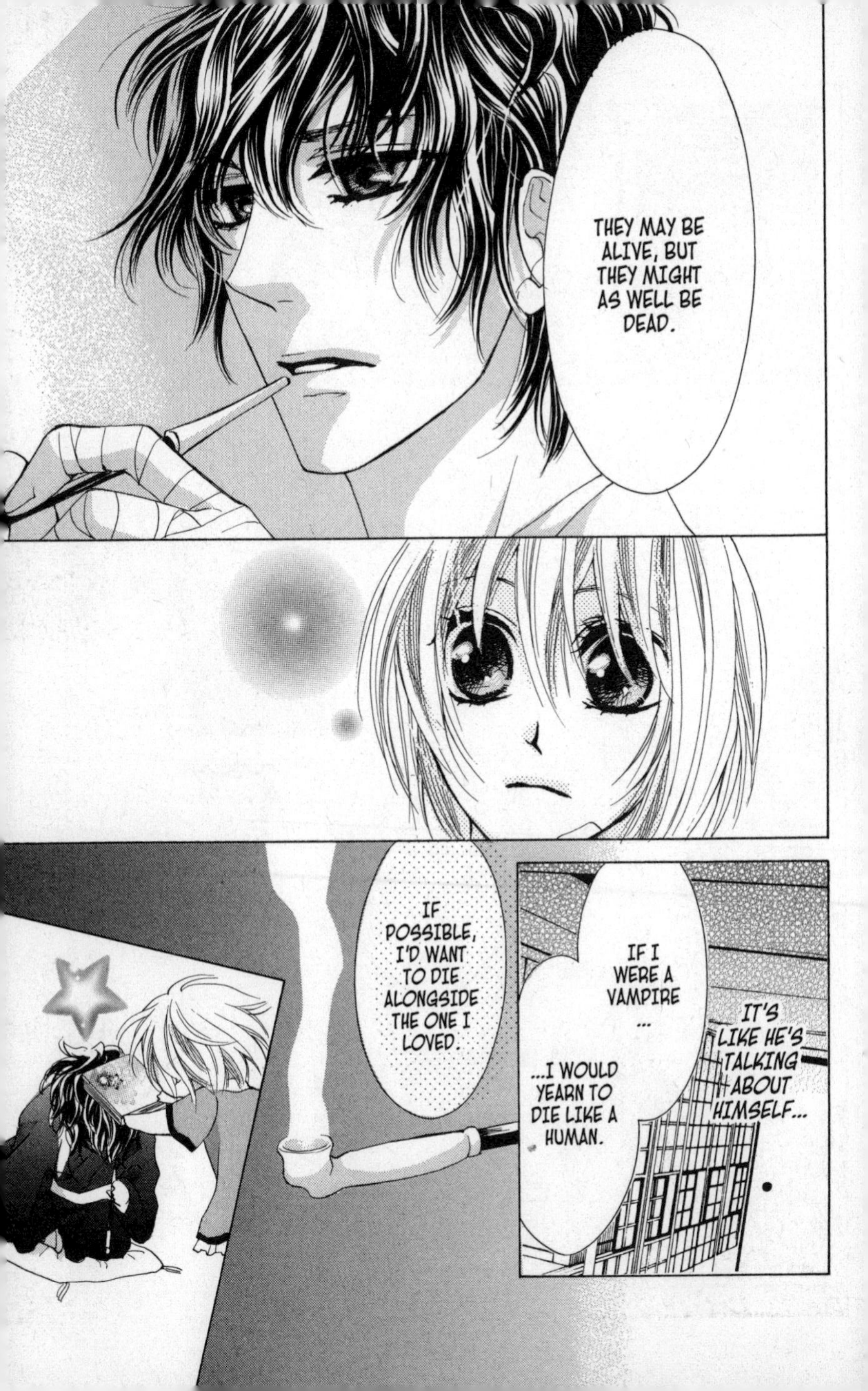
THEY MAY BE ALIVE, BUT THEY MIGHT AS WELL BE DEAD.
IF I WERE A VAMPIRE...
...I WOULD YEARN TO DIE LIKE A HUMAN.
IT'S LIKE HE'S TALKING ABOUT HIMSELF...
IF POSSIBLE, I'D WANT TO DIE ALONGSIDE THE ONE I LOVED.

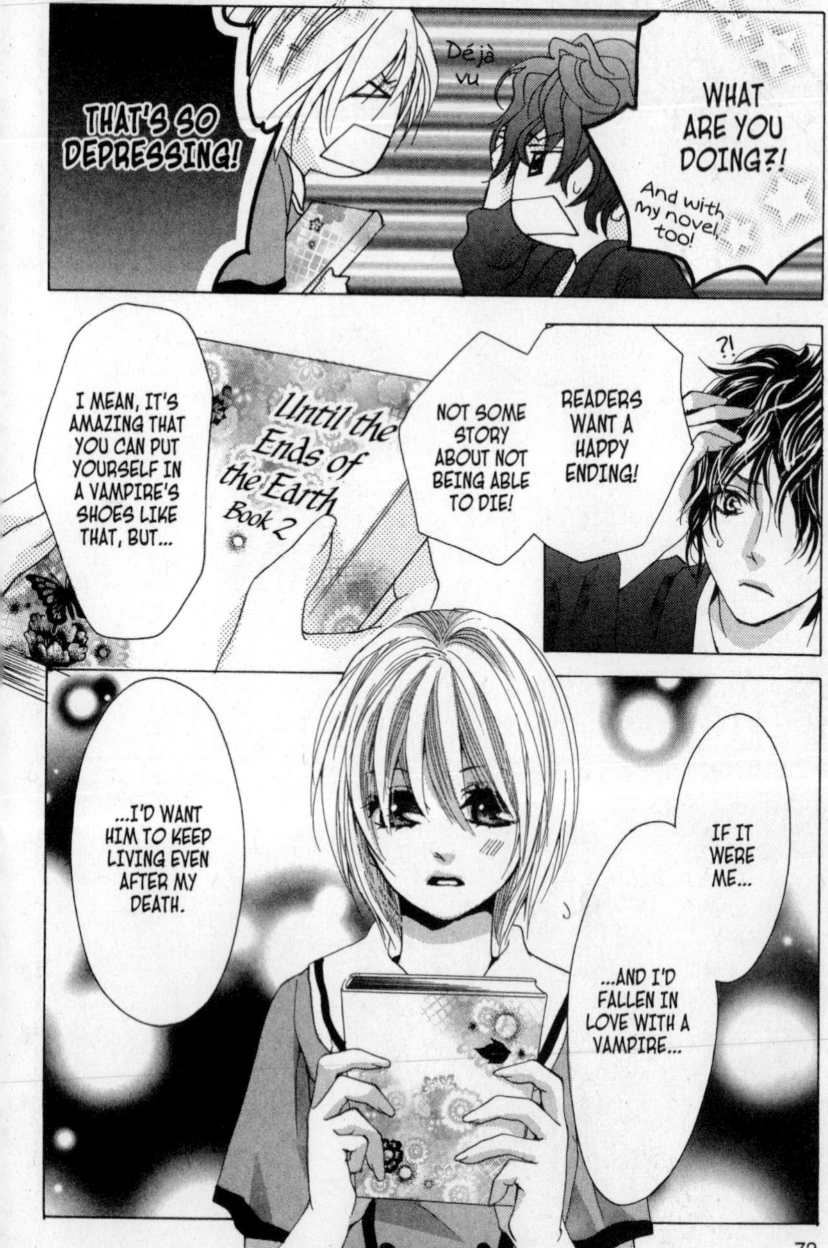
WHAT ARE YOU DOING?!
And with my novel, too!
Déjà vu
THAT'S SO DEPRESSING!
?!
READERS WANT A HAPPY ENDING!
NOT SOME STORY ABOUT NOT BEING ABLE TO DIE!
Until the Ends of the Earth Book 2
I MEAN, IT'S AMAZING THAT YOU CAN PUT YOURSELF IN A VAMPIRE'S SHOES LIKE THAT, BUT...
IF IT WERE ME...
...AND I'D FALLEN IN LOVE WITH A VAMPIRE...
...I'D WANT HIM TO KEEP LIVING EVEN AFTER MY DEATH.

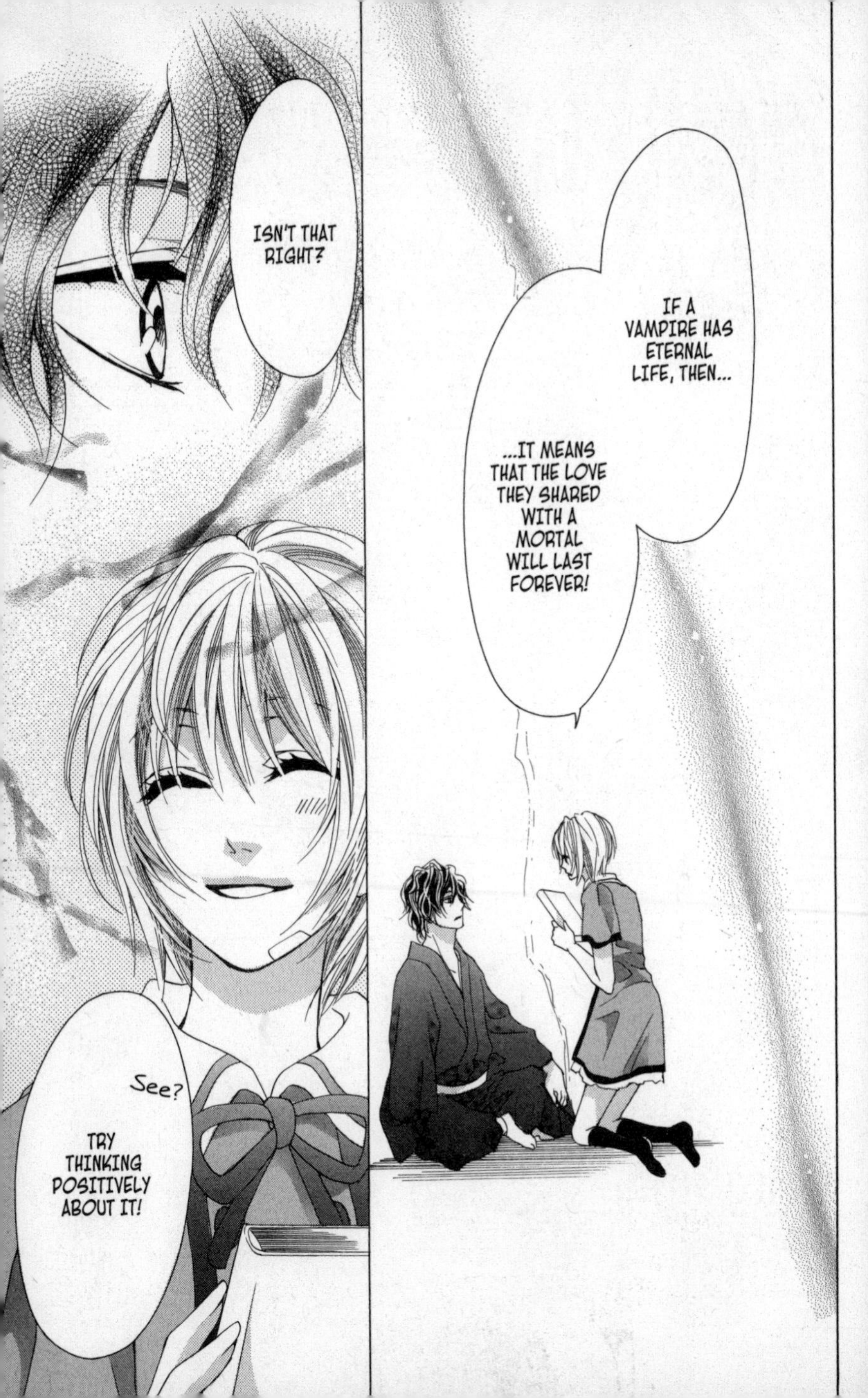
IF A VAMPIRE HAS ETERNAL LIFE, THEN...
...IT MEANS THAT THE LOVE THEY SHARED WITH A MORTAL WILL LAST FOREVER!
ISN'T THAT RIGHT?
See?
TRY THINKING POSITIVELY ABOUT IT!

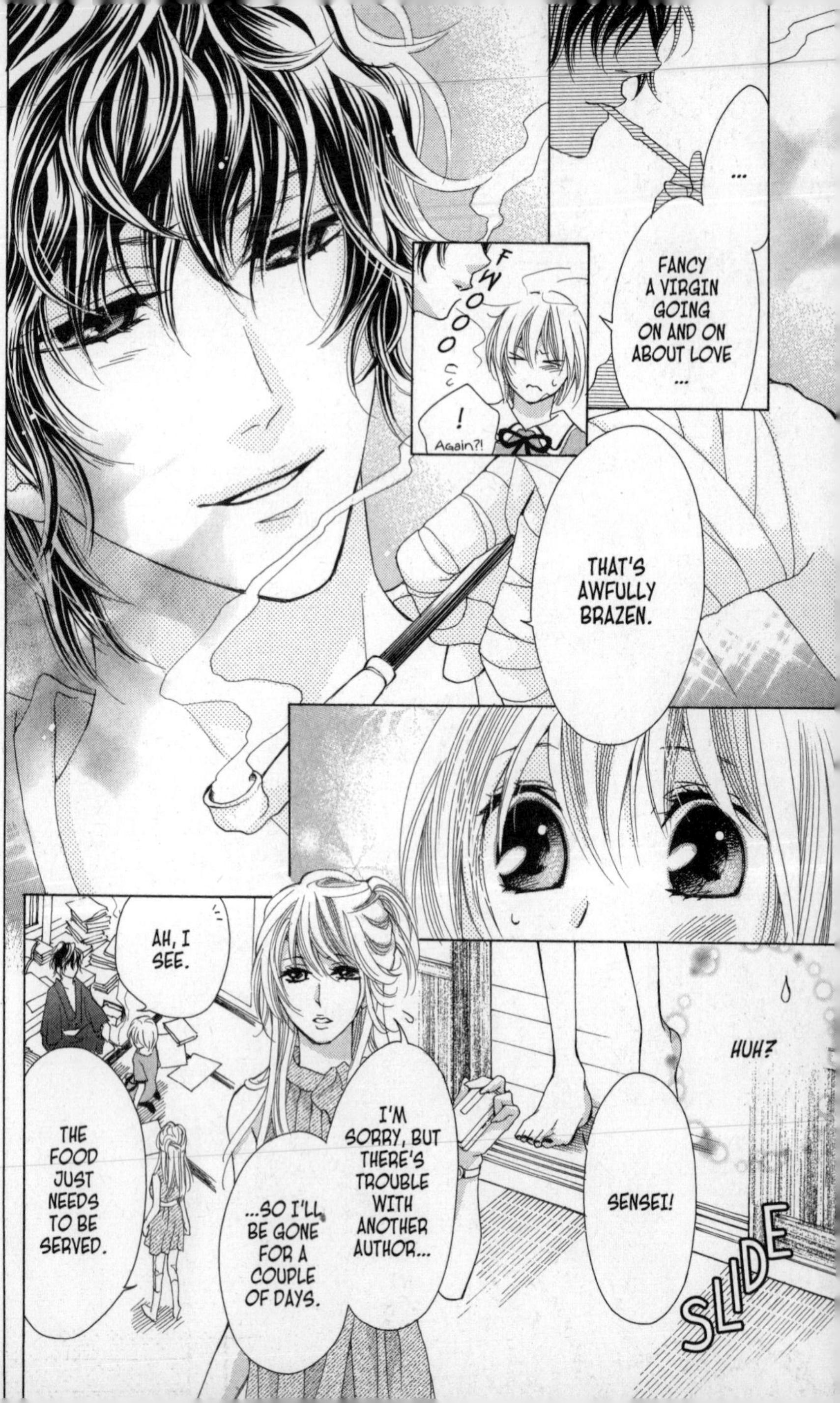
...
FANCY A VIRGIN GOING ON AND ON ABOUT LOVE ...
FWOOOO
!
Again?!
THAT'S AWFULLY BRAZEN.
HUH?
SENSEI!
SLIDE
I'M SORRY, BUT THERE'S TROUBLE WITH ANOTHER AUTHOR...
...SO I'LL BE GONE FOR A COUPLE OF DAYS.
AH, I SEE.
THE FOOD JUST NEEDS TO BE SERVED.

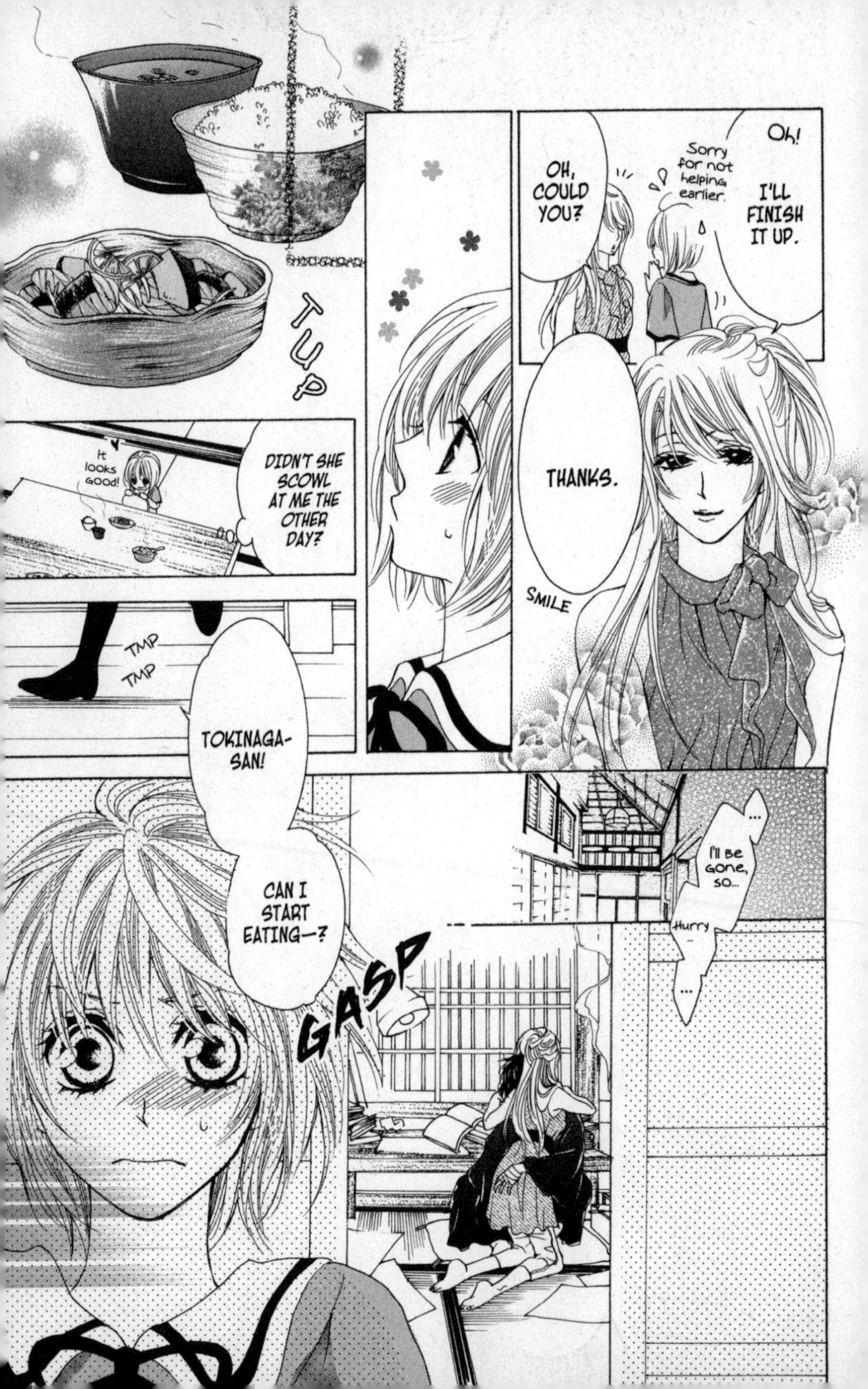
Oh! I'LL FINISH IT UP.
Sorry for not helping earlier.
OH, COULD YOU?
THANKS.
SMILE
TUP
DIDN'T SHE SCOWL AT ME THE OTHER DAY?
It looks good!
TMP
TMP
TOKINAGA-SAN!
CAN I START EATING—?
...
I'll be gone, so...
Hurry ...
...
GASP

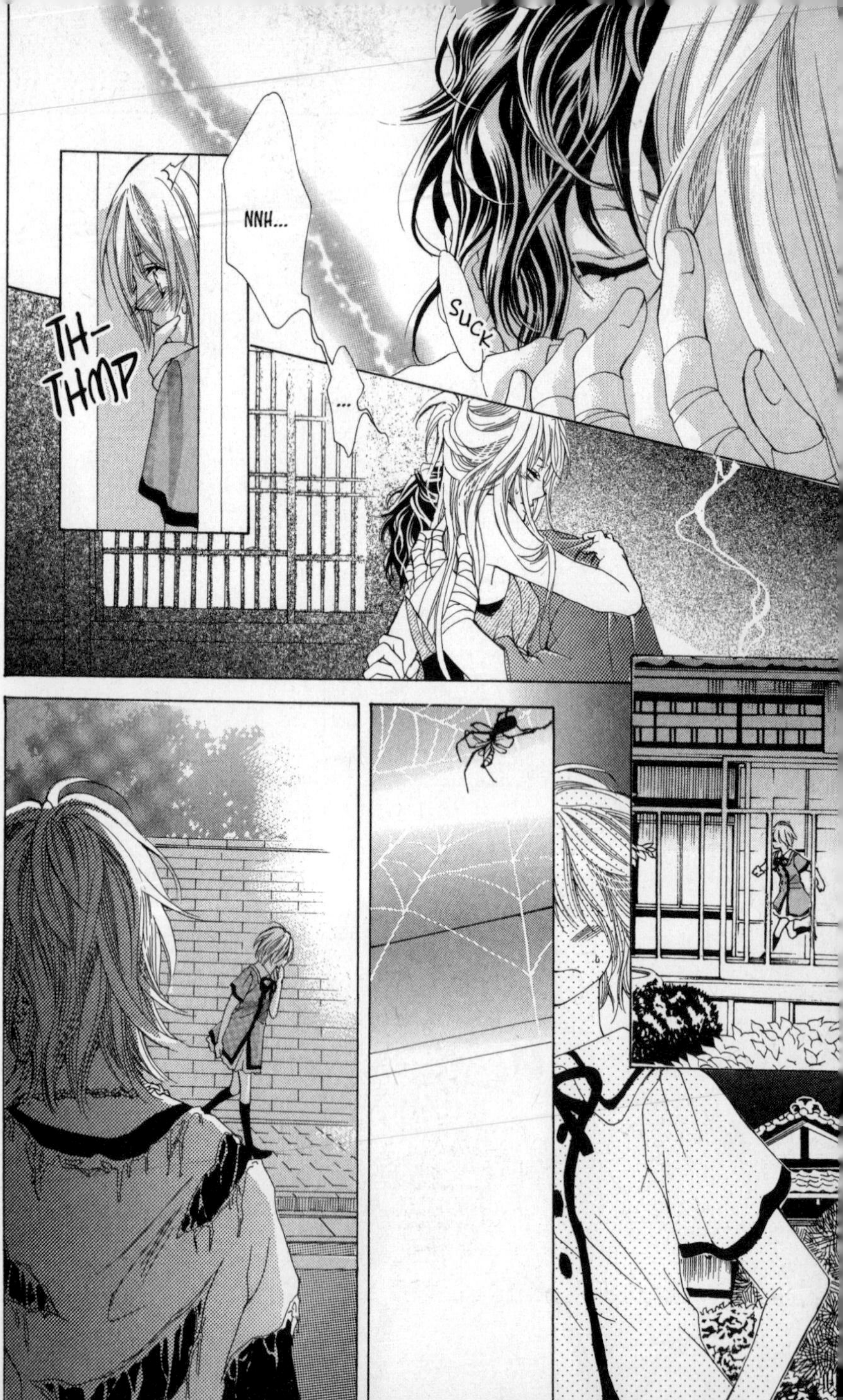
SUCK
NNH...
...
TH-THMP

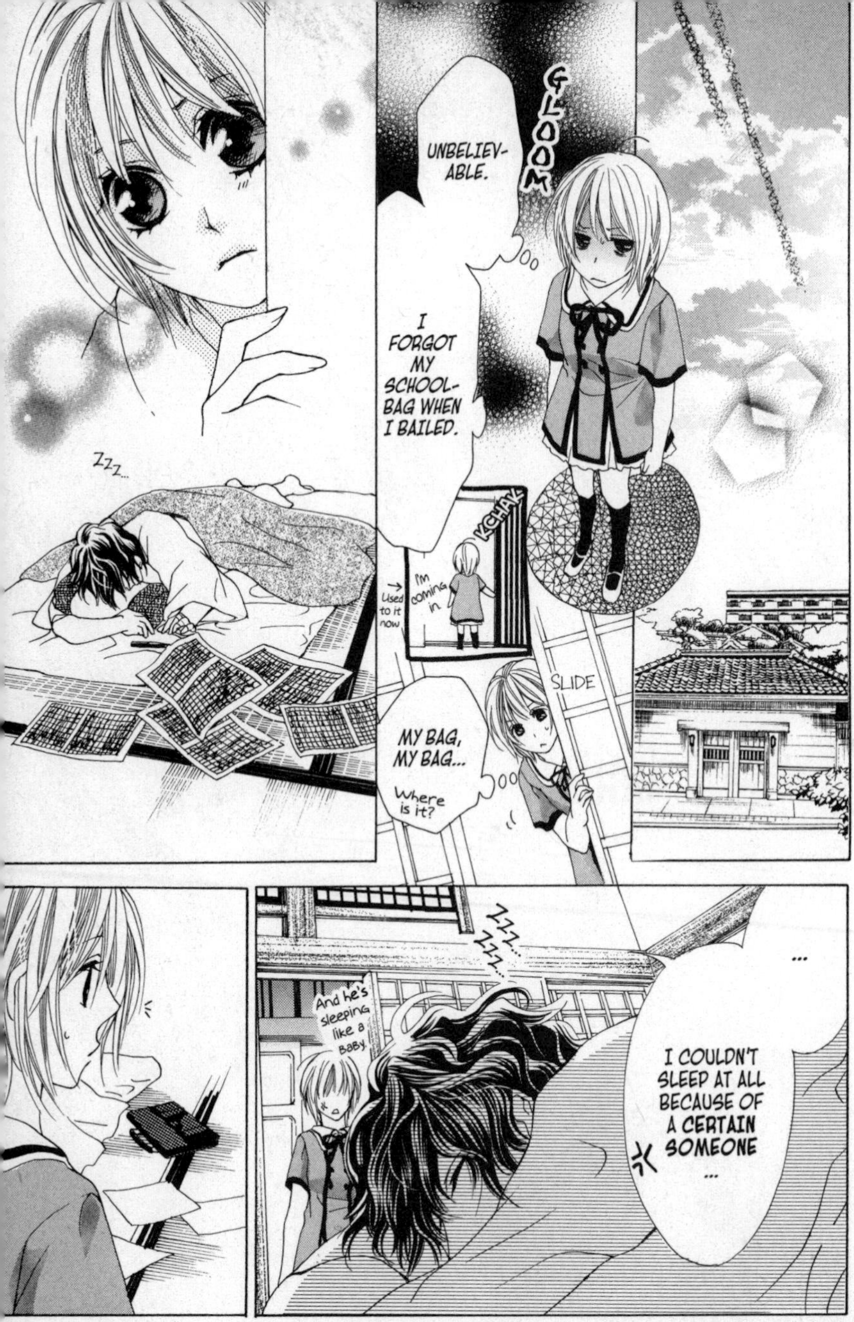
GLOOM
UNBELIEV-ABLE.
I FORGOT MY SCHOOL-BAG WHEN I BAILED.
KCHAK
I'm coming in.
Used to it now
SLIDE
MY BAG, MY BAG...
Where is it?
Zzz...
...
I COULDN'T SLEEP AT ALL BECAUSE OF A CERTAIN SOMEONE ...
ZZZ ZZZ...
And he's sleeping like a baby.

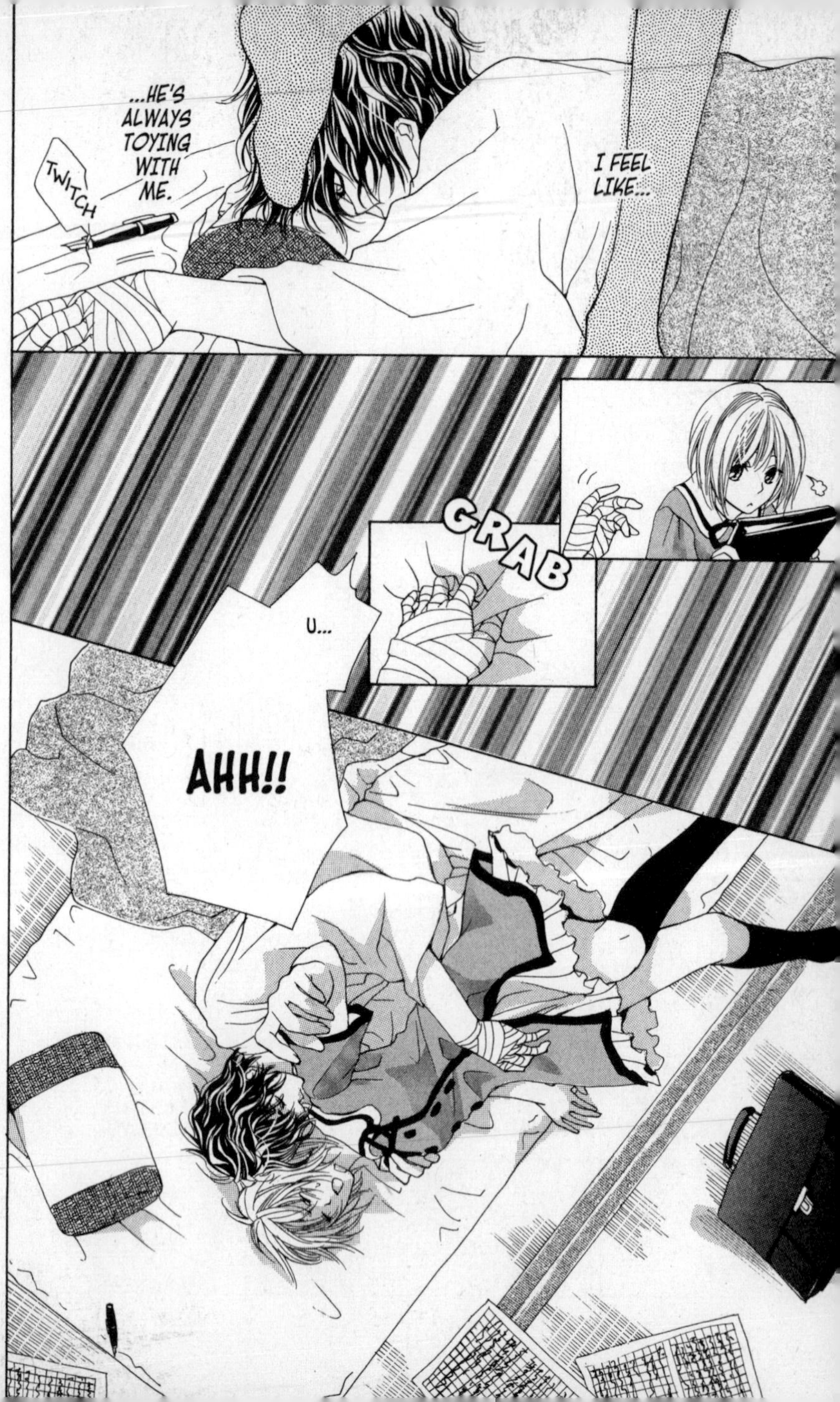
I FEEL LIKE...
...HE'S ALWAYS TOYING WITH ME.
TWITCH
GRAB
U...
AHH!!

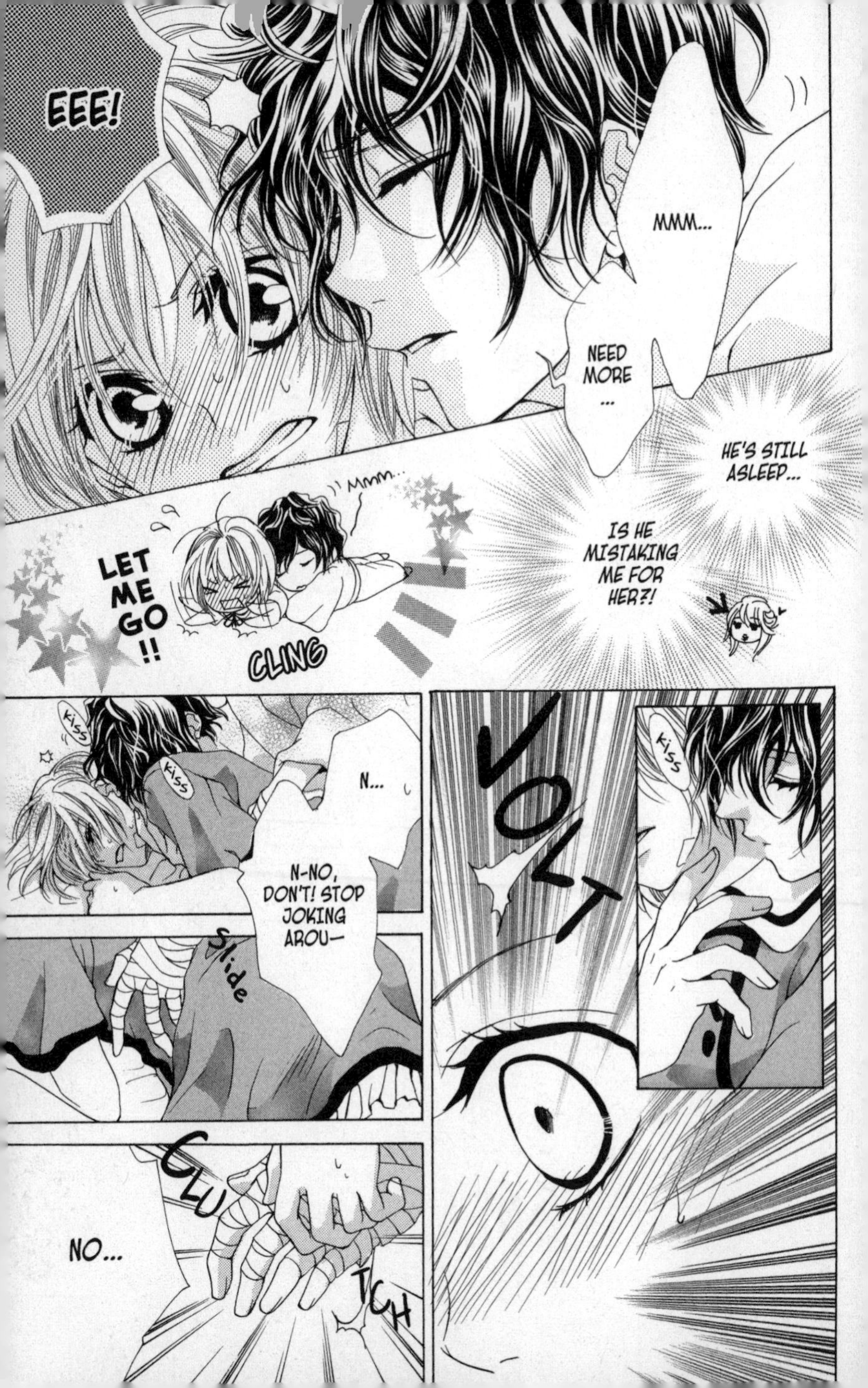
MMM...
NEED MORE ...
EEE!
HE'S STILL ASLEEP...
IS HE MISTAKING ME FOR HER?!
Mmm...
LET ME GO!!
CLING
kiss
VOLT
kiss
kiss
N...
N-NO, DON'T! STOP JOKING AROU—
slide
CLUTCH
NO...

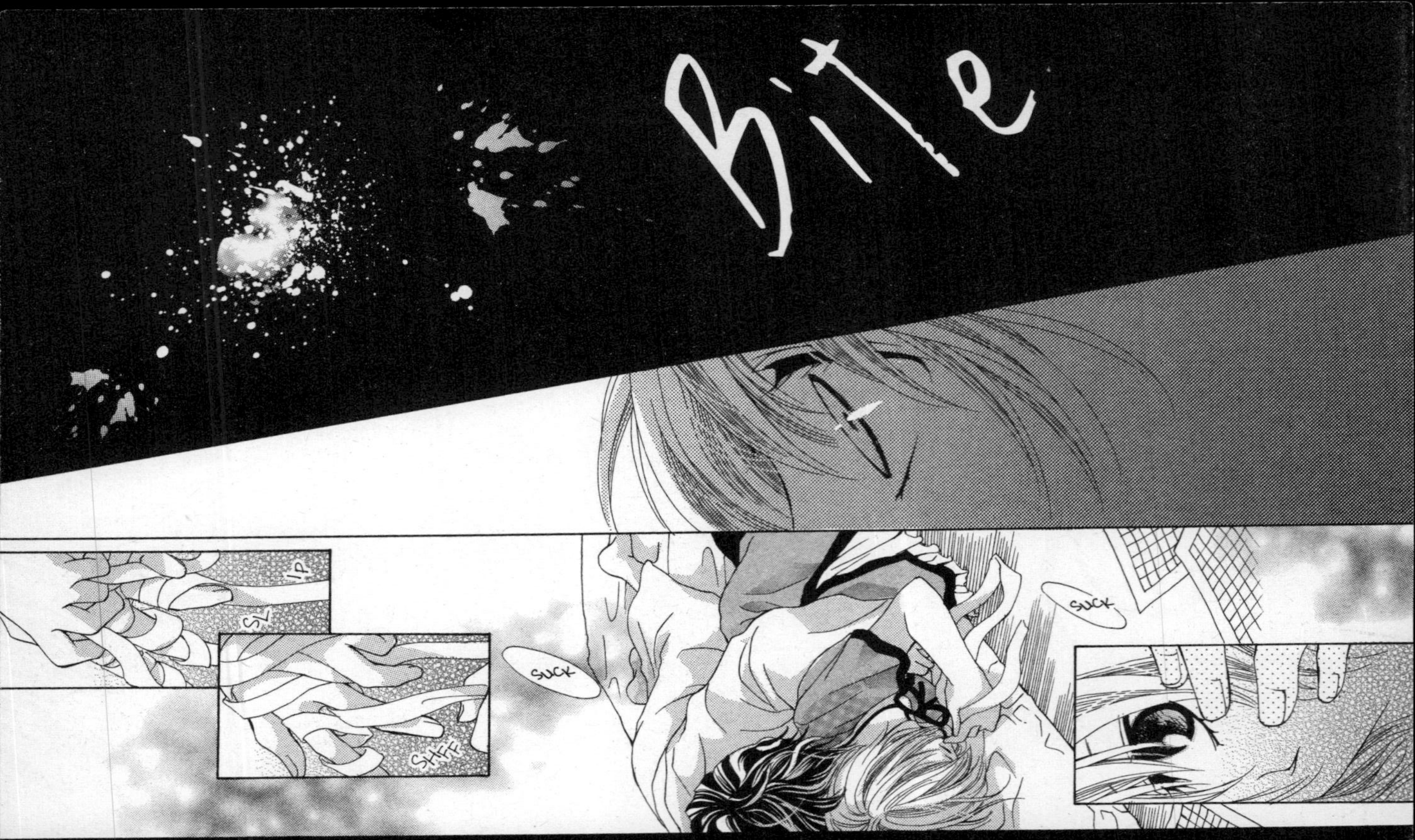
Bite
SUCK
SUCK
SLIP
SHFF

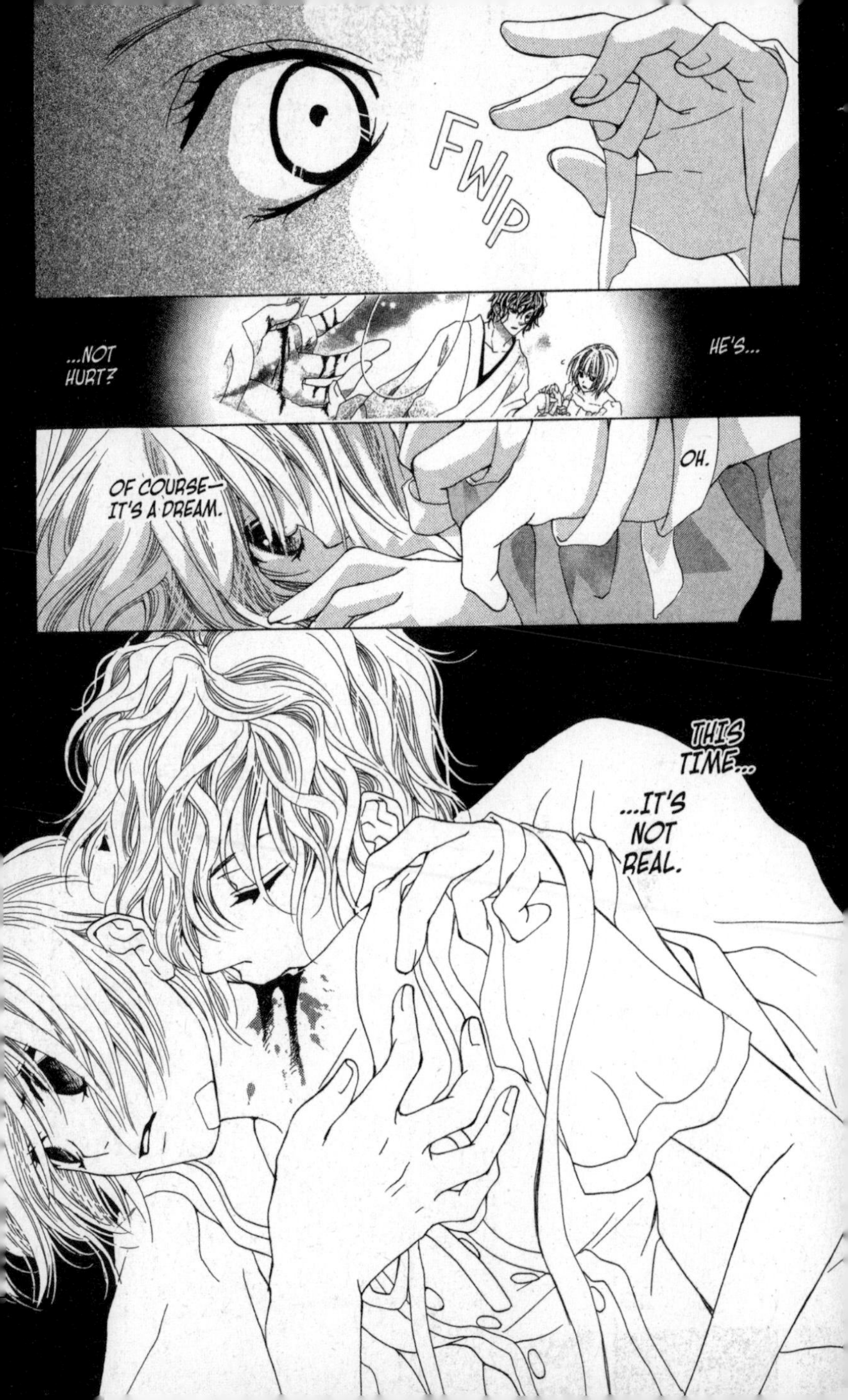
FWIP
HE'S...
...NOT HURT?
OH.
OF COURSE—IT'S A DREAM.
THIS TIME...
...IT'S NOT REAL.

Kimono

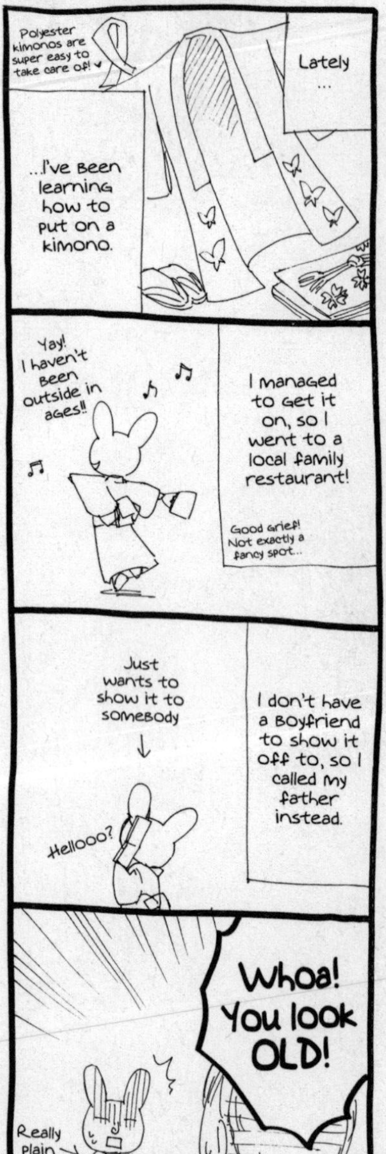
Lately …
Polyester kimonos are super easy to take care of! ♥
…I've been learning how to put on a kimono.
I managed to get it on, so I went to a local family restaurant!
Good grief! Not exactly a fancy spot…
Yay! I haven't been outside in ages!!
I don't have a boyfriend to show it off to, so I called my father instead.
Just wants to show it to somebody
Hellooo?
Whoa! You look OLD!
Like somebody's grandma!
Really plain

Chapter 3

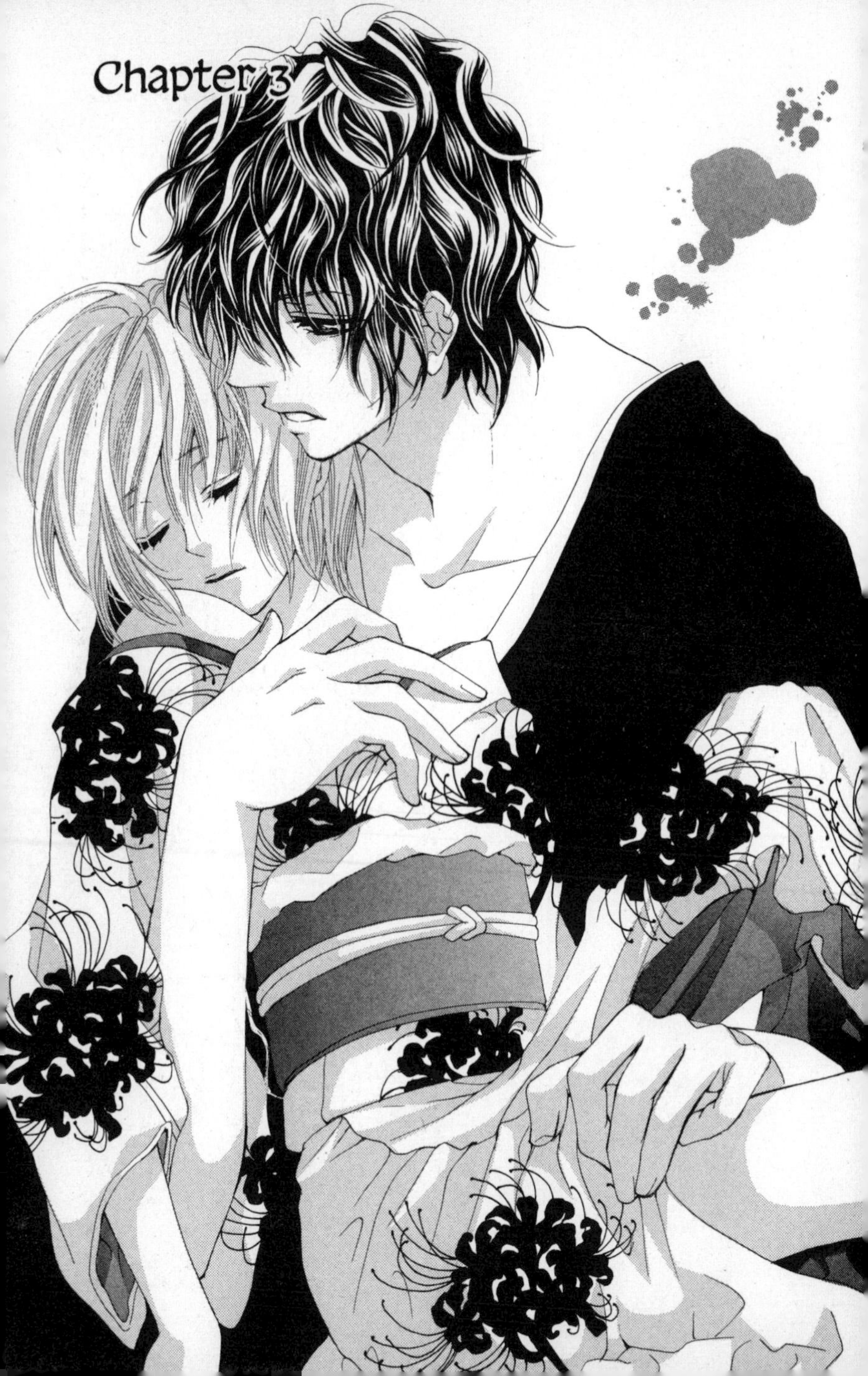

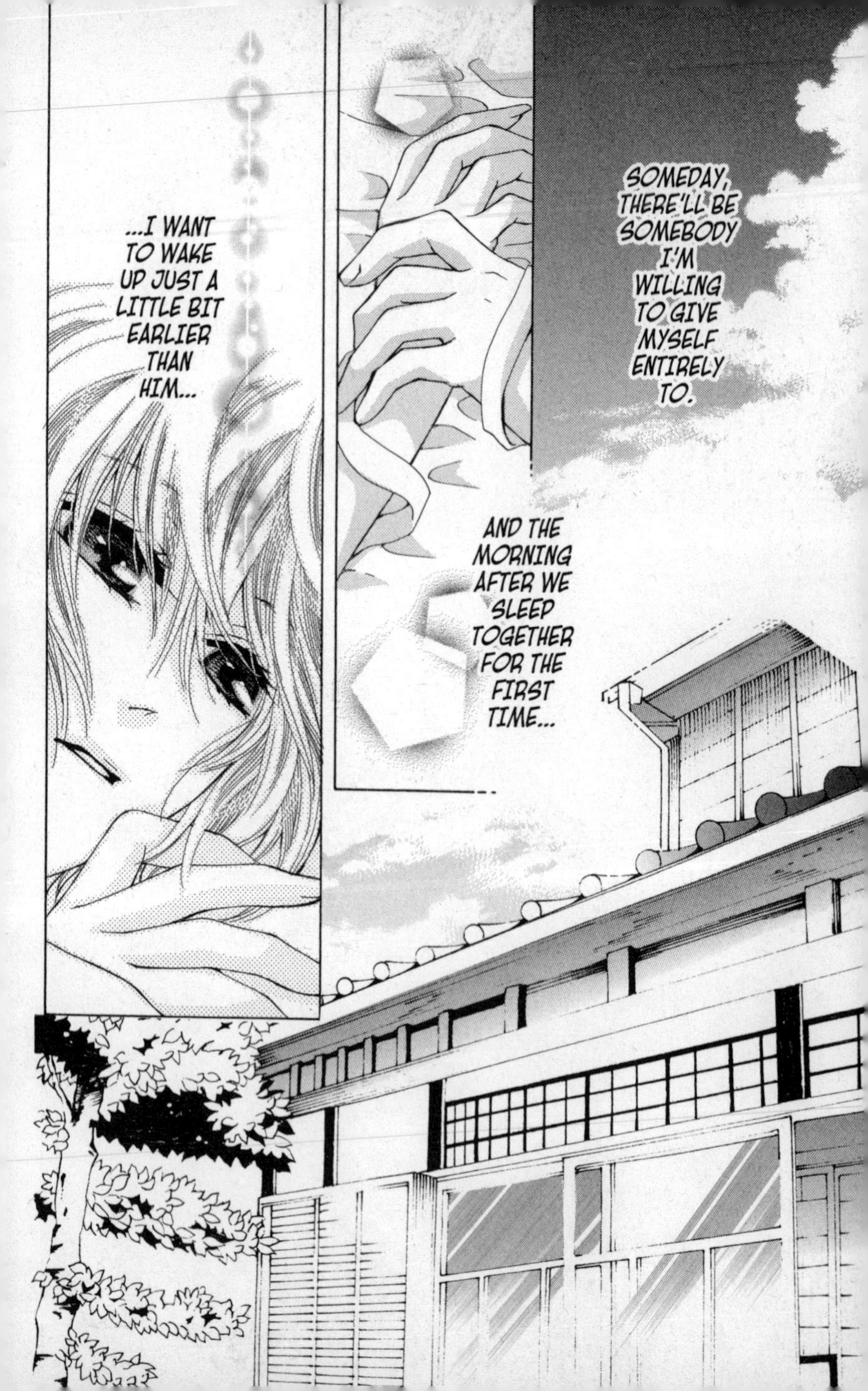
SOMEDAY, THERE'LL BE SOMEBODY I'M WILLING TO GIVE MYSELF ENTIRELY TO.
AND THE MORNING AFTER WE SLEEP TOGETHER FOR THE FIRST TIME...
...I WANT TO WAKE UP JUST A LITTLE BIT EARLIER THAN HIM...

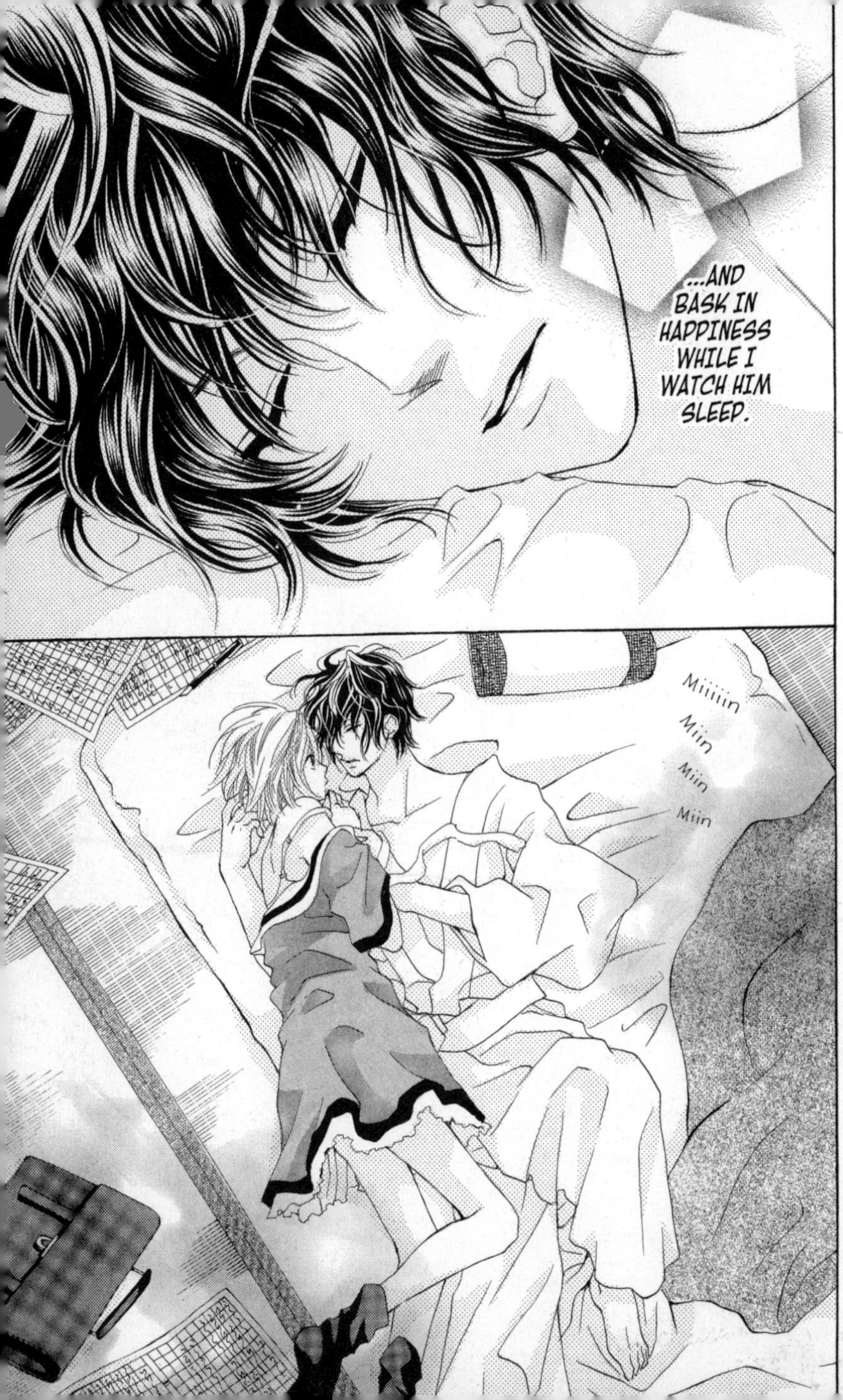
...AND BASK IN HAPPINESS WHILE I WATCH HIM SLEEP.
Miiiiin
Miin
Miin
Miin

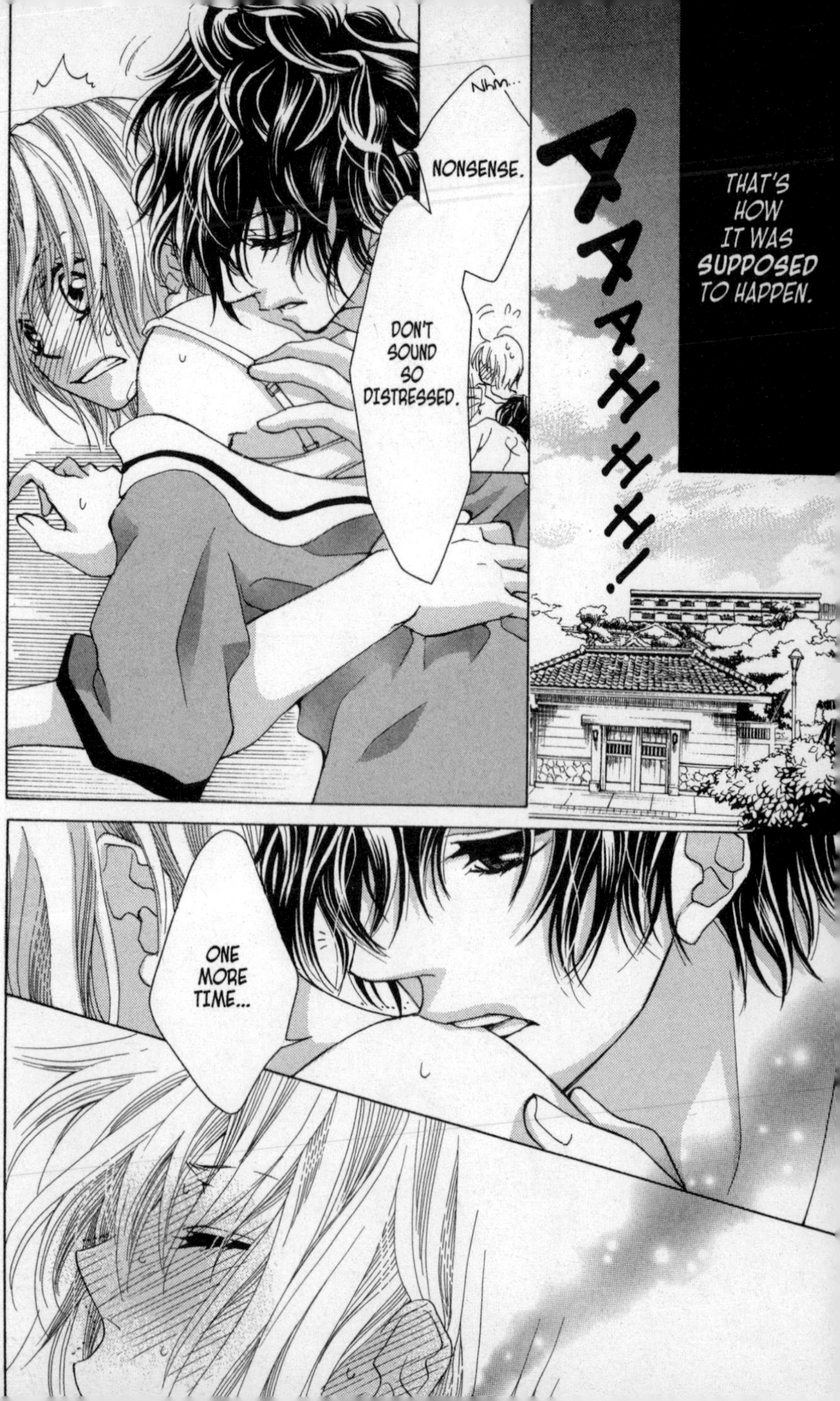
THAT'S HOW IT WAS SUPPOSED TO HAPPEN.
AAAHHH!
Nhm...
NONSENSE.
DON'T SOUND SO DISTRESSED.
ONE MORE TIME...

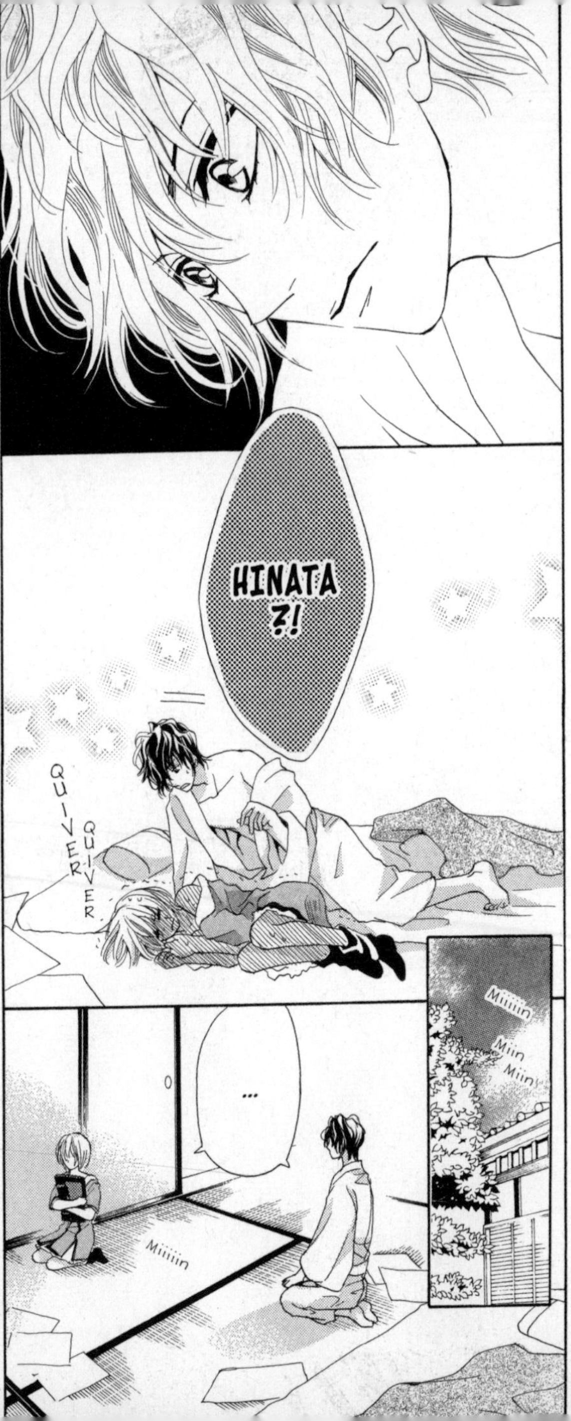
HINATA ?!
QUIVER
QUIVER
Miiiiin
Miin
Miin
...
Miiiiin

Small Talk

③

That's right, my friend I-chan is up next! She caught the bouquet. ♥

She's planning to get married next year!

I've been her friend for her whole life, and I'm so incredibly happy that she's finally found such happiness. ♥

Why "finally"? Well, because she's always dated bad guys.

She has it all together, so she's always attracted unreliable men who wanted to be taken care of. She used to talk to me about that a lot.

But her fiancé is a great, dependable guy!

I can rest easy knowing she's in such good hands. ♥

It's like she's my daughter or something... (Smile)

And Y is engaged now too, although she won't be getting married for a while yet.

← Continued in ④

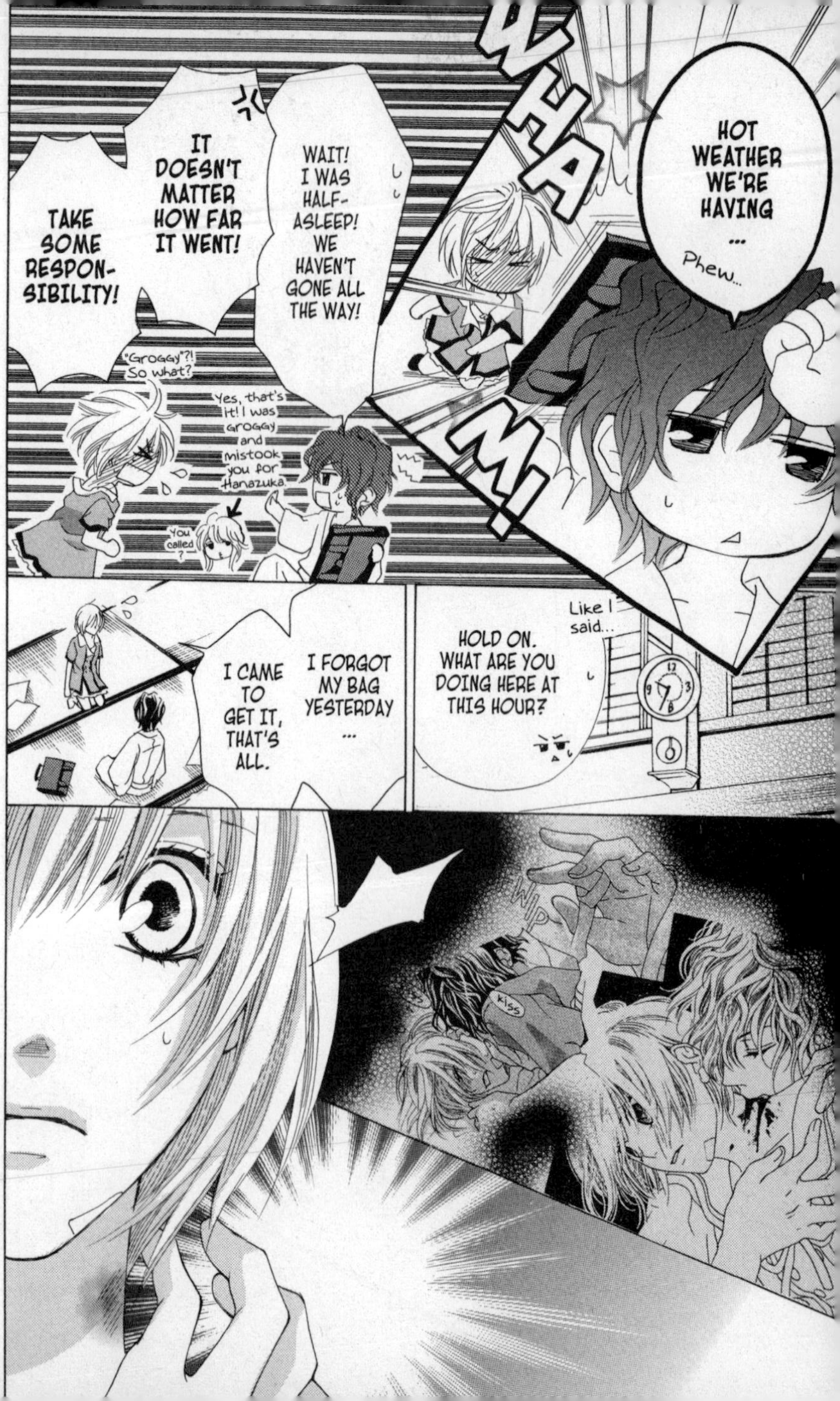
WHAM!
HOT WEATHER WE'RE HAVING ...
Phew...
WAIT! I WAS HALF-ASLEEP! WE HAVEN'T GONE ALL THE WAY!
IT DOESN'T MATTER HOW FAR IT WENT!
TAKE SOME RESPONSIBILITY!
Yes, that's it! I was groggy and mistook you for Hanazuka.
"Groggy"?! So what?
You called?
Like I said...
HOLD ON. WHAT ARE YOU DOING HERE AT THIS HOUR?
I FORGOT MY BAG YESTERDAY ...
I CAME TO GET IT, THAT'S ALL.
WIP
kiss

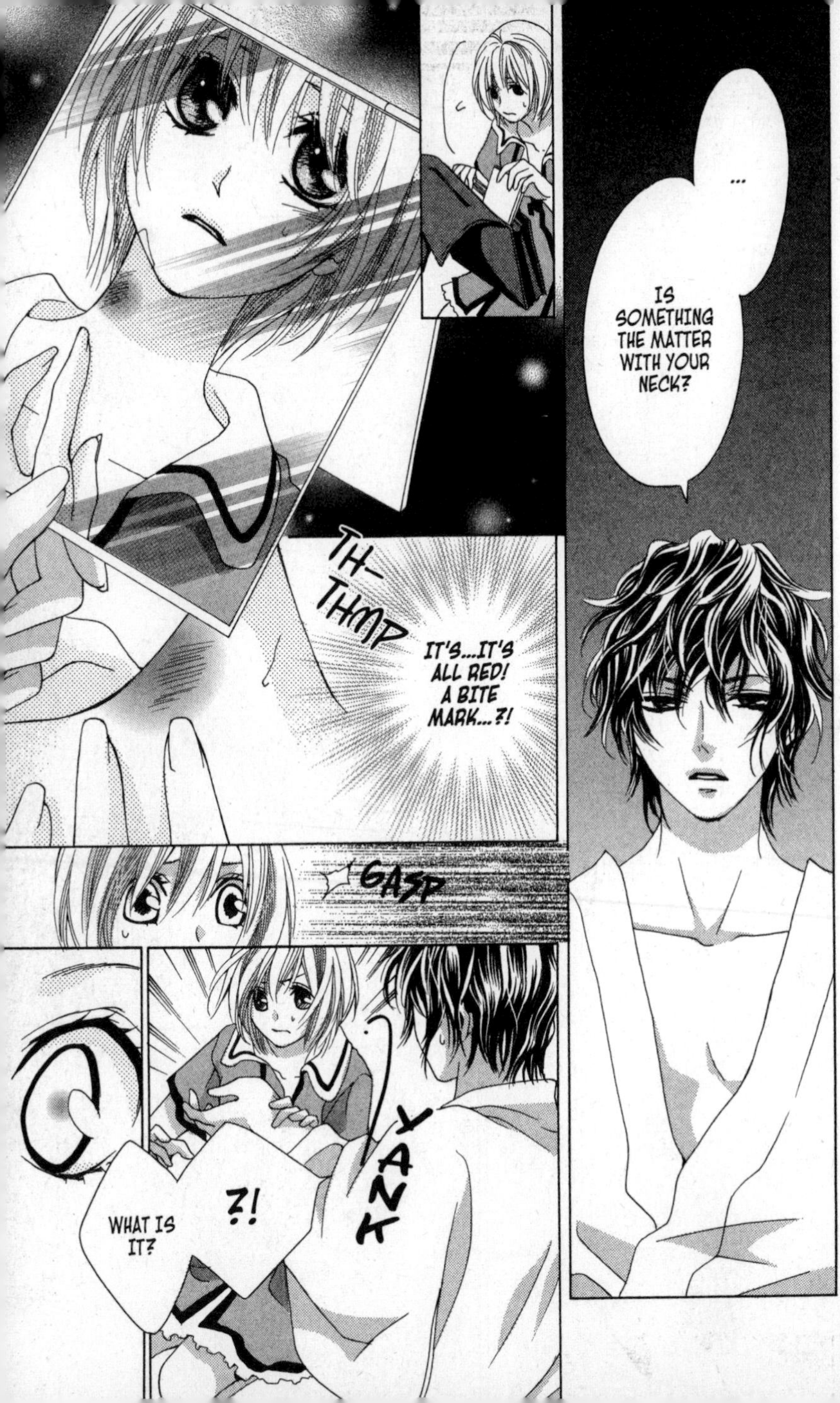
...
IS SOMETHING THE MATTER WITH YOUR NECK?
TH-THMP
IT'S...IT'S ALL RED! A BITE MARK...?!
GASP
YANK
?!
WHAT IS IT?

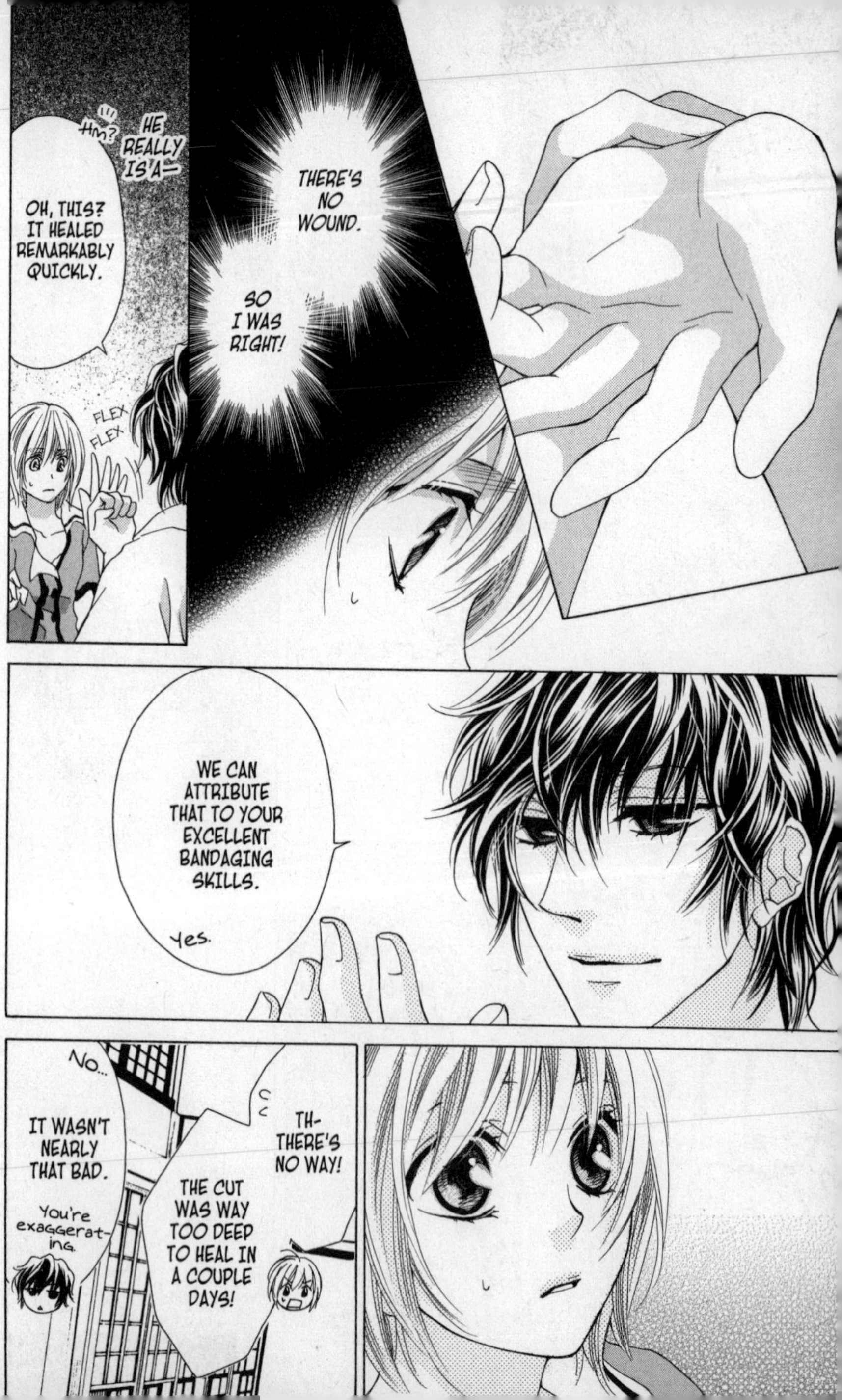
THERE'S NO WOUND.
SO I WAS RIGHT!
Hm?
HE REALLY IS A—
OH, THIS? IT HEALED REMARKABLY QUICKLY.
FLEX FLEX
WE CAN ATTRIBUTE THAT TO YOUR EXCELLENT BANDAGING SKILLS.
Yes.
TH-THERE'S NO WAY!
THE CUT WAS WAY TOO DEEP TO HEAL IN A COUPLE DAYS!
No...
IT WASN'T NEARLY THAT BAD.
You're exaggerat-ing.

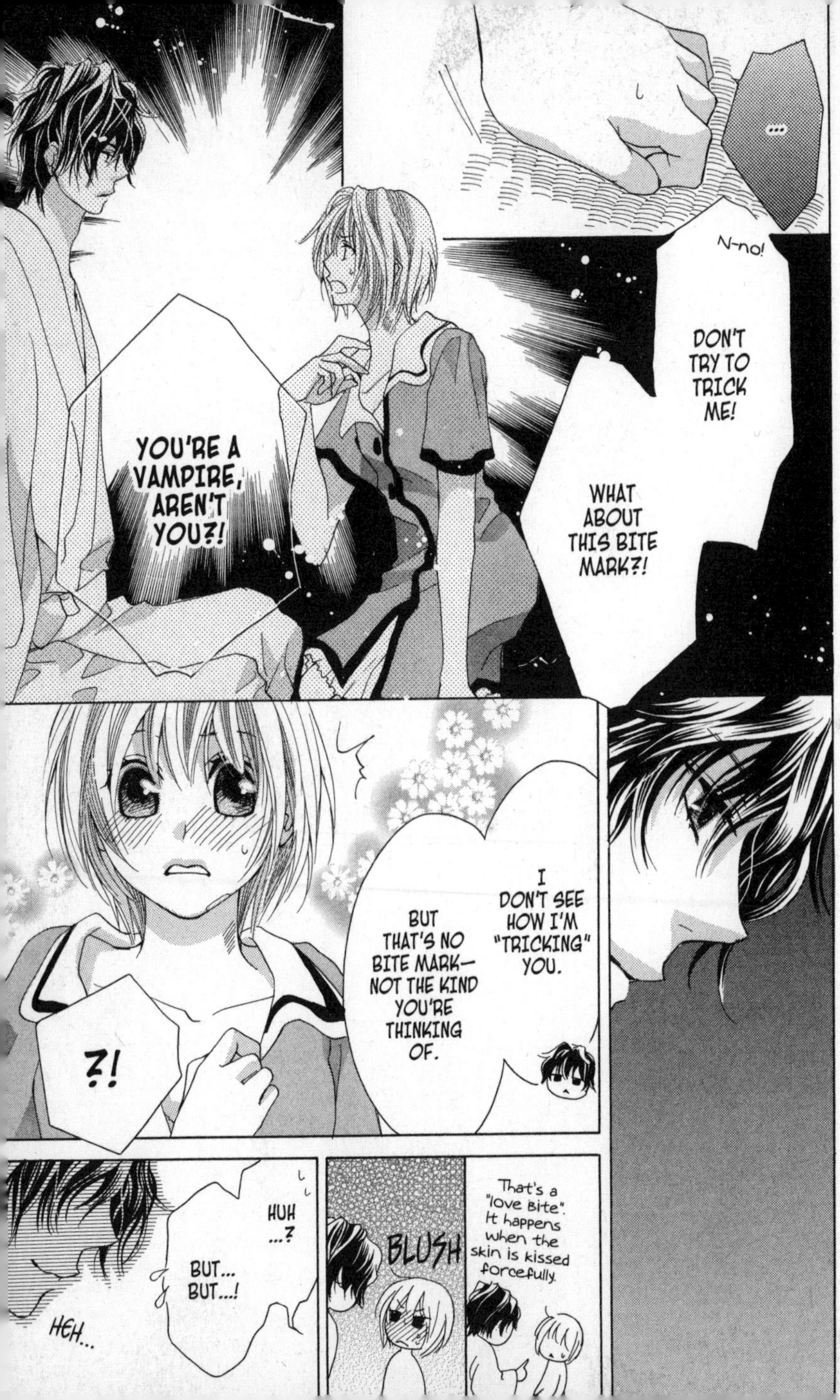
...
N-no!
DON'T TRY TO TRICK ME!
WHAT ABOUT THIS BITE MARK?!
YOU'RE A VAMPIRE, AREN'T YOU?!
I DON'T SEE HOW I'M "TRICKING" YOU.
BUT THAT'S NO BITE MARK— NOT THE KIND YOU'RE THINKING OF.
?!
That's a "love bite". It happens when the skin is kissed forcefully.
BLUSH
HUH ...?
BUT... BUT...!
HEH...

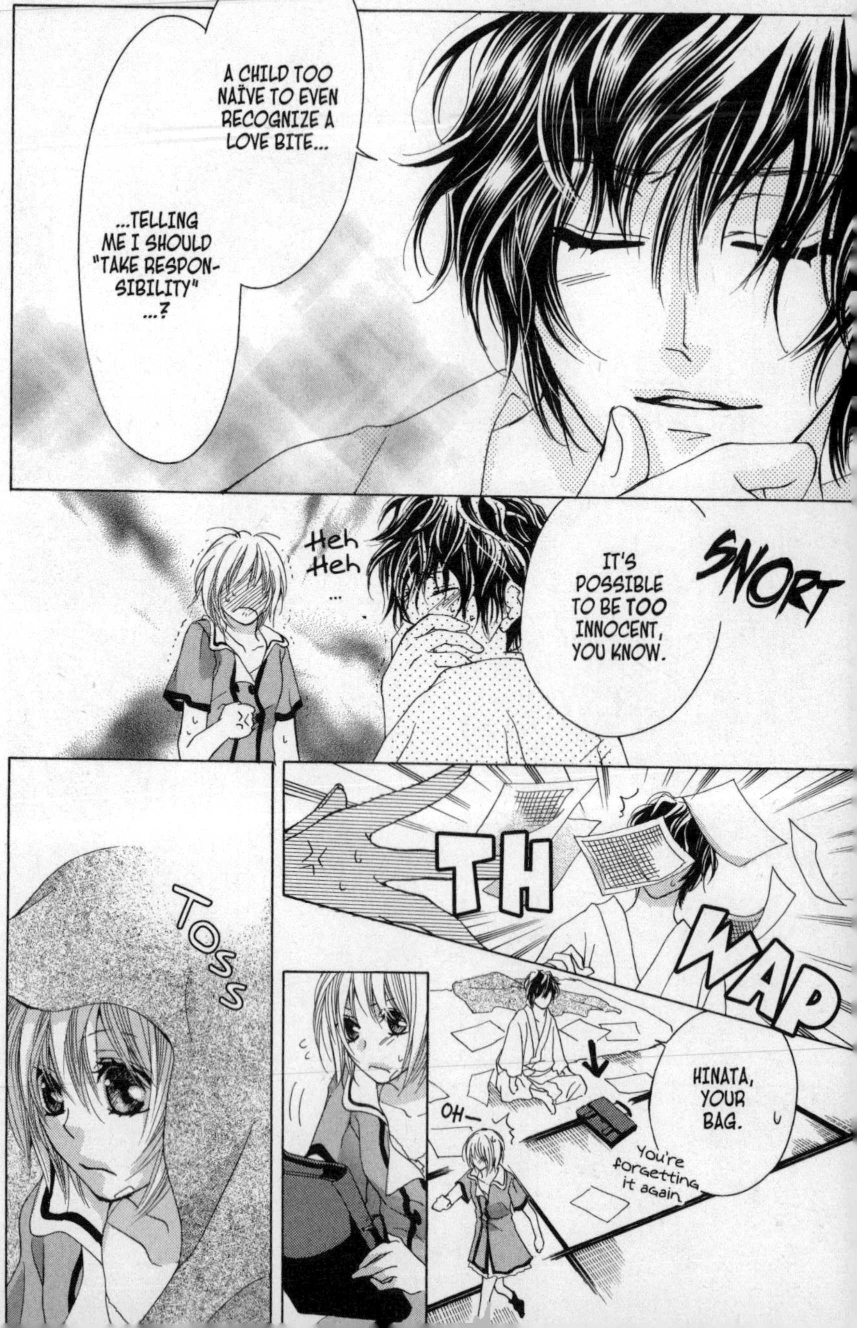
A CHILD TOO NAÏVE TO EVEN RECOGNIZE A LOVE BITE...
...TELLING ME I SHOULD "TAKE RESPON-SIBILITY" ...?
SNORT
IT'S POSSIBLE TO BE TOO INNOCENT, YOU KNOW.
Heh Heh ...
THWAP
HINATA, YOUR BAG.
You're forgetting it again.
OH—
TOSS

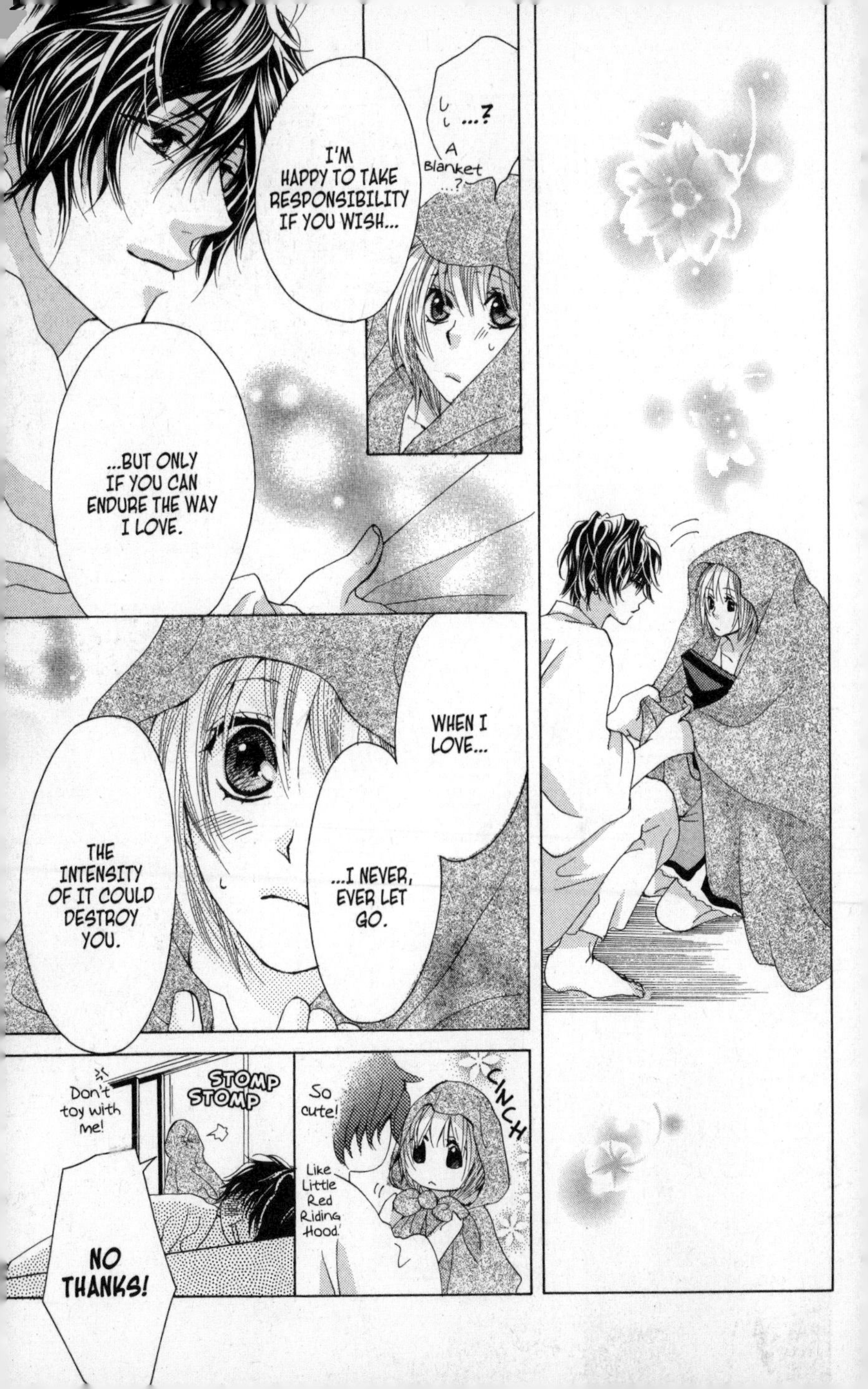
...?
A Blanket ...?
I'M HAPPY TO TAKE RESPONSIBILITY IF YOU WISH...
...BUT ONLY IF YOU CAN ENDURE THE WAY I LOVE.
WHEN I LOVE...
...I NEVER, EVER LET GO.
THE INTENSITY OF IT COULD DESTROY YOU.
CINCH
So cute!
Like Little Red Riding Hood!
STOMP STOMP
Don't toy with me!
NO THANKS!

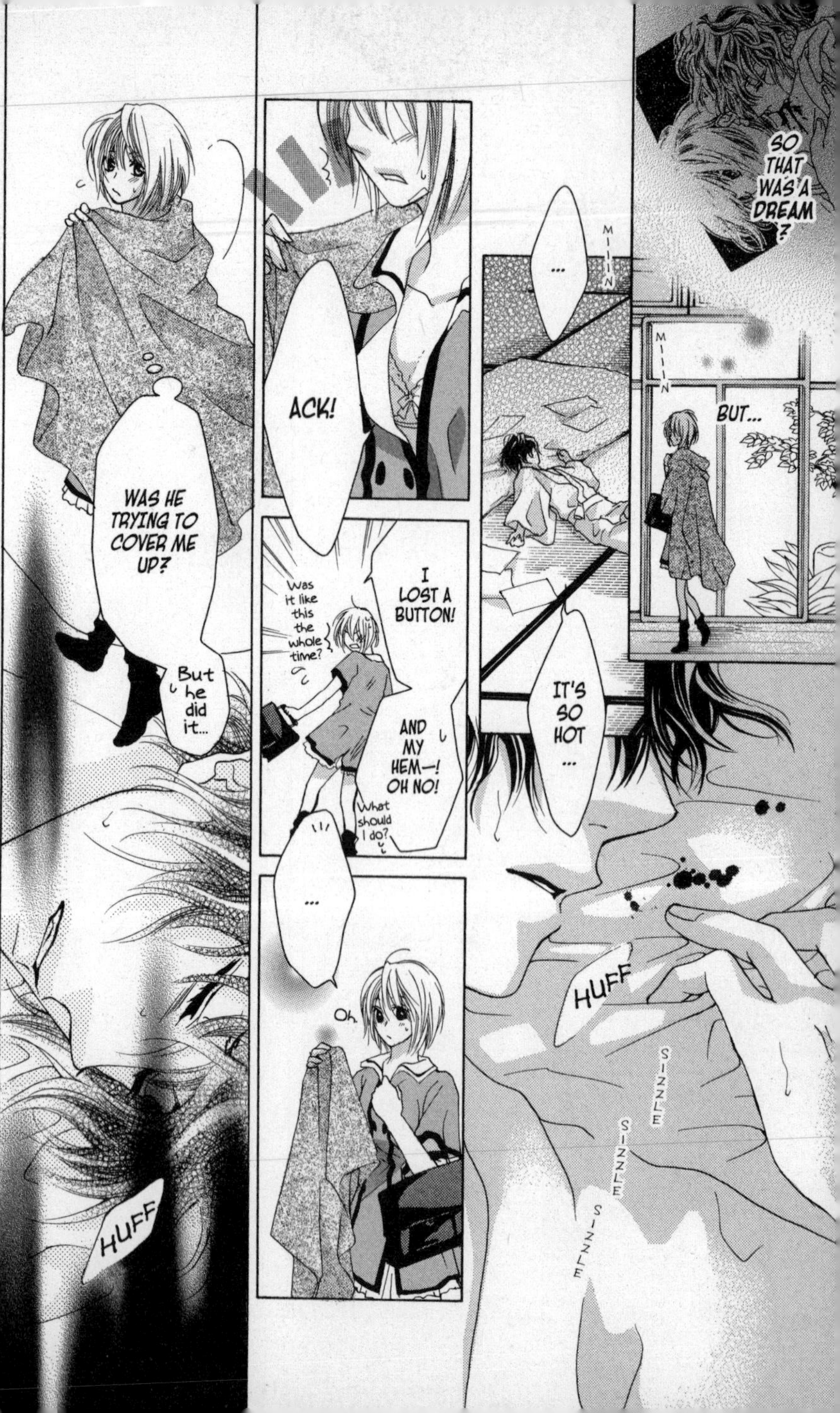
SO THAT WAS A DREAM?
MIIIN
BUT...
MIIIN
...
IT'S SO HOT...
HUFF
SIZZLE
SIZZLE
SIZZLE
ACK!
I LOST A BUTTON!
Was it like this the whole time?
AND MY HEM—! OH NO!
What should I do?
...
Oh.
WAS HE TRYING TO COVER ME UP?
But he did it...
HUFF

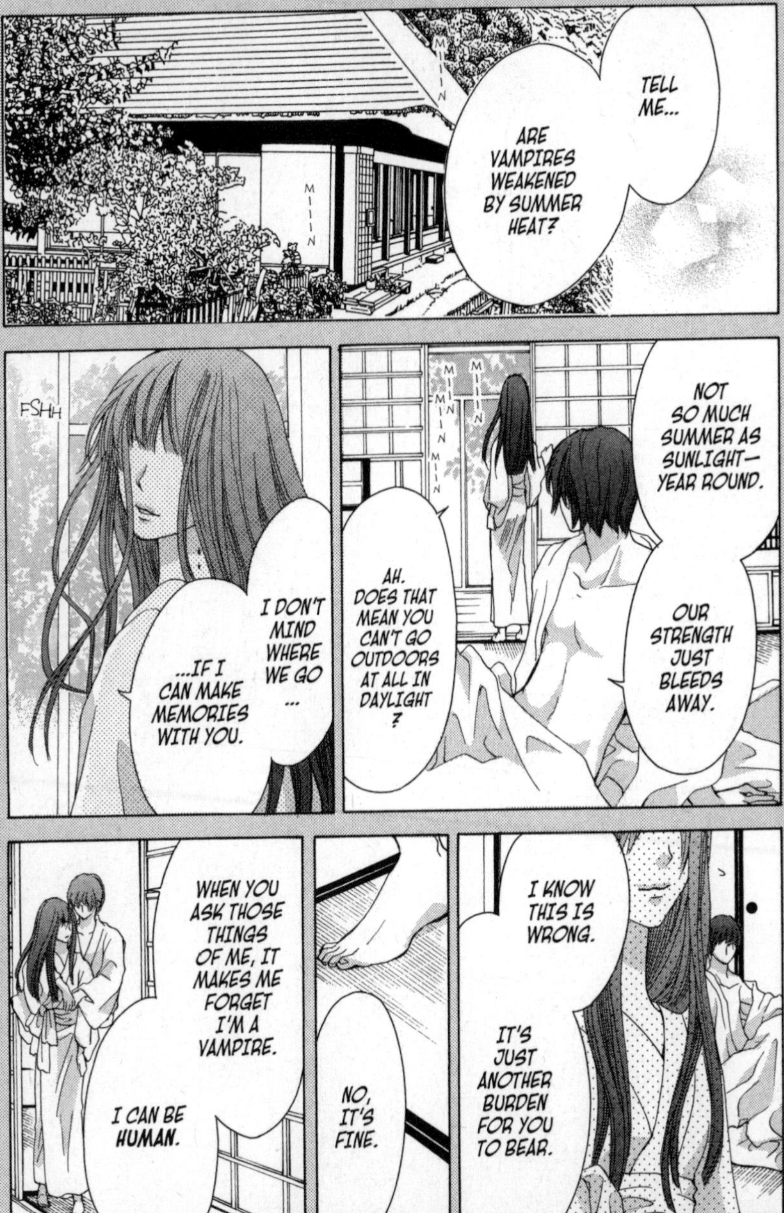
MIIN
MIIN
TELL ME...
ARE VAMPIRES WEAKENED BY SUMMER HEAT?
MIIN
MIIN
MIIN
NOT SO MUCH SUMMER AS SUNLIGHT— YEAR ROUND.
OUR STRENGTH JUST BLEEDS AWAY.
AH. DOES THAT MEAN YOU CAN'T GO OUTDOORS AT ALL IN DAYLIGHT?
FSHH
I DON'T MIND WHERE WE GO...
...IF I CAN MAKE MEMORIES WITH YOU.
I KNOW THIS IS WRONG.
IT'S JUST ANOTHER BURDEN FOR YOU TO BEAR.
NO, IT'S FINE.
WHEN YOU ASK THOSE THINGS OF ME, IT MAKES ME FORGET I'M A VAMPIRE.
I CAN BE HUMAN.

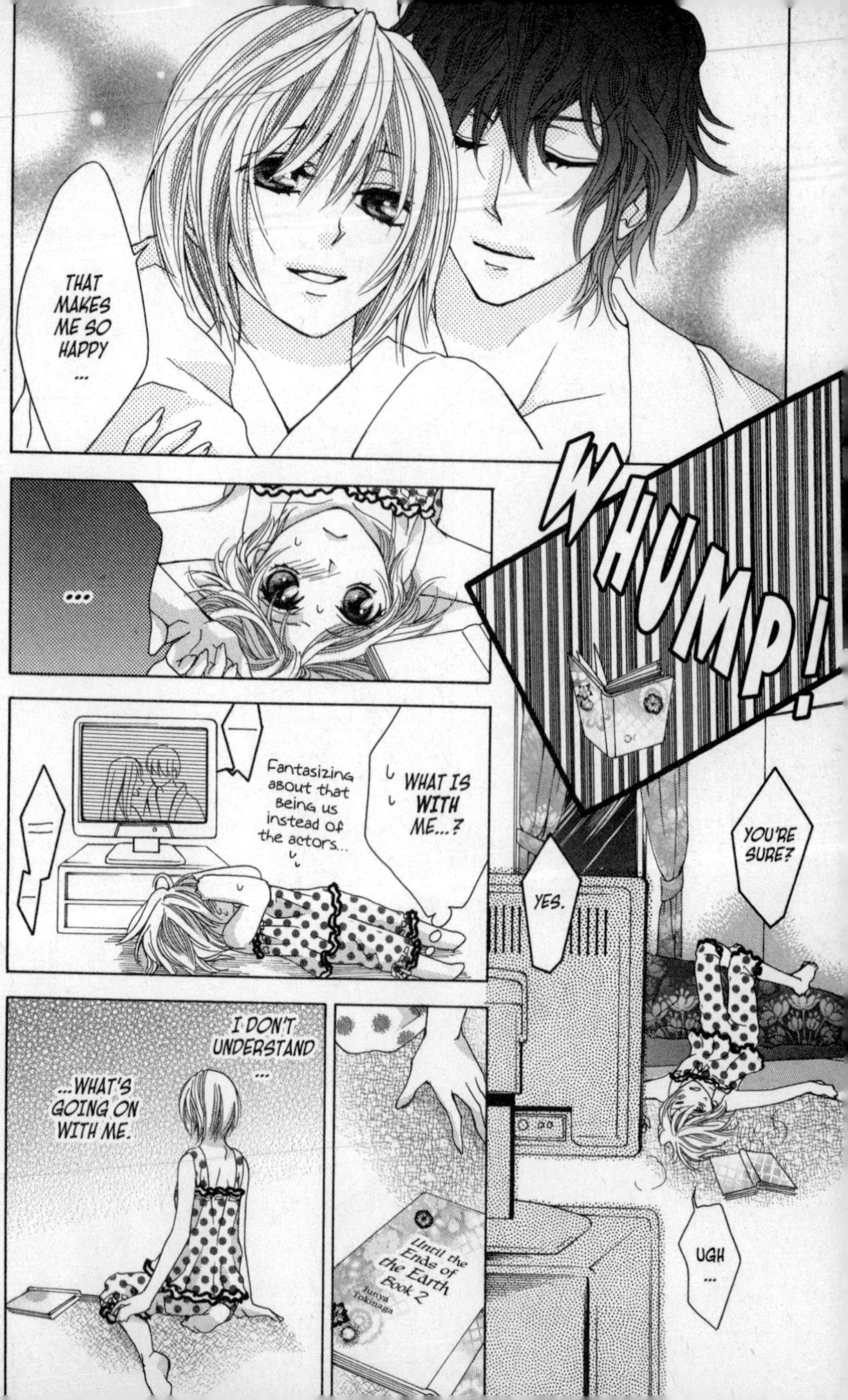
YOU'RE SURE?
YES.
THAT MAKES ME SO HAPPY...
WHUMP!
UGH...
...
WHAT IS WITH ME...?
Fantasizing about that being us instead of the actors...
Until the Ends of the Earth Book 2 Junya Tokinaga
I DON'T UNDERSTAND...
...WHAT'S GOING ON WITH ME.

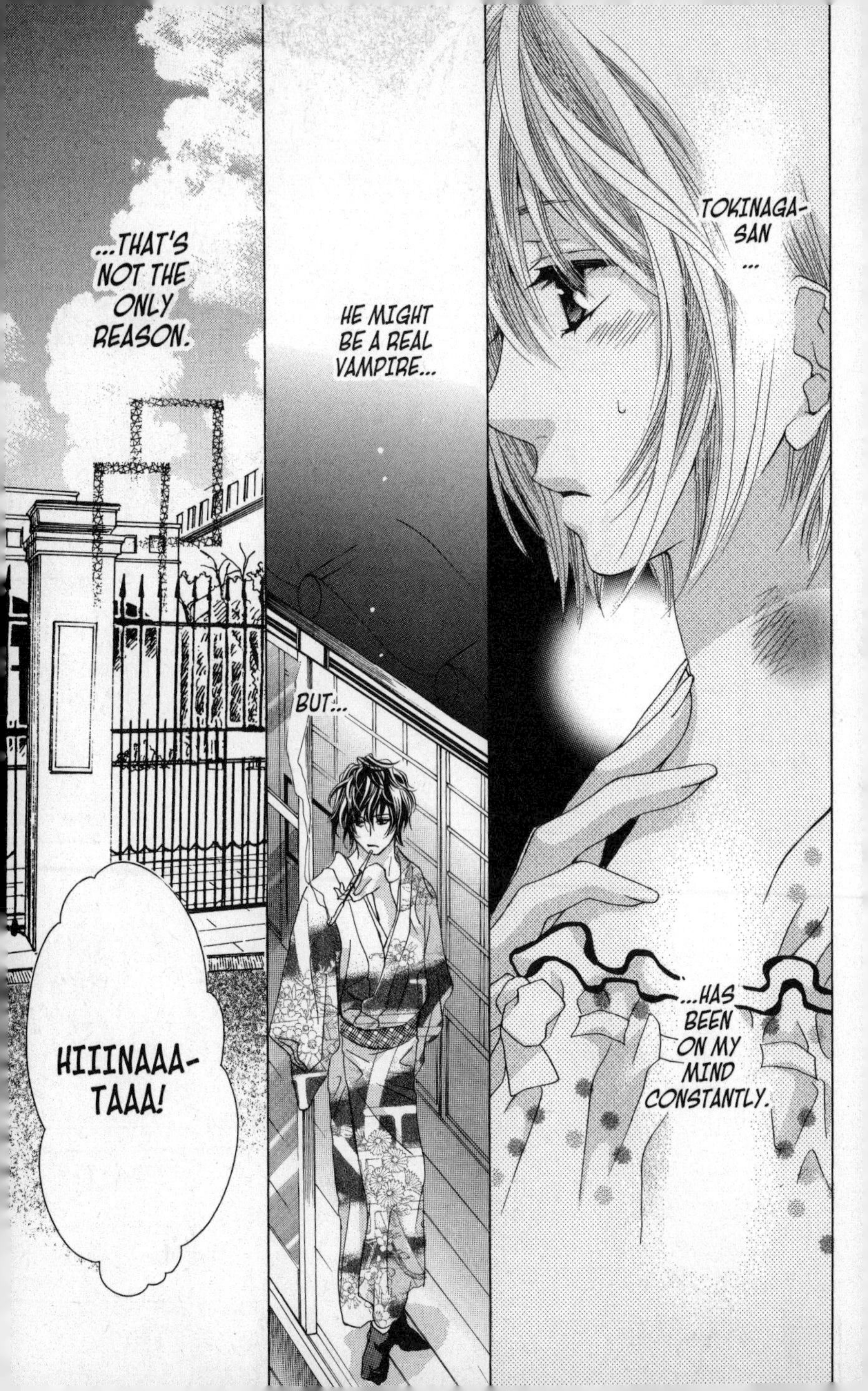
TOKINAGA-SAN ...
...HAS BEEN ON MY MIND CONSTANTLY.
HE MIGHT BE A REAL VAMPIRE...
BUT...
...THAT'S NOT THE ONLY REASON.
HIIINAAA-TAAA!

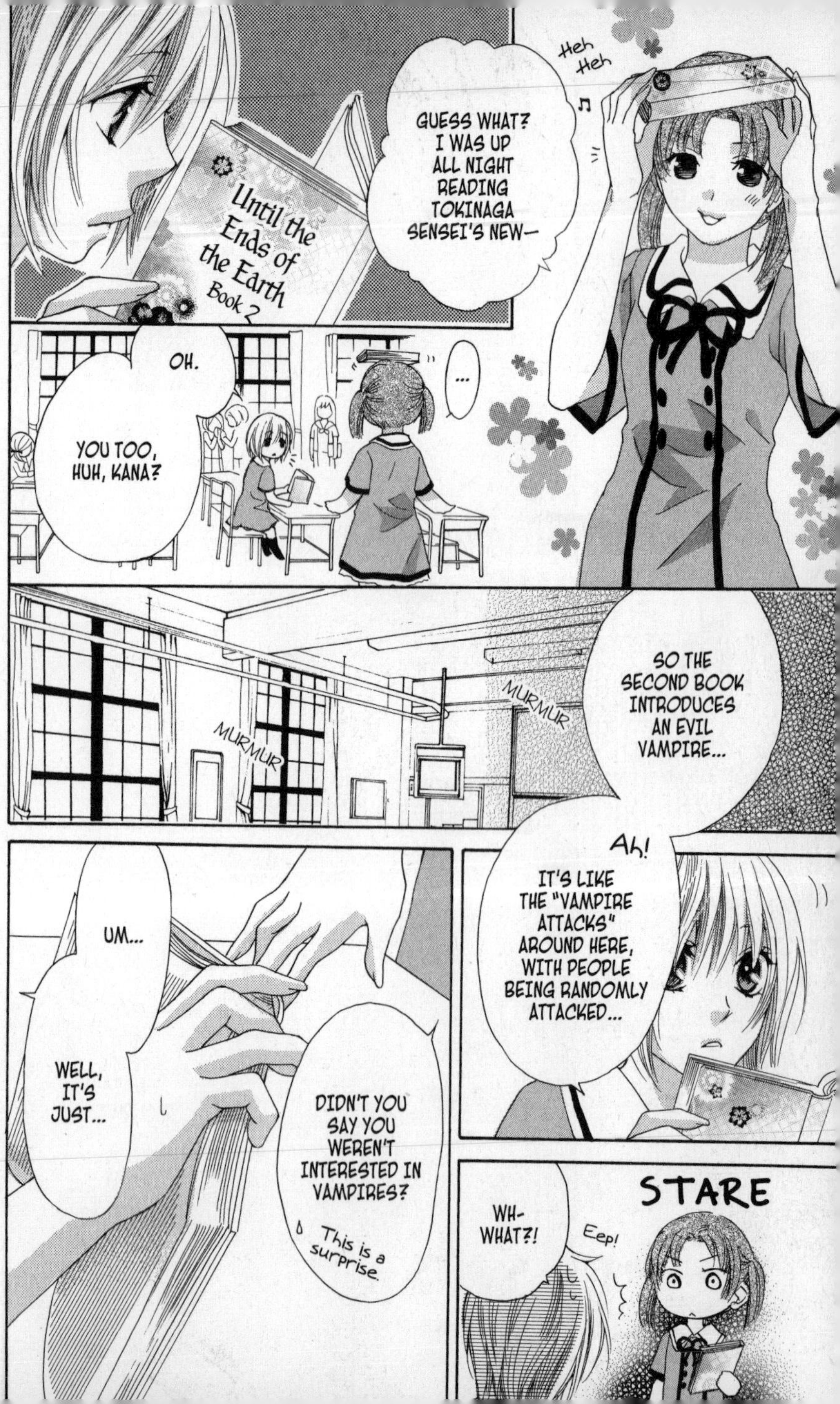
Heh Heh
GUESS WHAT? I WAS UP ALL NIGHT READING TOKINAGA SENSEI'S NEW—
Until the Ends of the Earth Book 2
...
OH.
YOU TOO, HUH, KANA?
SO THE SECOND BOOK INTRODUCES AN EVIL VAMPIRE...
MURMUR
MURMUR
Ah!
IT'S LIKE THE "VAMPIRE ATTACKS" AROUND HERE, WITH PEOPLE BEING RANDOMLY ATTACKED...
STARE
Eep!
WH-WHAT?!
DIDN'T YOU SAY YOU WEREN'T INTERESTED IN VAMPIRES?
This is a surprise.
UM...
WELL, IT'S JUST...

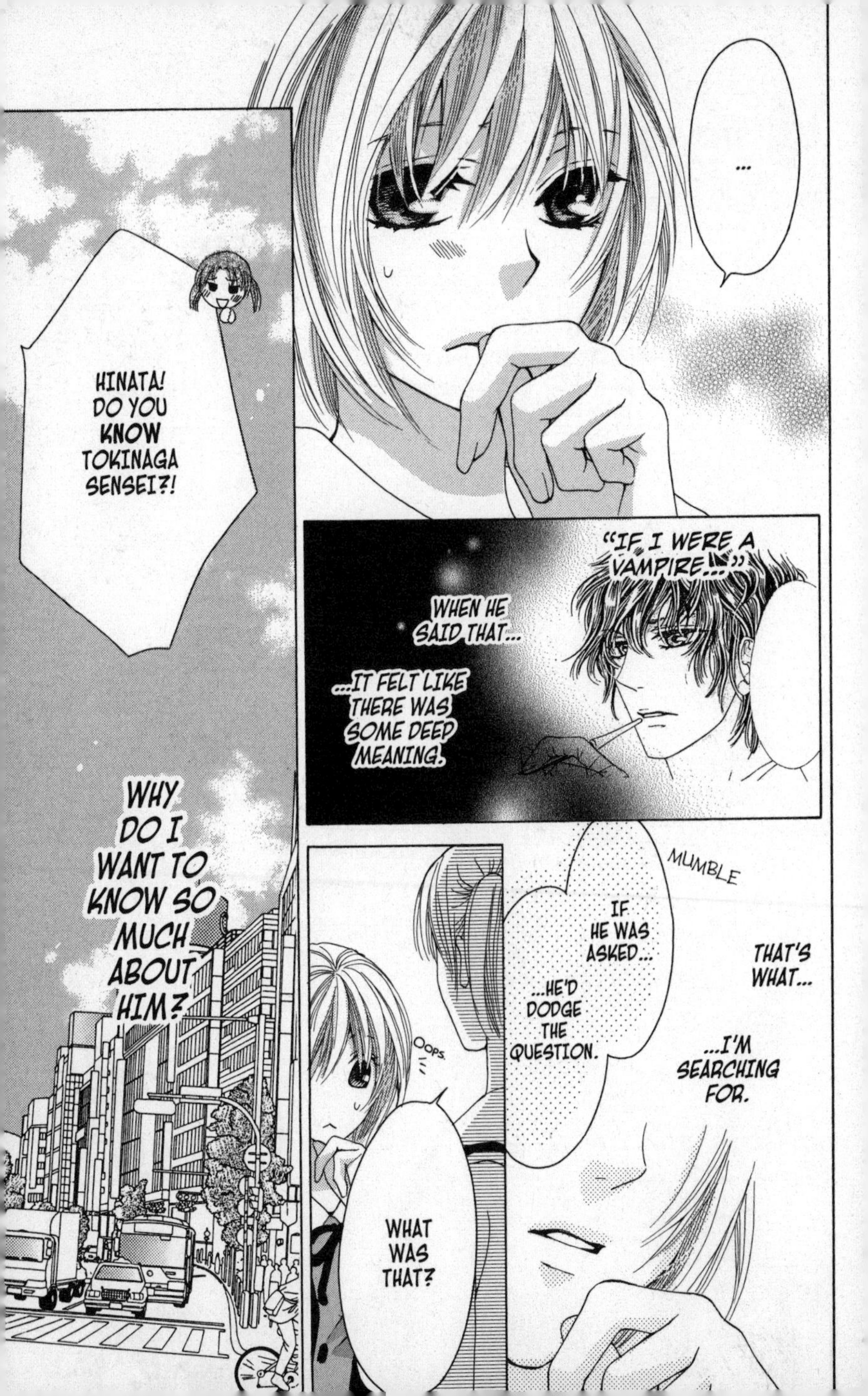
...
"IF I WERE A VAMPIRE..."
WHEN HE SAID THAT...
...IT FELT LIKE THERE WAS SOME DEEP MEANING.
THAT'S WHAT...
...I'M SEARCHING FOR.
MUMBLE
IF HE WAS ASKED...
...HE'D DODGE THE QUESTION.
OOPS.
WHAT WAS THAT?
HINATA! DO YOU KNOW TOKINAGA SENSEI?!
WHY DO I WANT TO KNOW SO MUCH ABOUT HIM?

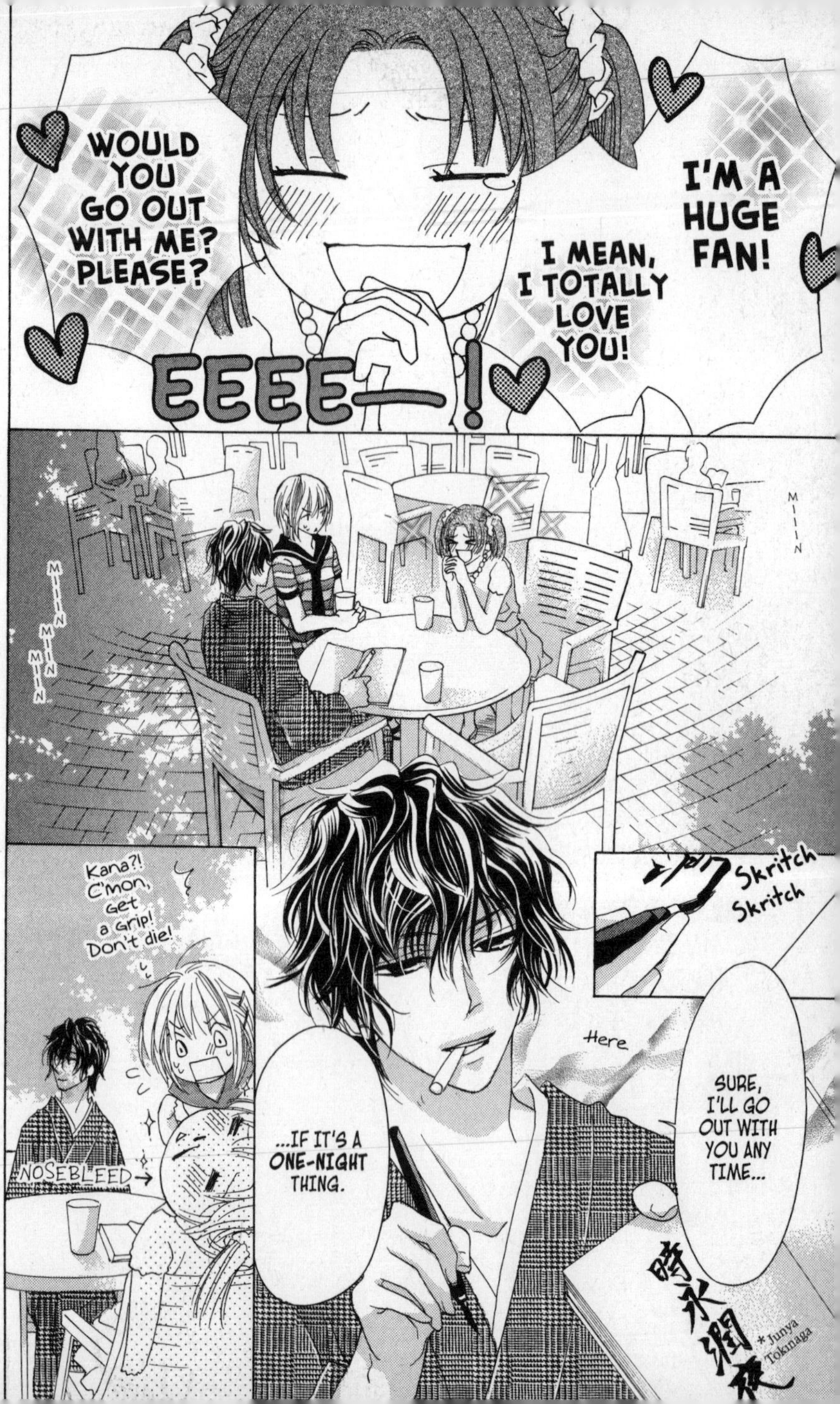
I'M A HUGE FAN!
I MEAN, I TOTALLY LOVE YOU!
WOULD YOU GO OUT WITH ME? PLEASE?
EEEE—!
MIIN
MIIN
MIIN
MIIN
Skritch Skritch
SURE, I'LL GO OUT WITH YOU ANY TIME...
Here
...IF IT'S A ONE-NIGHT THING.
時永潤夜
*Junya Tokinaga
Kana?! C'mon, get a grip! Don't die!
NOSEBLEED

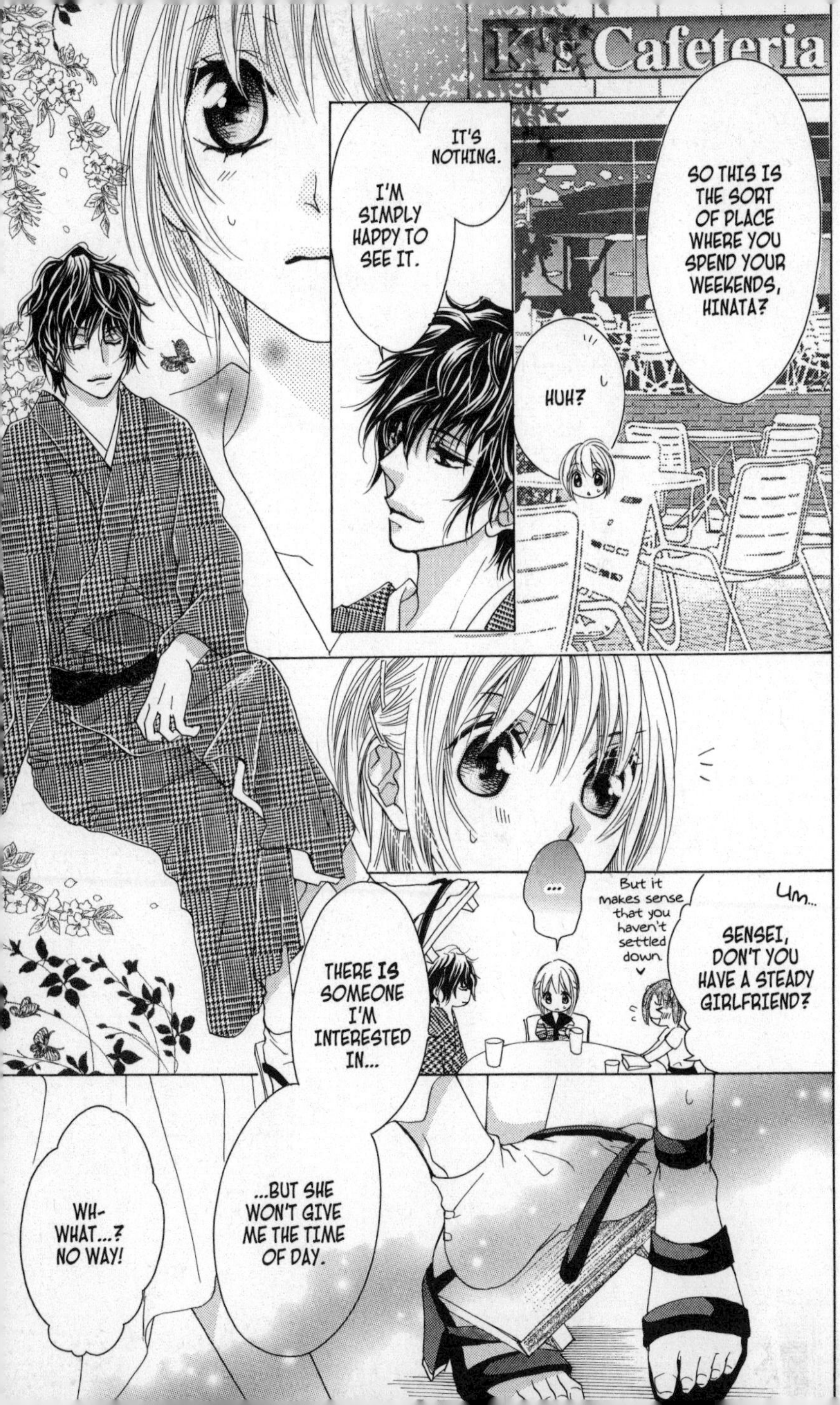
K's Cafeteria
SO THIS IS THE SORT OF PLACE WHERE YOU SPEND YOUR WEEKENDS, HINATA?
HUH?
IT'S NOTHING.
I'M SIMPLY HAPPY TO SEE IT.
Um...
SENSEI, DON'T YOU HAVE A STEADY GIRLFRIEND?
But it makes sense that you haven't settled down.
...
THERE IS SOMEONE I'M INTERESTED IN...
...BUT SHE WON'T GIVE ME THE TIME OF DAY.
WH- WHAT...? NO WAY!

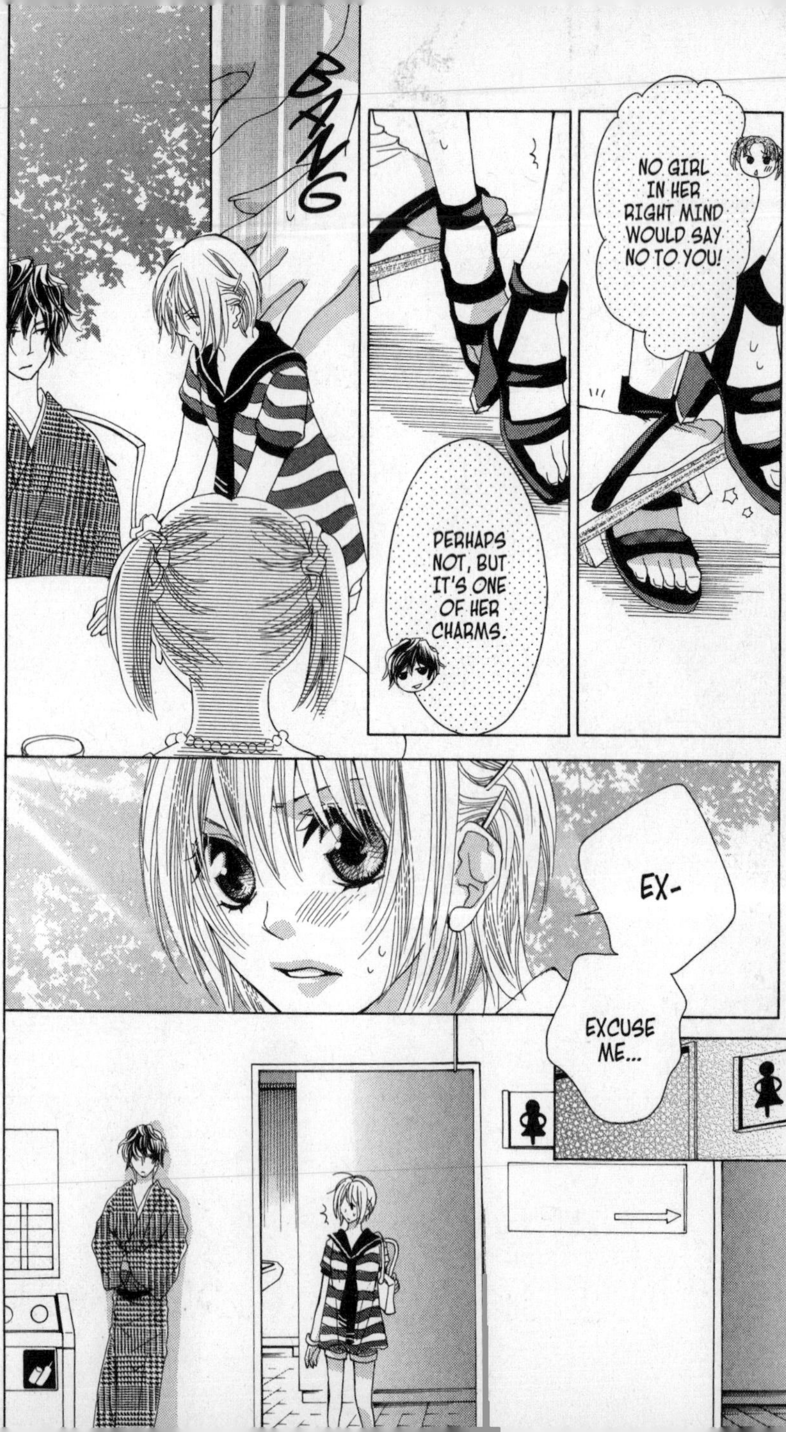
NO GIRL IN HER RIGHT MIND WOULD SAY NO TO YOU!
PERHAPS NOT, BUT IT'S ONE OF HER CHARMS.
BANG
EX-
EXCUSE ME...

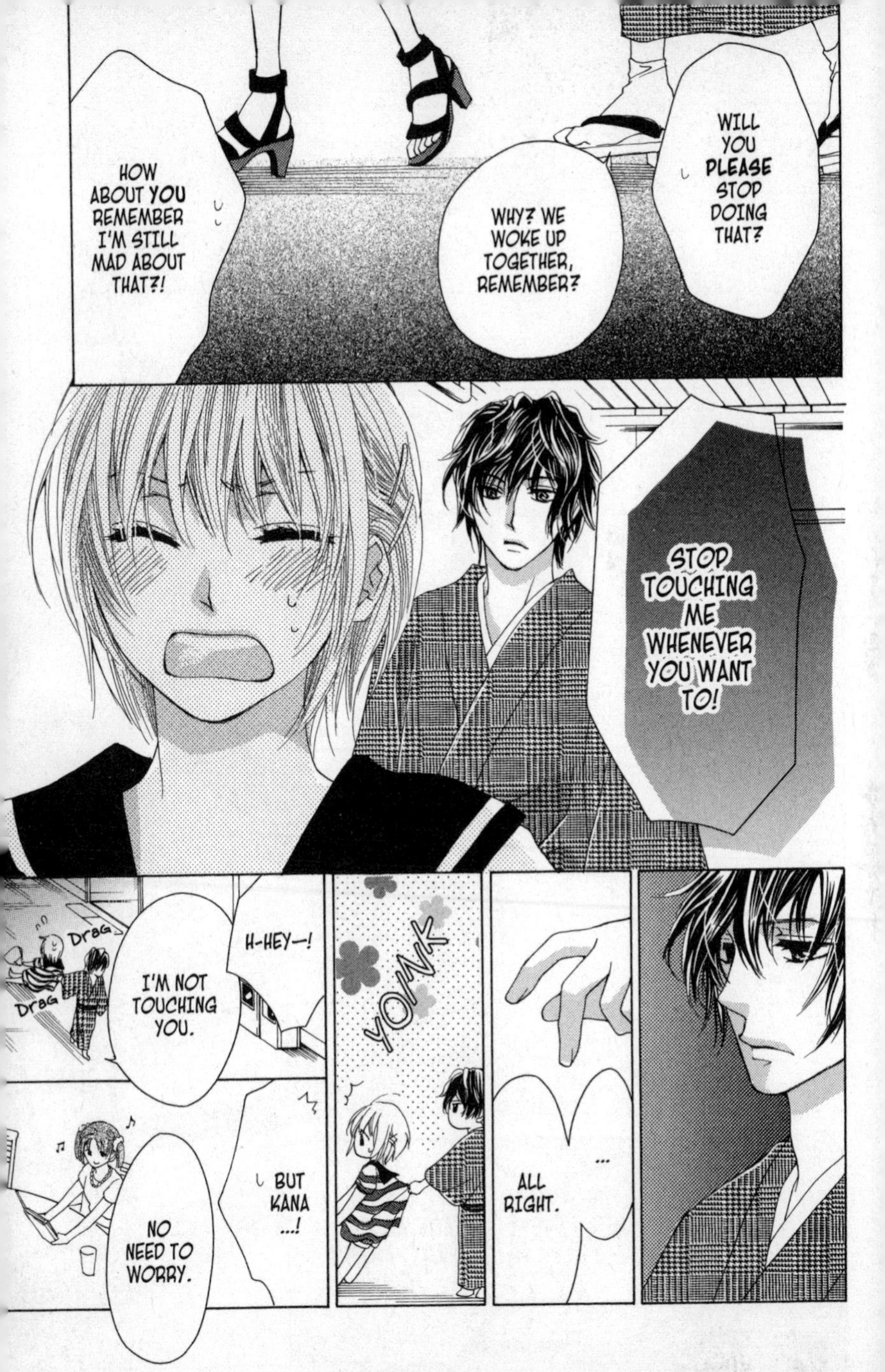
WILL YOU PLEASE STOP DOING THAT?
WHY? WE WOKE UP TOGETHER, REMEMBER?
HOW ABOUT YOU REMEMBER I'M STILL MAD ABOUT THAT?!
STOP TOUCHING ME WHENEVER YOU WANT TO!
... ALL RIGHT.
YOINK
BUT KANA ...!
H-HEY—!
I'M NOT TOUCHING YOU.
DRAG
DRAG
NO NEED TO WORRY.

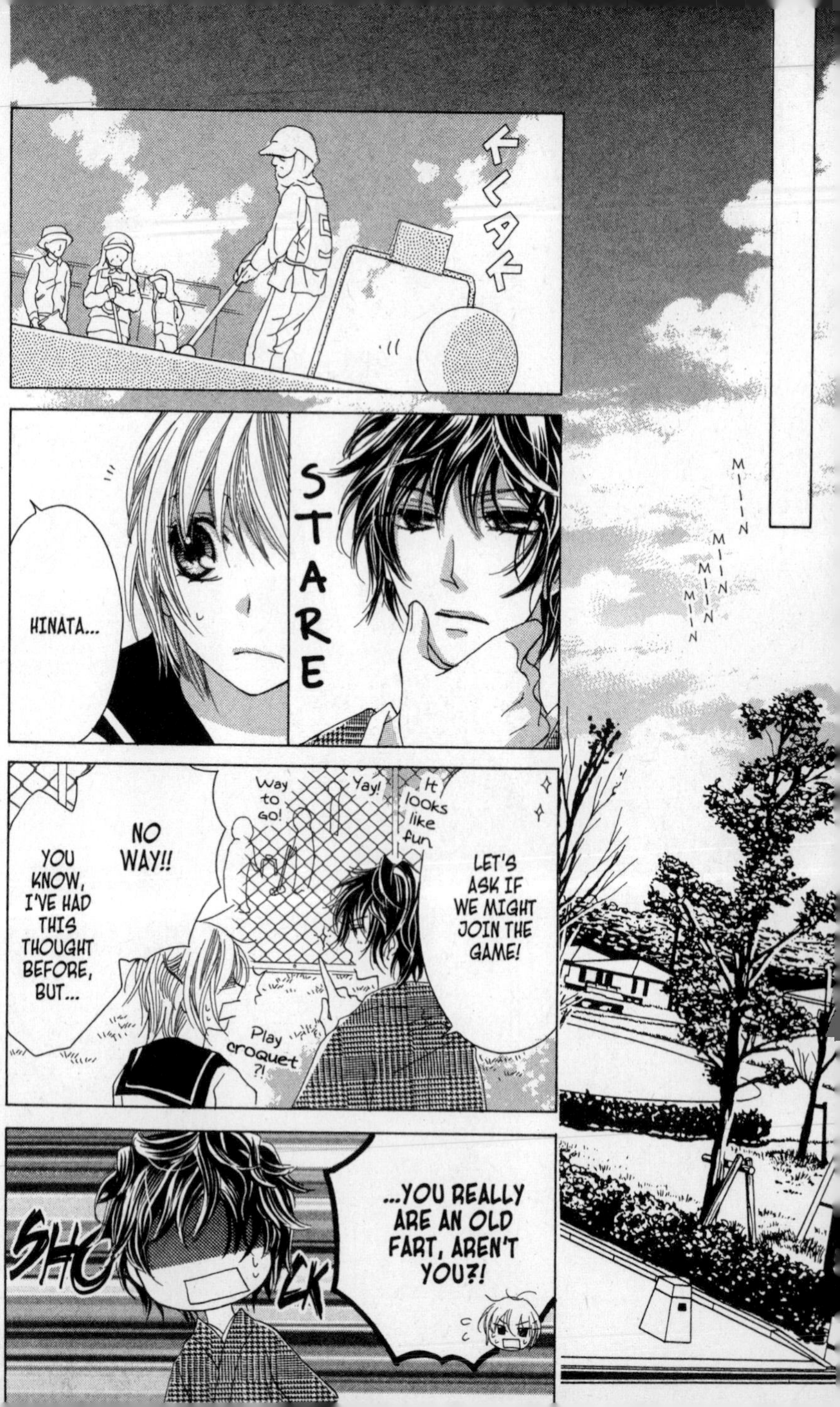
MIIN
MIIN
MIIN
MIIN
KLAK
STARE
HINATA...
LET'S ASK IF WE MIGHT JOIN THE GAME!
It looks like fun
Yay!
Way to go!
Play croquet?!
NO WAY!!
YOU KNOW, I'VE HAD THIS THOUGHT BEFORE, BUT...
...YOU REALLY ARE AN OLD FART, AREN'T YOU?!
SHOCK

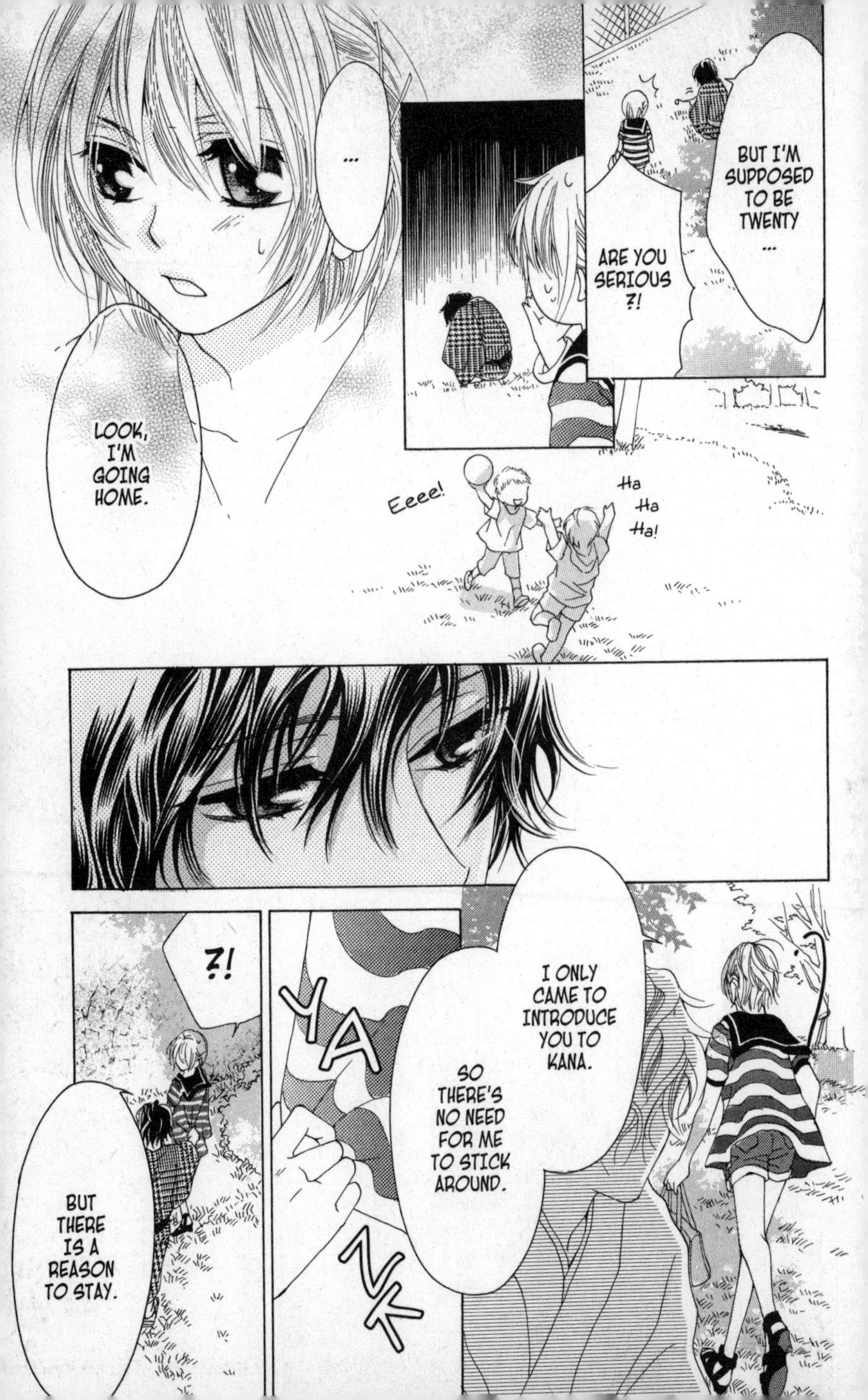
BUT I'M SUPPOSED TO BE TWENTY ...
ARE YOU SERIOUS ?!
...
LOOK, I'M GOING HOME.
Ha Ha Ha!
Eeee!
I ONLY CAME TO INTRODUCE YOU TO KANA.
SO THERE'S NO NEED FOR ME TO STICK AROUND.
YANK
?!
BUT THERE IS A REASON TO STAY.

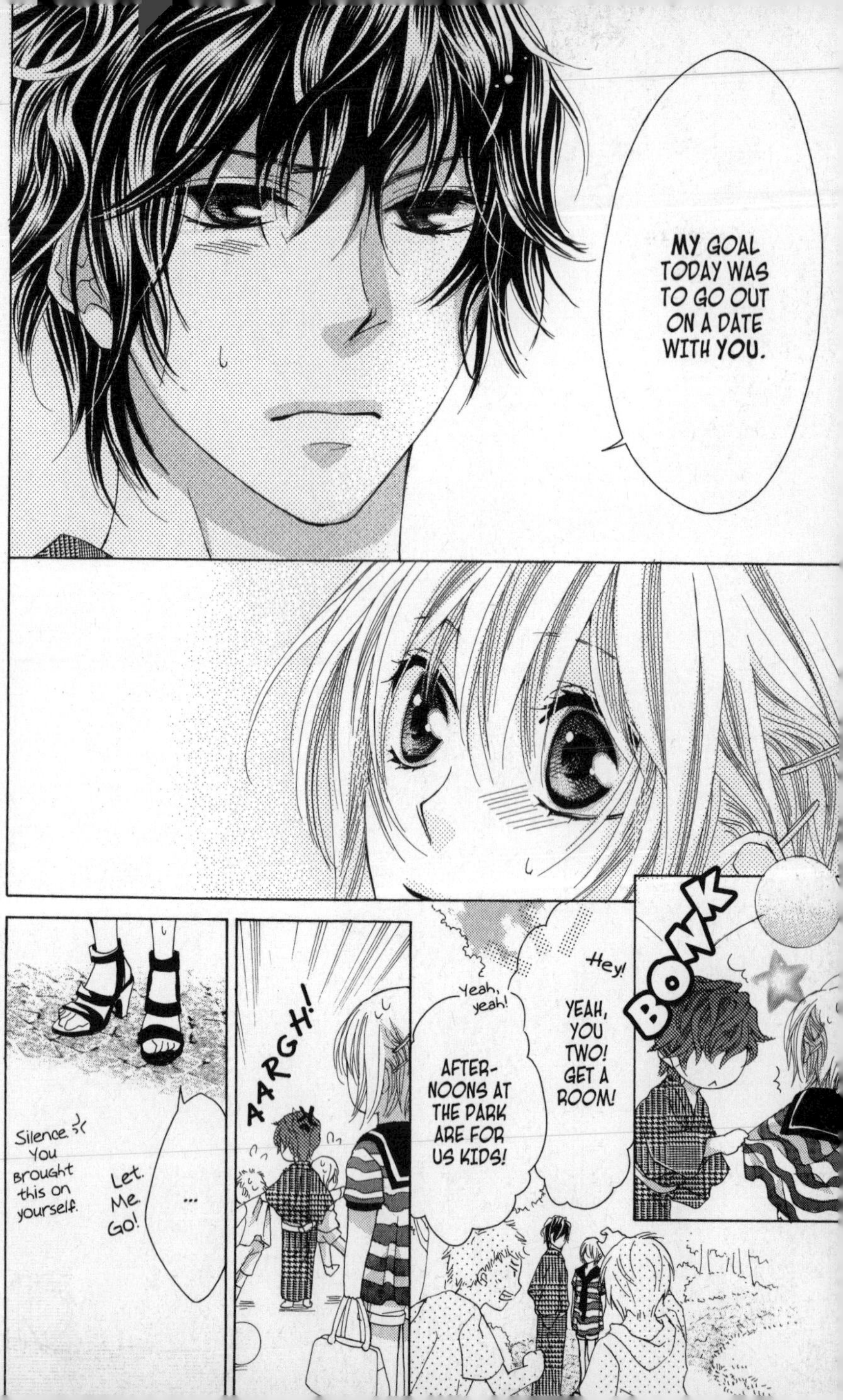
MY GOAL TODAY WAS TO GO OUT ON A DATE WITH YOU.
BONK
Hey!
YEAH, YOU TWO! GET A ROOM!
Yeah, yeah!
AFTER-NOONS AT THE PARK ARE FOR US KIDS!
AARGH!
...
Let. Me. Go!
Silence. You brought this on yourself.

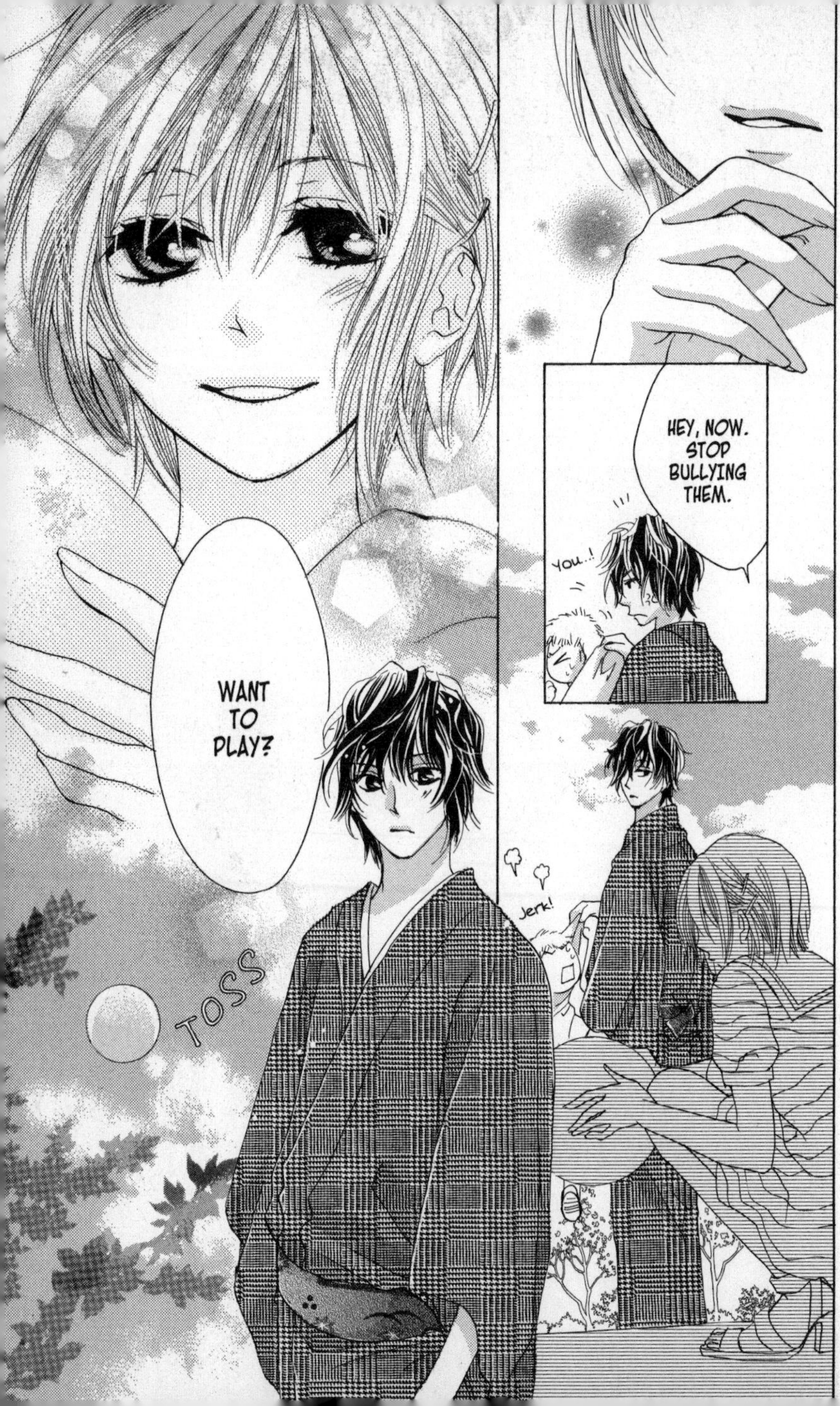
HEY, NOW. STOP BULLYING THEM.
You...!
Jerk!
WANT TO PLAY?
TOSS

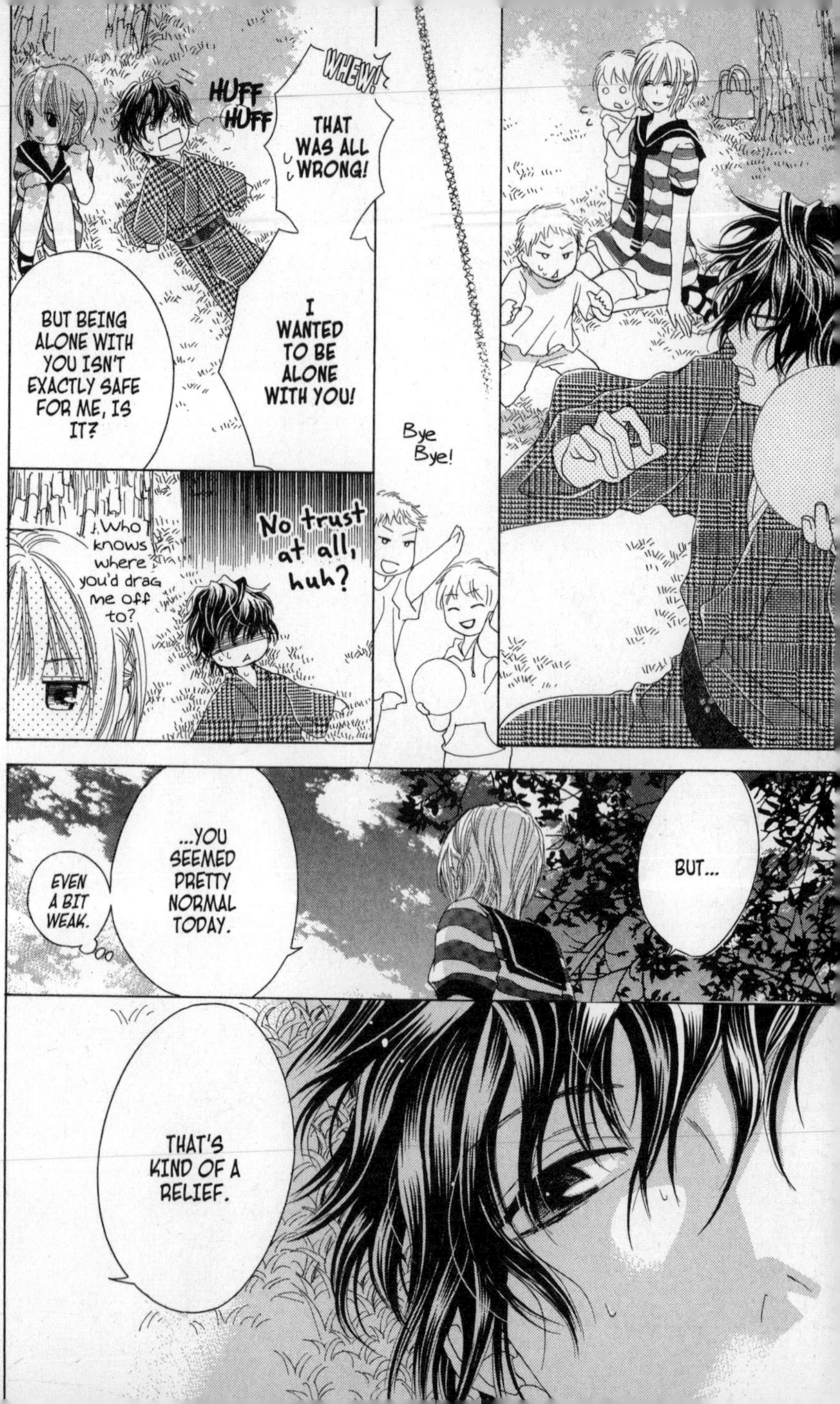
Bye Bye!
WHEW!
THAT WAS ALL WRONG!
I WANTED TO BE ALONE WITH YOU!
HUFF HUFF
BUT BEING ALONE WITH YOU ISN'T EXACTLY SAFE FOR ME, IS IT?
No trust at all, huh?
Who knows where you'd drag me off to?
BUT...
...YOU SEEMED PRETTY NORMAL TODAY.
EVEN A BIT WEAK.
THAT'S KIND OF A RELIEF.

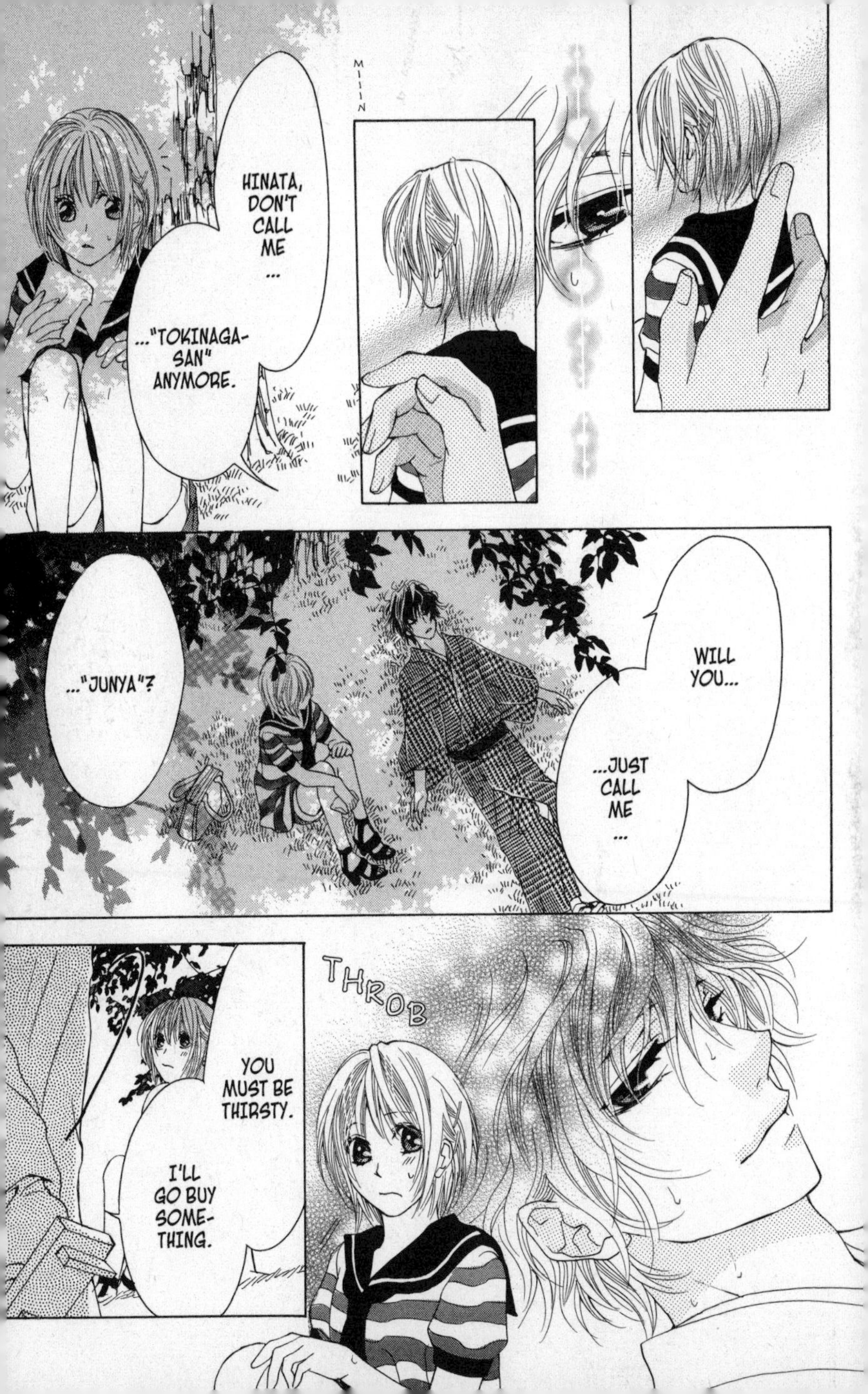
MIIIN
HINATA, DON'T CALL ME ...
..."TOKINAGA-SAN" ANYMORE.
WILL YOU...
...JUST CALL ME ...
..."JUNYA"?
THROB
YOU MUST BE THIRSTY.
I'LL GO BUY SOME-THING.

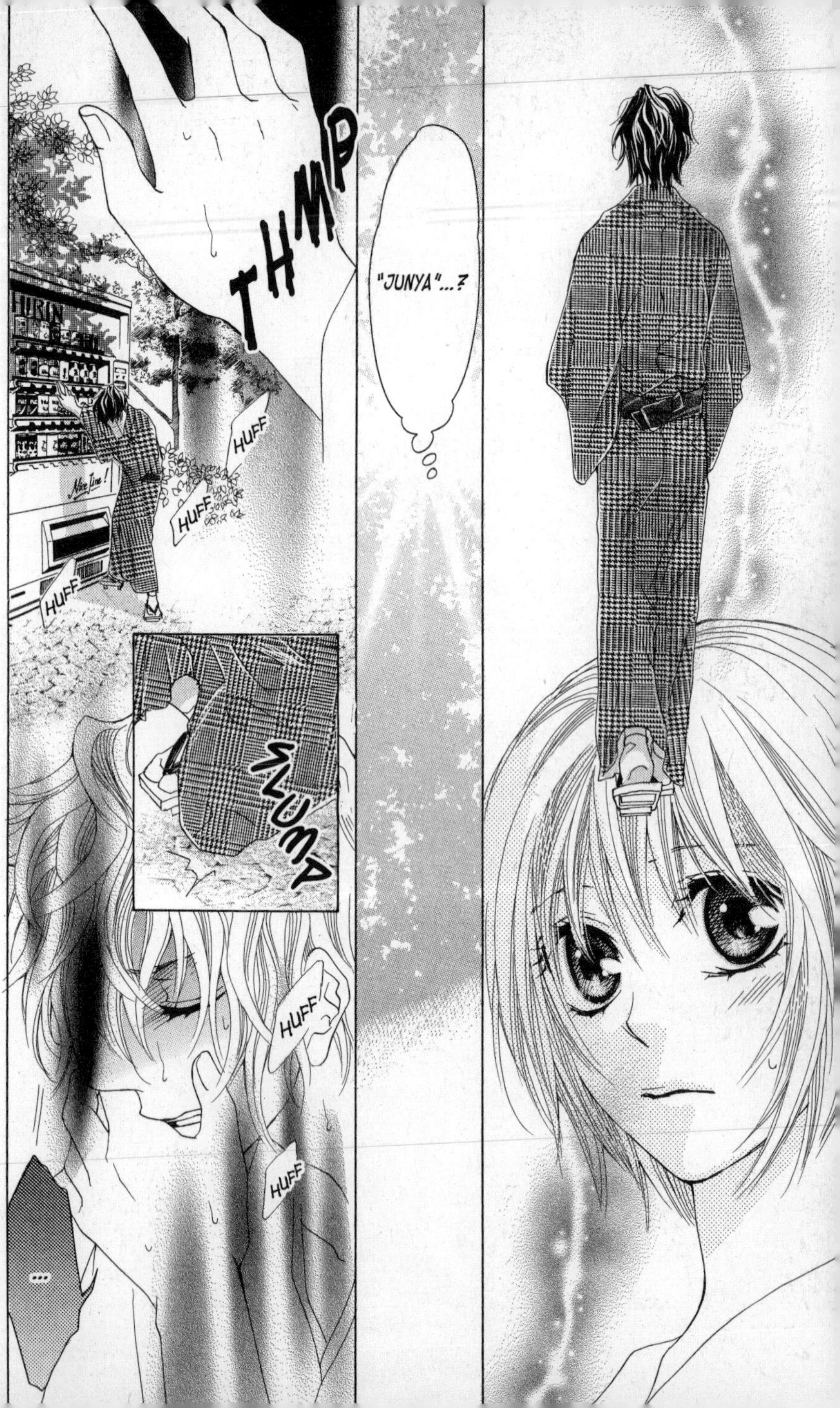
"JUNYA"...?
THMP
HUFF
HUFF
HUFF
SLUMP
HUFF
HUFF
...

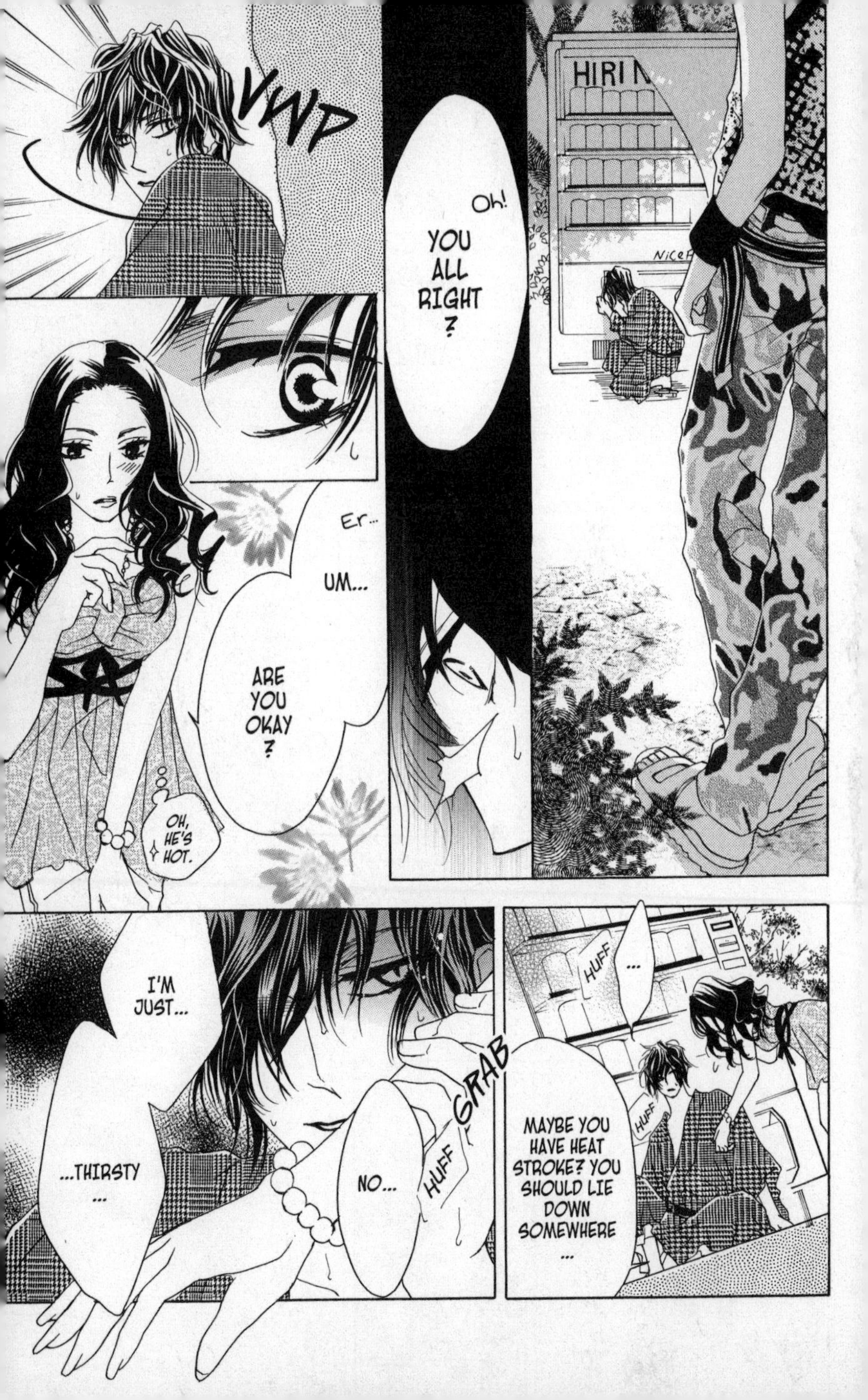
HIRI N
NiceF
Oh!
YOU ALL RIGHT?
VWP
Er...
UM...
ARE YOU OKAY?
OH, HE'S HOT.
HUFF
...
HUFF
MAYBE YOU HAVE HEAT STROKE? YOU SHOULD LIE DOWN SOMEWHERE...
GRAB
HUFF
NO...
I'M JUST...
...THIRSTY...

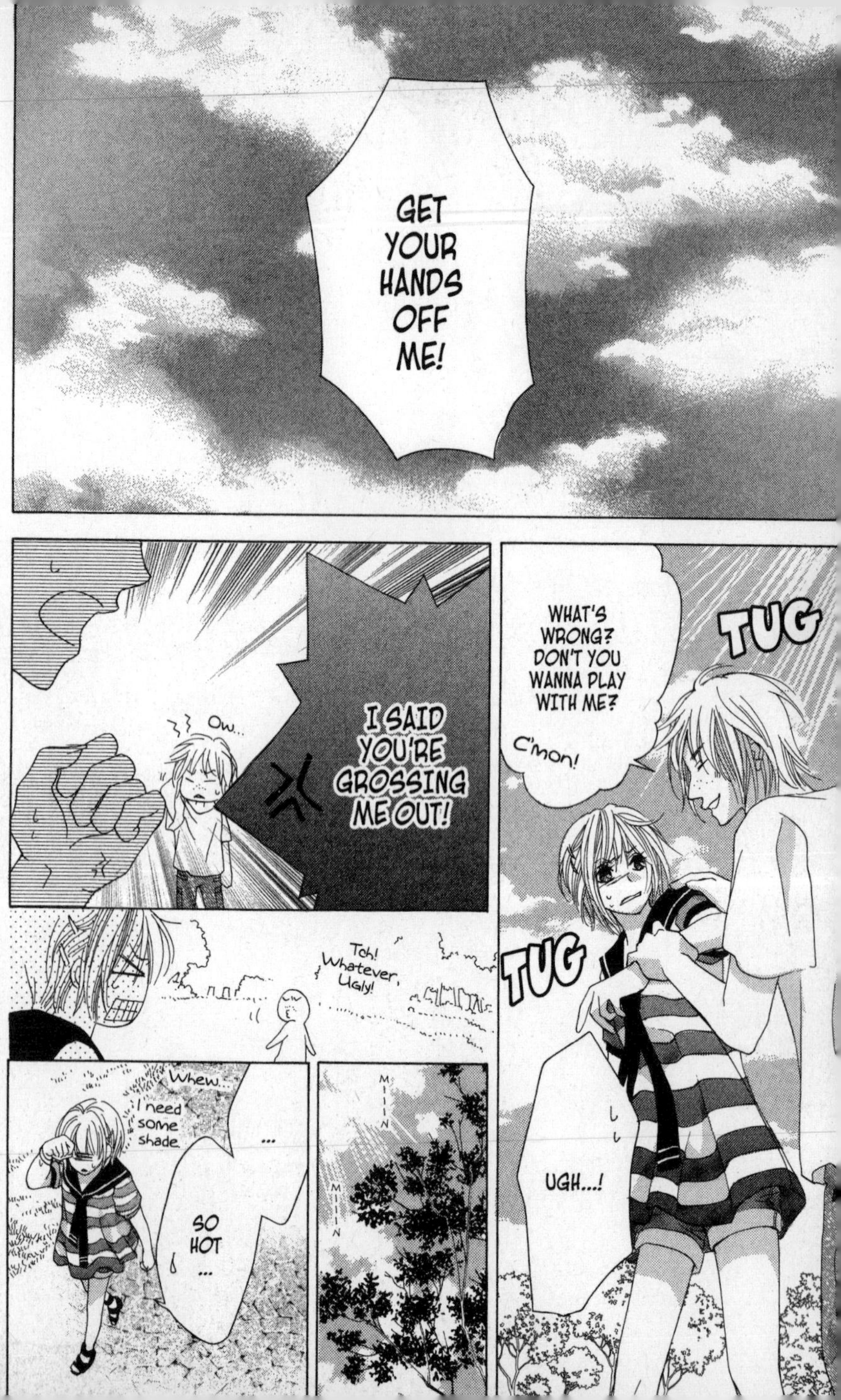
GET YOUR HANDS OFF ME!
WHAT'S WRONG? DON'T YOU WANNA PLAY WITH ME?
C'mon!
TUG
TUG
UGH...!
I SAID YOU'RE GROSSING ME OUT!
Ow...
Tch! Whatever, Ugly!
M-I-I-N
M-I-I-N
Whew... I need some shade.
...
SO HOT ...

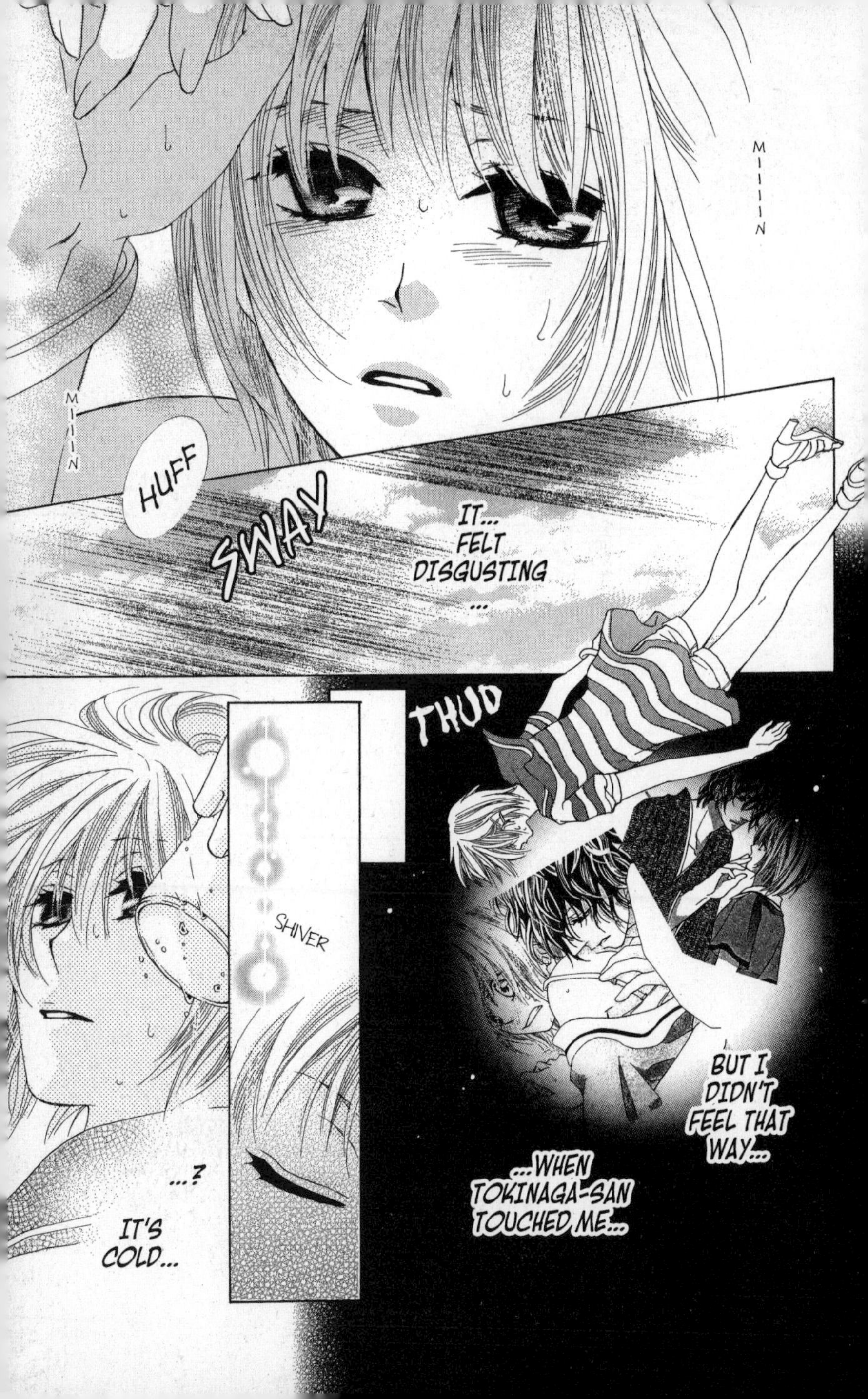
MIIIN
MIIIN
HUFF
IT... FELT DISGUSTING...
SWAY
THUD
BUT I DIDN'T FEEL THAT WAY...
...WHEN TOKINAGA-SAN TOUCHED ME...
SHIVER
...?
IT'S COLD...

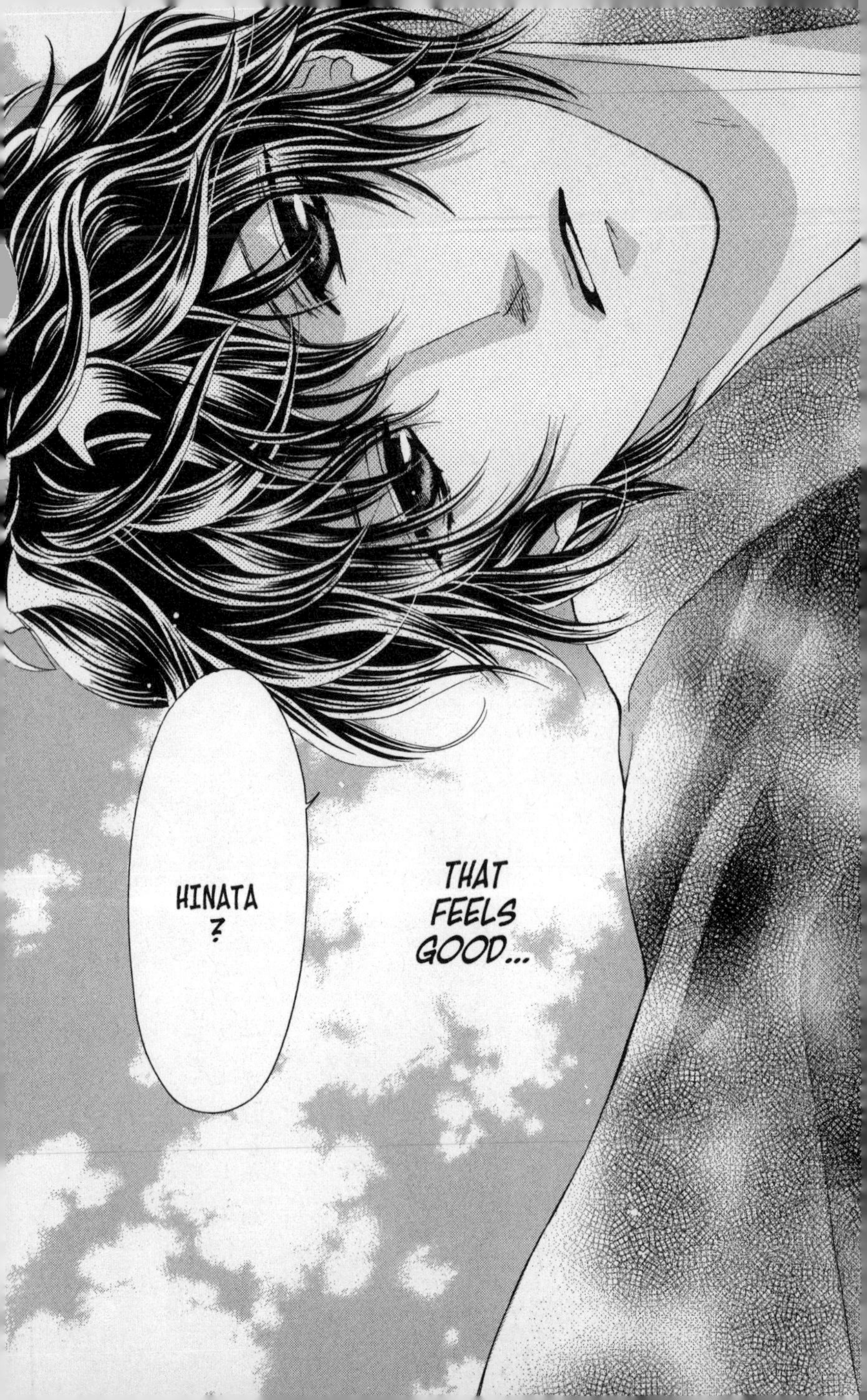
THAT FEELS GOOD...
HINATA?

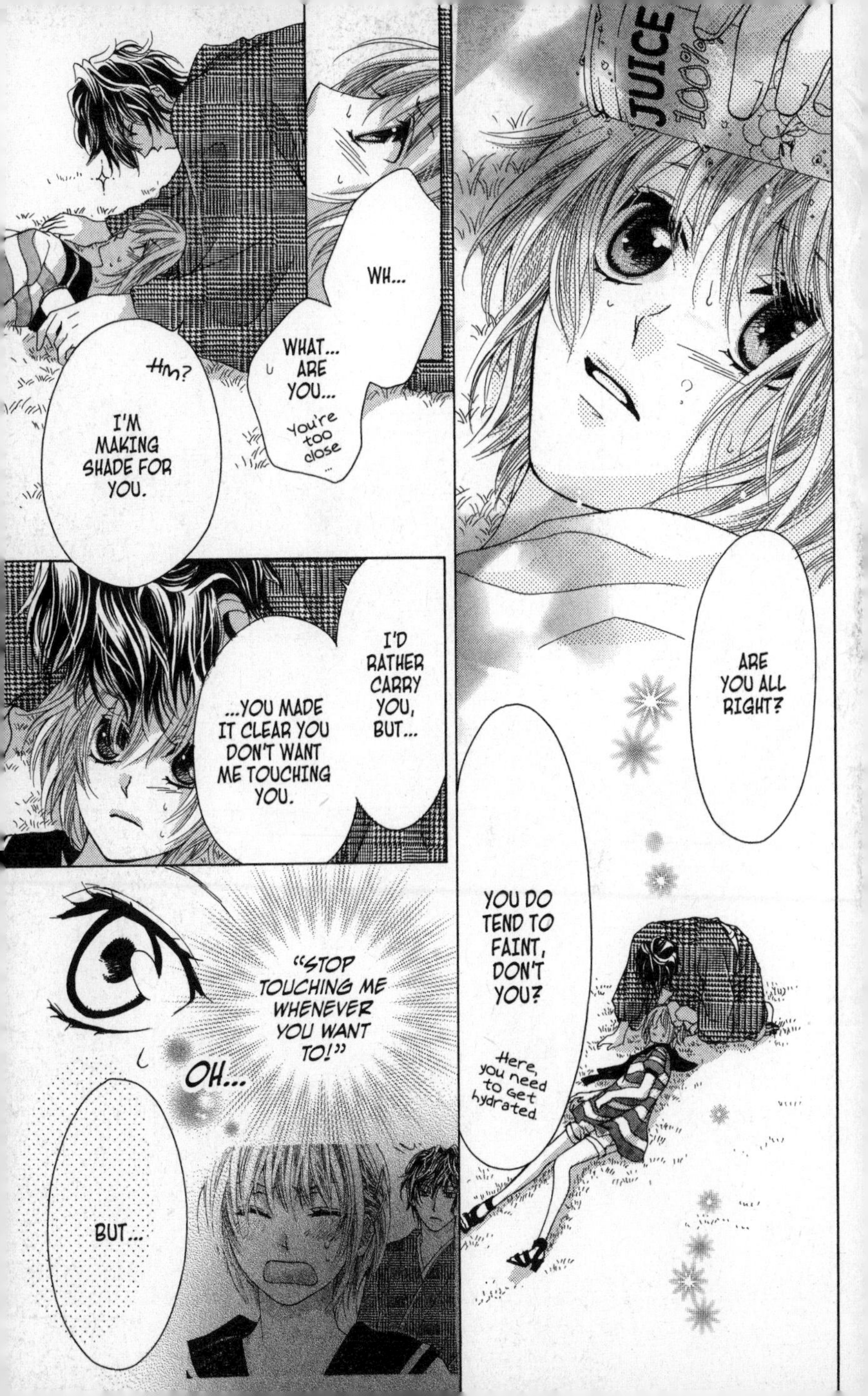
JUICE 100%
ARE YOU ALL RIGHT?
YOU DO TEND TO FAINT, DON'T YOU?
Here, you need to get hydrated.
WH...
WHAT... ARE YOU...
You're too close...
Hm?
I'M MAKING SHADE FOR YOU.
I'D RATHER CARRY YOU, BUT...
...YOU MADE IT CLEAR YOU DON'T WANT ME TOUCHING YOU.
"STOP TOUCHING ME WHENEVER YOU WANT TO!"
OH...
BUT...

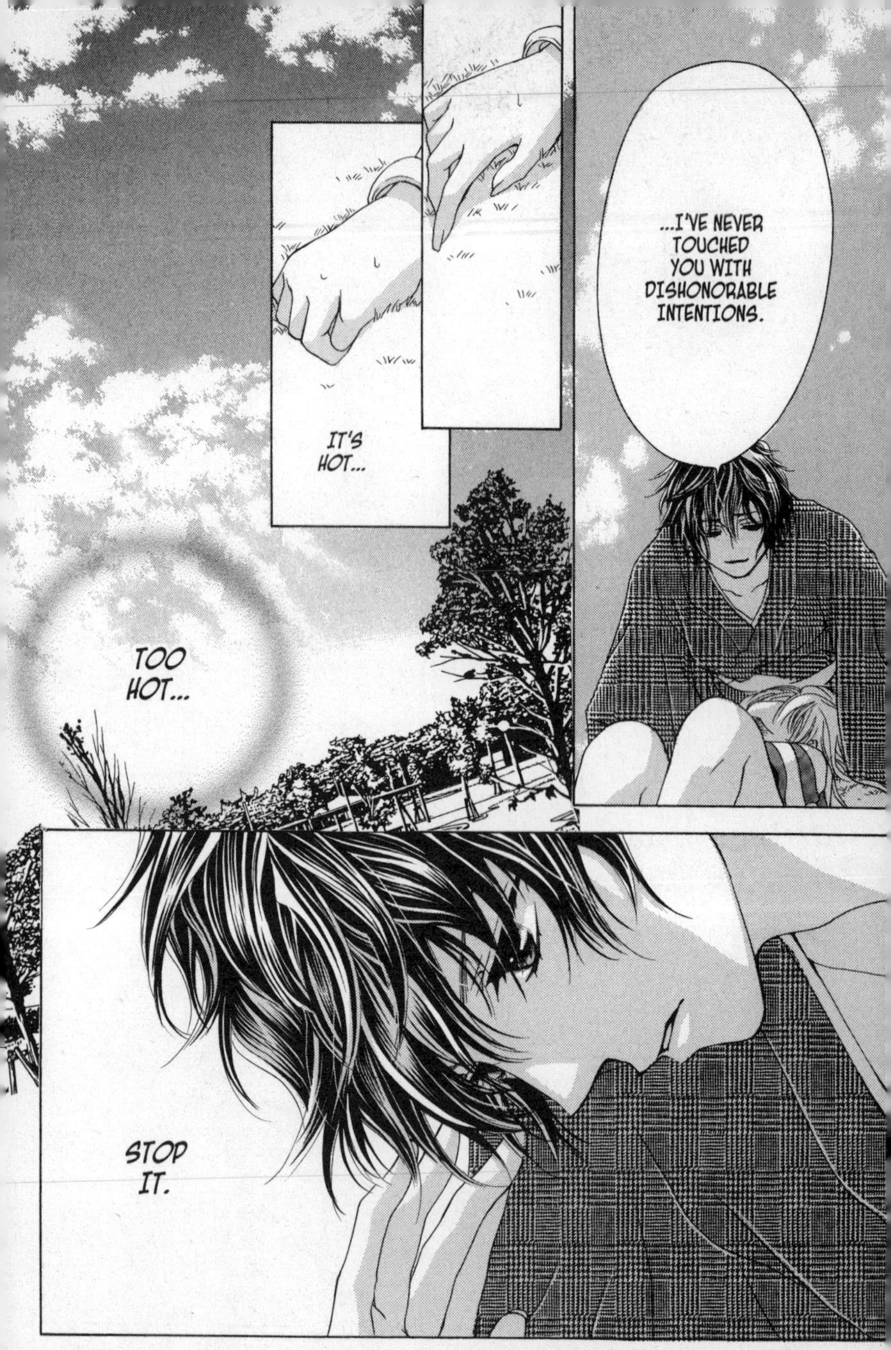
...I'VE NEVER TOUCHED YOU WITH DISHONORABLE INTENTIONS.
IT'S HOT...
TOO HOT...
STOP IT.

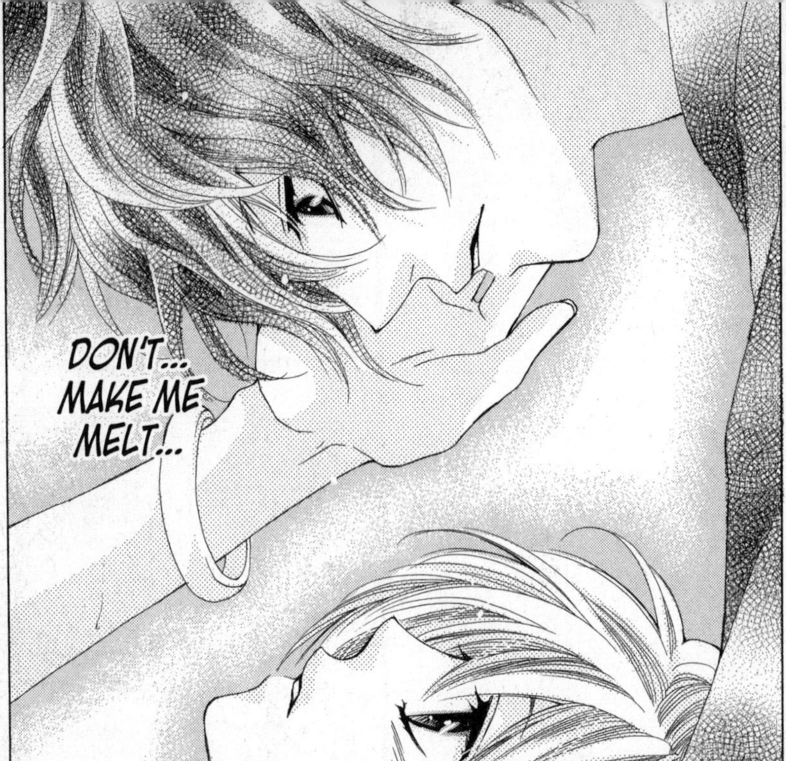
DON'T... MAKE ME MELT!...

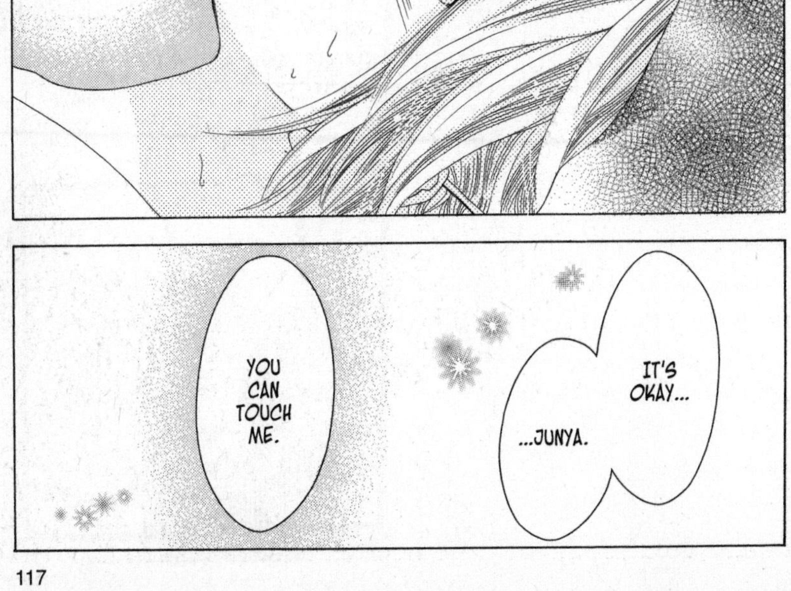
IT'S OKAY...
...JUNYA.
YOU CAN TOUCH ME.

A Source of Embarrassment

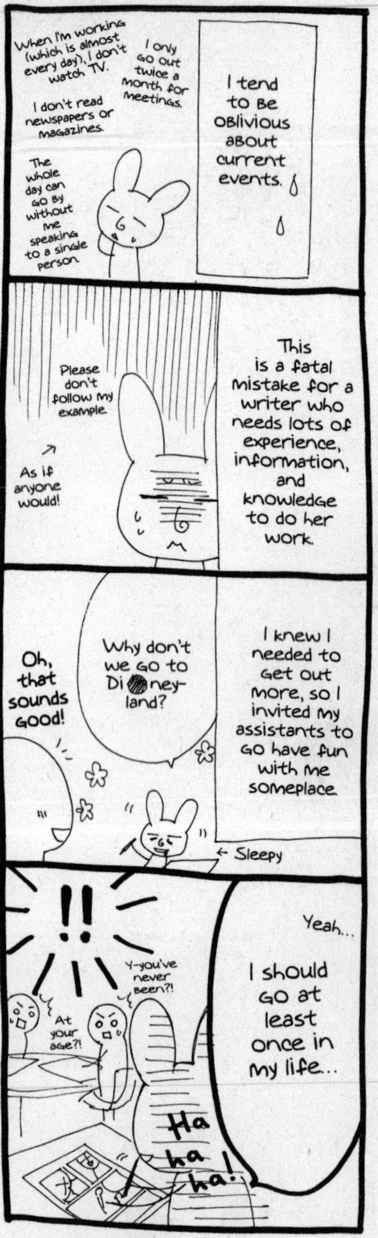
I tend to be oblivious about current events.
I only go out twice a month for meetings.
When I'm working (which is almost every day), I don't watch TV.
I don't read newspapers or magazines.
The whole day can go by without me speaking to a single person.
This is a fatal mistake for a writer who needs lots of experience, information, and knowledge to do her work.
Please don't follow my example.
As if anyone would!
I knew I needed to get out more, so I invited my assistants to go have fun with me someplace.
Why don't we go to Di[redacted]ney-land?
Oh, that sounds good!
Sleepy
Yeah...
I should go at least once in my life...
!!
Y-you've never been?!
At your age?!
Ha ha ha!

They were VERY surprised.

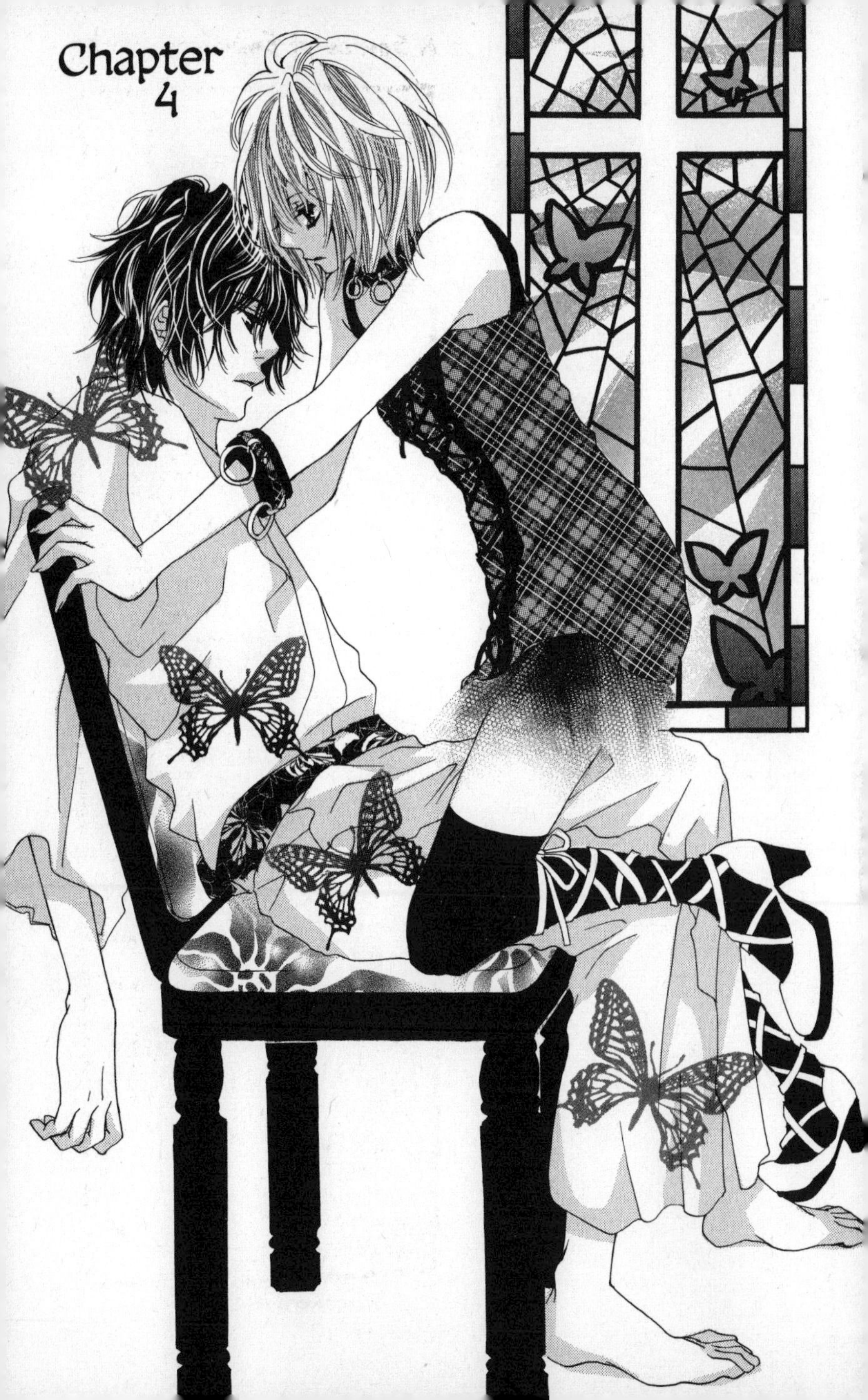
Chapter
4

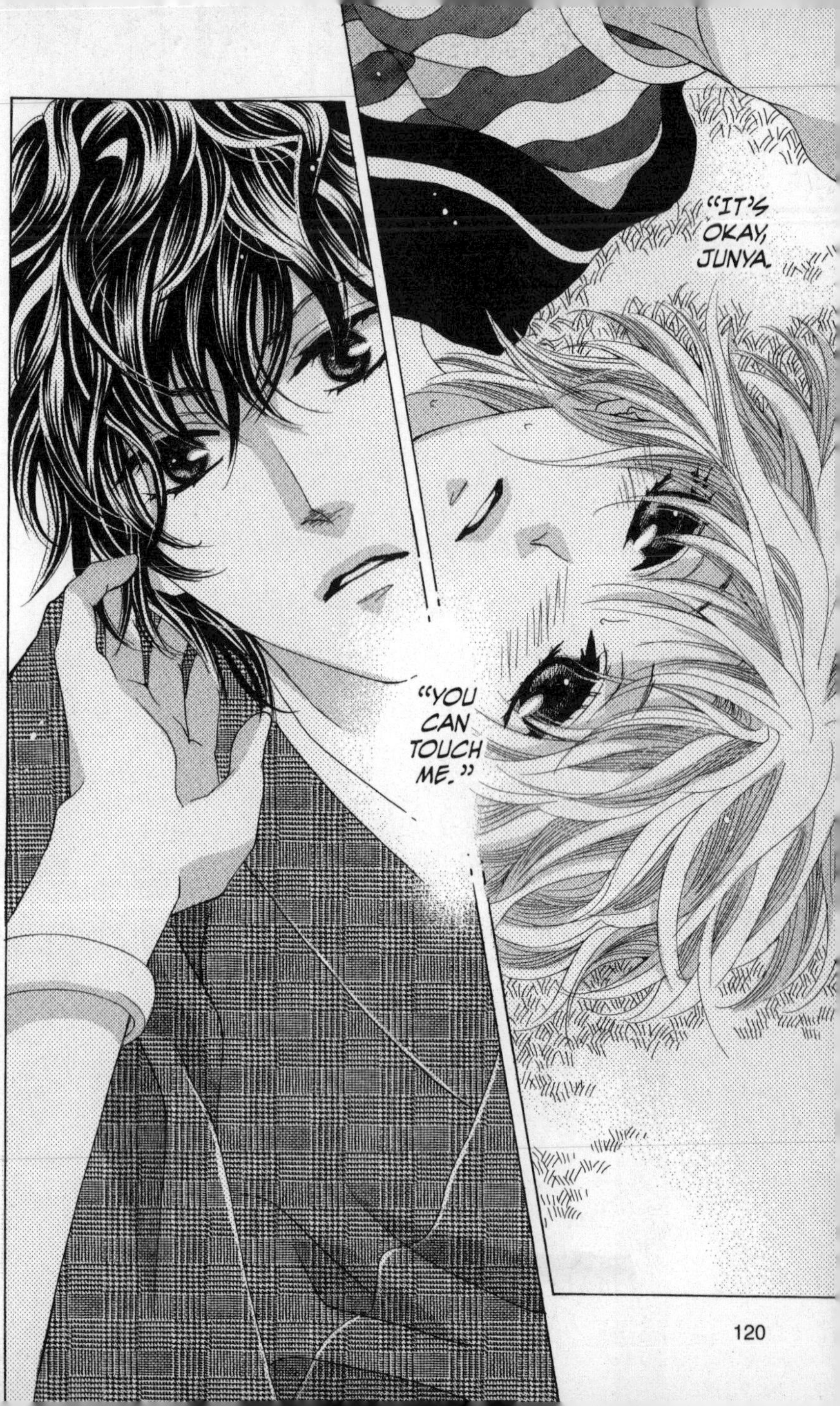
"IT'S OKAY, JUNYA.
"YOU CAN TOUCH ME."

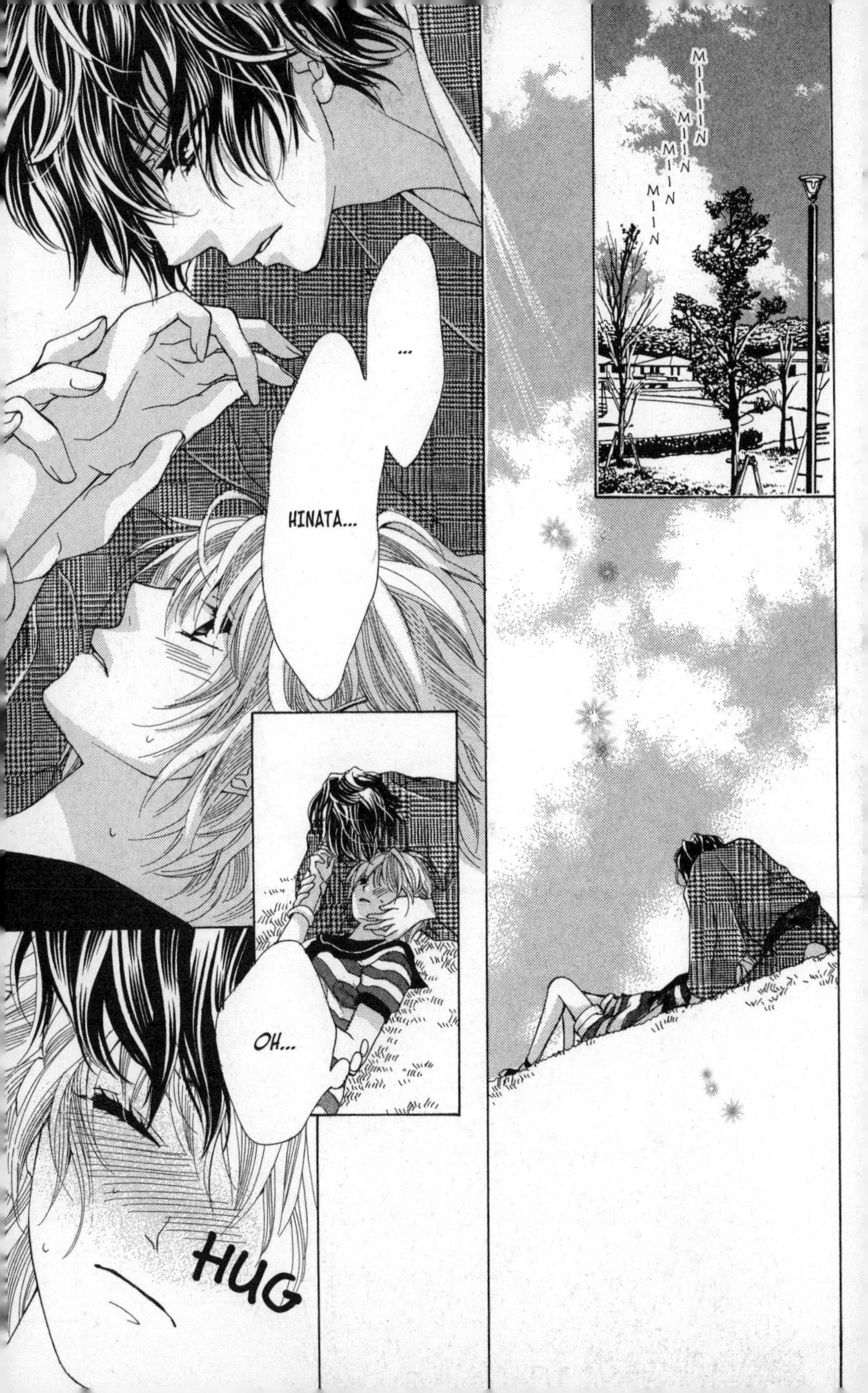
MIIN
MIIN
MIIN
MIIN
...
HINATA...
OH...
HUG

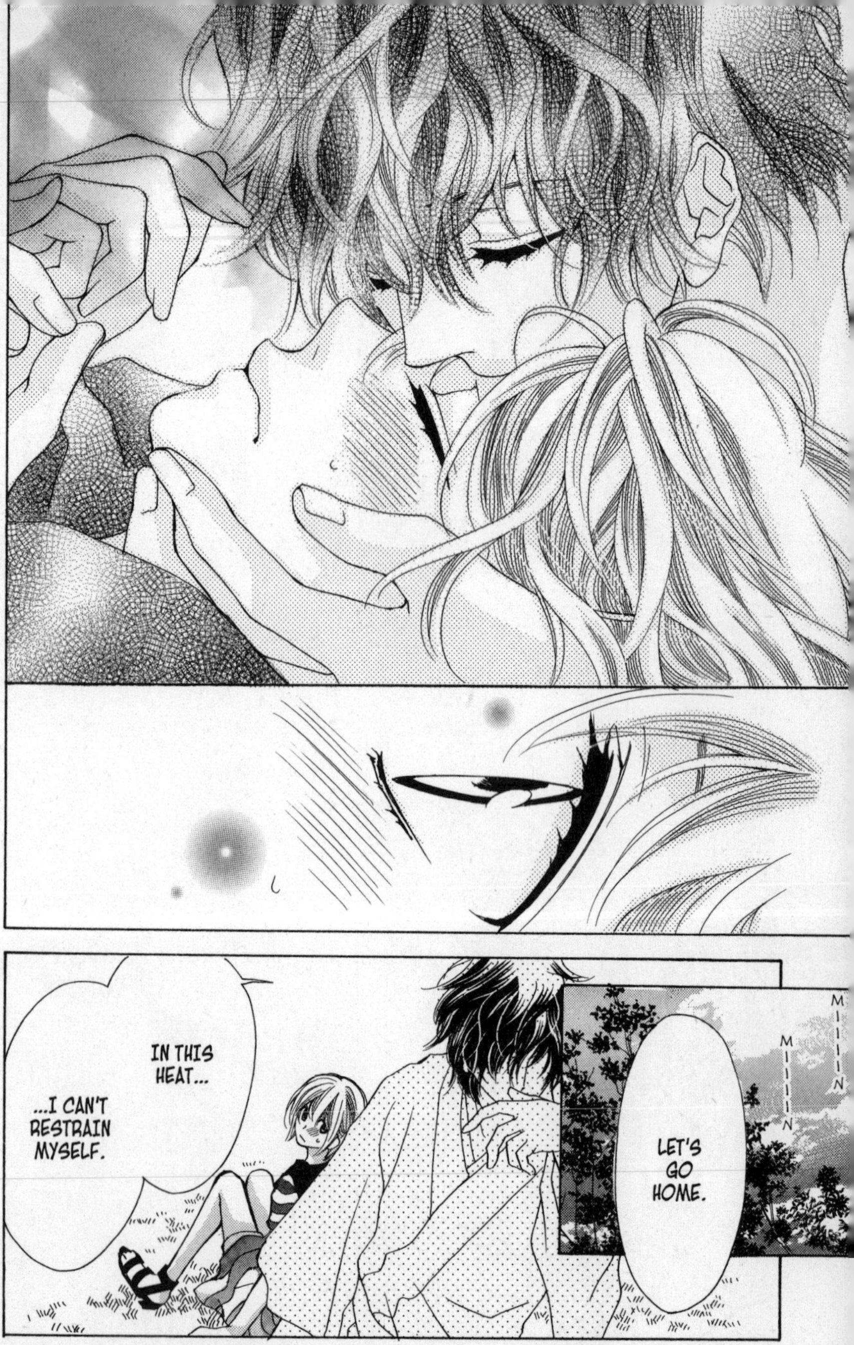
MIIIN
MIIIN
LET'S GO HOME.
IN THIS HEAT...
...I CAN'T RESTRAIN MYSELF.

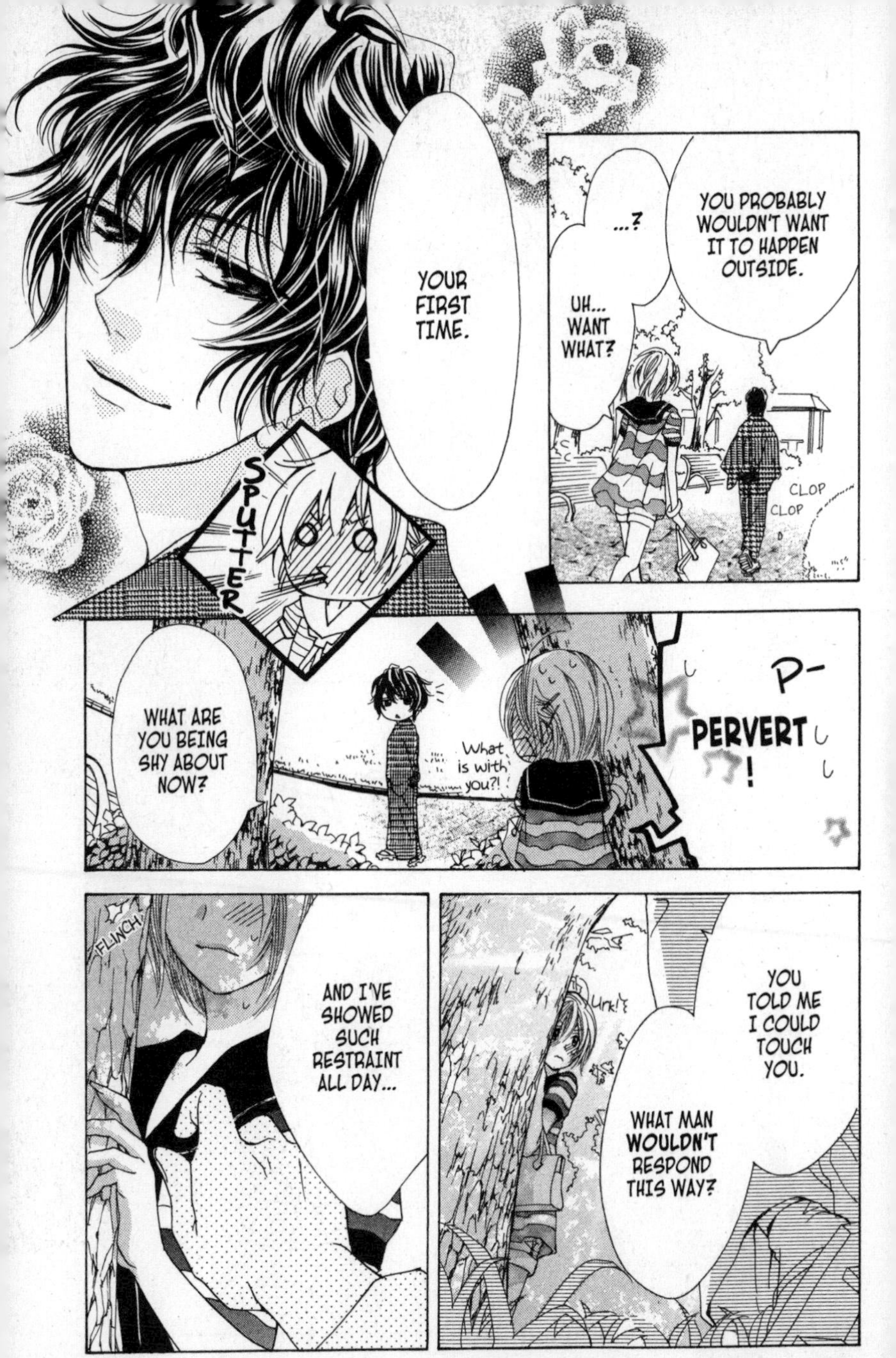
YOU PROBABLY WOULDN'T WANT IT TO HAPPEN OUTSIDE.
...?
UH... WANT WHAT?
CLOP
CLOP
YOUR FIRST TIME.
SPUTTER
P- PERVERT!
What is with you?!
WHAT ARE YOU BEING SHY ABOUT NOW?
YOU TOLD ME I COULD TOUCH YOU.
Urk!
WHAT MAN WOULDN'T RESPOND THIS WAY?
FLINCH
AND I'VE SHOWED SUCH RESTRAINT ALL DAY...

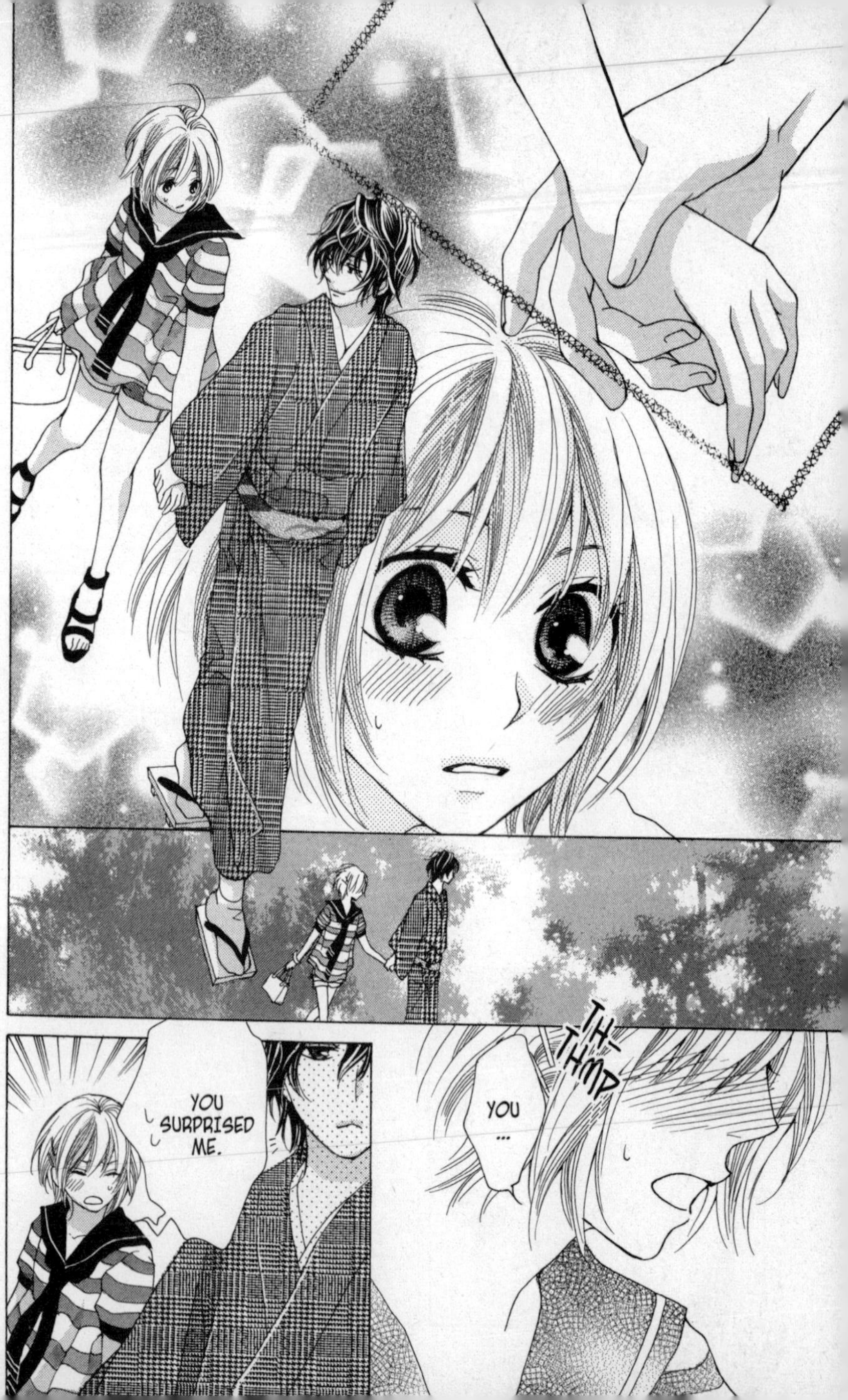
TH-THMP
YOU ...
YOU SURPRISED ME.

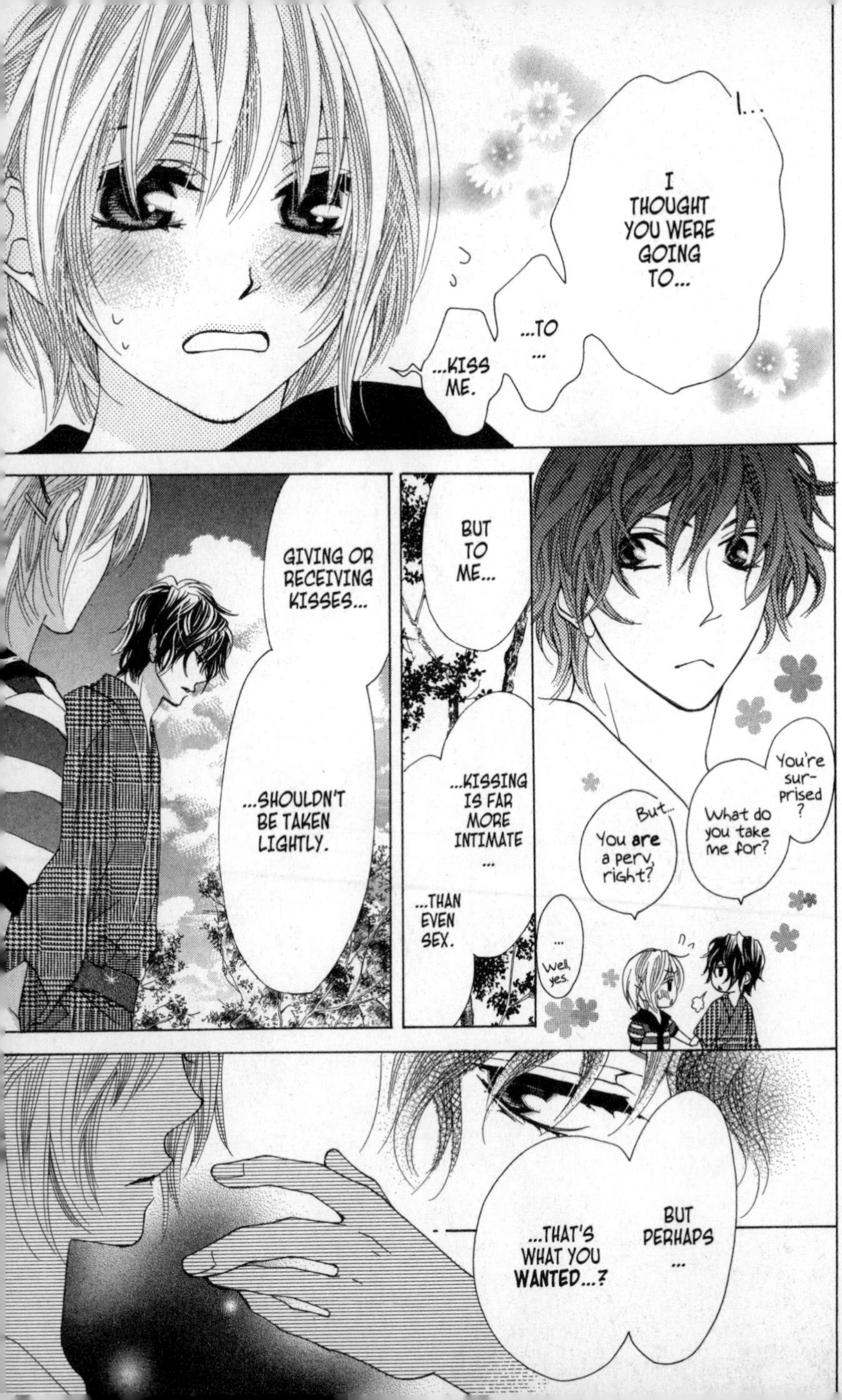
I...
I THOUGHT YOU WERE GOING TO...
...TO ...
...KISS ME.
You're sur-prised?
What do you take me for?
But... You are a perv, right?
... Well, yes.
BUT TO ME...
...KISSING IS FAR MORE INTIMATE ...
...THAN EVEN SEX.
GIVING OR RECEIVING KISSES...
...SHOULDN'T BE TAKEN LIGHTLY.
BUT PERHAPS ...
...THAT'S WHAT YOU WANTED...?

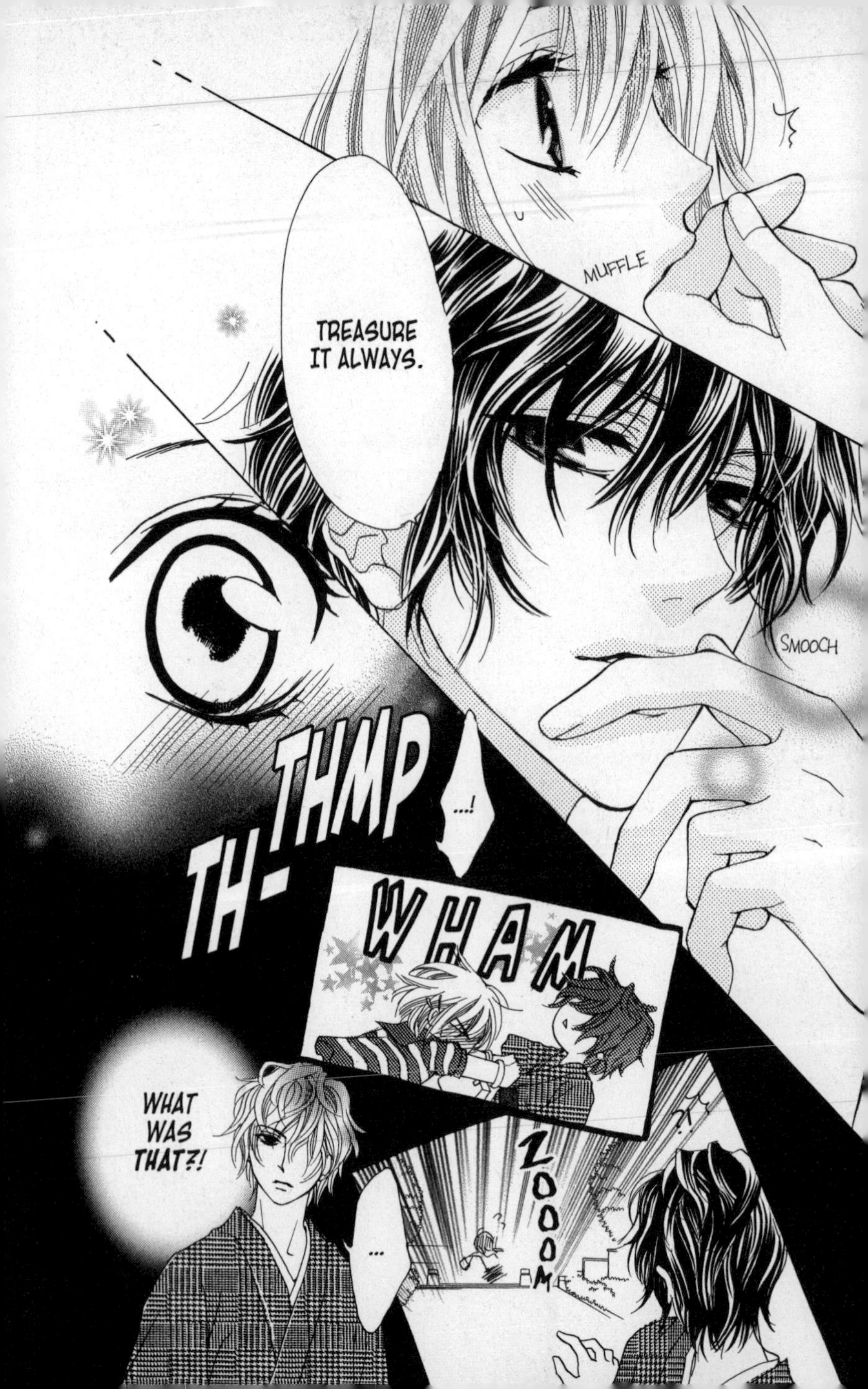
MUFFLE
TREASURE IT ALWAYS.
SMOOCH
...!
TH-THMP
WHAM
ZOOOOM
WHAT WAS THAT?!
...

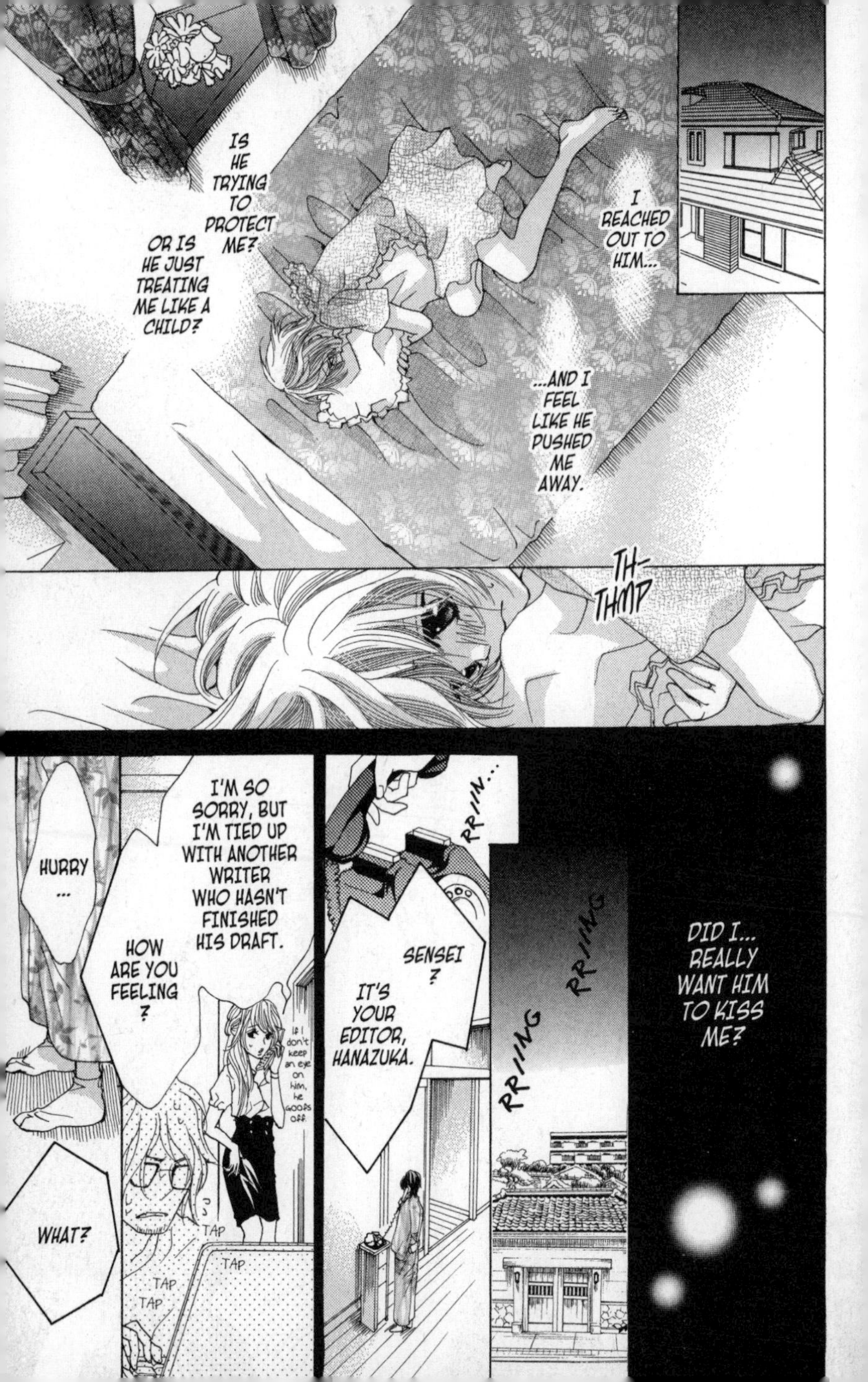
I REACHED OUT TO HIM...
...AND I FEEL LIKE HE PUSHED ME AWAY.
IS HE TRYING TO PROTECT ME?
OR IS HE JUST TREATING ME LIKE A CHILD?
TH-THMP
DID I... REALLY WANT HIM TO KISS ME?
RRIIING
RRIIING
RRIIN...
SENSEI?
IT'S YOUR EDITOR, HANAZUKA.
I'M SO SORRY, BUT I'M TIED UP WITH ANOTHER WRITER WHO HASN'T FINISHED HIS DRAFT.
HOW ARE YOU FEELING?
If I don't keep an eye on him, he GOOFS off.
TAP
TAP
TAP
TAP
HURRY...
WHAT?

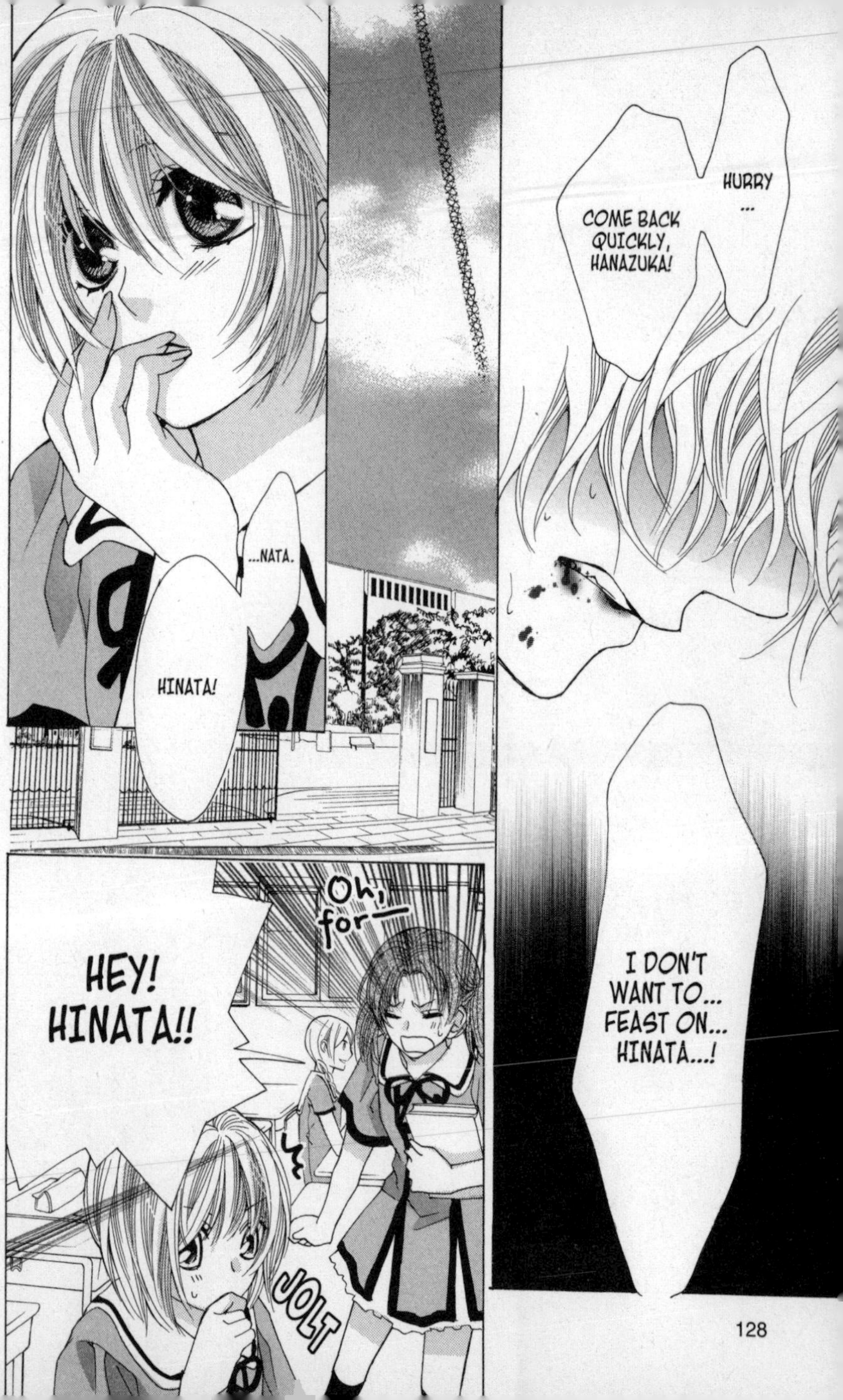
HURRY ...
COME BACK QUICKLY, HANAZUKA!
I DON'T WANT TO... FEAST ON... HINATA...!
...NATA.
HINATA!
Oh, for—
HEY! HINATA!!
JOLT

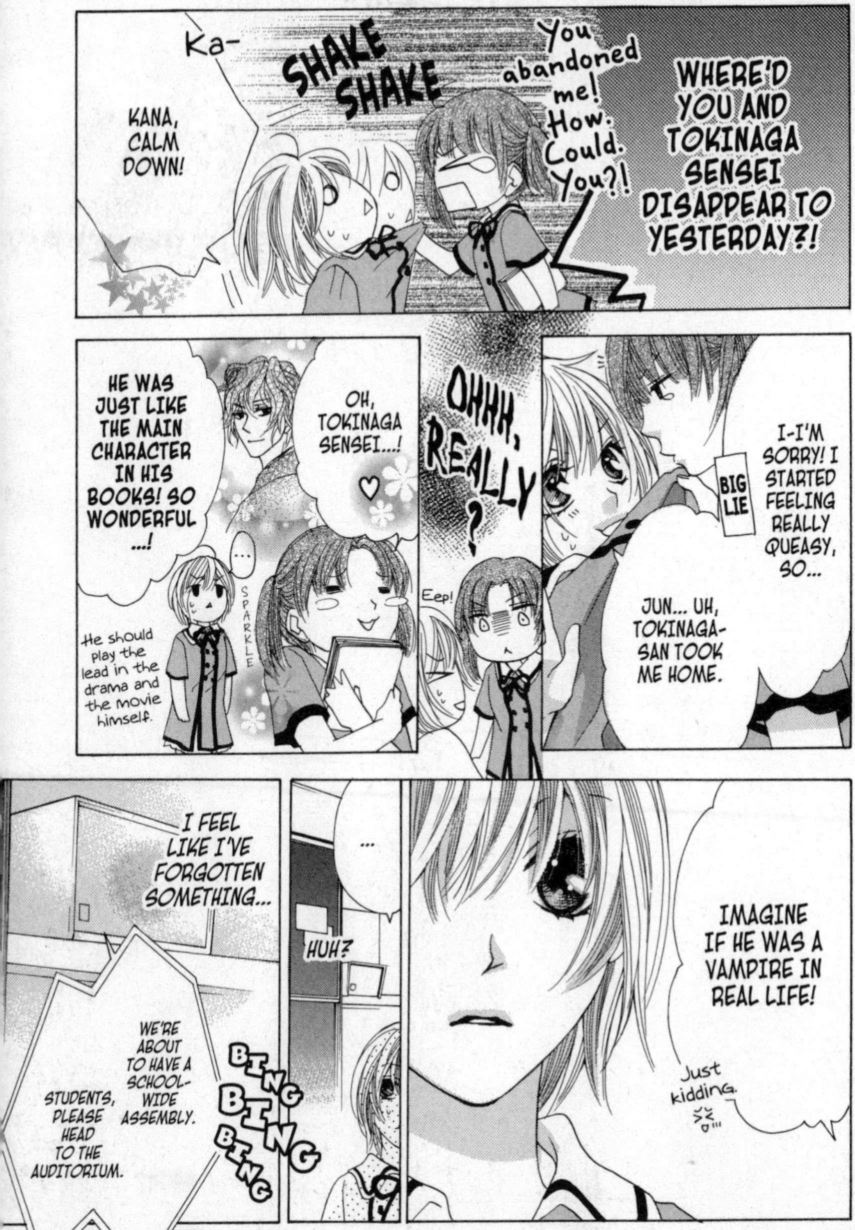
WHERE'D YOU AND TOKINAGA SENSEI DISAPPEAR TO YESTERDAY?!
You abandoned me! How. Could. You?!
SHAKE SHAKE
Ka-
KANA, CALM DOWN!
I-I'M SORRY! I STARTED FEELING REALLY QUEASY, SO...
BIG LIE
JUN... UH, TOKINAGA-SAN TOOK ME HOME.
OHHH, REALLY?
Eep!
OH, TOKINAGA SENSEI...!
HE WAS JUST LIKE THE MAIN CHARACTER IN HIS BOOKS! SO WONDERFUL...!
SPARKLE
...
He should play the lead in the drama and the movie himself.
IMAGINE IF HE WAS A VAMPIRE IN REAL LIFE!
Just kidding.
...
HUH?
I FEEL LIKE I'VE FORGOTTEN SOMETHING...
BING BING BING
WE'RE ABOUT TO HAVE A SCHOOL-WIDE ASSEMBLY.
STUDENTS, PLEASE HEAD TO THE AUDITORIUM.

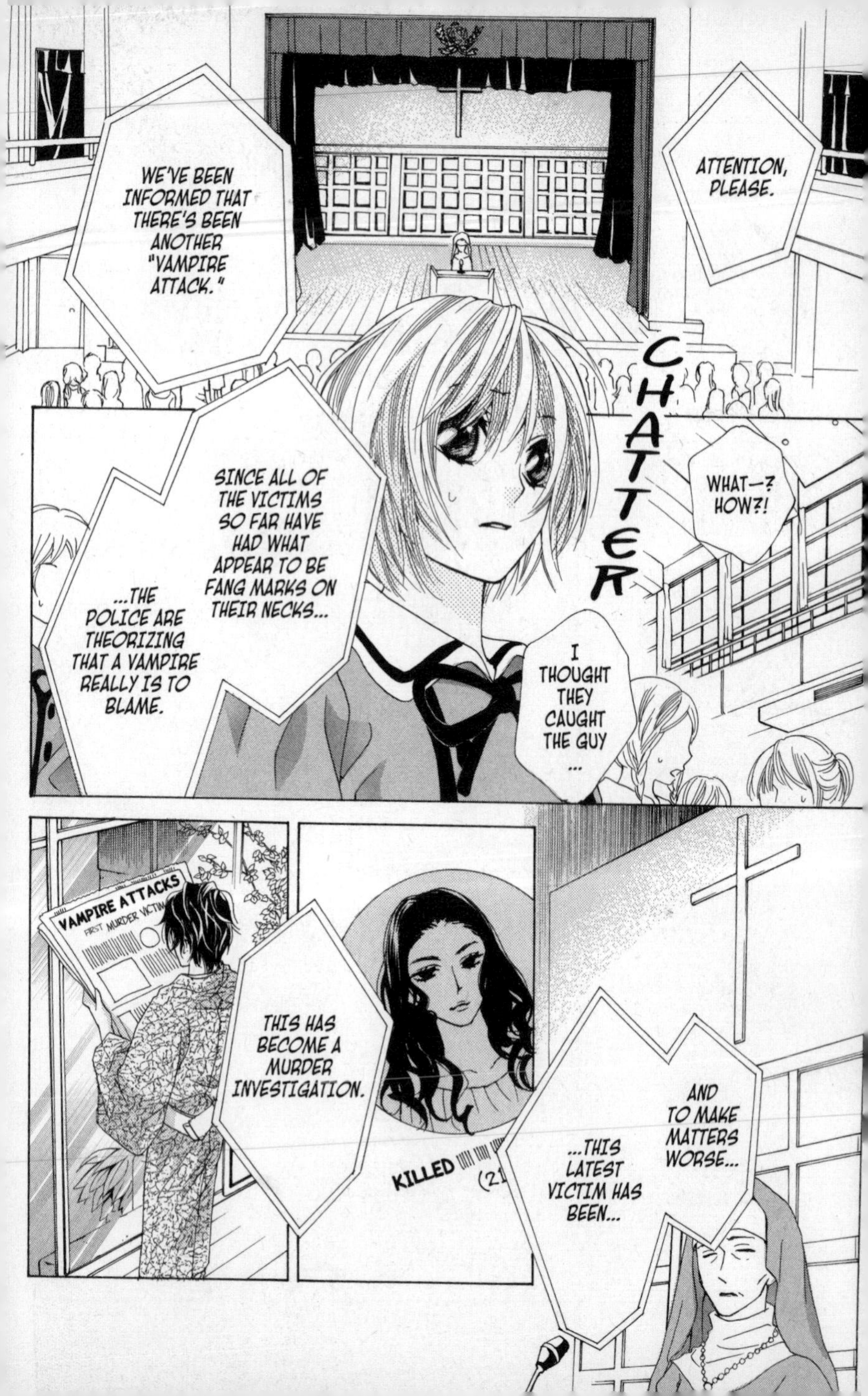
ATTENTION, PLEASE.
WE'VE BEEN INFORMED THAT THERE'S BEEN ANOTHER "VAMPIRE ATTACK."
CHATTER
WHAT—?! HOW?!
I THOUGHT THEY CAUGHT THE GUY...
SINCE ALL OF THE VICTIMS SO FAR HAVE HAD WHAT APPEAR TO BE FANG MARKS ON THEIR NECKS...
...THE POLICE ARE THEORIZING THAT A VAMPIRE REALLY IS TO BLAME.
AND TO MAKE MATTERS WORSE...
...THIS LATEST VICTIM HAS BEEN...
KILLED
THIS HAS BECOME A MURDER INVESTIGATION.
VAMPIRE ATTACKS
FIRST MURDER VICTIM

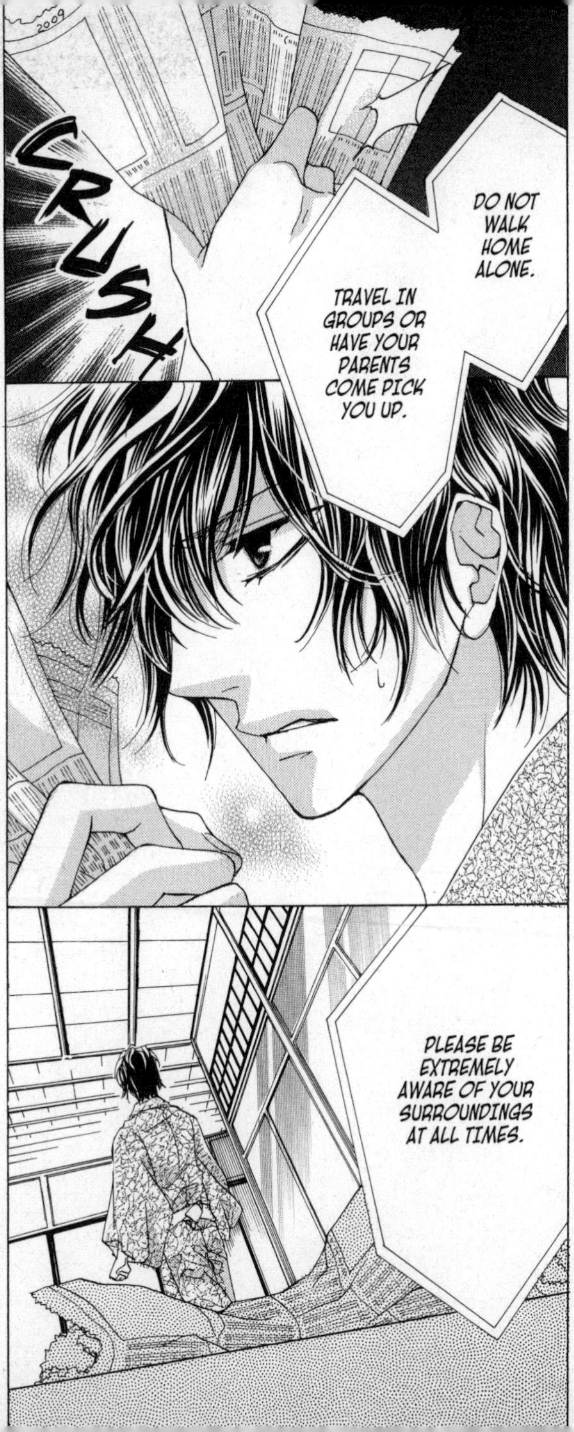
DO NOT WALK HOME ALONE.
TRAVEL IN GROUPS OR HAVE YOUR PARENTS COME PICK YOU UP.
CRUSH
PLEASE BE EXTREMELY AWARE OF YOUR SURROUNDINGS AT ALL TIMES.

Small Talk

④

Y and her boyfriend had a long, leisurely courtship. Even when there were periods of time when they couldn't be together, they trusted each other. It was like they were already married! (*Ha ha*)

They're my ideal couple. ♥

As a side note: Y sometimes sends a care package of food to my house. (Grin)

It's a big help, because I live such a haphazard lifestyle.

So that leaves K, M and me. We're all very stoic and reserved, so our love lives don't come up much.

That said, my former editor and my current editor went from dating to being married in under six months! So it's all up to fate.

For now, I'll just be married to my work.♥ (*Heh*)

Since I'm writing romantic manga, I should apologize for the lack of romance in my life...

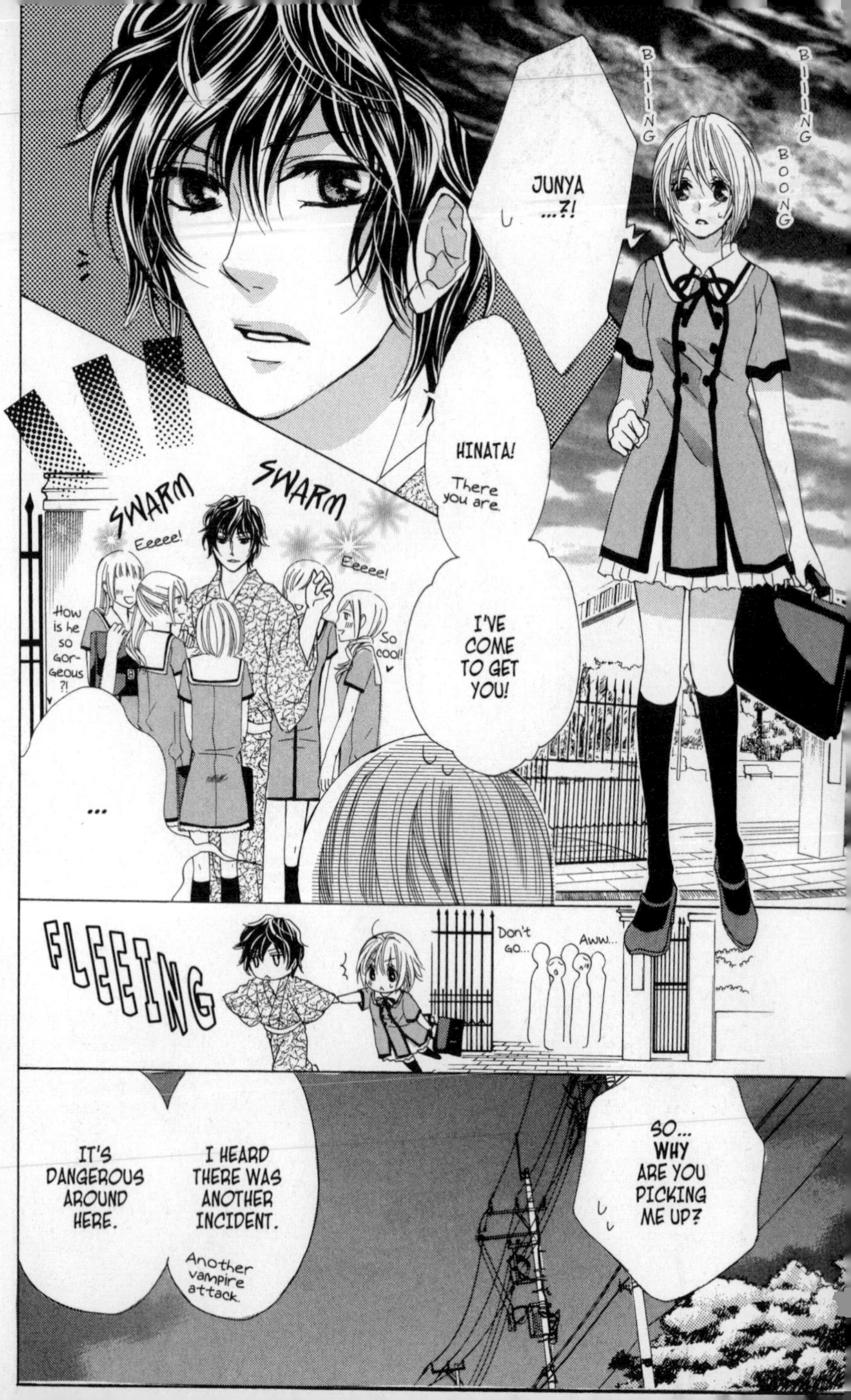
BIIING
BIIING
BOONG
JUNYA ...?!
HINATA!
There you are.
I'VE COME TO GET YOU!
SWARM
SWARM
Eeeee!
Eeeee!
So cool!
How is he so gorgeous?!
...
Aww...
Don't go...
FLEEING
SO... WHY ARE YOU PICKING ME UP?
I HEARD THERE WAS ANOTHER INCIDENT.
Another vampire attack.
IT'S DANGEROUS AROUND HERE.

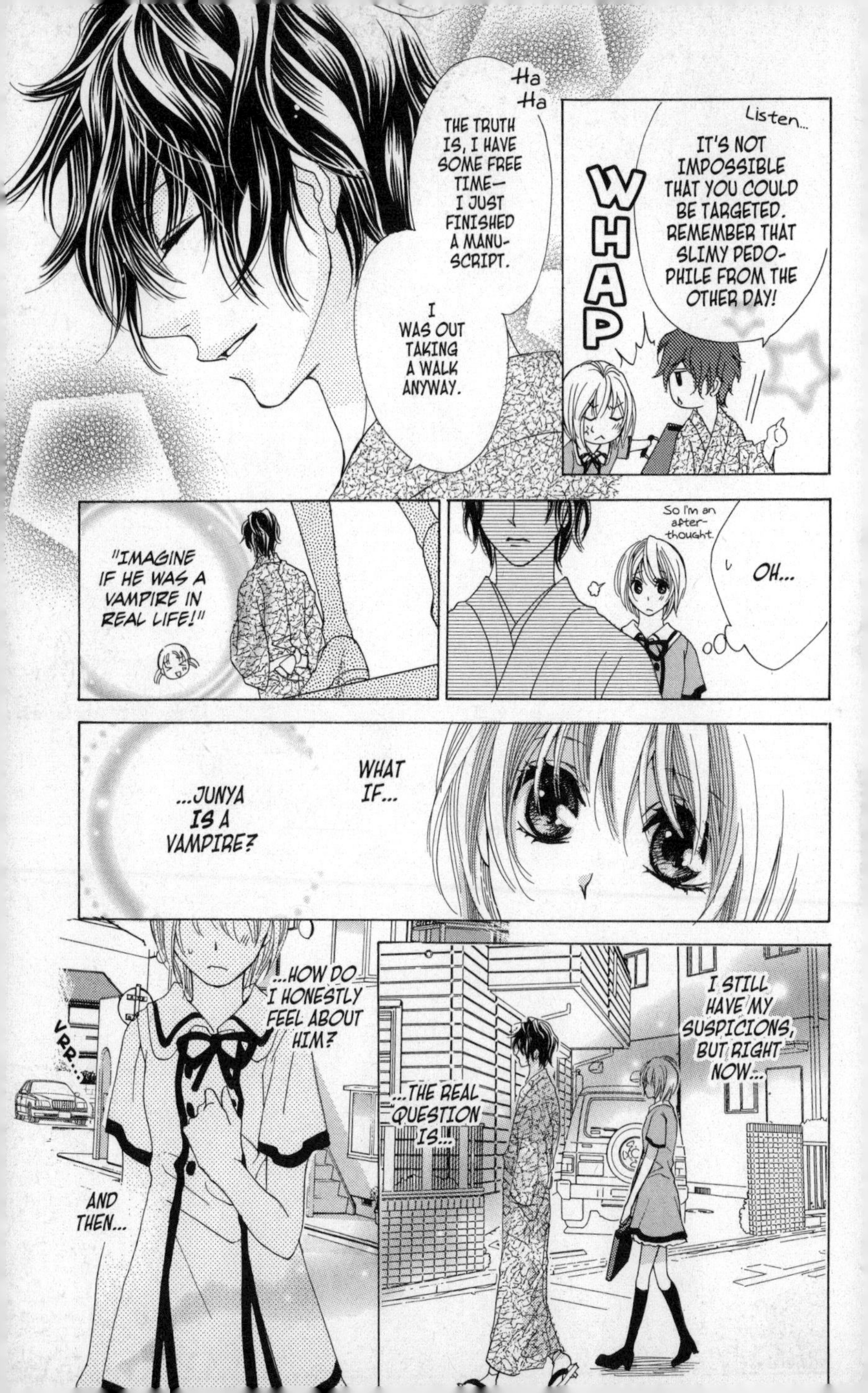

Listen...
IT'S NOT IMPOSSIBLE THAT YOU COULD BE TARGETED. REMEMBER THAT SLIMY PEDO-PHILE FROM THE OTHER DAY!
WHAP
Ha Ha
THE TRUTH IS, I HAVE SOME FREE TIME— I JUST FINISHED A MANU-SCRIPT.
I WAS OUT TAKING A WALK ANYWAY.
So I'm an after-thought.
OH...
"IMAGINE IF HE WAS A VAMPIRE IN REAL LIFE!"
WHAT IF...
...JUNYA IS A VAMPIRE?
I STILL HAVE MY SUSPICIONS, BUT RIGHT NOW...
...THE REAL QUESTION IS...
...HOW DO I HONESTLY FEEL ABOUT HIM?
VRR...
AND THEN...

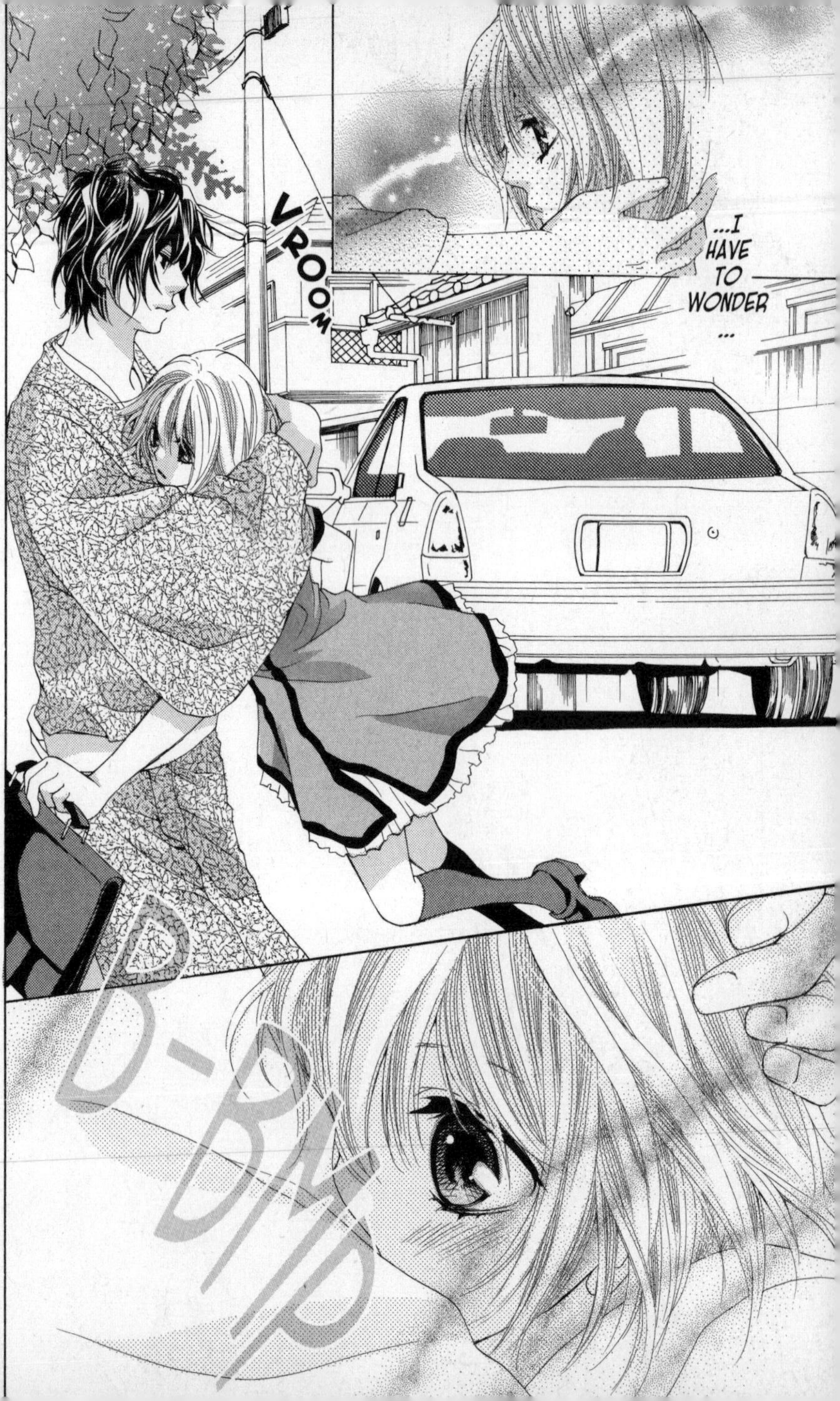
...I HAVE TO WONDER ...
VROOM
B-BMP

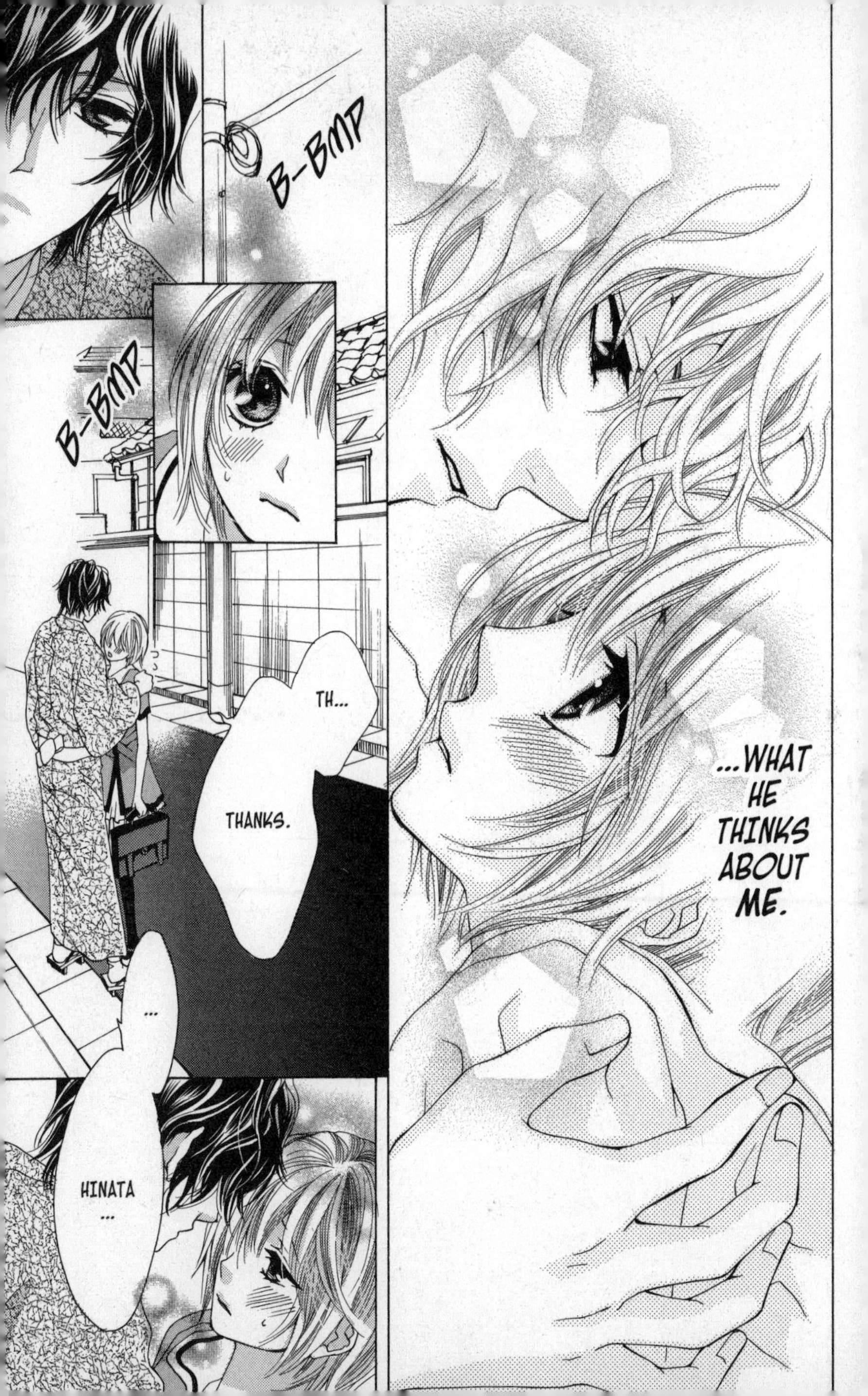
...WHAT HE THINKS ABOUT ME.
B-BMP
B-BMP
TH...
THANKS.
...
HINATA ...

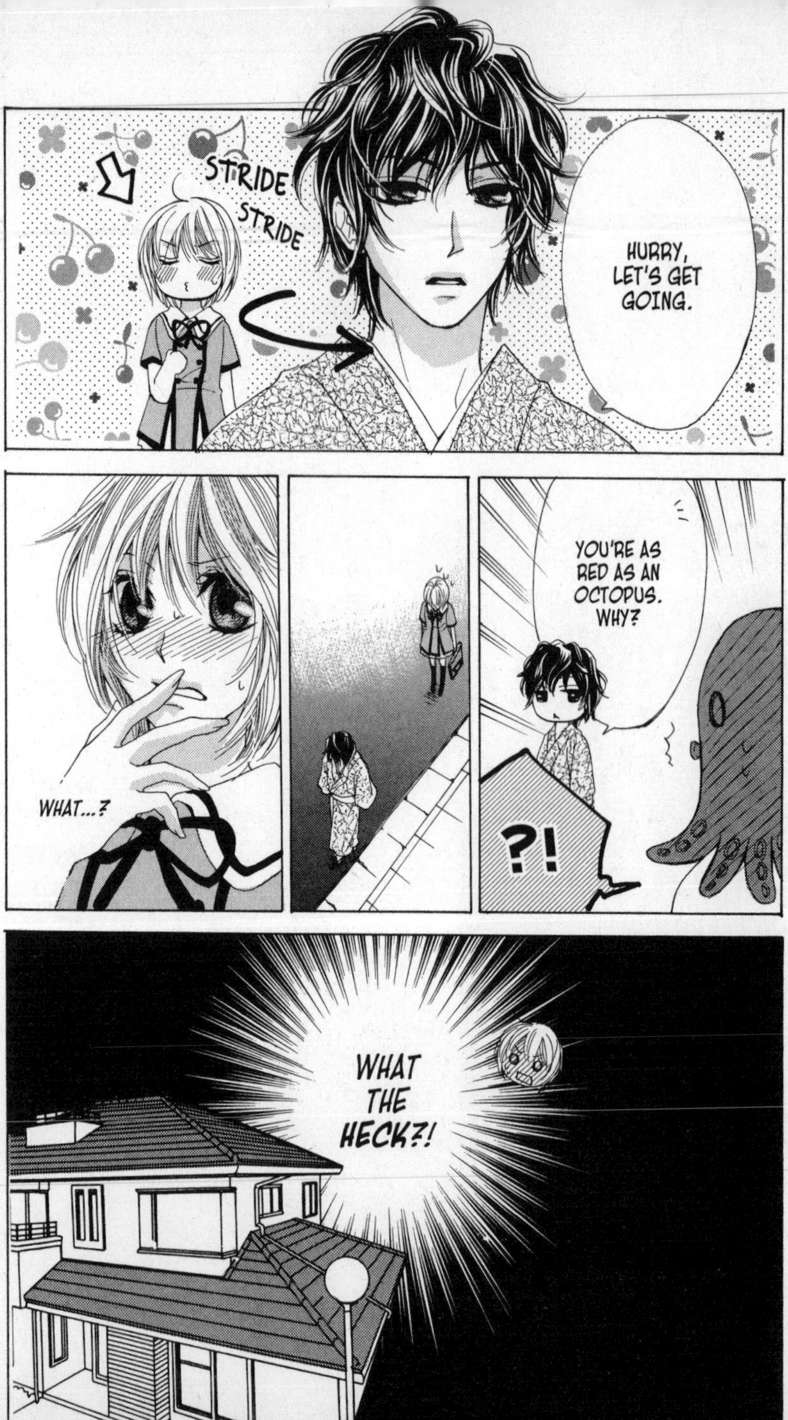
HURRY, LET'S GET GOING.
STRIDE
STRIDE
YOU'RE AS RED AS AN OCTOPUS. WHY?
?!
WHAT...?
WHAT THE HECK?!

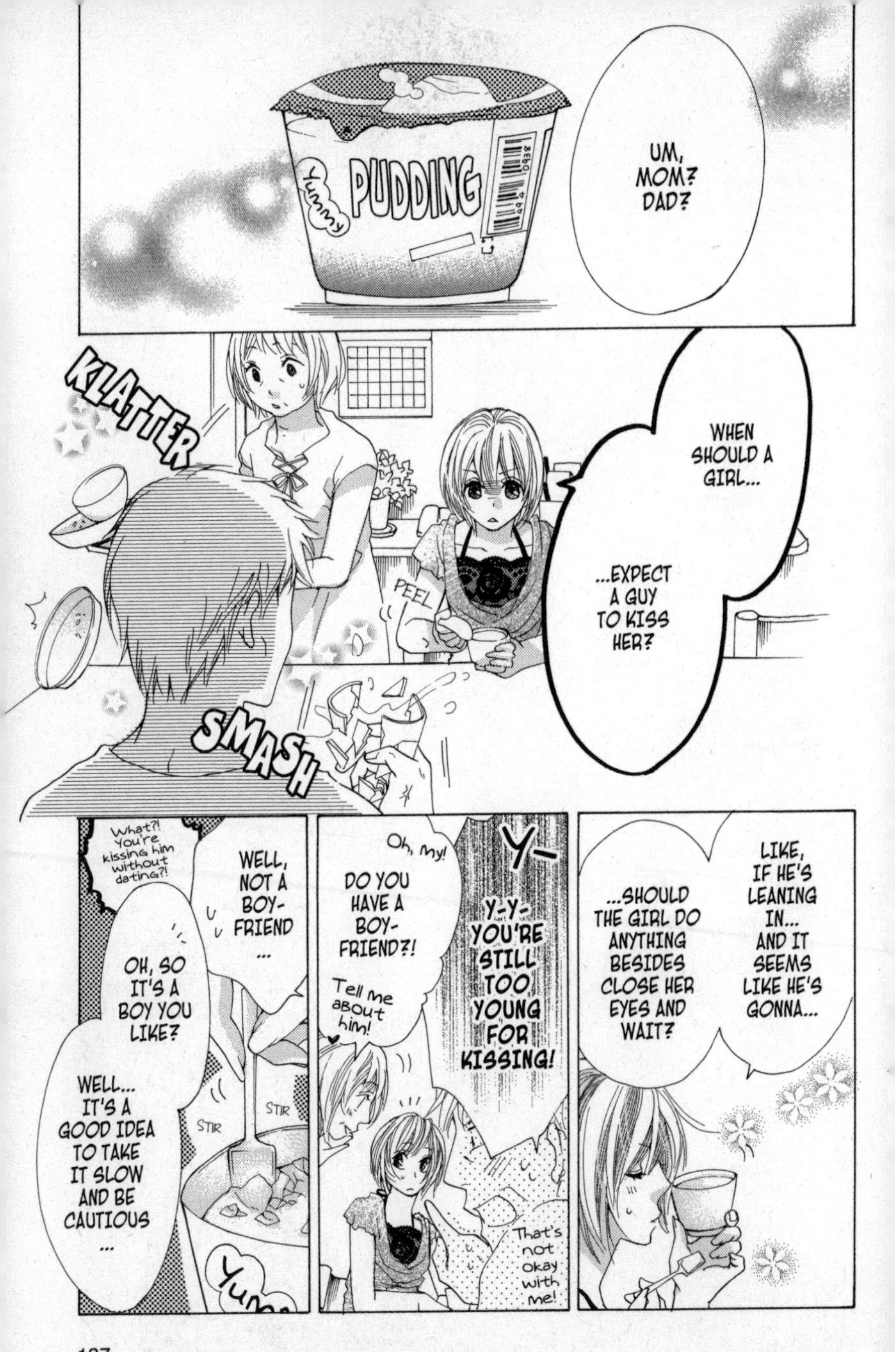
PUDDING
Yummy
UM, MOM? DAD?
WHEN SHOULD A GIRL...
...EXPECT A GUY TO KISS HER?
KLATTER
PEEL
SMASH
LIKE, IF HE'S LEANING IN... AND IT SEEMS LIKE HE'S GONNA...
...SHOULD THE GIRL DO ANYTHING BESIDES CLOSE HER EYES AND WAIT?
Y-
Y-Y-YOU'RE STILL TOO YOUNG FOR KISSING!
That's not okay with me!
Oh, my!
DO YOU HAVE A BOY-FRIEND?!
Tell me about him!
WELL, NOT A BOY-FRIEND...
What?! You're kissing him without dating?!
OH, SO IT'S A BOY YOU LIKE?
WELL... IT'S A GOOD IDEA TO TAKE IT SLOW AND BE CAUTIOUS...
STIR
STIR

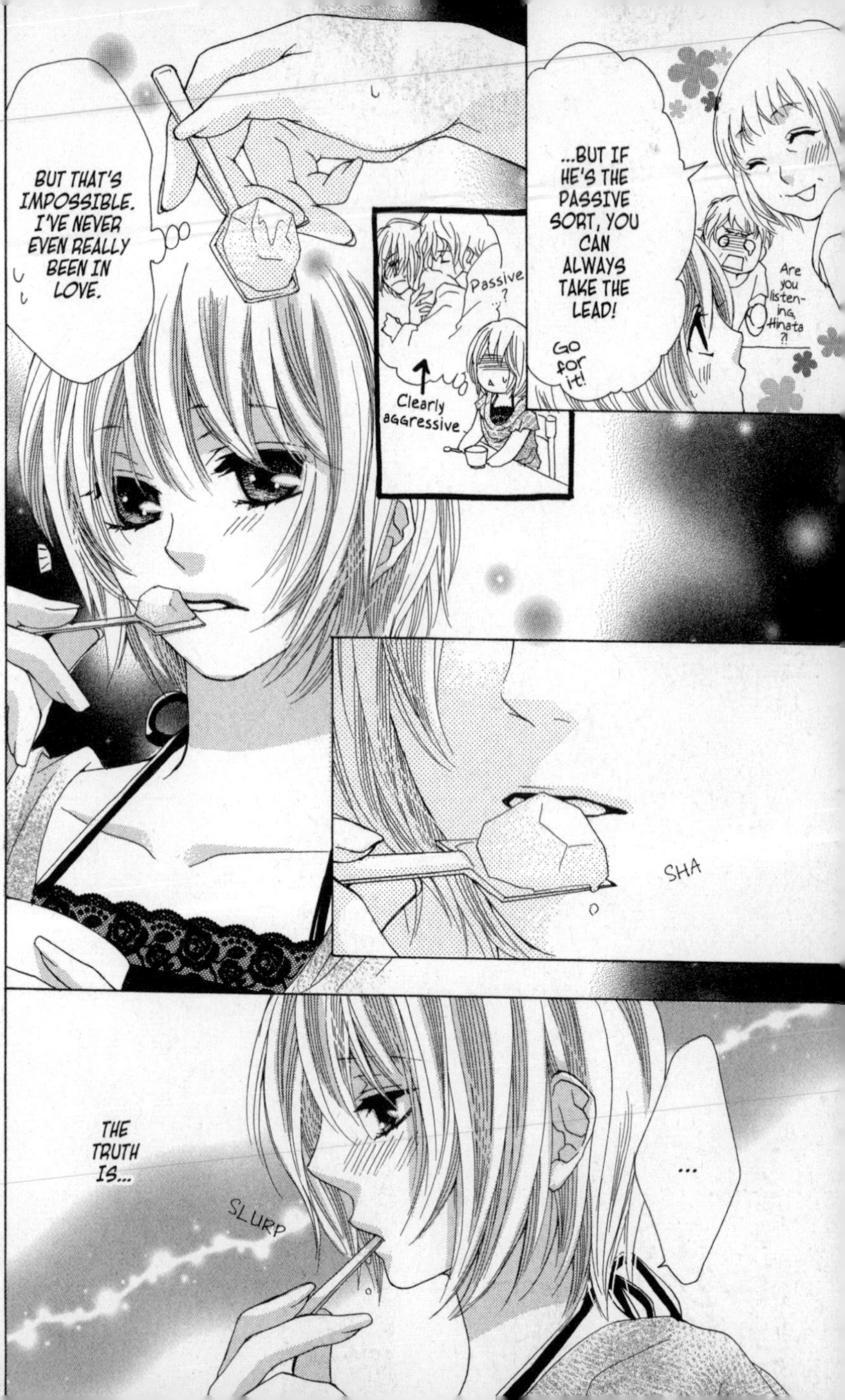
...BUT IF HE'S THE PASSIVE SORT, YOU CAN ALWAYS TAKE THE LEAD!
Go for it!
Are you listening, Hinata?!
Passive...?
Clearly aggressive
BUT THAT'S IMPOSSIBLE. I'VE NEVER EVEN REALLY BEEN IN LOVE.
SHA
THE TRUTH IS...
SLURP
...

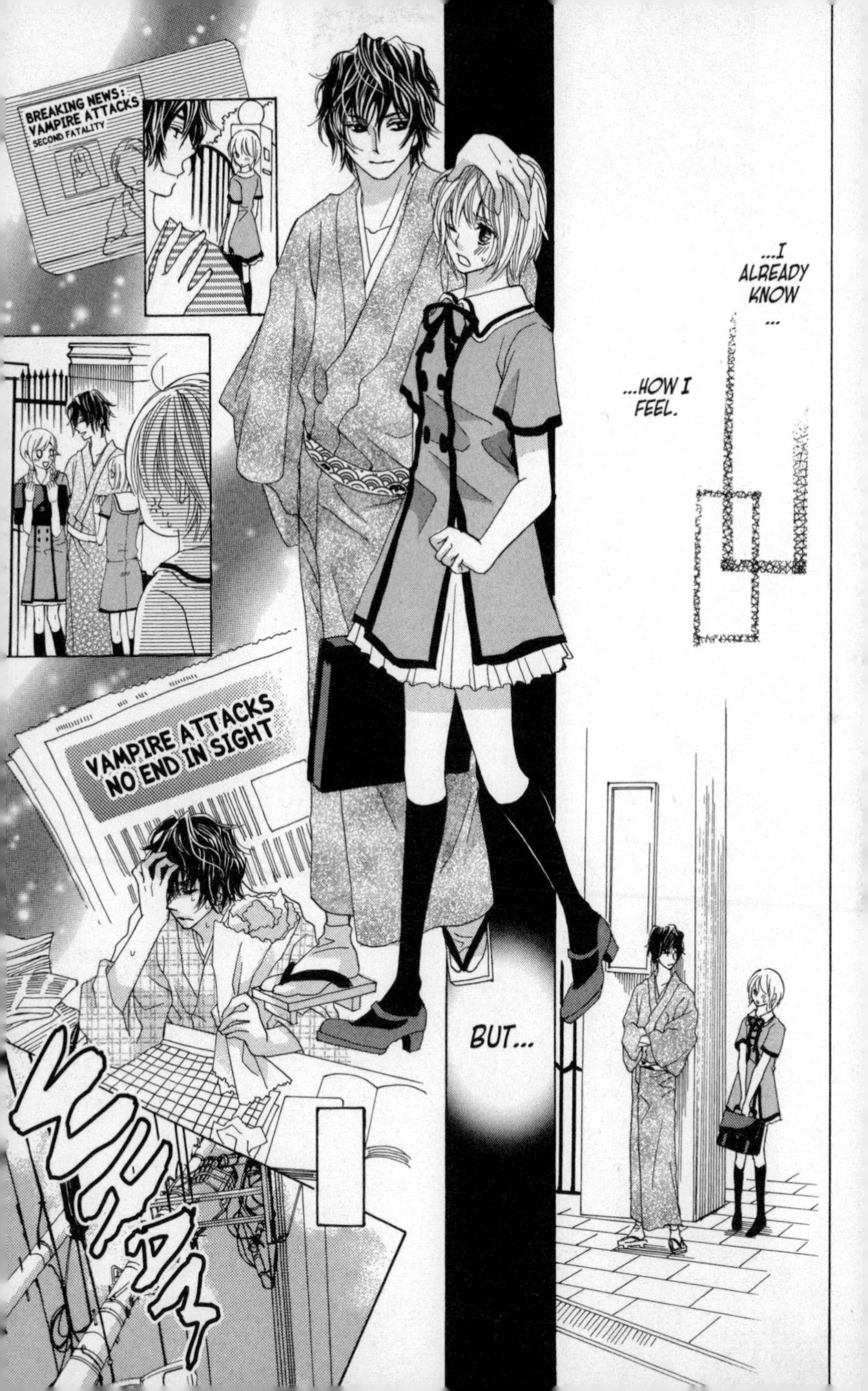

...I ALREADY KNOW ...
...HOW I FEEL.
BUT...
BREAKING NEWS: VAMPIRE ATTACKS
SECOND FATALITY
VAMPIRE ATTACKS NO END IN SIGHT

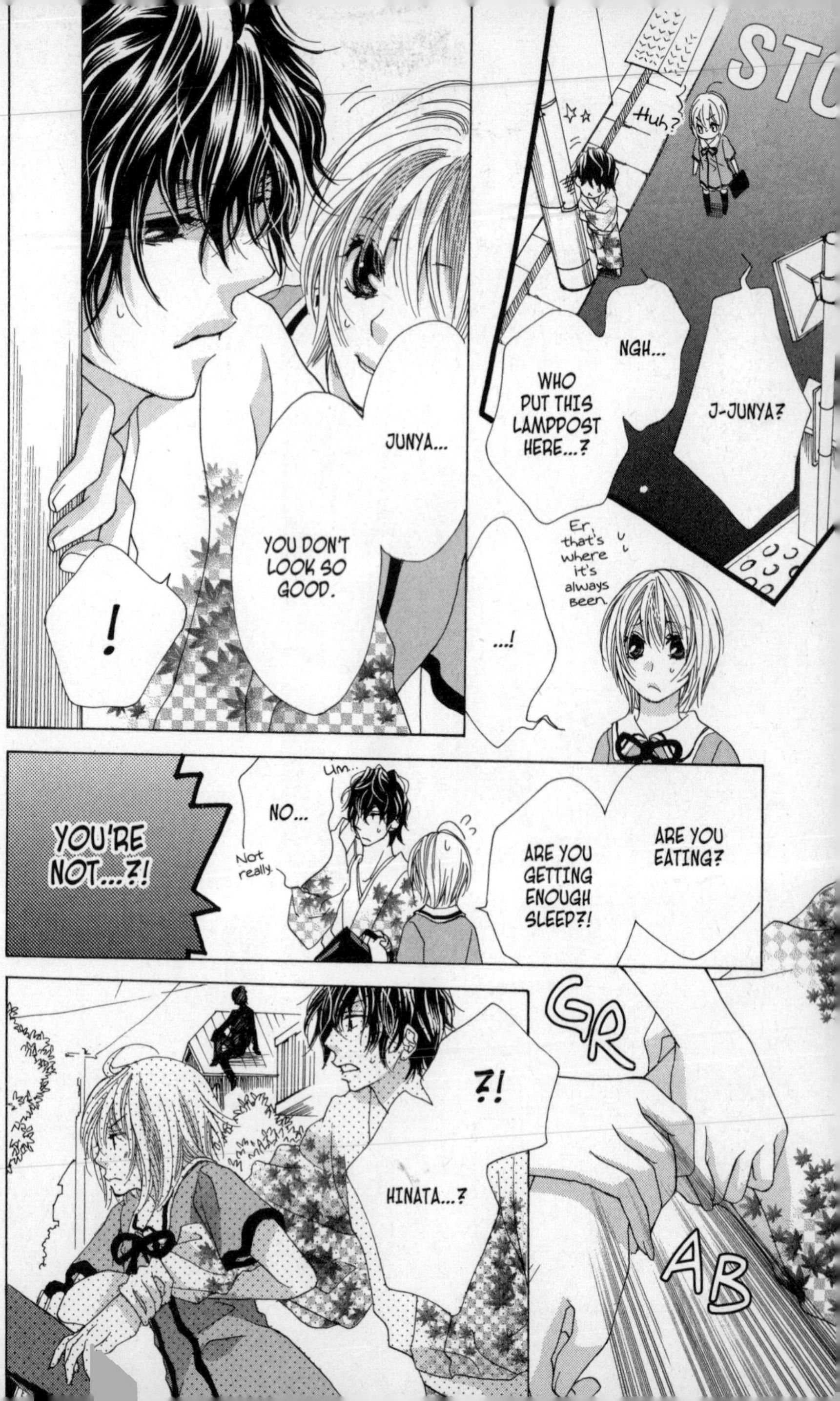
Huh?
NGH...
J-JUNYA?
WHO PUT THIS LAMPPOST HERE...?
Er, that's where it's always been.
...!
JUNYA...
YOU DON'T LOOK SO GOOD.
!
ARE YOU EATING?
ARE YOU GETTING ENOUGH SLEEP?!
Um...
NO...
Not really.
YOU'RE NOT...?!
GR
AB
?!
HINATA...?

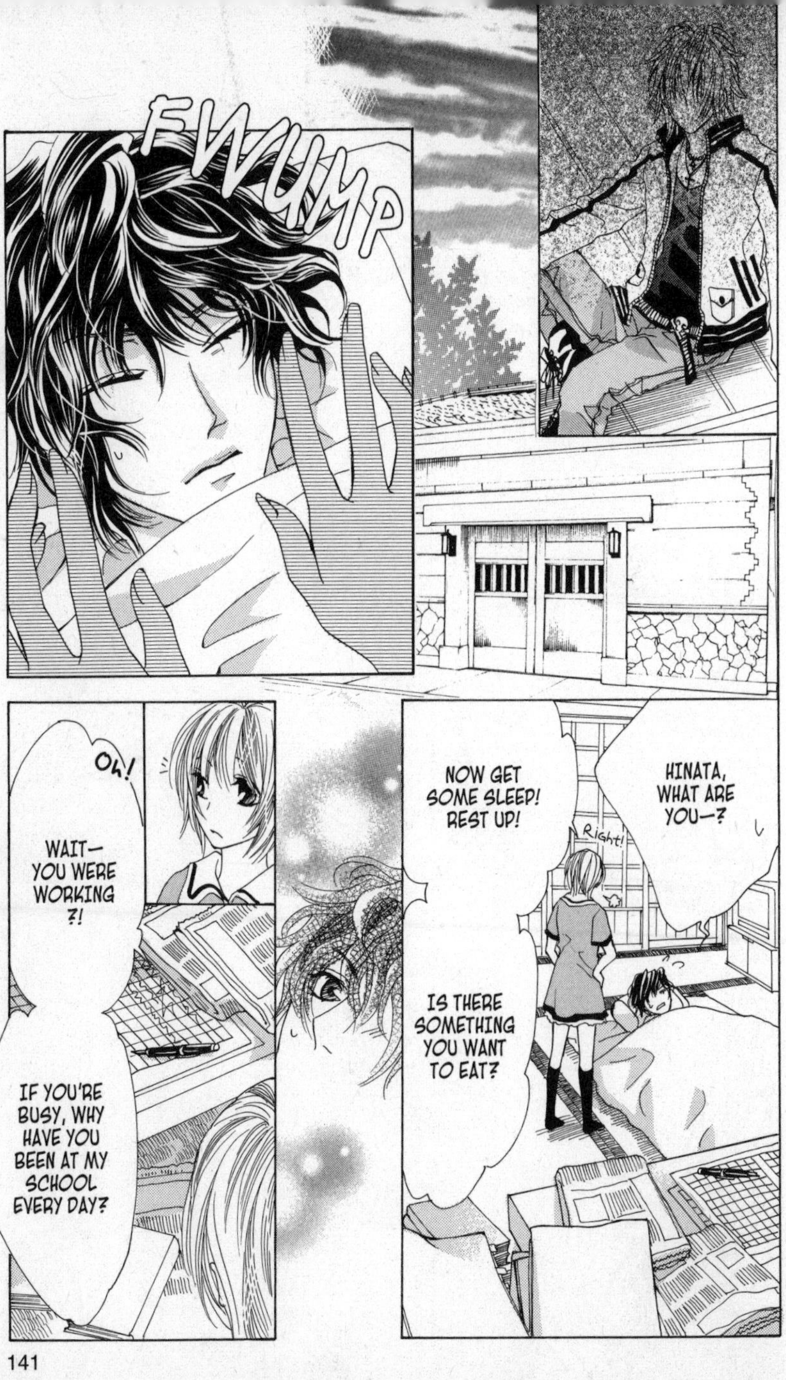
FWUMP
HINATA, WHAT ARE YOU—?
NOW GET SOME SLEEP! REST UP!
Right!
IS THERE SOMETHING YOU WANT TO EAT?
Oh!
WAIT— YOU WERE WORKING?!
IF YOU'RE BUSY, WHY HAVE YOU BEEN AT MY SCHOOL EVERY DAY?

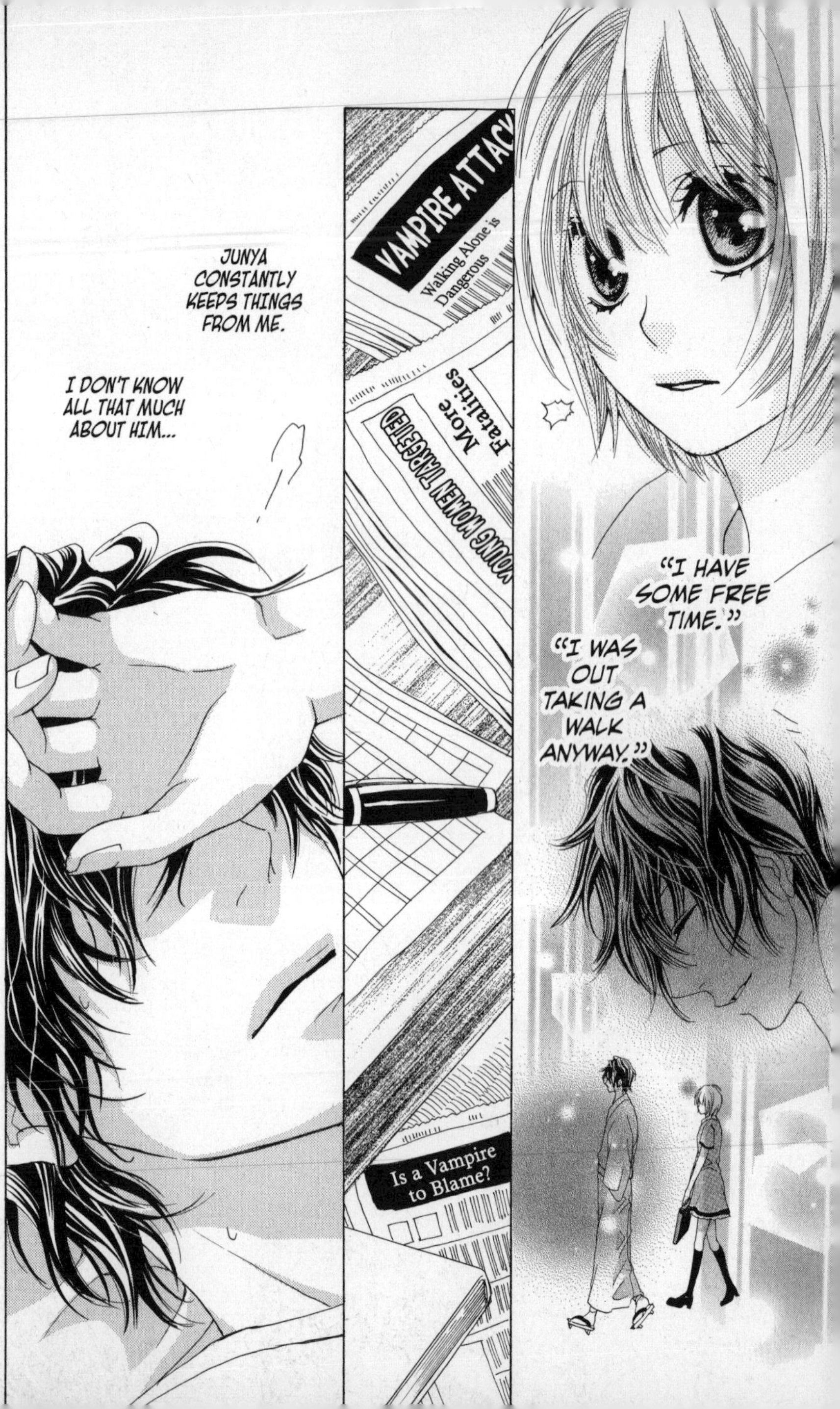
"I HAVE SOME FREE TIME."
"I WAS OUT TAKING A WALK ANYWAY."
VAMPIRE ATTACK
Walking Alone is Dangerous
More Fatalities
YOUNG WOMEN TARGETED
Is a Vampire to Blame?
JUNYA CONSTANTLY KEEPS THINGS FROM ME.
I DON'T KNOW ALL THAT MUCH ABOUT HIM...

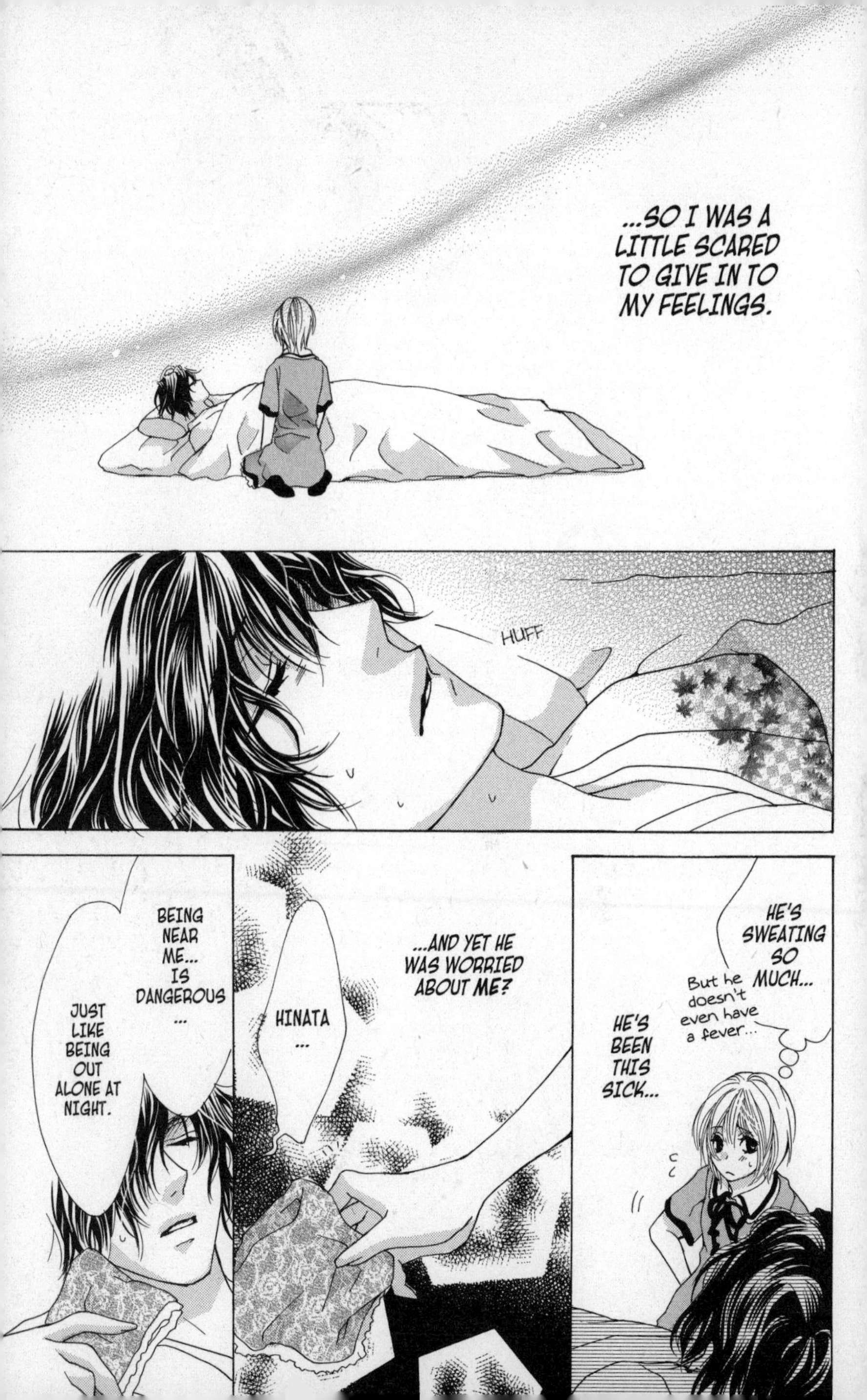
...SO I WAS A LITTLE SCARED TO GIVE IN TO MY FEELINGS.
HUFF
HE'S SWEATING SO MUCH...
But he doesn't even have a fever...
HE'S BEEN THIS SICK...
...AND YET HE WAS WORRIED ABOUT ME?
HINATA...
BEING NEAR ME... IS DANGEROUS...
JUST LIKE BEING OUT ALONE AT NIGHT.

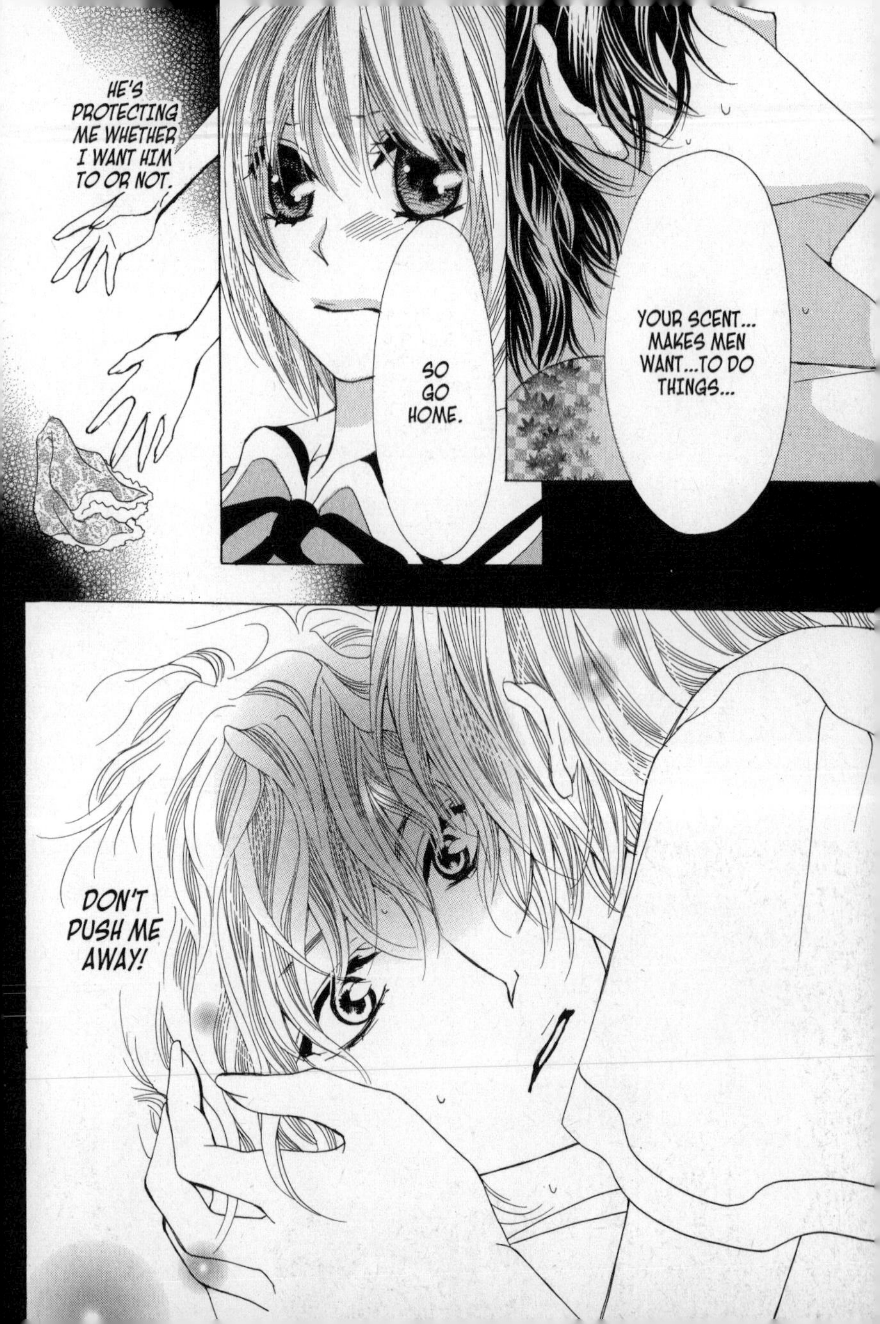
YOUR SCENT... MAKES MEN WANT...TO DO THINGS...
SO GO HOME.
HE'S PROTECTING ME WHETHER I WANT HIM TO OR NOT.
DON'T PUSH ME AWAY!

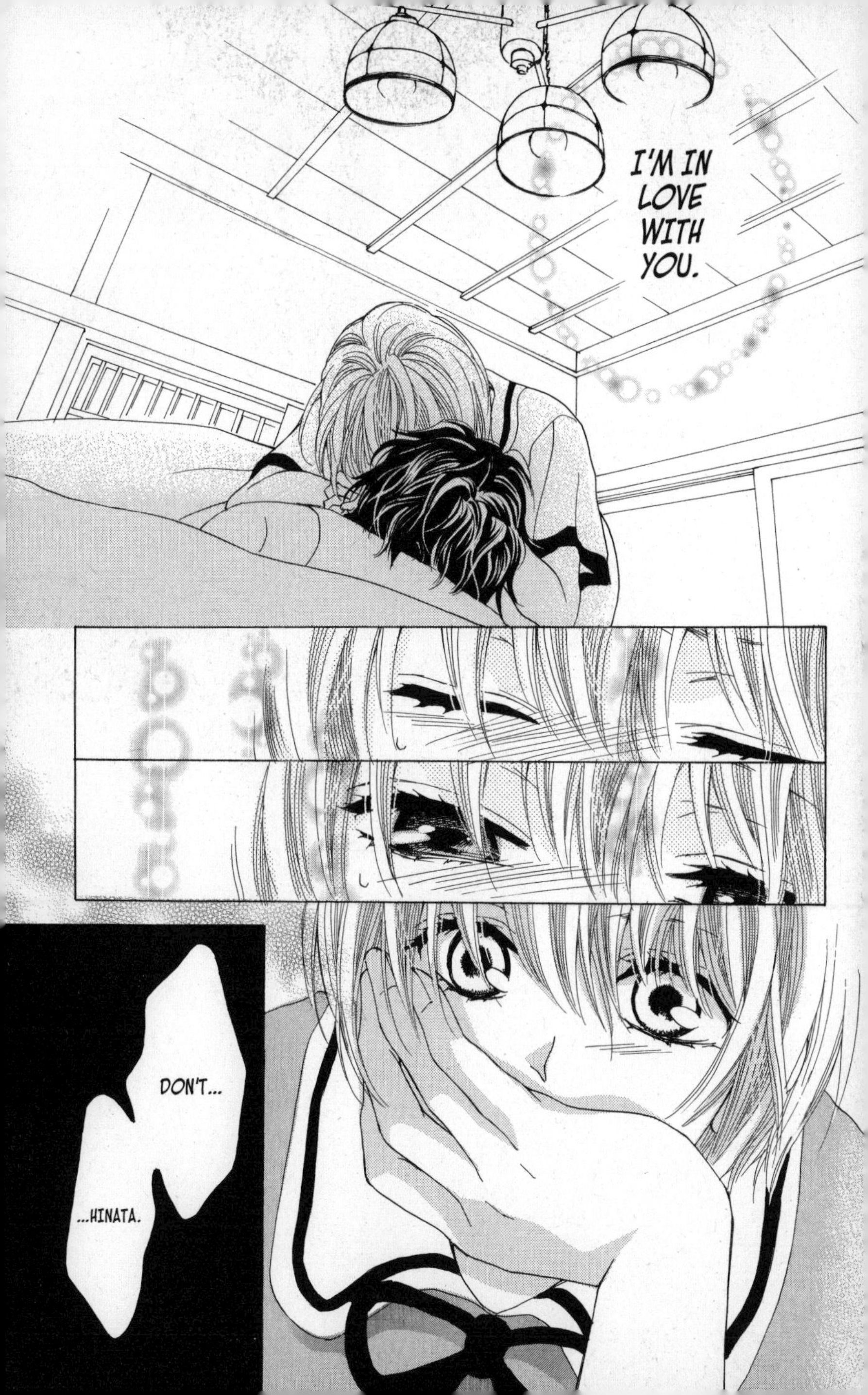
I'M IN LOVE WITH YOU.
DON'T...
...HINATA.

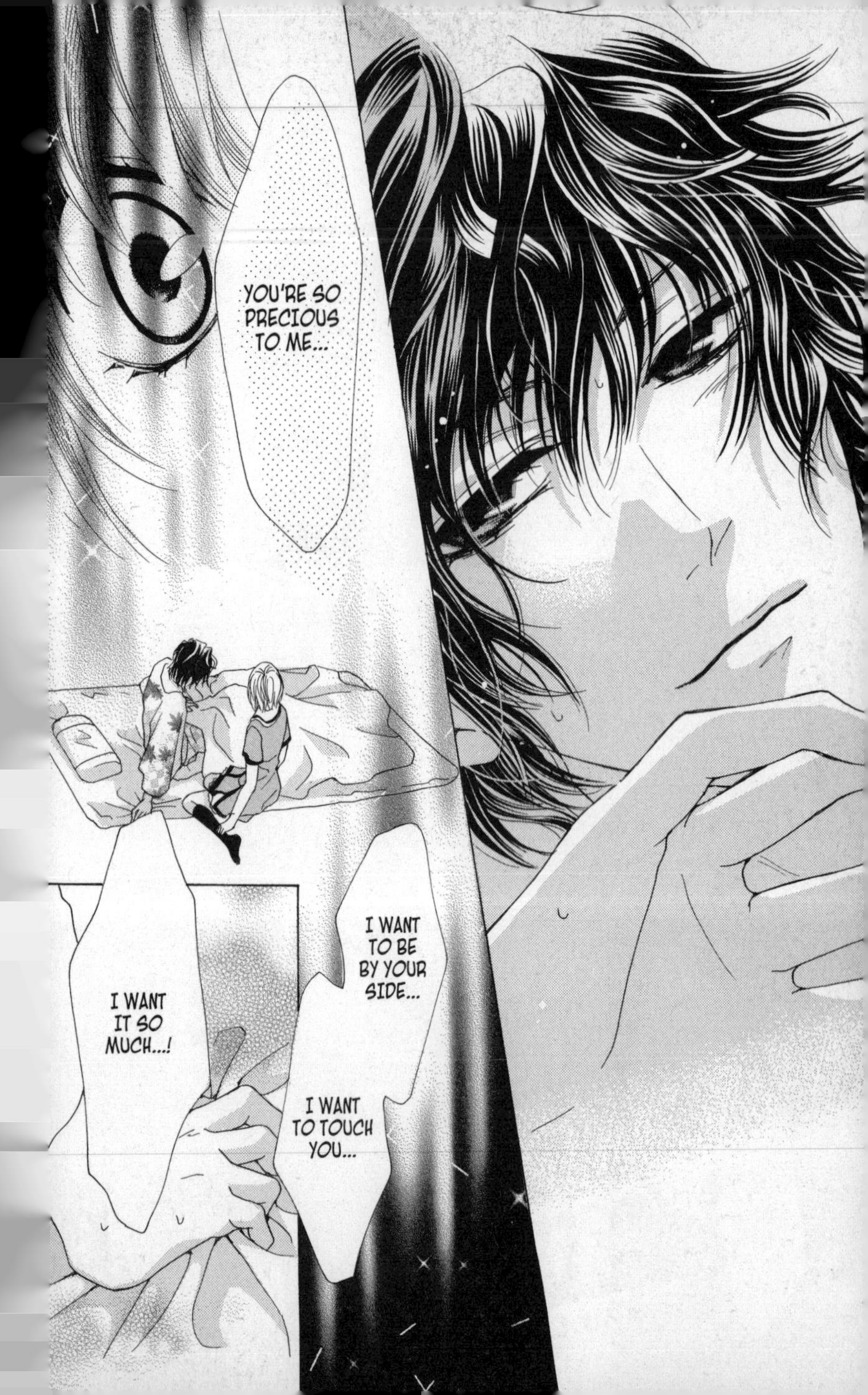
YOU'RE SO PRECIOUS TO ME...
I WANT TO BE BY YOUR SIDE...
I WANT TO TOUCH YOU...
I WANT IT SO MUCH...!

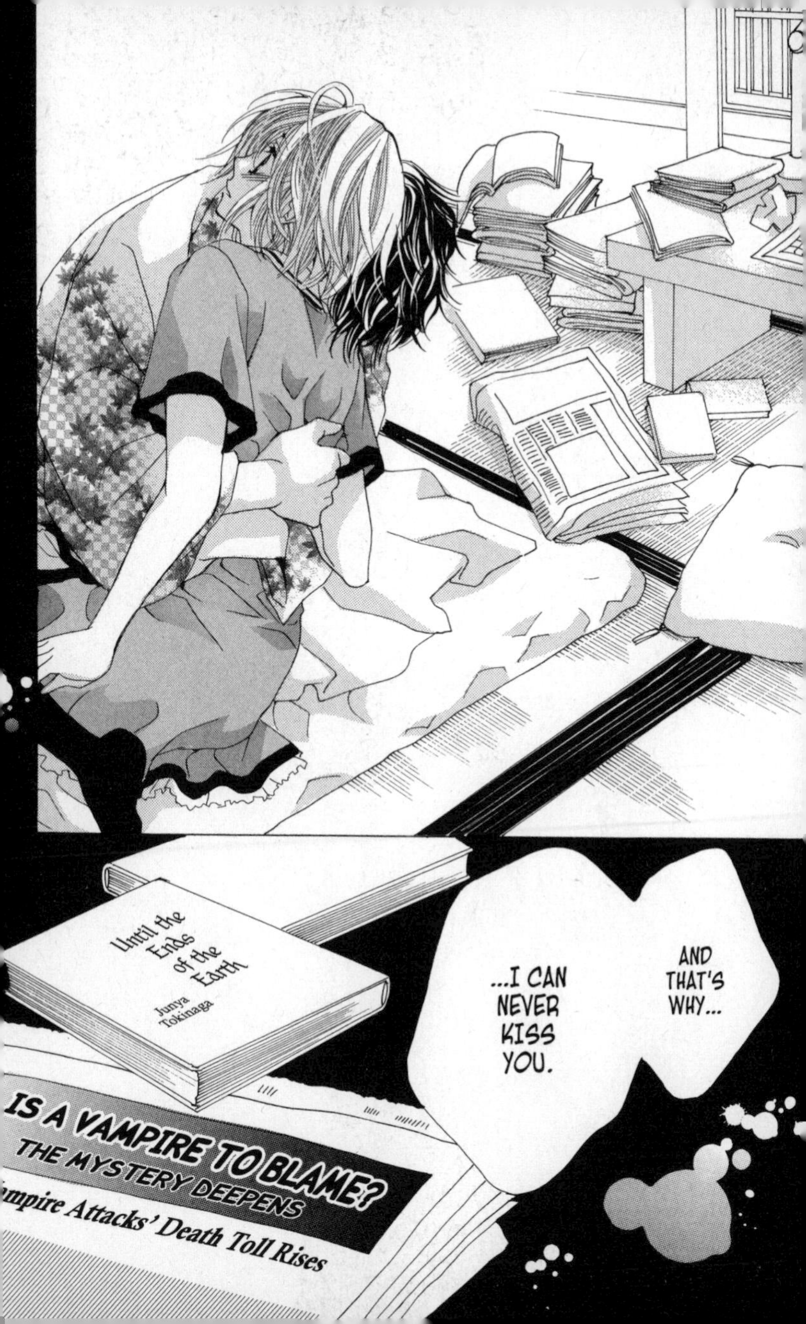
AND THAT'S WHY...
...I CAN NEVER KISS YOU.
Until the Ends of the Earth
Junya Tokinaga
IS A VAMPIRE TO BLAME?
THE MYSTERY DEEPENS
mpire Attacks' Death Toll Rises

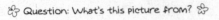
🌸 Question: What's this picture from? 🌸

🌸 Answer: It's a congratulatory drawing for my editors' wedding! 🌸

This was on the cover of their
wedding program! They used my art
for such a momentous occasion! I
wasn't at all sure I was up to it, But I
did my very Best! 🎵 It doesn't do justice
to the handsome couple at all though.

I always dreamed aBout doing an
illustration for my editors' wedding,
so I was thrilled when they asked.
Thank you so much! ♥

F-sama
from
the same
editorial
department
↙

My
editor →

I wish you eternal happiness together! ♥

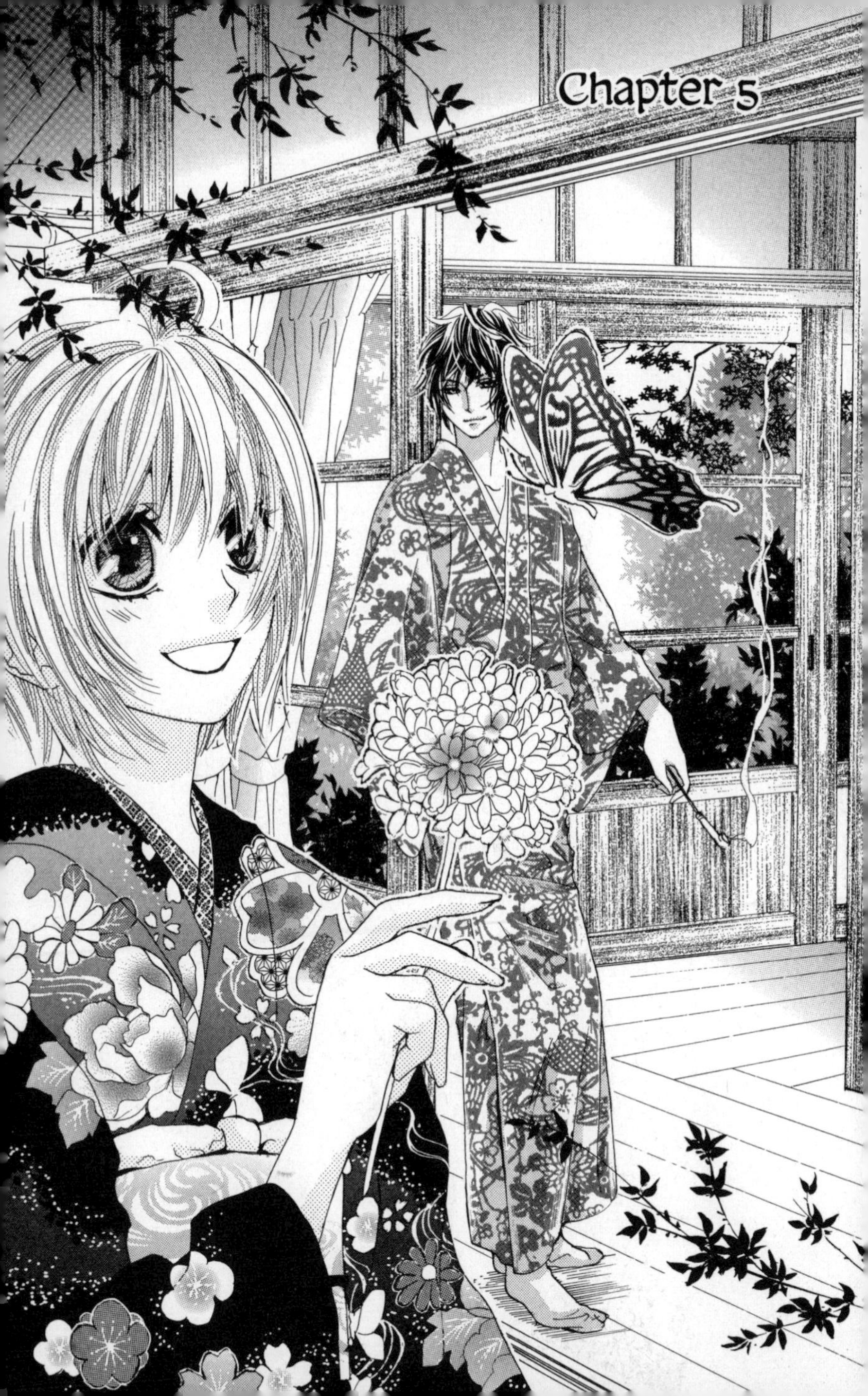
Chapter 5

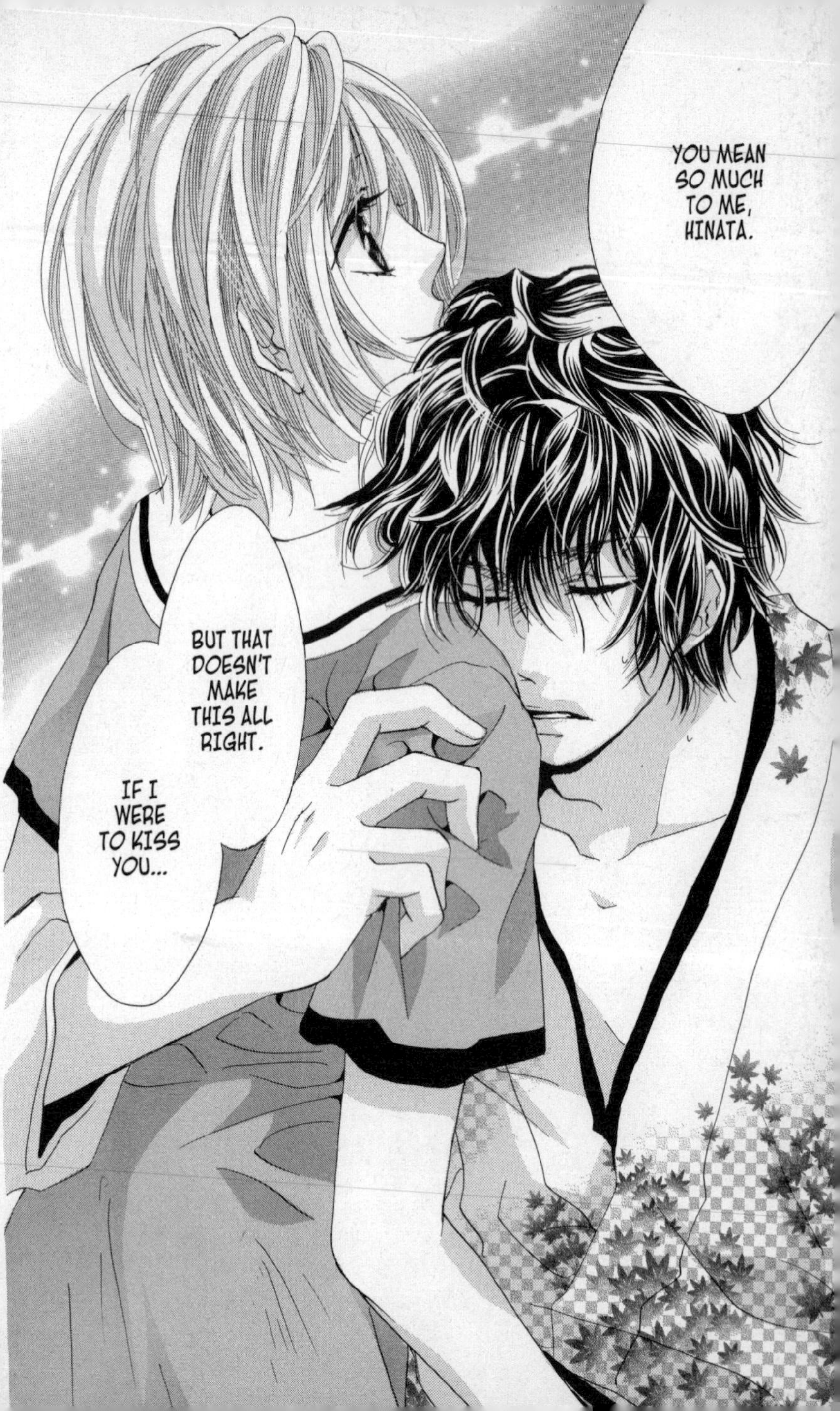
YOU MEAN SO MUCH TO ME, HINATA.
BUT THAT DOESN'T MAKE THIS ALL RIGHT.
IF I WERE TO KISS YOU...

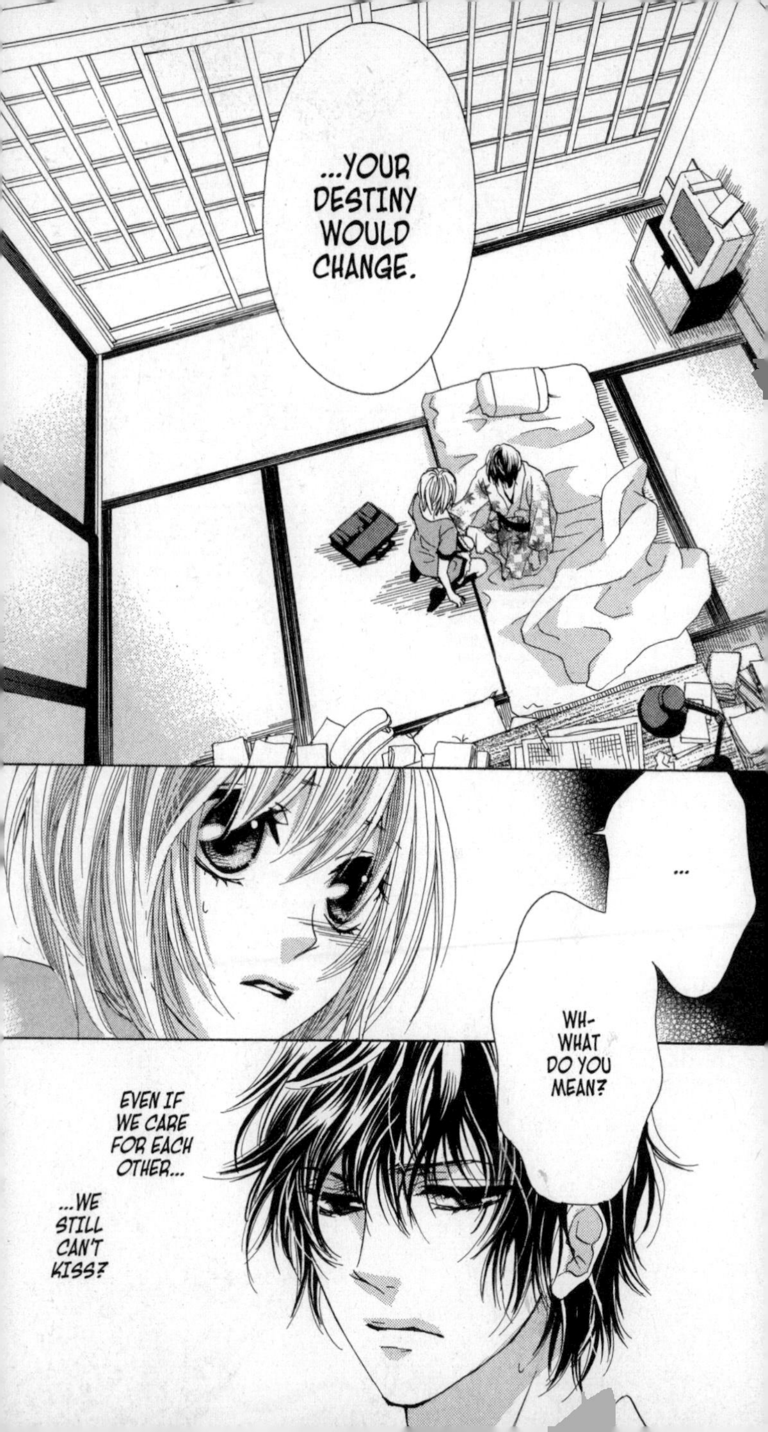
...YOUR DESTINY WOULD CHANGE.
...
WH-WHAT DO YOU MEAN?
EVEN IF WE CARE FOR EACH OTHER...
...WE STILL CAN'T KISS?

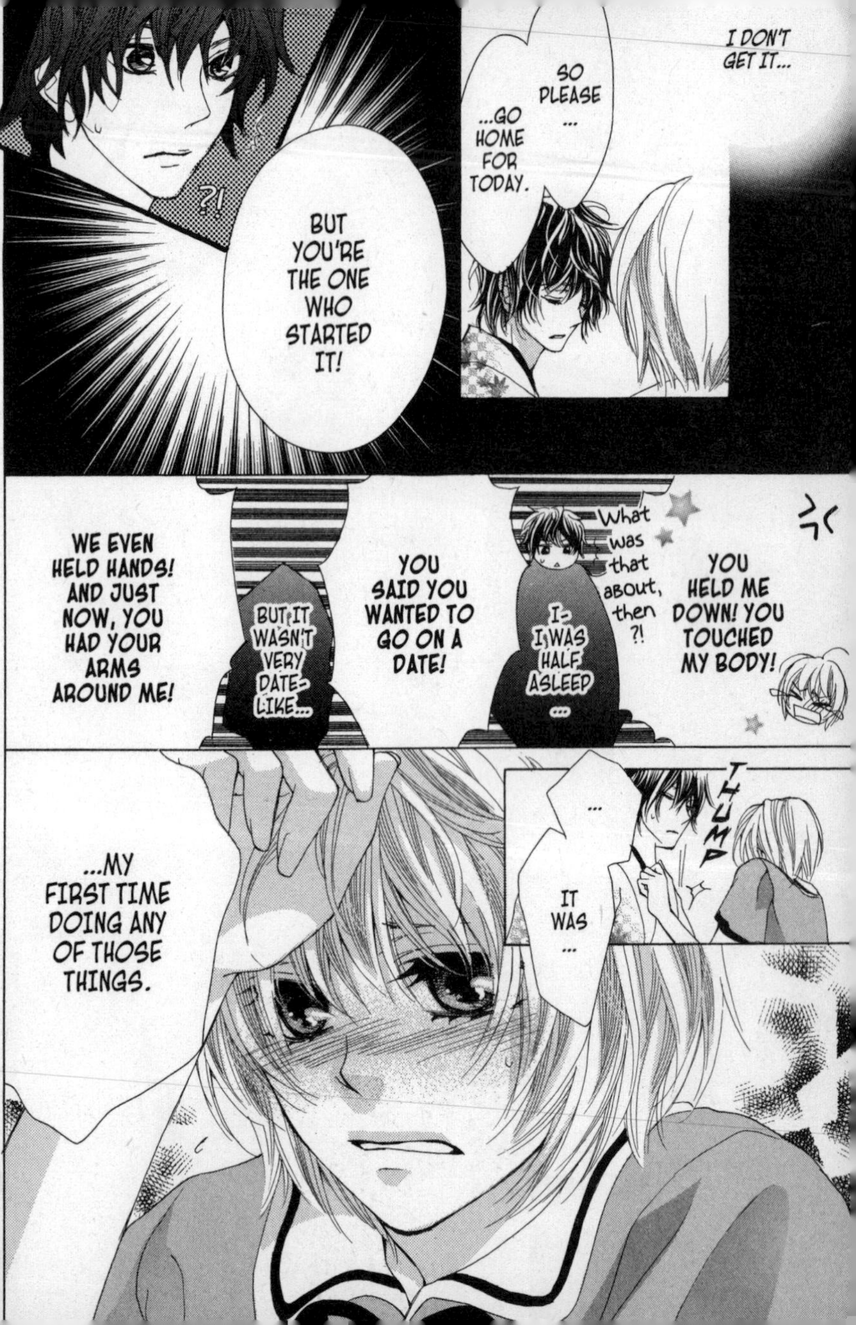
I DON'T GET IT...
SO PLEASE ...
...GO HOME FOR TODAY.
?!
BUT YOU'RE THE ONE WHO STARTED IT!
YOU HELD ME DOWN! YOU TOUCHED MY BODY!
What was that about, then?!
I- I WAS HALF ASLEEP ...
YOU SAID YOU WANTED TO GO ON A DATE!
BUT IT WASN'T VERY DATE-LIKE...
WE EVEN HELD HANDS! AND JUST NOW, YOU HAD YOUR ARMS AROUND ME!
THUMP
...
IT WAS ...
...MY FIRST TIME DOING ANY OF THOSE THINGS.

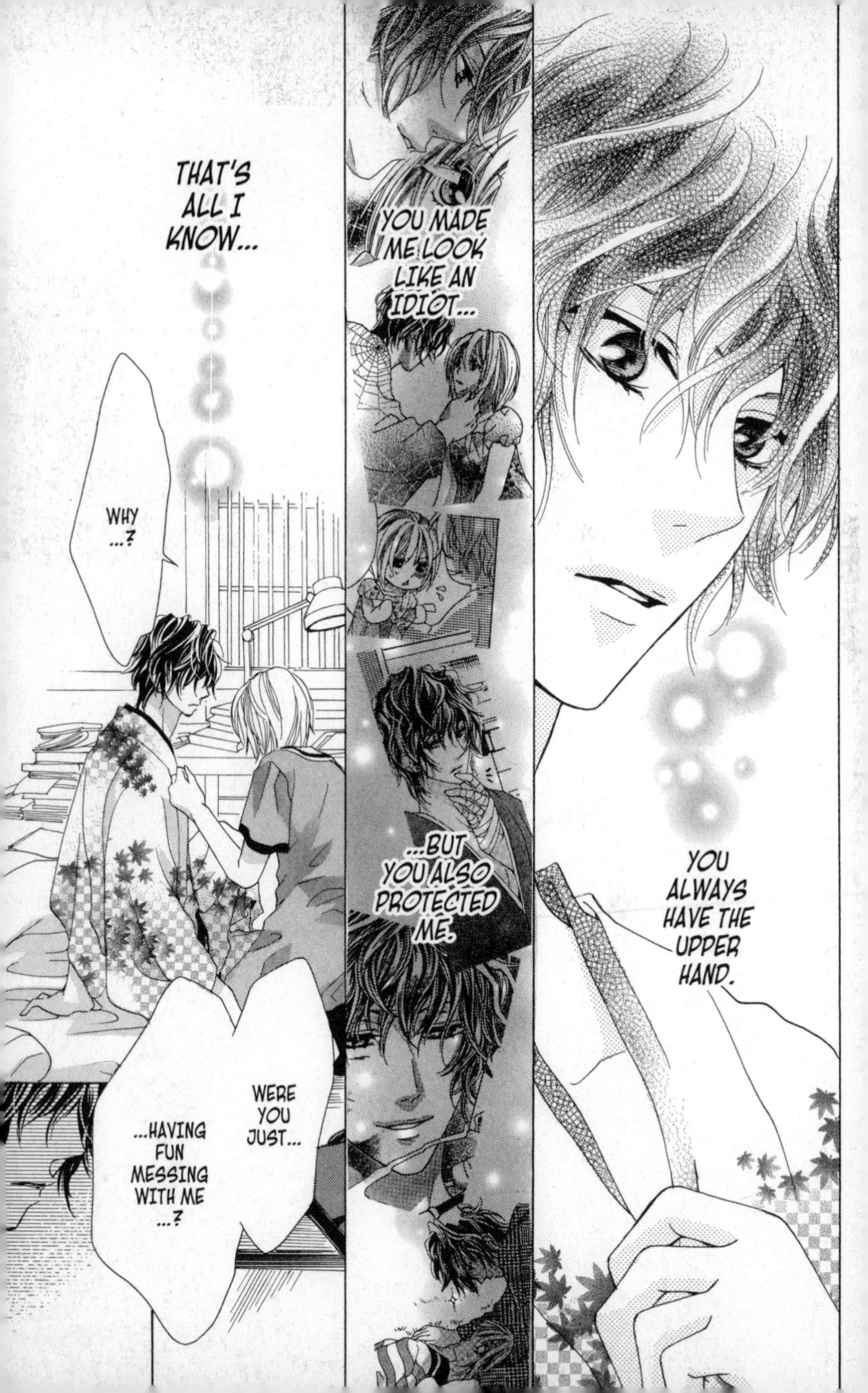
YOU ALWAYS HAVE THE UPPER HAND.
YOU MADE ME LOOK LIKE AN IDIOT...
...BUT YOU ALSO PROTECTED ME.
THAT'S ALL I KNOW...
WHY ...?
WERE YOU JUST...
...HAVING FUN MESSING WITH ME ...?

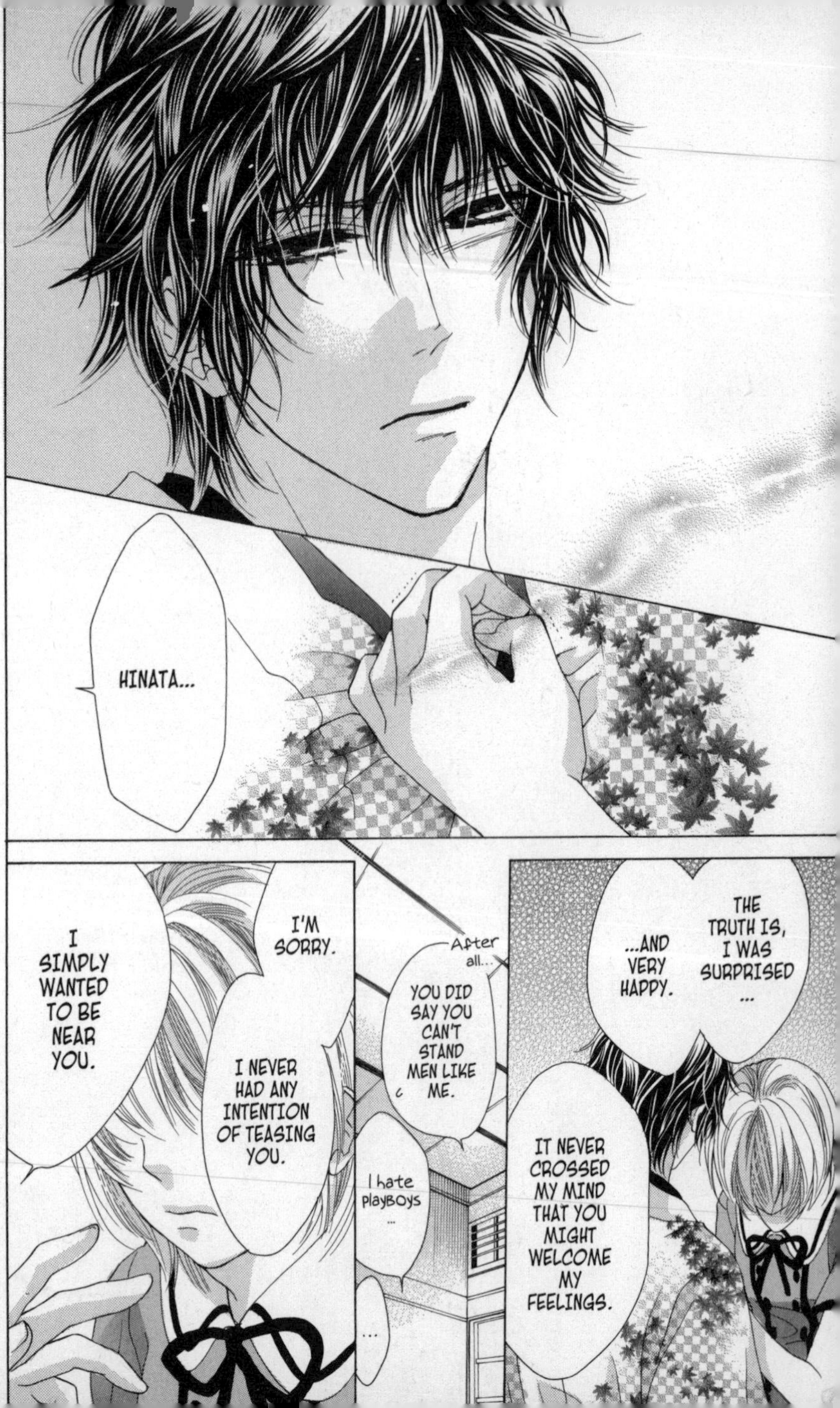
HINATA...
THE TRUTH IS, I WAS SURPRISED...
...AND VERY HAPPY.
IT NEVER CROSSED MY MIND THAT YOU MIGHT WELCOME MY FEELINGS.
After all...
YOU DID SAY YOU CAN'T STAND MEN LIKE ME.
I hate playboys...
...
I'M SORRY.
I NEVER HAD ANY INTENTION OF TEASING YOU.
I SIMPLY WANTED TO BE NEAR YOU.

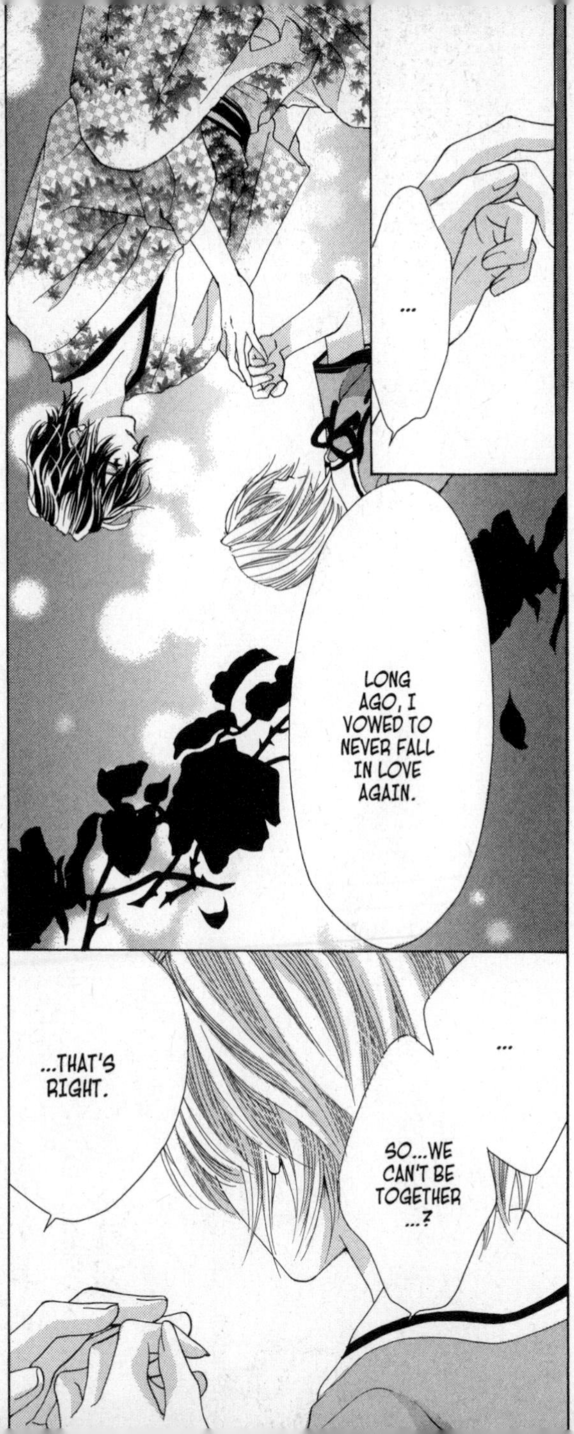
...
LONG AGO, I VOWED TO NEVER FALL IN LOVE AGAIN.
...
SO...WE CAN'T BE TOGETHER...?
...THAT'S RIGHT.

Small Talk

5

Hmm...
I'm running out of things to talk about.

Um... Let me see...

Oh, I know!
I'm planning to move this year.

I've been living by myself, but I'm thinking of moving to a bigger place so I can live with my mom.

I didn't grow up well off, so I don't tend to splurge.

Tokyo's high cost of living is bad for my heart.

Seriously, it's astonishing.

I'm going to do my best to find a cheap place.

(Cheapskate)

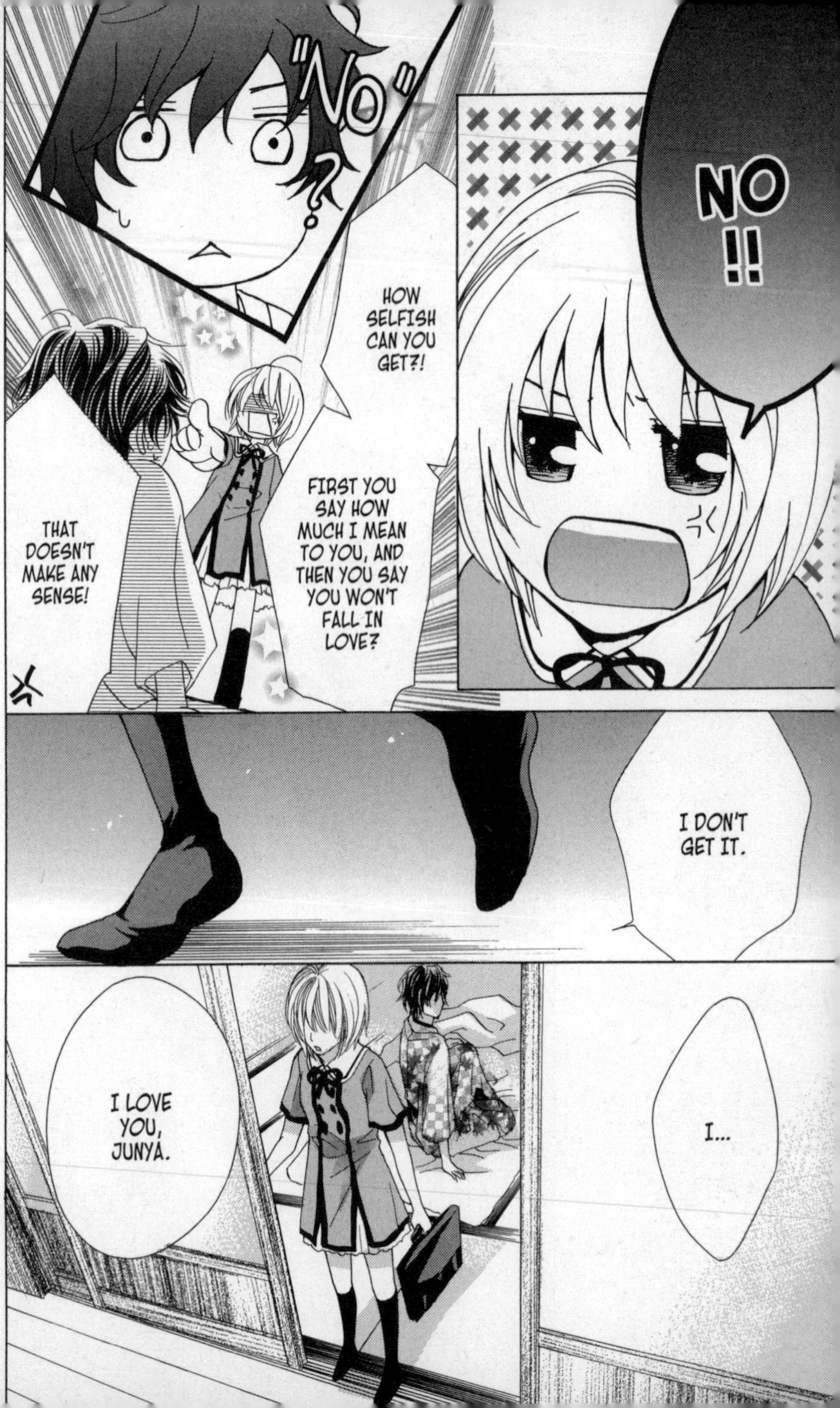
NO !!
"NO"?
HOW SELFISH CAN YOU GET?!
FIRST YOU SAY HOW MUCH I MEAN TO YOU, AND THEN YOU SAY YOU WON'T FALL IN LOVE?
THAT DOESN'T MAKE ANY SENSE!
I DON'T GET IT.
I...
I LOVE YOU, JUNYA.

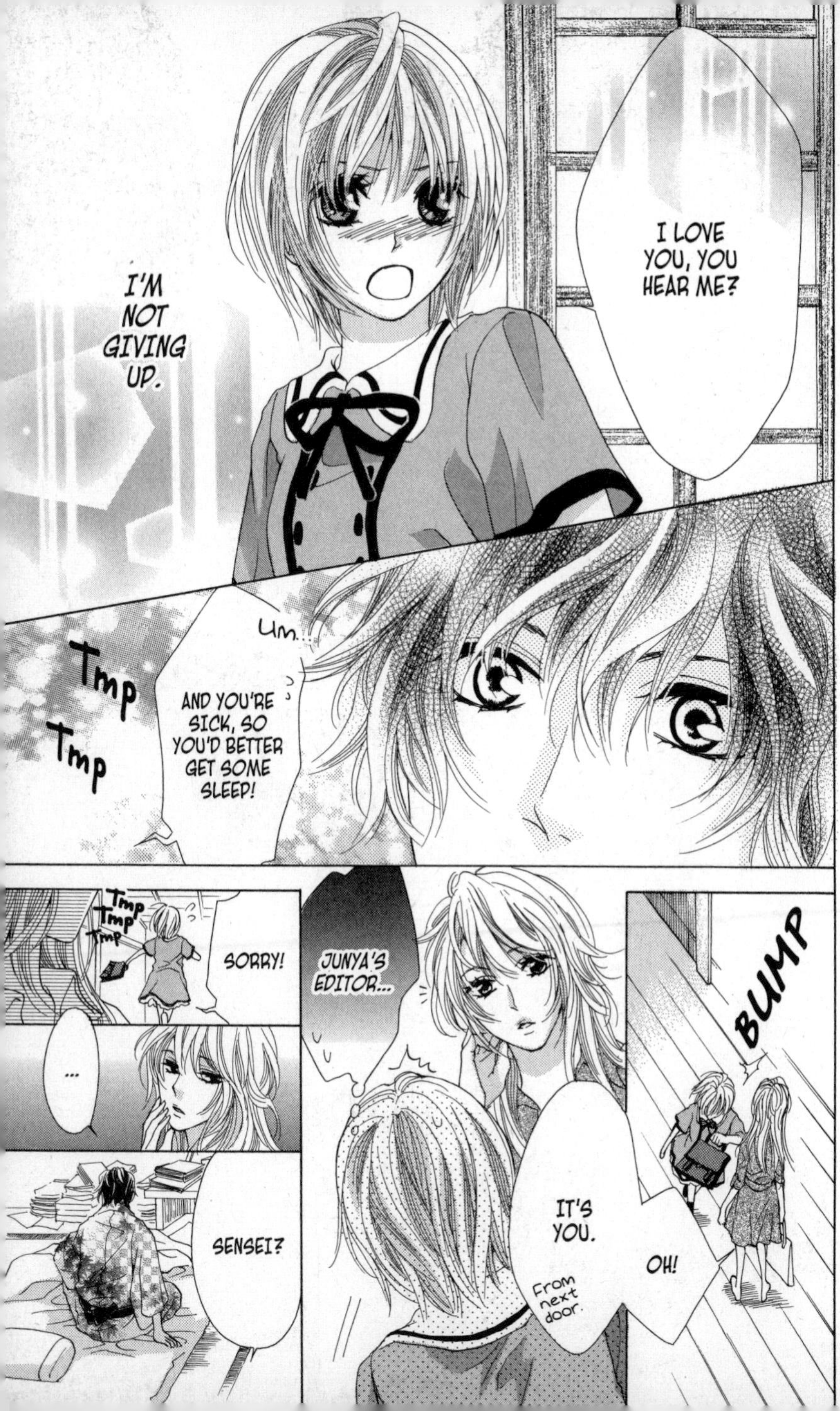
I LOVE YOU, YOU HEAR ME?
I'M NOT GIVING UP.
Um...
AND YOU'RE SICK, SO YOU'D BETTER GET SOME SLEEP!
Tmp
Tmp
BUMP
OH!
JUNYA'S EDITOR...
IT'S YOU.
From next door.
Tmp
Tmp
Tmp
SORRY!
...
SENSEI?

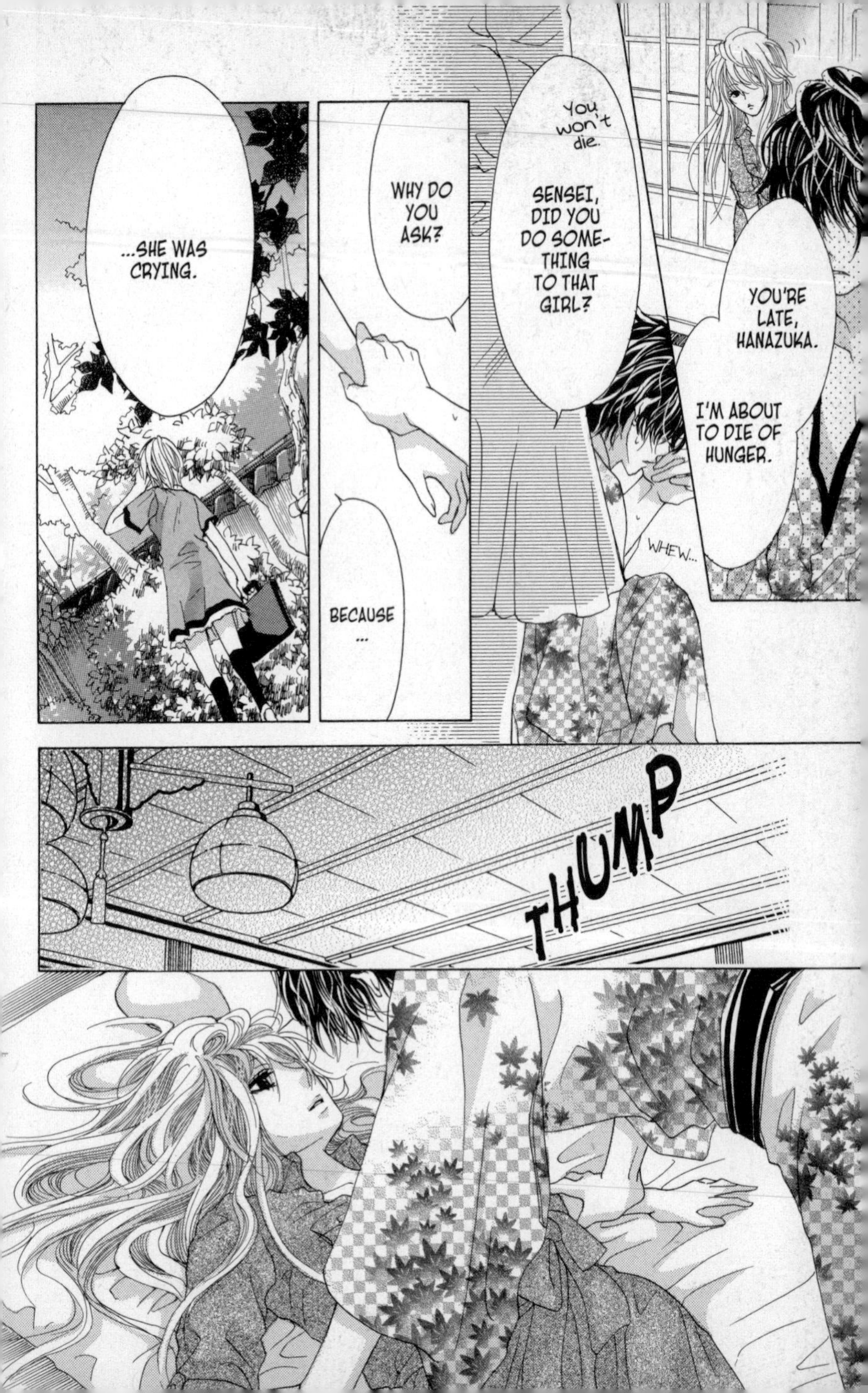

YOU'RE LATE, HANAZUKA.
I'M ABOUT TO DIE OF HUNGER.
WHEW...
You won't die.
SENSEI, DID YOU DO SOME-THING TO THAT GIRL?
WHY DO YOU ASK?
BECAUSE ...
...SHE WAS CRYING.
THUMP

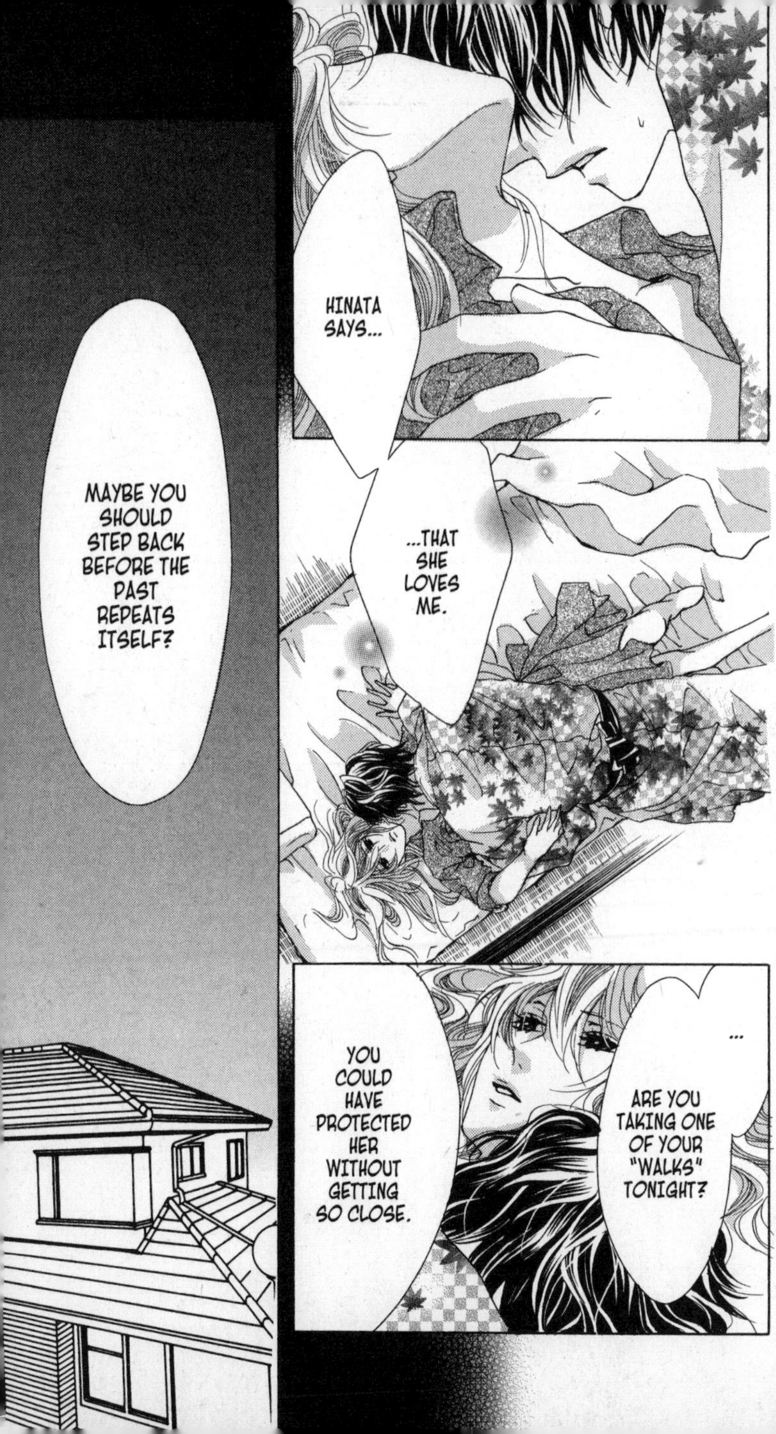
HINATA SAYS...
...THAT SHE LOVES ME.
...
ARE YOU TAKING ONE OF YOUR "WALKS" TONIGHT?
YOU COULD HAVE PROTECTED HER WITHOUT GETTING SO CLOSE.
MAYBE YOU SHOULD STEP BACK BEFORE THE PAST REPEATS ITSELF?

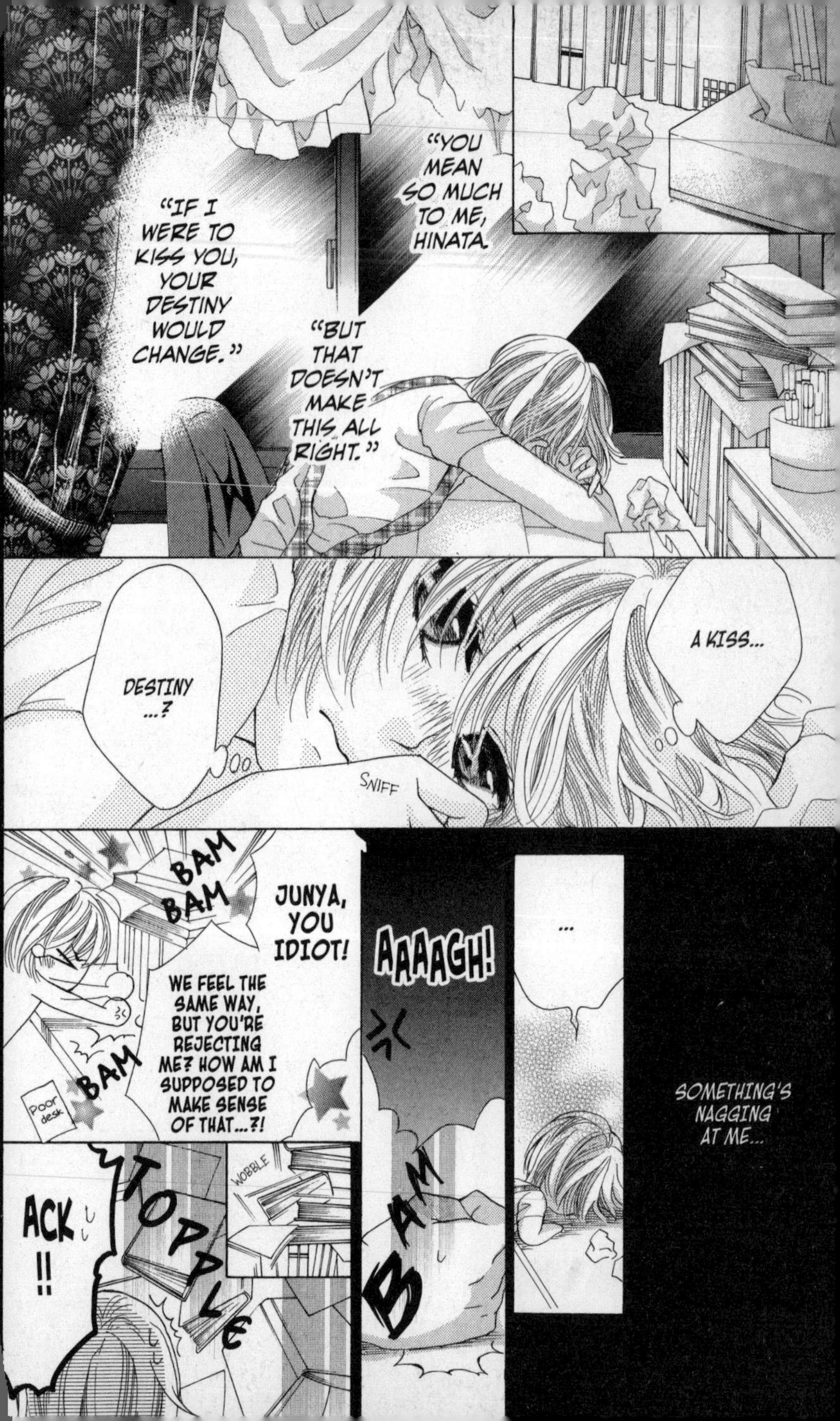
"YOU MEAN SO MUCH TO ME, HINATA.
"IF I WERE TO KISS YOU, YOUR DESTINY WOULD CHANGE."
"BUT THAT DOESN'T MAKE THIS ALL RIGHT."
A KISS...
SNIFF
DESTINY ...?
SOMETHING'S NAGGING AT ME...
...
AAAAGH!
BAM
JUNYA, YOU IDIOT!
BAM BAM
WE FEEL THE SAME WAY, BUT YOU'RE REJECTING ME? HOW AM I SUPPOSED TO MAKE SENSE OF THAT...?!
BAM
Poor desk
WOBBLE
TOPPLE
ACK !!

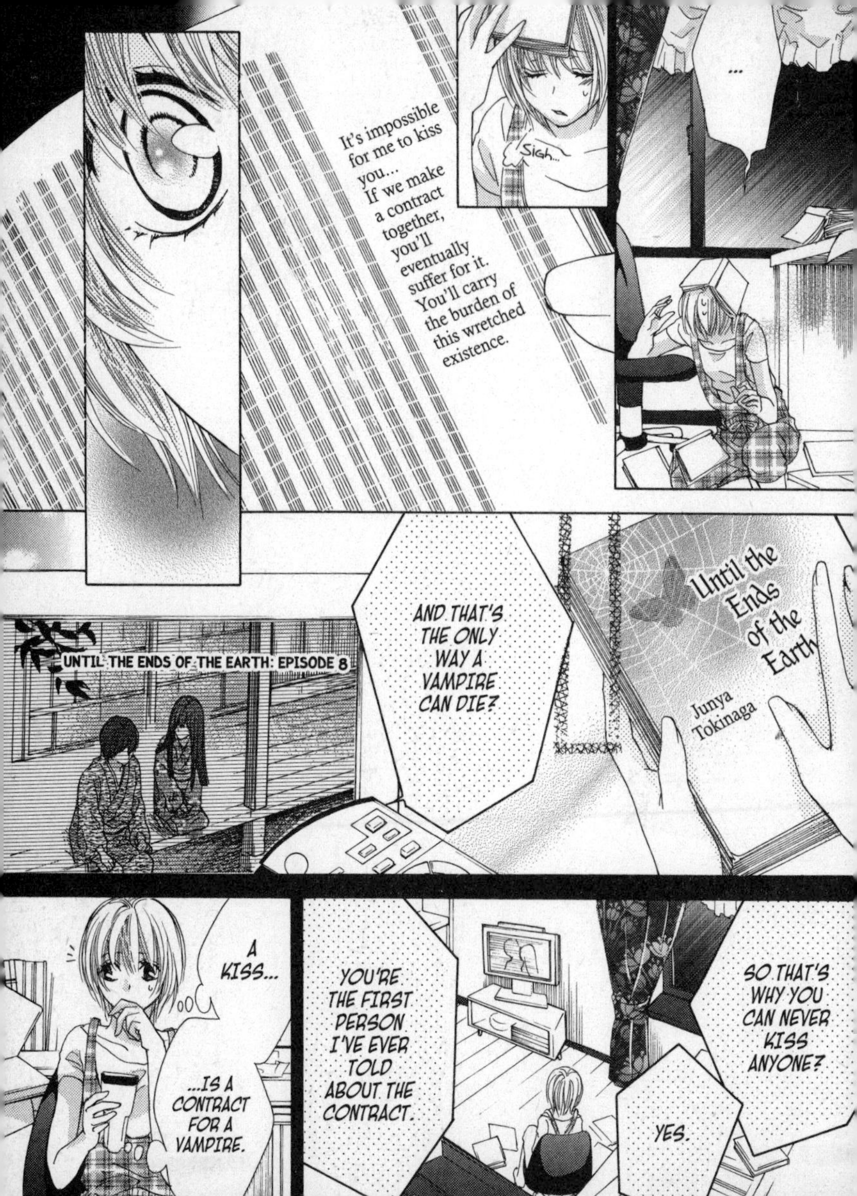
...
Sigh...
It's impossible for me to kiss you... If we make a contract together, you'll eventually suffer for it. You'll carry the burden of this wretched existence.
Until the Ends of the Earth
Junya Tokinaga
AND THAT'S THE ONLY WAY A VAMPIRE CAN DIE?
UNTIL THE ENDS OF THE EARTH: EPISODE 8
SO THAT'S WHY YOU CAN NEVER KISS ANYONE?
YES.
YOU'RE THE FIRST PERSON I'VE EVER TOLD ABOUT THE CONTRACT.
A KISS...
...IS A CONTRACT FOR A VAMPIRE.

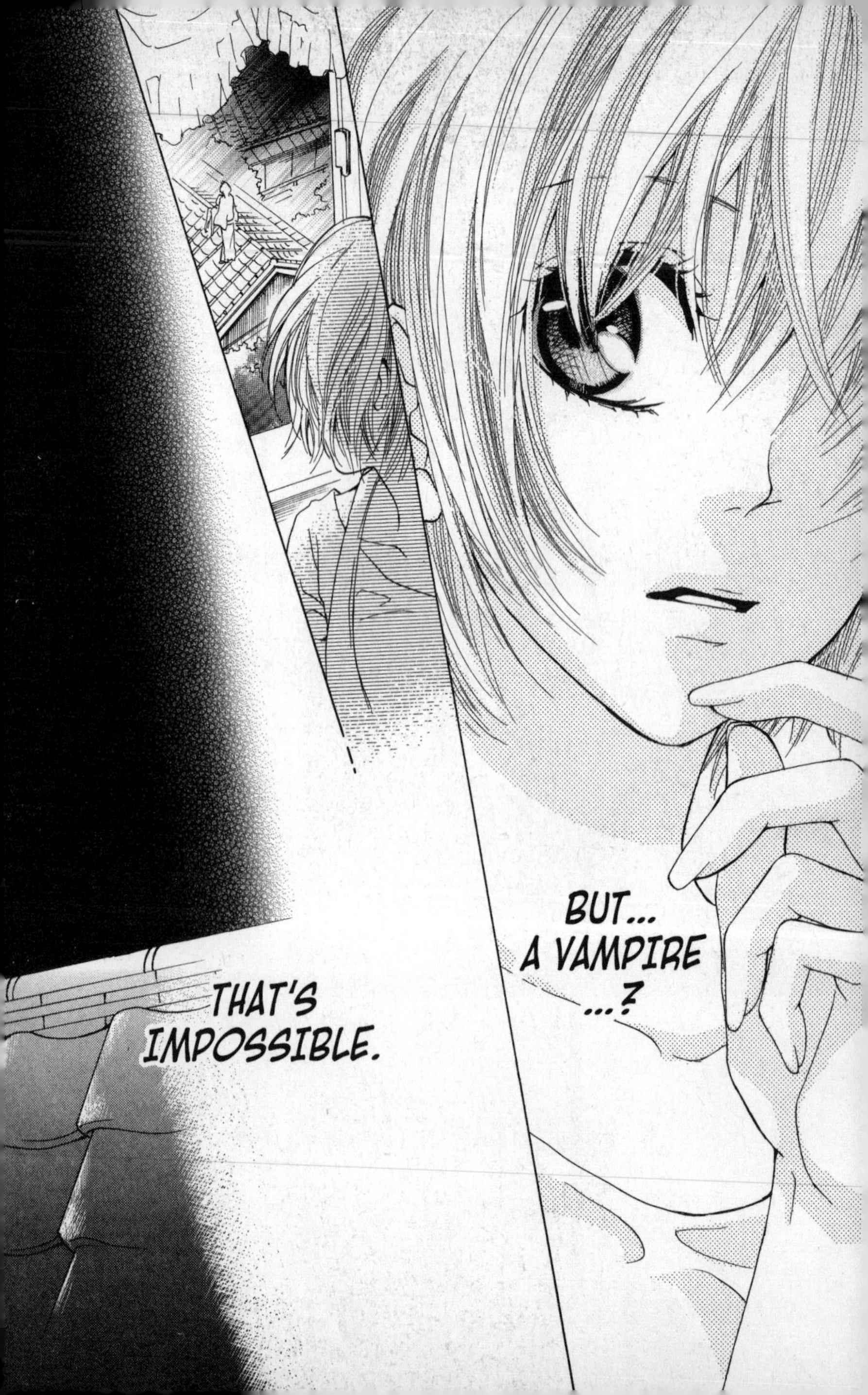
BUT... A VAMPIRE ...?
THAT'S IMPOSSIBLE.

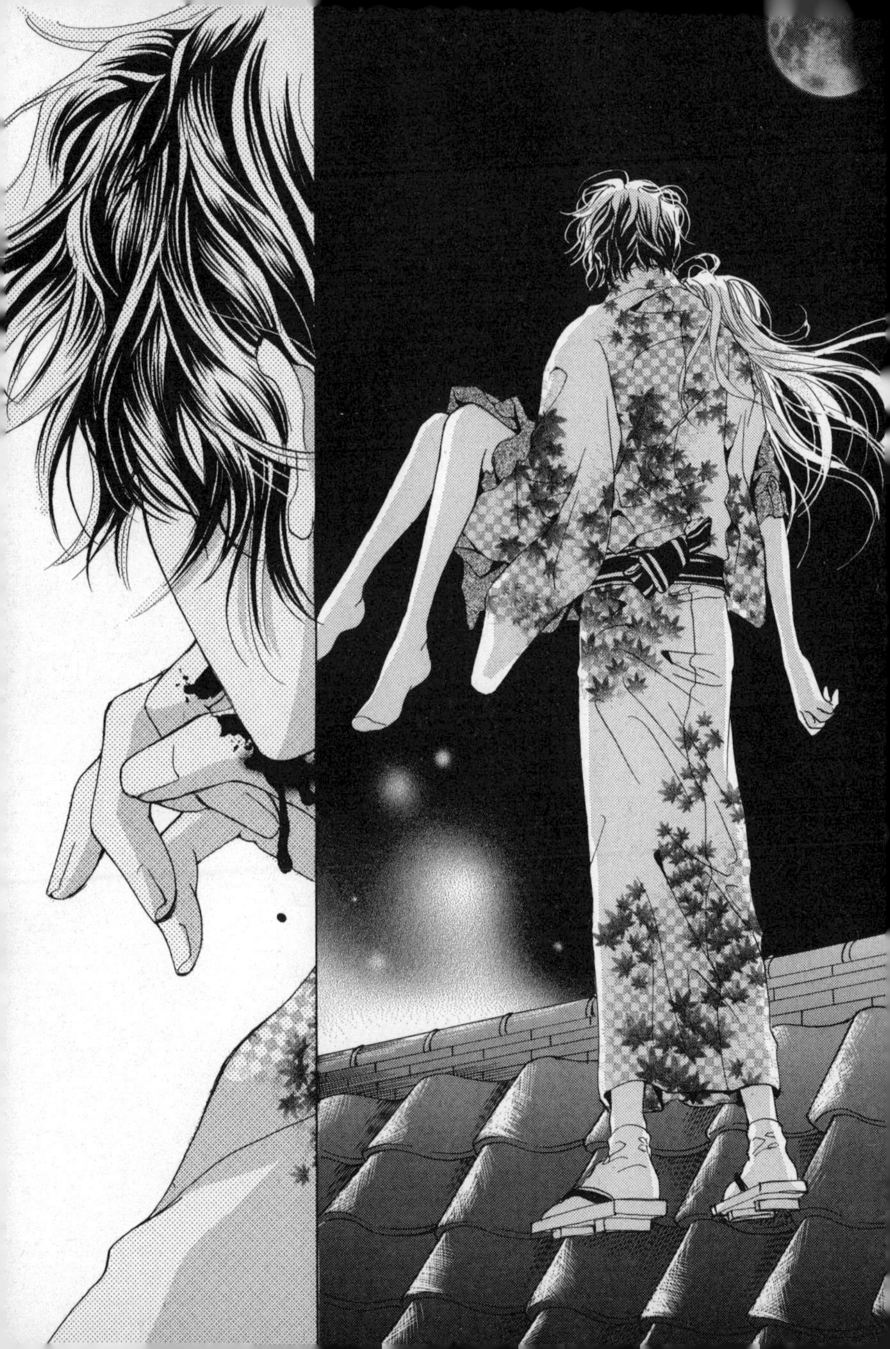

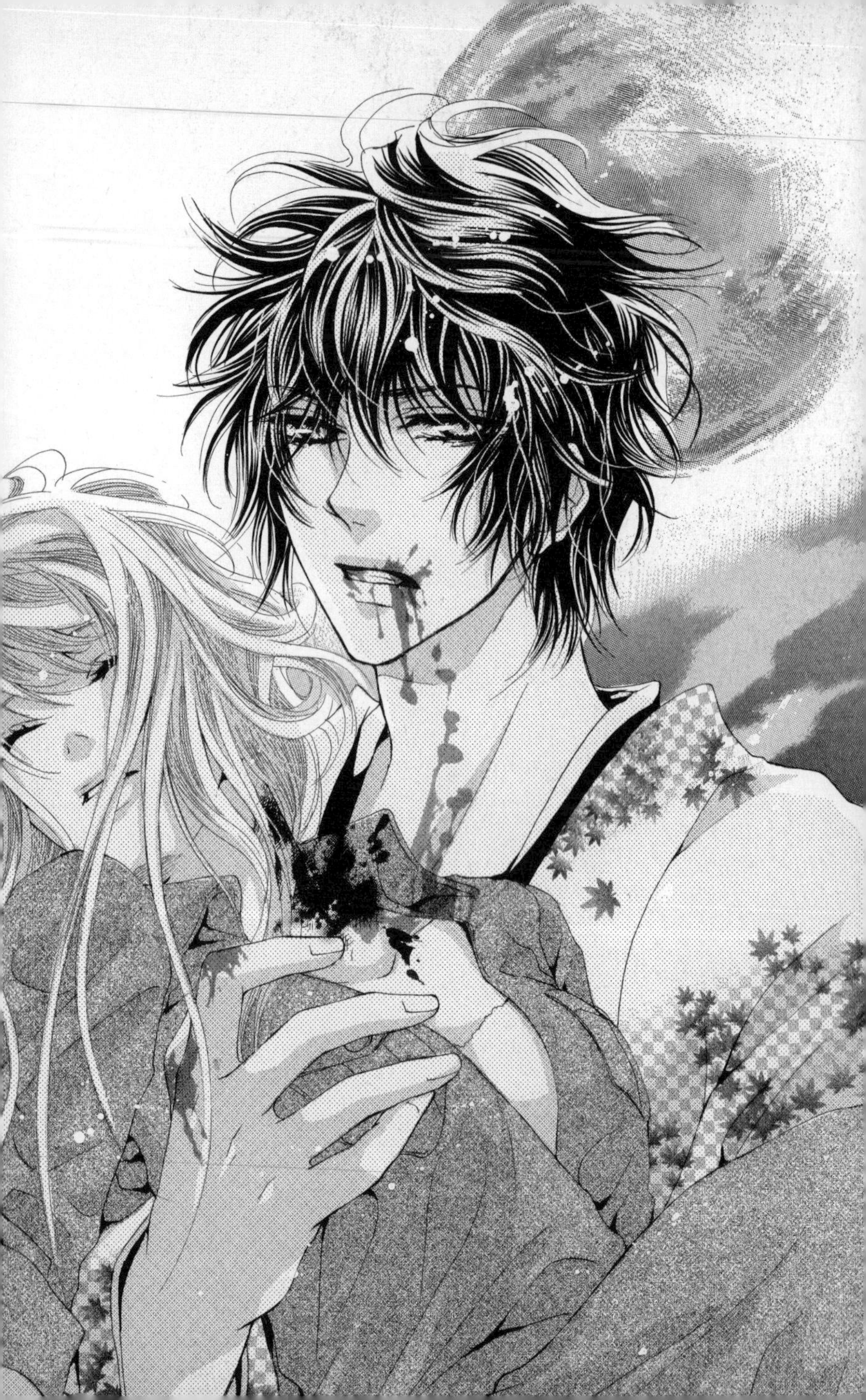

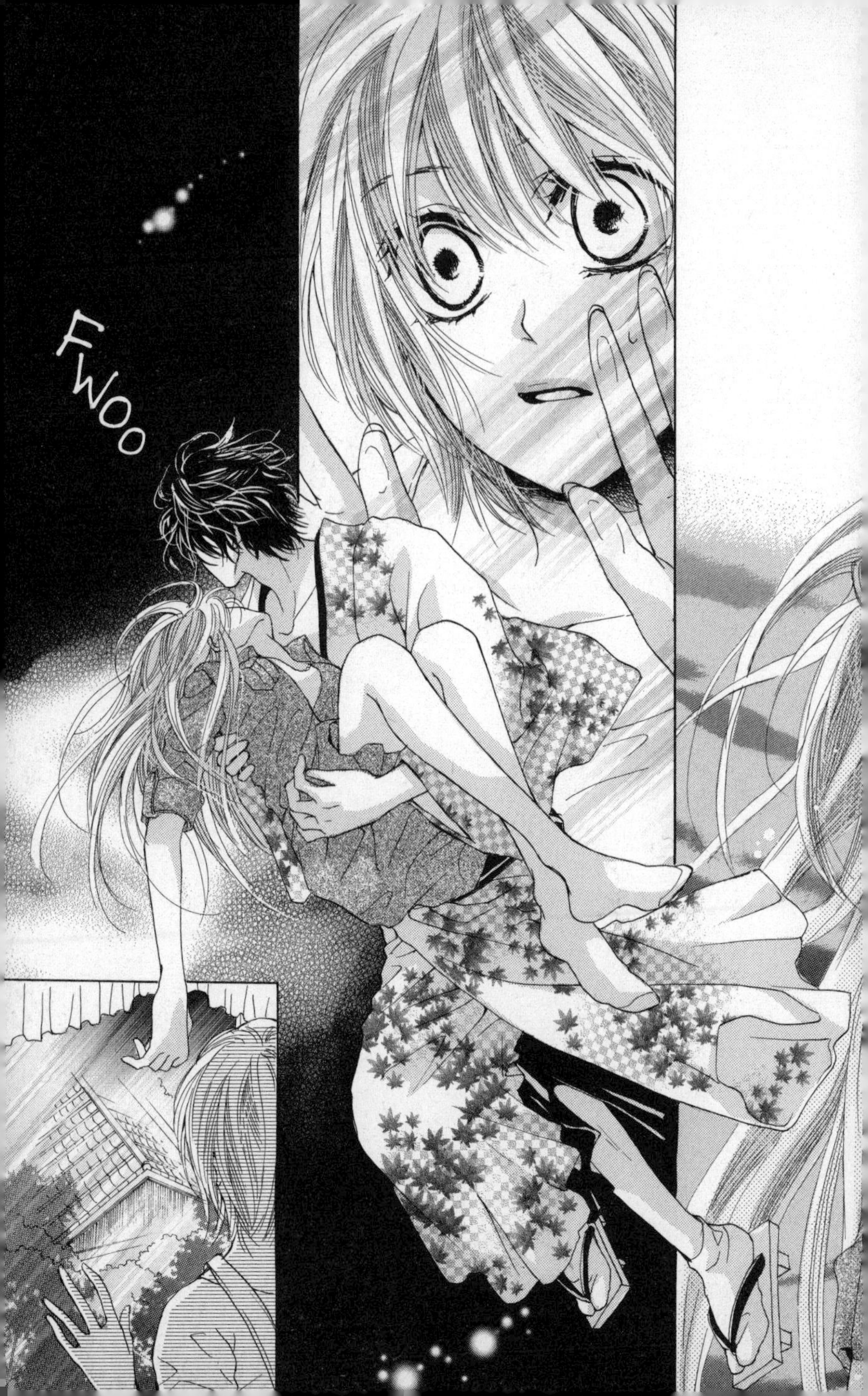
FWOO

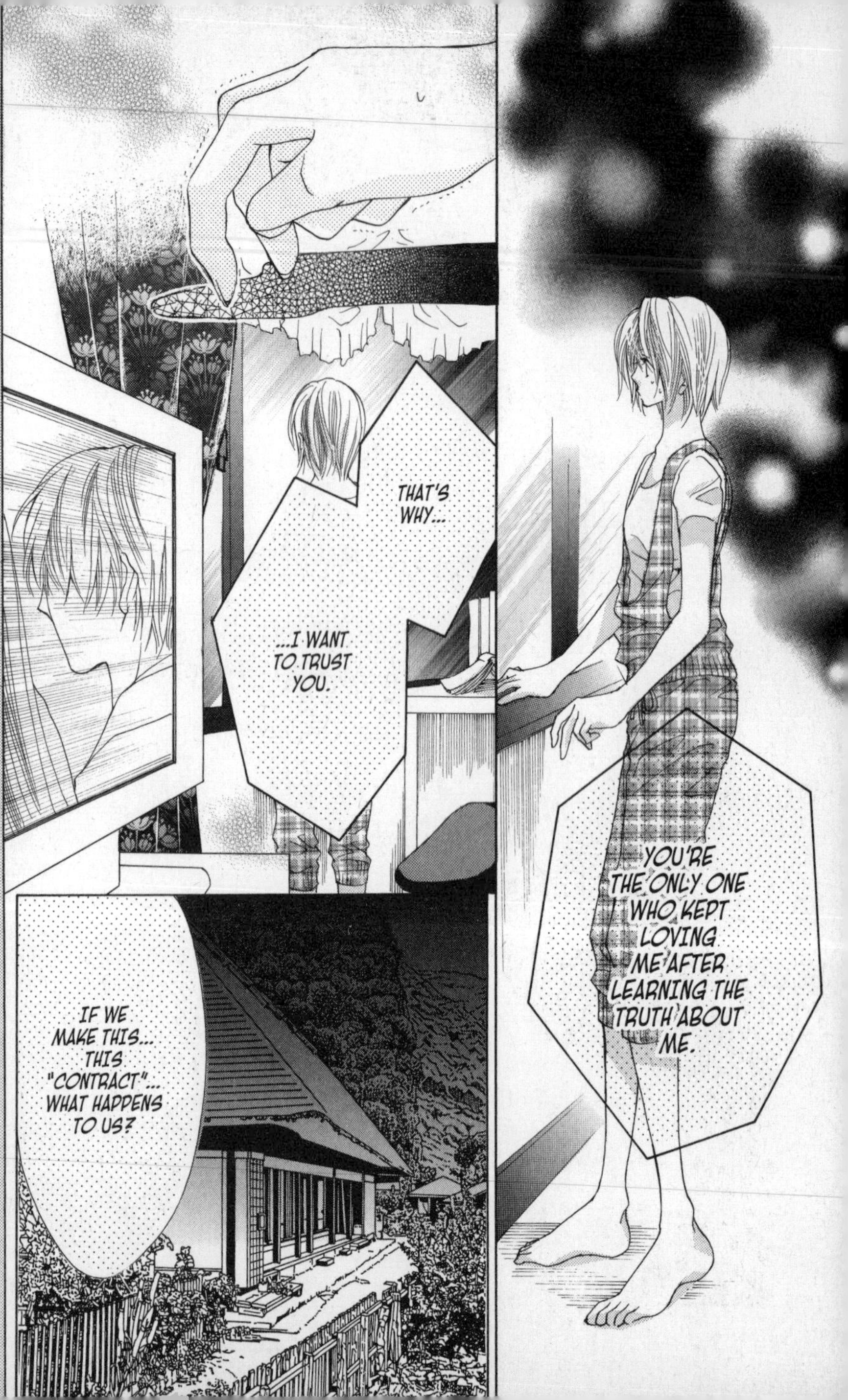
YOU'RE THE ONLY ONE WHO KEPT LOVING ME AFTER LEARNING THE TRUTH ABOUT ME.
THAT'S WHY...
...I WANT TO TRUST YOU.
IF WE MAKE THIS... THIS "CONTRACT"... WHAT HAPPENS TO US?

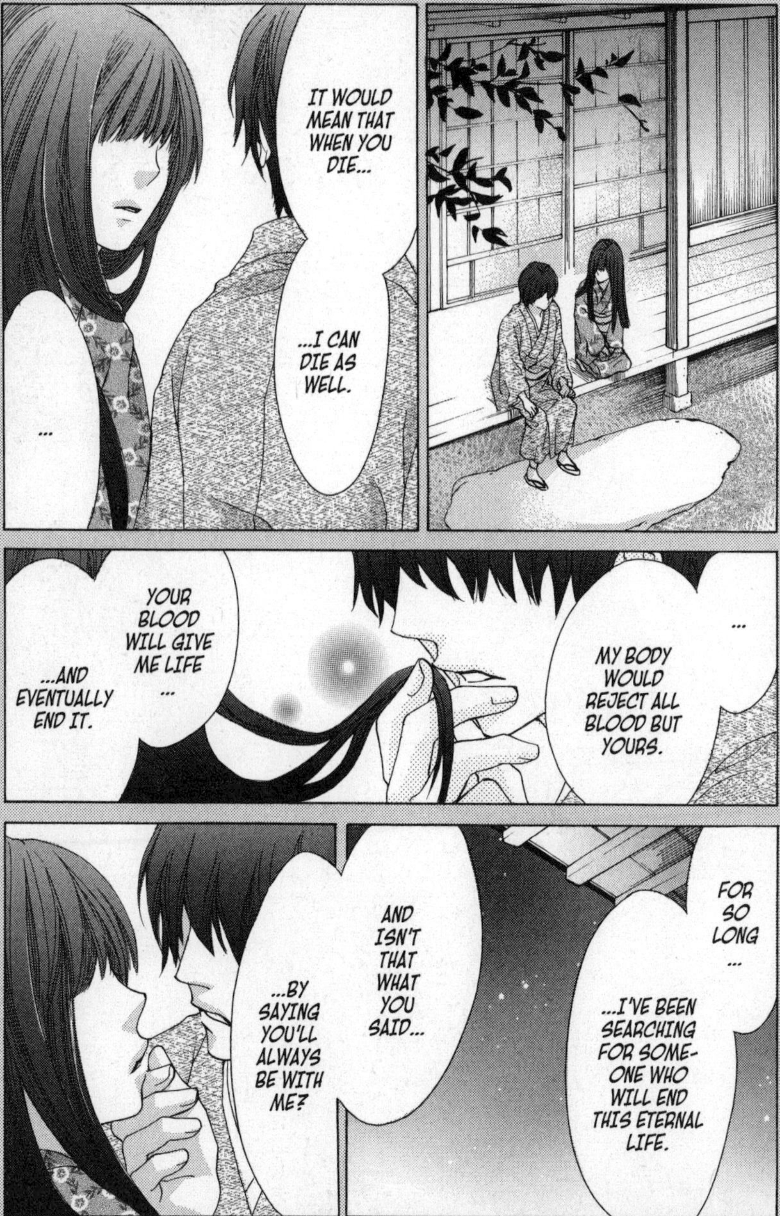
IT WOULD MEAN THAT WHEN YOU DIE...
...I CAN DIE AS WELL.
...
...
MY BODY WOULD REJECT ALL BLOOD BUT YOURS.
YOUR BLOOD WILL GIVE ME LIFE ...
...AND EVENTUALLY END IT.
FOR SO LONG ...
...I'VE BEEN SEARCHING FOR SOME-ONE WHO WILL END THIS ETERNAL LIFE.
AND ISN'T THAT WHAT YOU SAID...
...BY SAYING YOU'LL ALWAYS BE WITH ME?

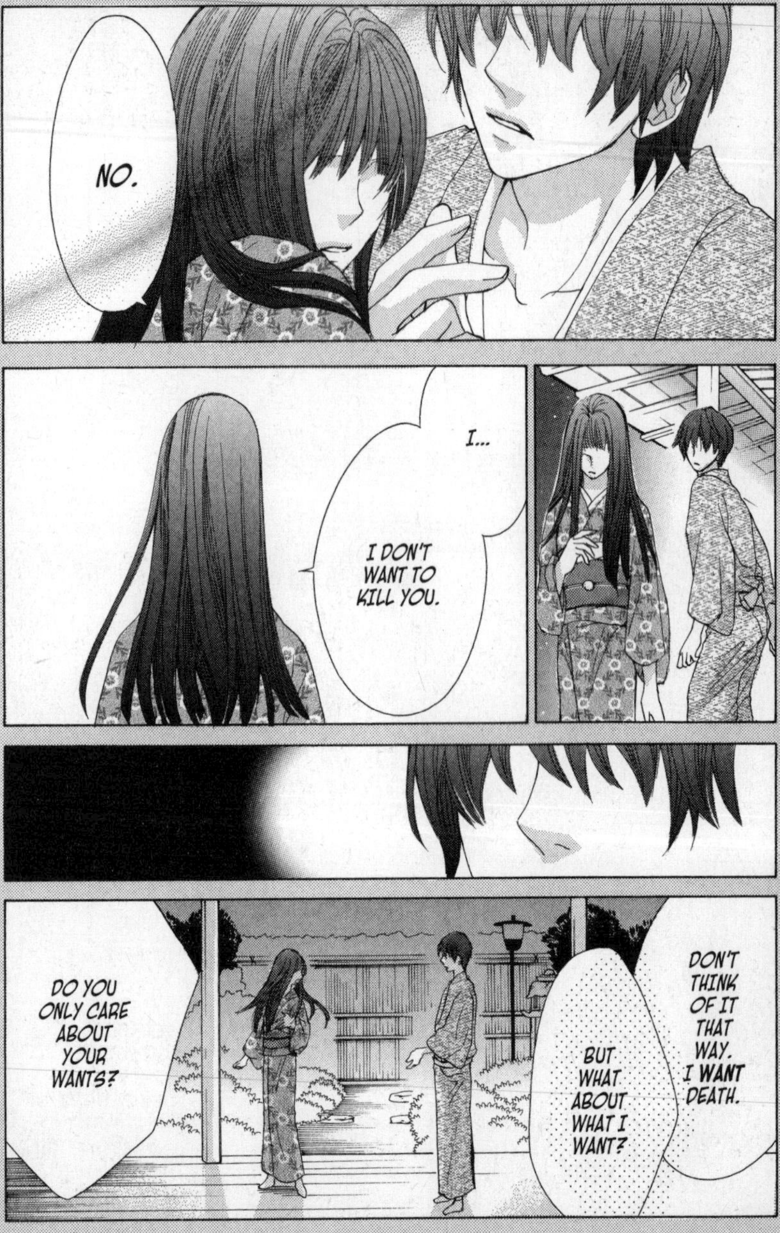
NO.
I...
I DON'T WANT TO KILL YOU.
DON'T THINK OF IT THAT WAY. I WANT DEATH.
BUT WHAT ABOUT WHAT I WANT?
DO YOU ONLY CARE ABOUT YOUR WANTS?

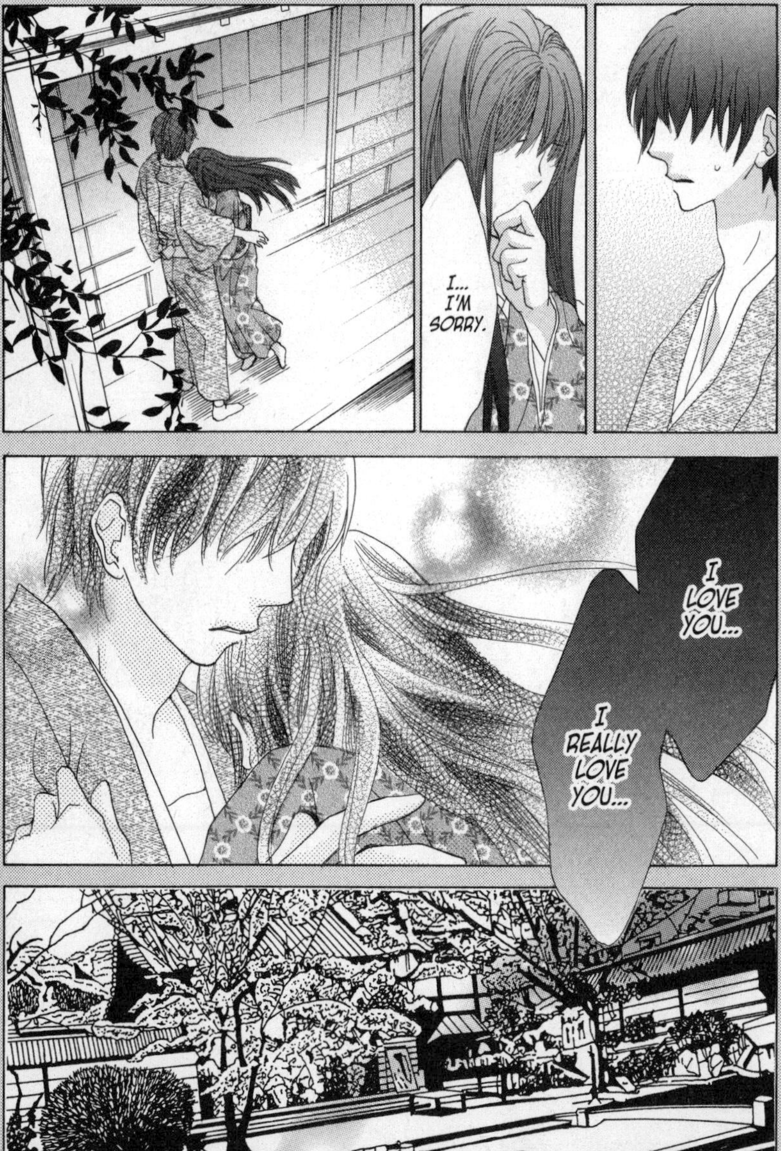
I... I'M SORRY.
I LOVE YOU...
I REALLY LOVE YOU...

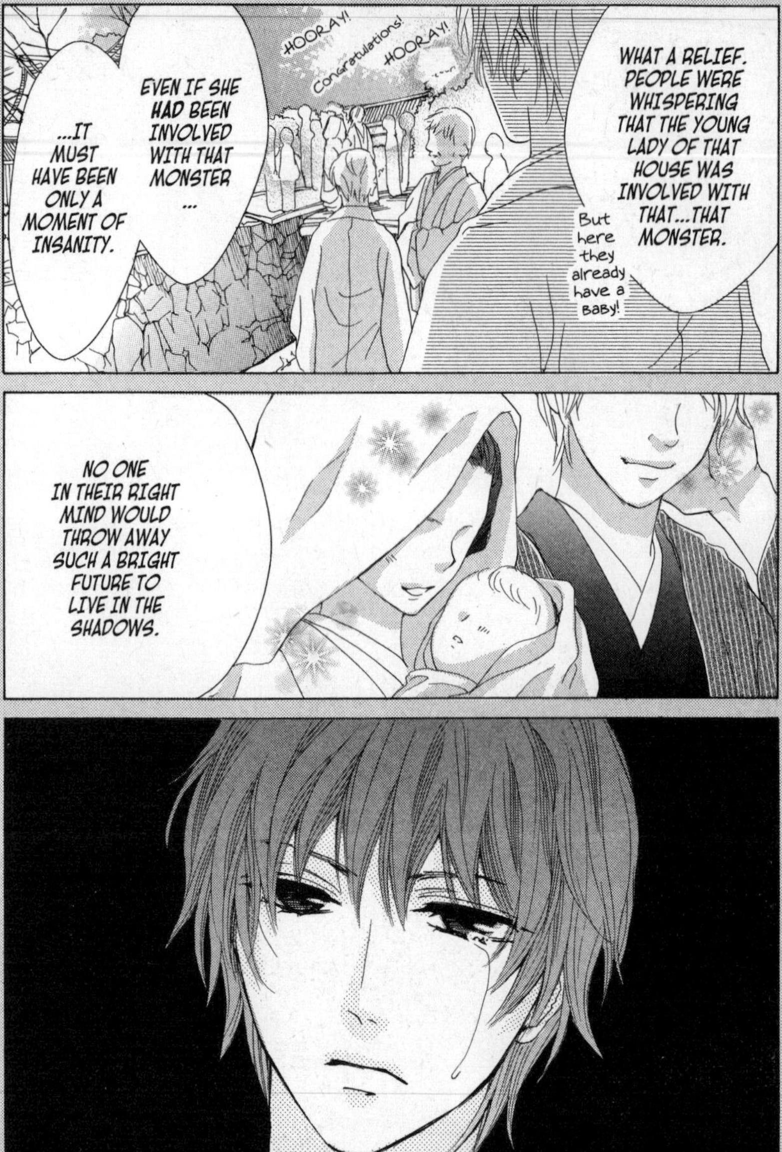
WHAT A RELIEF. PEOPLE WERE WHISPERING THAT THE YOUNG LADY OF THAT HOUSE WAS INVOLVED WITH THAT...THAT MONSTER.
But here they already have a baby!
HOORAY!
Congratulations!
HOORAY!
HOORAY!
EVEN IF SHE HAD BEEN INVOLVED WITH THAT MONSTER...
...IT MUST HAVE BEEN ONLY A MOMENT OF INSANITY.
NO ONE IN THEIR RIGHT MIND WOULD THROW AWAY SUCH A BRIGHT FUTURE TO LIVE IN THE SHADOWS.

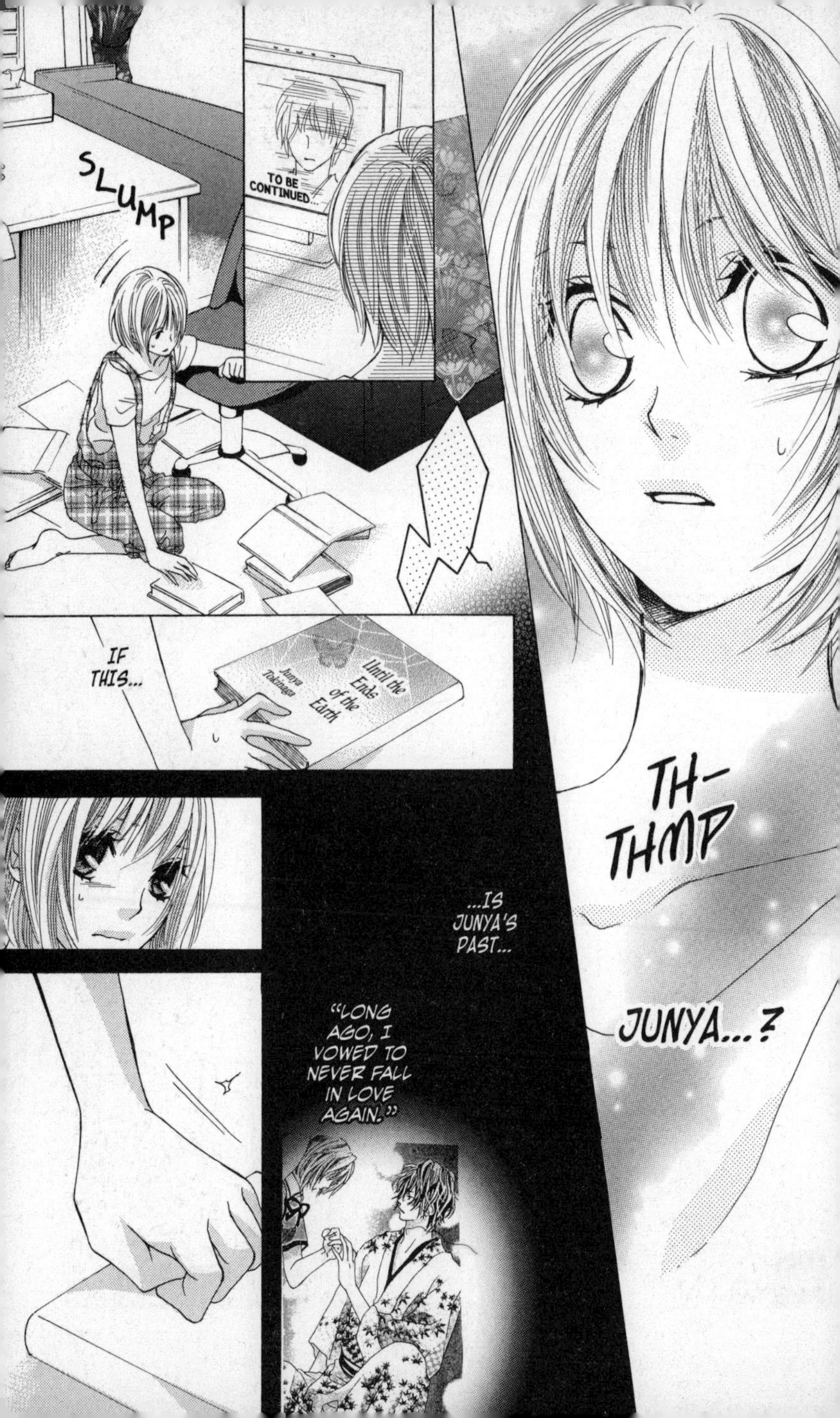
TH-THMP
JUNYA...?
TO BE CONTINUED...
SLUMP
IF THIS...
Until the Ends of the Earth
Junya Tokinaga
...IS JUNYA'S PAST...
"LONG AGO, I VOWED TO NEVER FALL IN LOVE AGAIN."

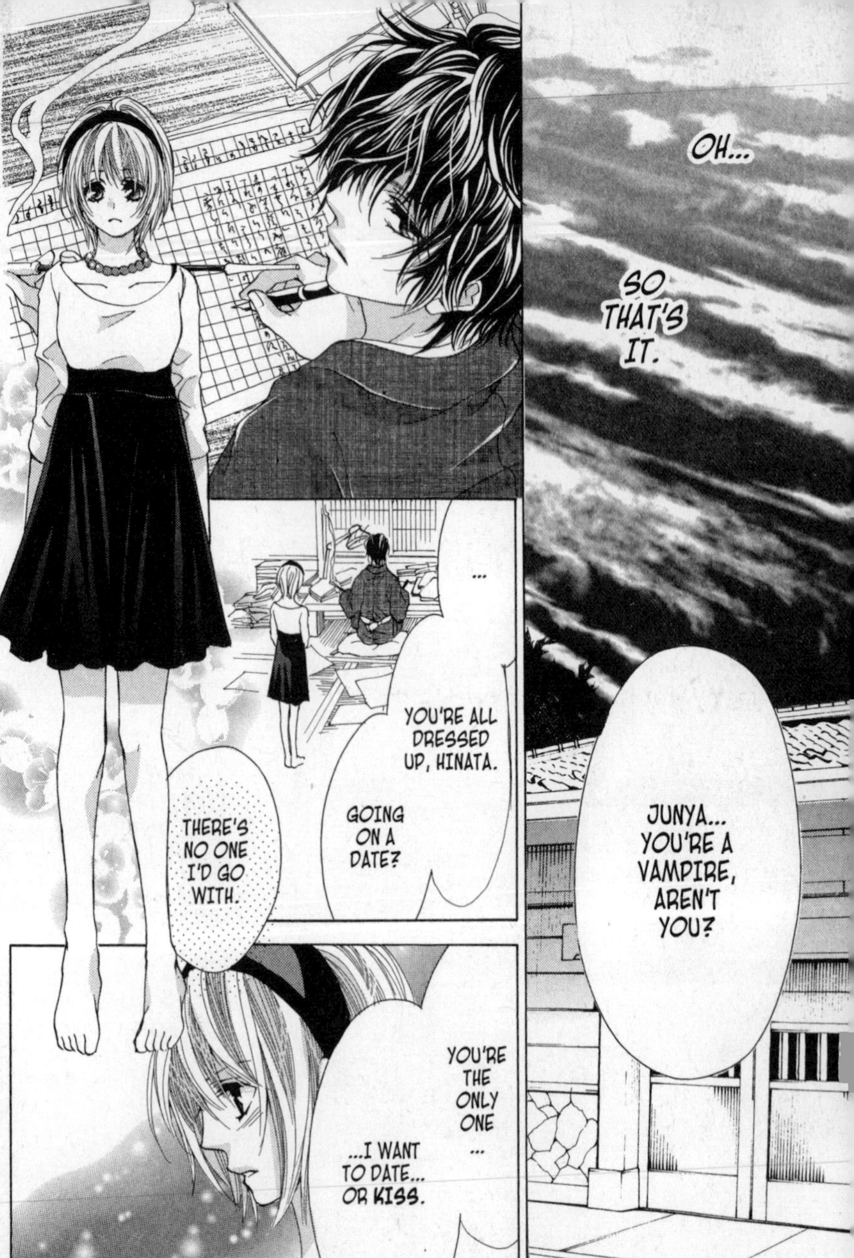
OH...
SO THAT'S IT.
JUNYA... YOU'RE A VAMPIRE, AREN'T YOU?
...
YOU'RE ALL DRESSED UP, HINATA.
GOING ON A DATE?
THERE'S NO ONE I'D GO WITH.
YOU'RE THE ONLY ONE ...
...I WANT TO DATE... OR KISS.

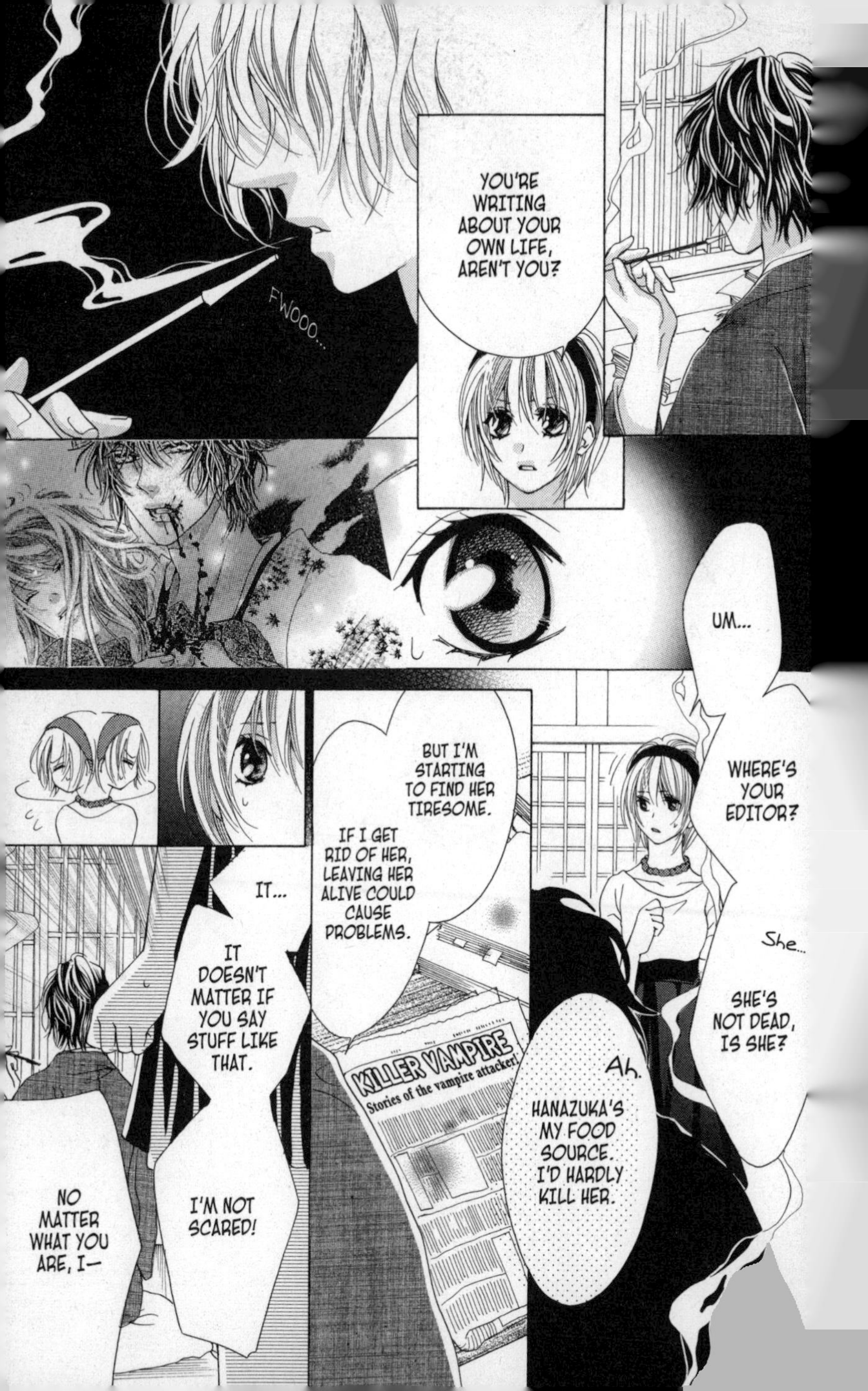
YOU'RE WRITING ABOUT YOUR OWN LIFE, AREN'T YOU?
FWOOO...
UM...
WHERE'S YOUR EDITOR?
She...
SHE'S NOT DEAD, IS SHE?
Ah.
HANAZUKA'S MY FOOD SOURCE. I'D HARDLY KILL HER.
BUT I'M STARTING TO FIND HER TIRESOME.
IF I GET RID OF HER, LEAVING HER ALIVE COULD CAUSE PROBLEMS.
KILLER VAMPIRE
Stories of the vampire attacker!
IT...
IT DOESN'T MATTER IF YOU SAY STUFF LIKE THAT.
I'M NOT SCARED!
NO MATTER WHAT YOU ARE, I—

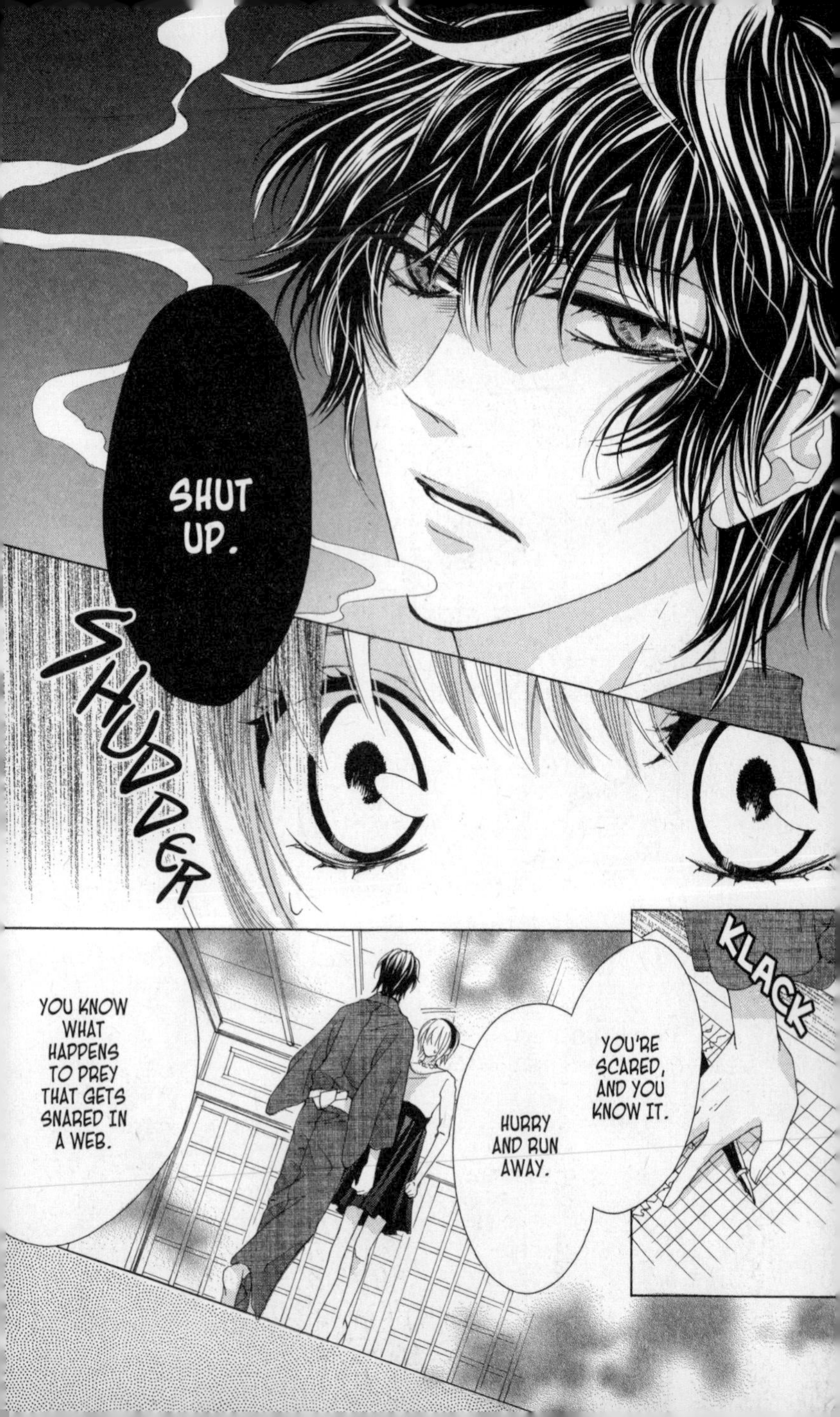
SHUT UP.
SHUDDER
KLACK
YOU'RE SCARED, AND YOU KNOW IT.
HURRY AND RUN AWAY.
YOU KNOW WHAT HAPPENS TO PREY THAT GETS SNARED IN A WEB.

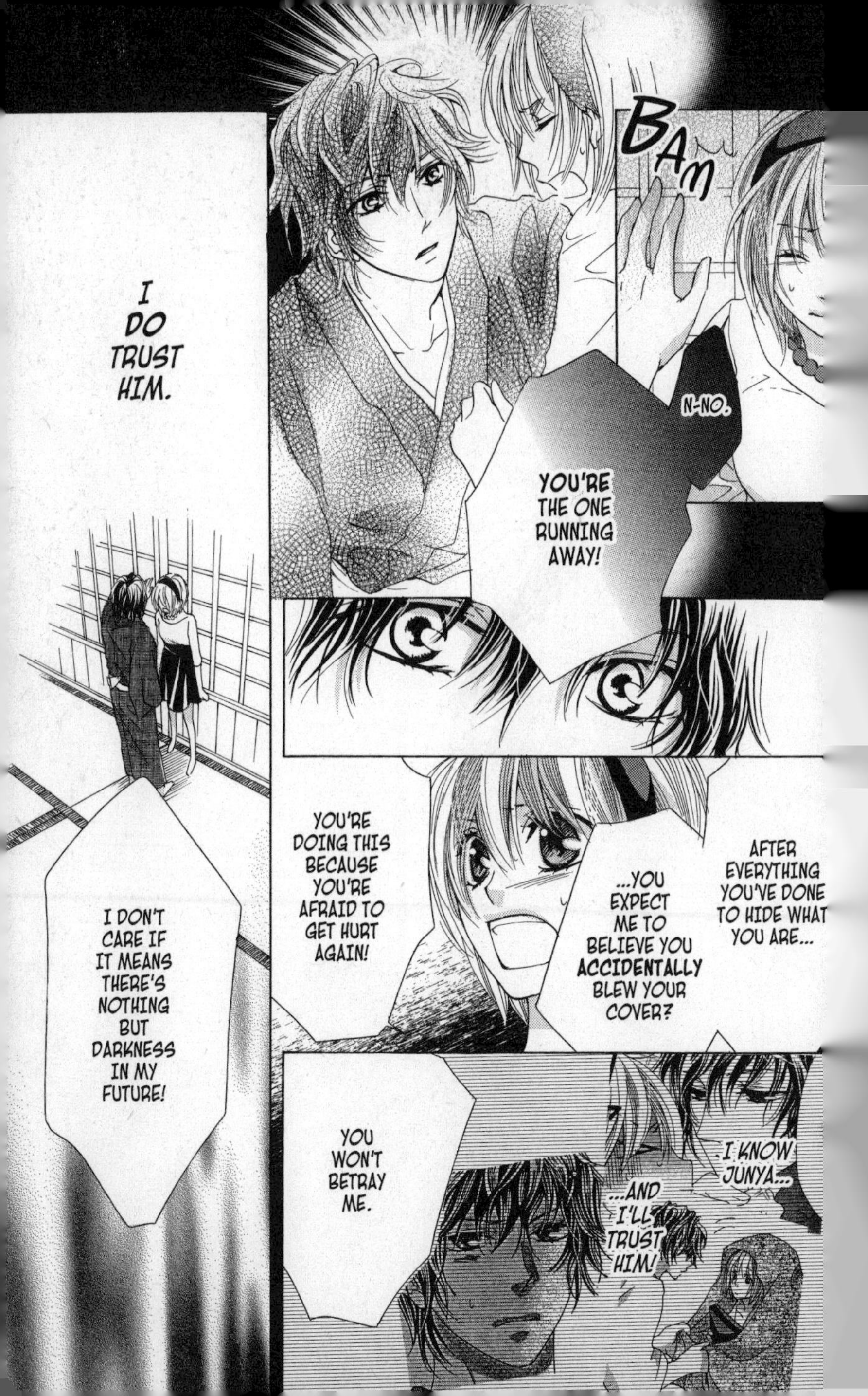
BAM
N-NO.
YOU'RE THE ONE RUNNING AWAY!
AFTER EVERYTHING YOU'VE DONE TO HIDE WHAT YOU ARE...
...YOU EXPECT ME TO BELIEVE YOU ACCIDENTALLY BLEW YOUR COVER?
YOU'RE DOING THIS BECAUSE YOU'RE AFRAID TO GET HURT AGAIN!
I KNOW JUNYA...
...AND I'LL TRUST HIM!
YOU WON'T BETRAY ME.
I DO TRUST HIM.
I DON'T CARE IF IT MEANS THERE'S NOTHING BUT DARKNESS IN MY FUTURE!

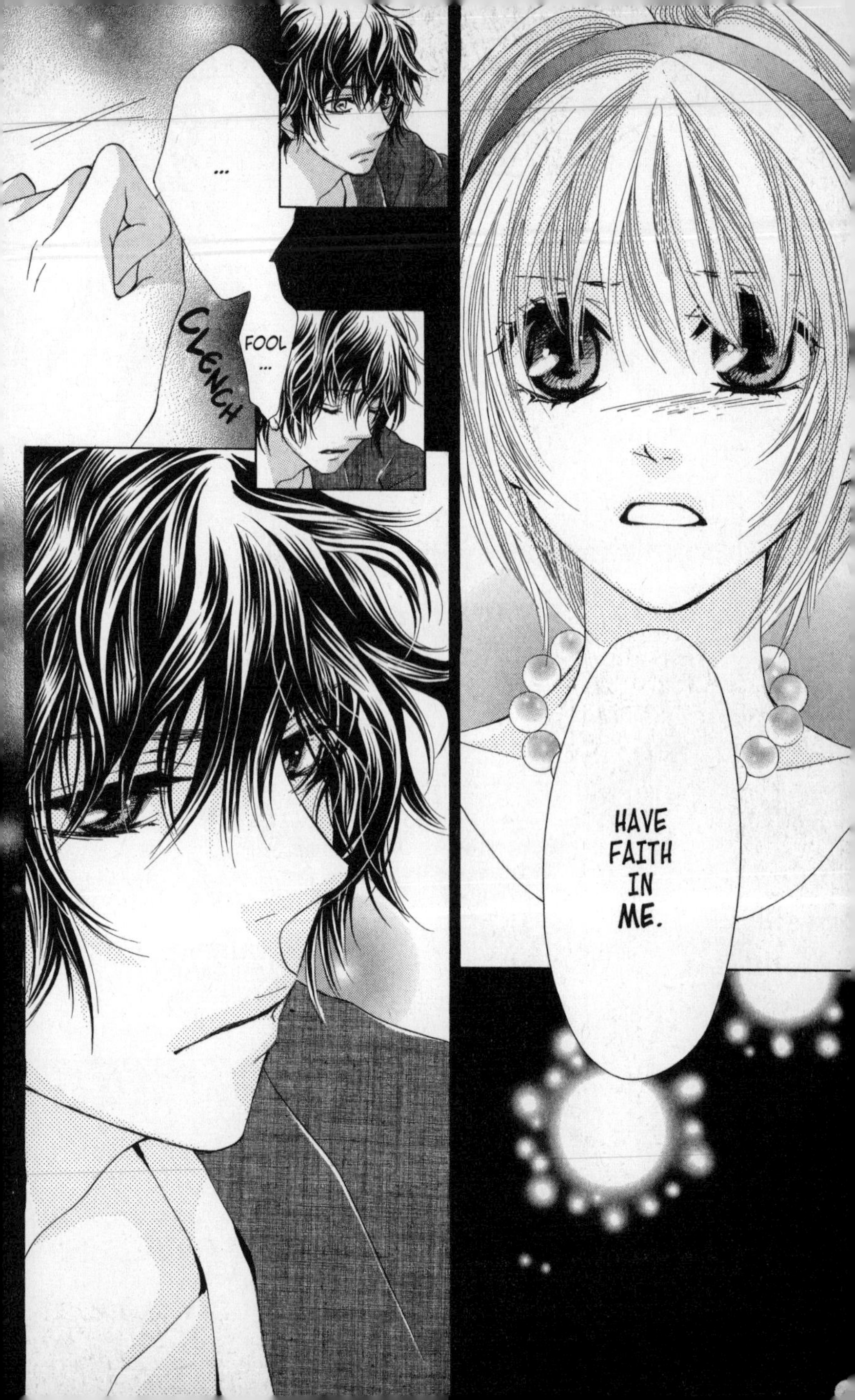
HAVE FAITH IN ME.
...
CLENCH
FOOL ...

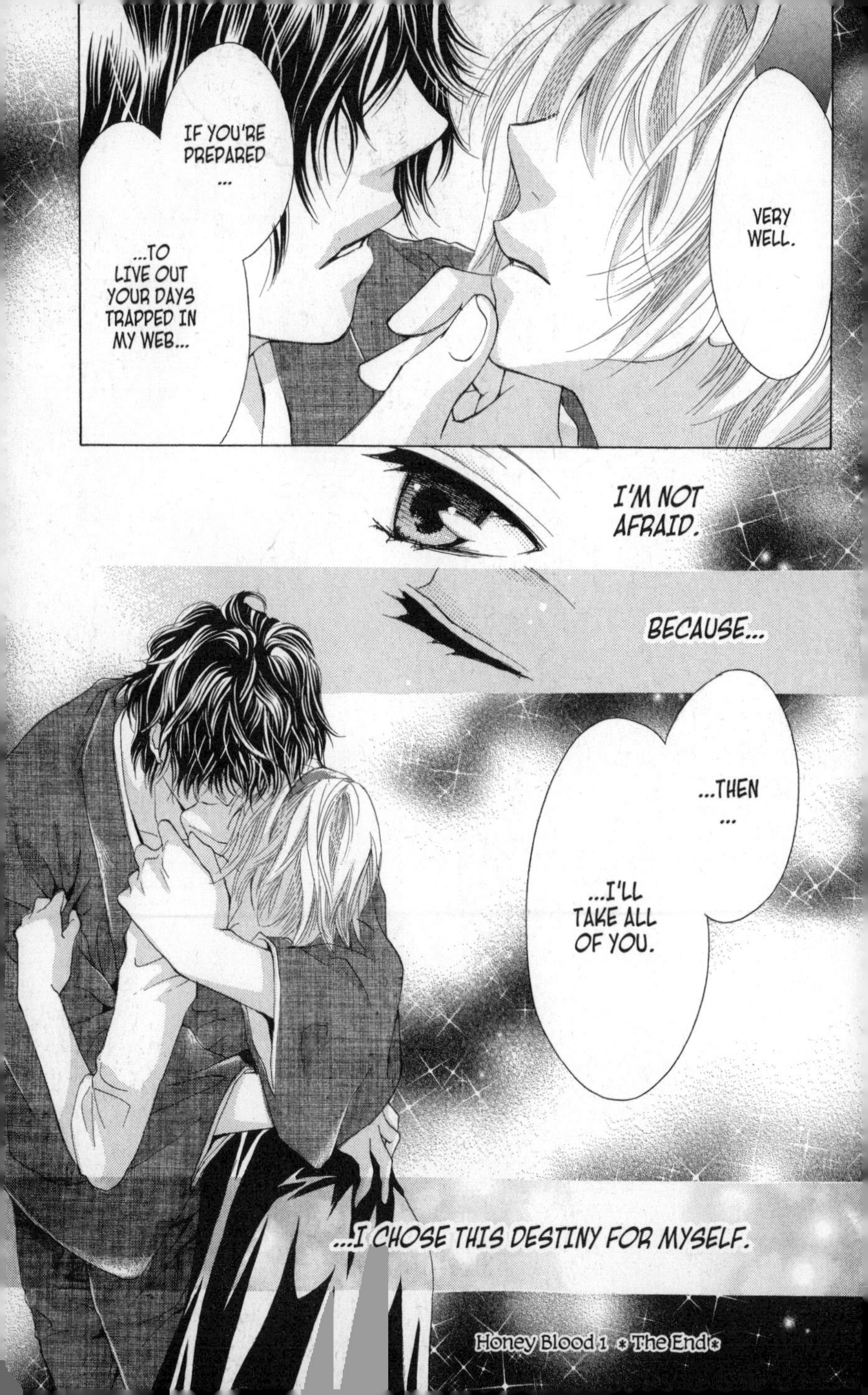
IF YOU'RE PREPARED ...
...TO LIVE OUT YOUR DAYS TRAPPED IN MY WEB...
VERY WELL.
I'M NOT AFRAID.
BECAUSE...
...THEN ...
...I'LL TAKE ALL OF YOU.
...I CHOSE THIS DESTINY FOR MYSELF.
Honey Blood 1 * The End *

Bonus Material!

Thank you for reading! I hope you liked it..
We'll get back to the serious events of
the main story in volume 2, but for now,
here are some silly bonus pages. Please
check them out if you have the time!

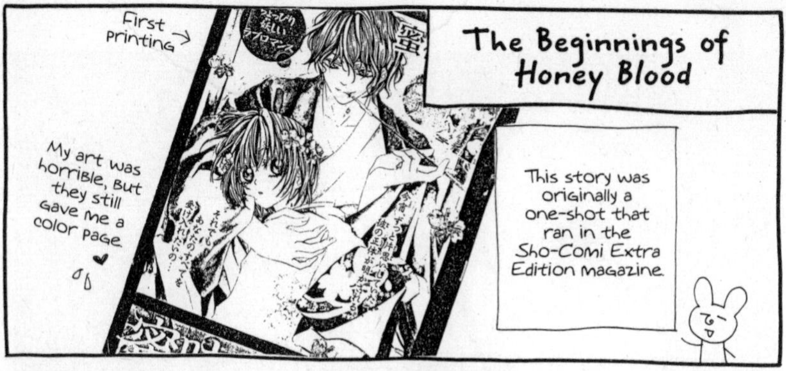
The Beginnings of Honey Blood
This story was originally a one-shot that ran in the Sho-Comi Extra Edition magazine.
First printing
My art was horrible, but they still gave me a color page.

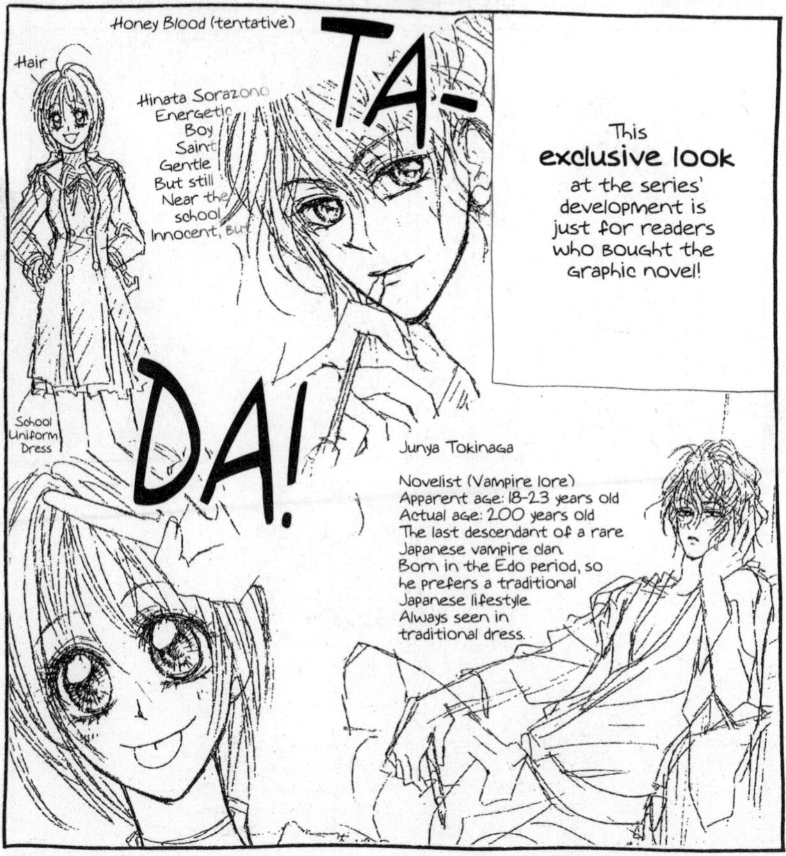
This exclusive look at the series' development is just for readers who bought the graphic novel!
TA-DA!
Honey Blood (tentative)
Hair
Hinata Sorazono
Energetic
Boy
Saint
Gentle
But still
Near the
school
Innocent, but
School Uniform Dress
Junya Tokinaga
Novelist (Vampire lore)
Apparent age: 18-23 years old
Actual age: 200 years old
The last descendant of a rare Japanese vampire clan.
Born in the Edo period, so he prefers a traditional Japanese lifestyle.
Always seen in traditional dress.

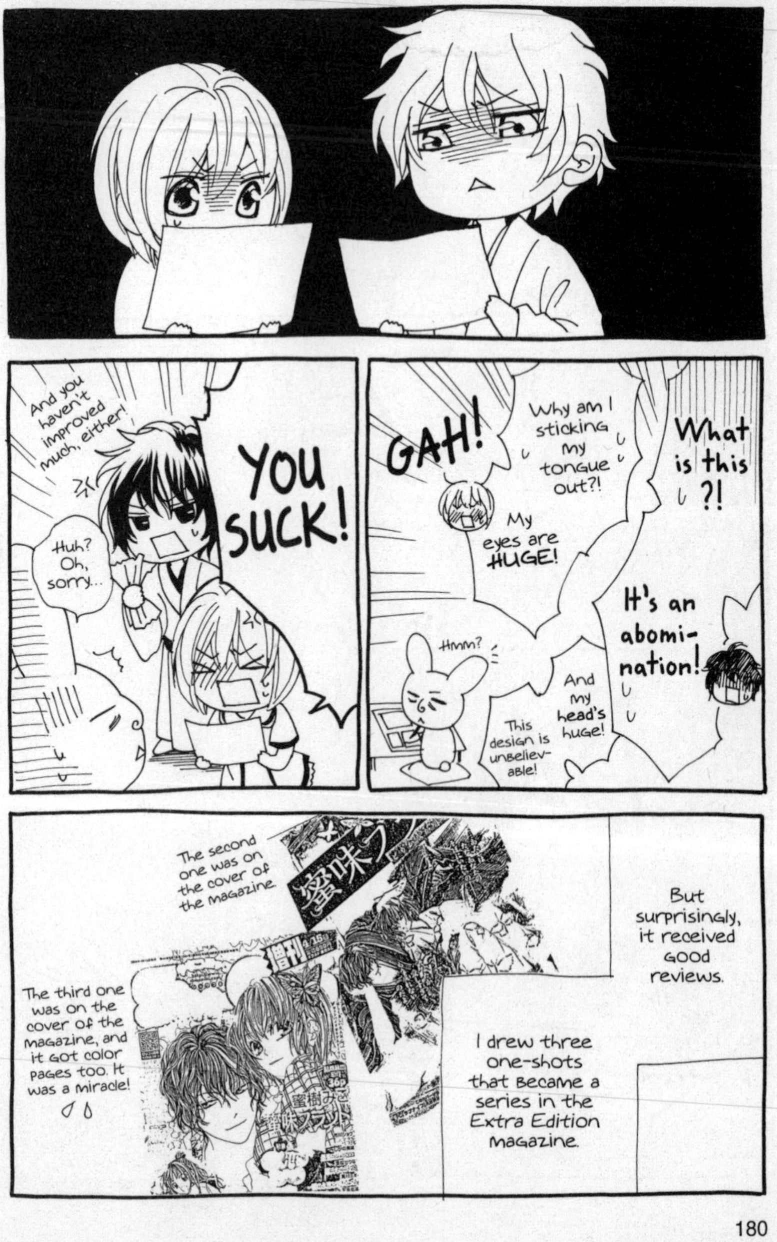
What is this ?!
Why am I sticking my tongue out?!
GAH!
My eyes are HUGE!
It's an abomination!
Hmm?
And my head's huge!
This design is unbeliev-able!
YOU SUCK!
And you haven't improved much, either!
Huh? Oh, sorry...
But surprisingly, it received good reviews.
I drew three one-shots that became a series in the Extra Edition magazine.
The second one was on the cover of the magazine.
The third one was on the cover of the magazine, and it got color pages too. It was a miracle!

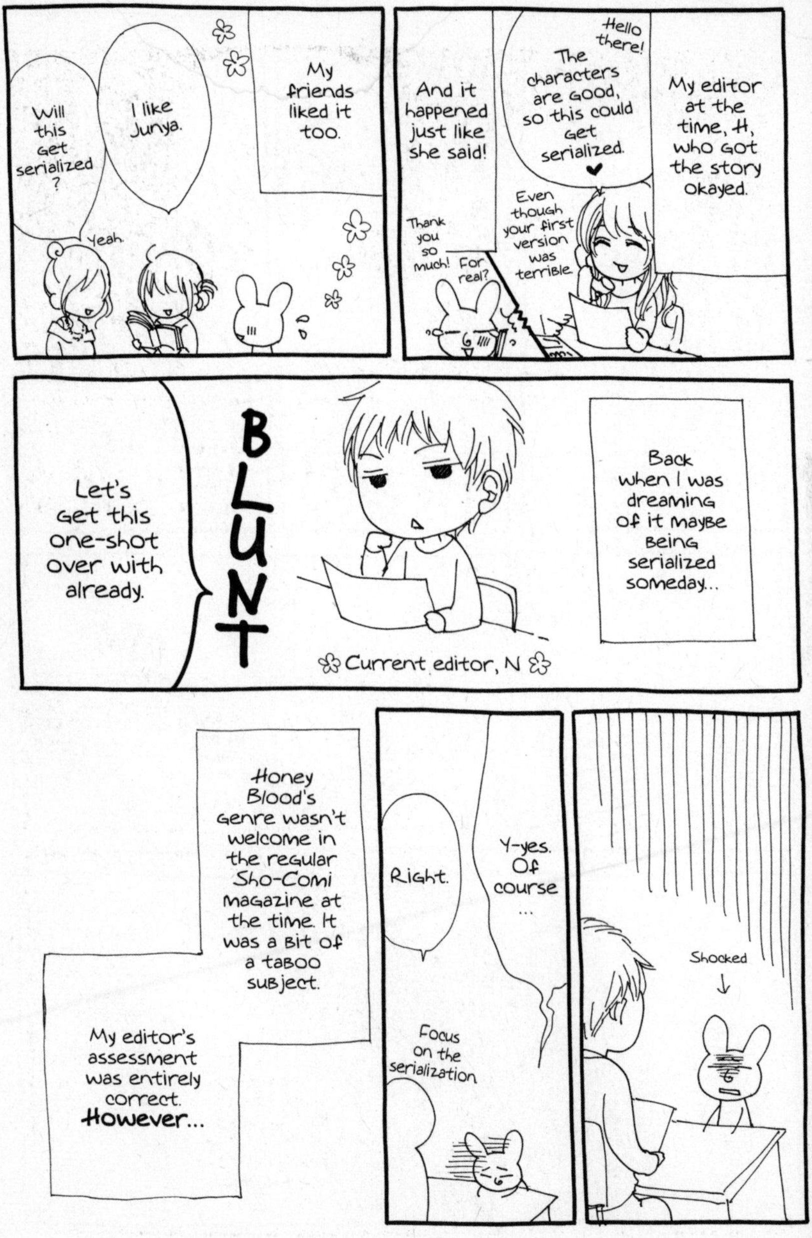
My editor at the time, H, who got the story okayed.
Hello there!
The characters are good, so this could get serialized. ♥
Even though your first version was terrible.
And it happened just like she said!
Thank you so much!
For real?
My friends liked it too.
I like Junya.
Will this get serialized?
Yeah.
Back when I was dreaming of it maybe being serialized someday...
BLUNT
Let's get this one-shot over with already.
Current editor, N
Shocked
Y-yes. Of course...
Right.
Focus on the serialization
Honey Blood's genre wasn't welcome in the regular Sho-Comi magazine at the time. It was a bit of a taboo subject.
My editor's assessment was entirely correct. **However...**

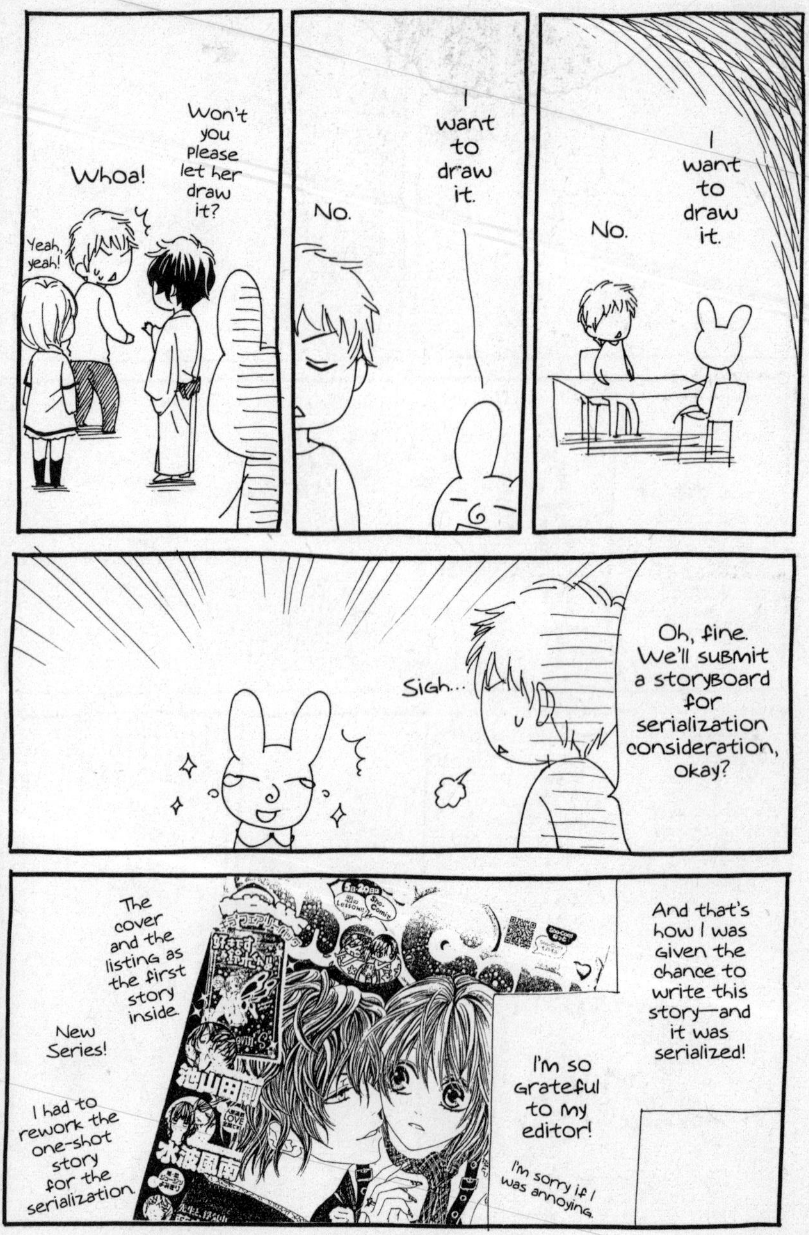
I want to draw it.
No.
I want to draw it.
No.
Won't you please let her draw it?
Whoa!
Yeah, yeah!
Oh, fine. We'll submit a storyboard for serialization consideration, okay?
Sigh...
And that's how I was given the chance to write this story—and it was serialized!
I'm so grateful to my editor!
I'm sorry if I was annoying.
The cover and the listing as the first story inside.
New Series!
I had to rework the one-shot story for the serialization.

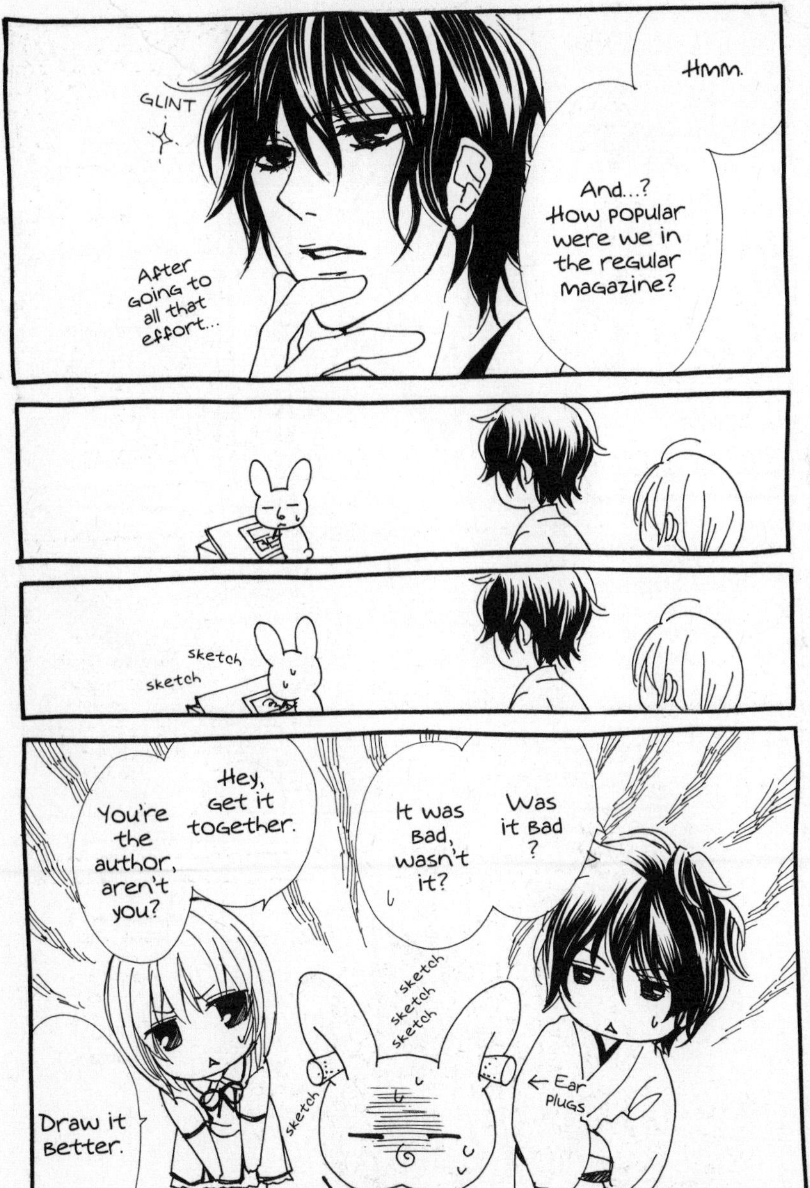

Hmm.
And...? How popular were we in the regular magazine?
GLINT
After going to all that effort...
sketch
sketch
Was it bad?
It was bad, wasn't it?
Hey, get it together.
You're the author, aren't you?
sketch sketch sketch
← Ear plugs
sketch
Draw it better.

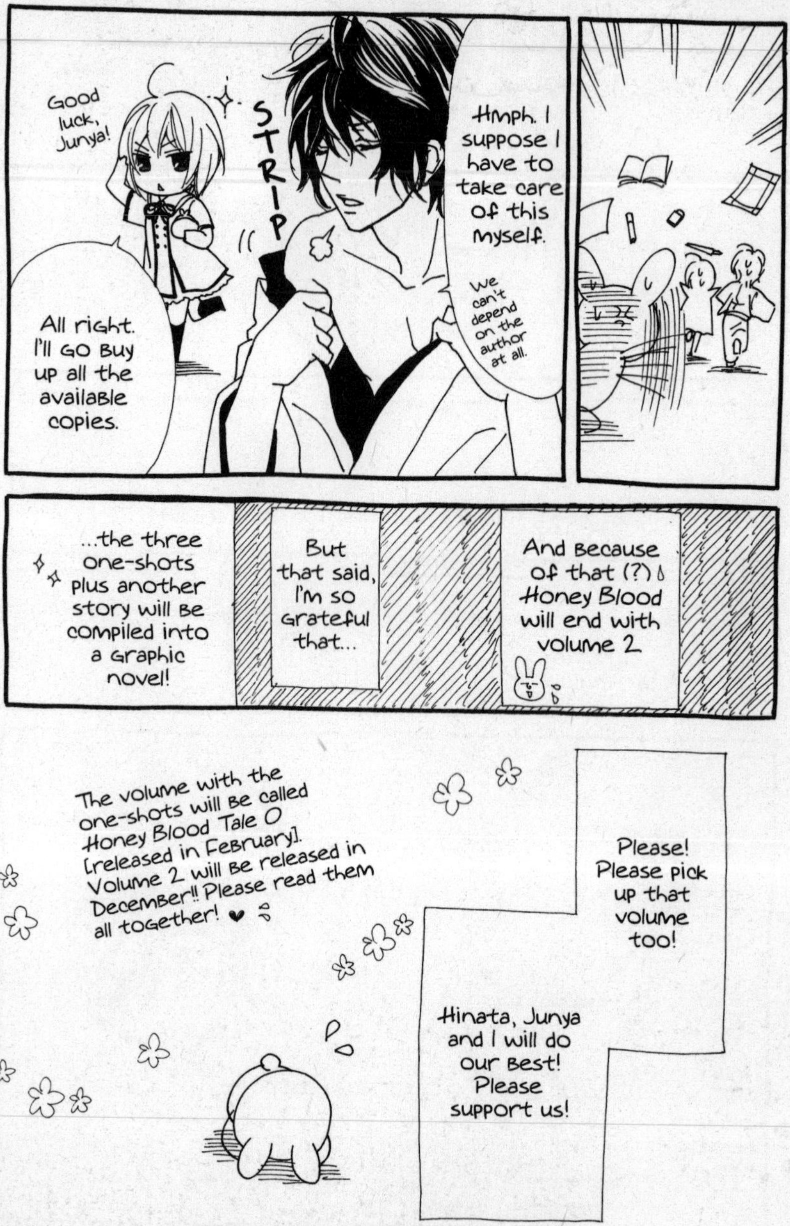
Hmph. I suppose I have to take care of this myself.
We can't depend on the author at all.
STRIP
Good luck, Junya!
All right. I'll go buy up all the available copies.
And because of that (?) Honey Blood will end with volume 2.
But that said, I'm so grateful that...
...the three one-shots plus another story will be compiled into a graphic novel!
Please! Please pick up that volume too!
Hinata, Junya and I will do our best! Please support us!
The volume with the one-shots will be called Honey Blood Tale 0 [released in February]. Volume 2 will be released in December!! Please read them all together!

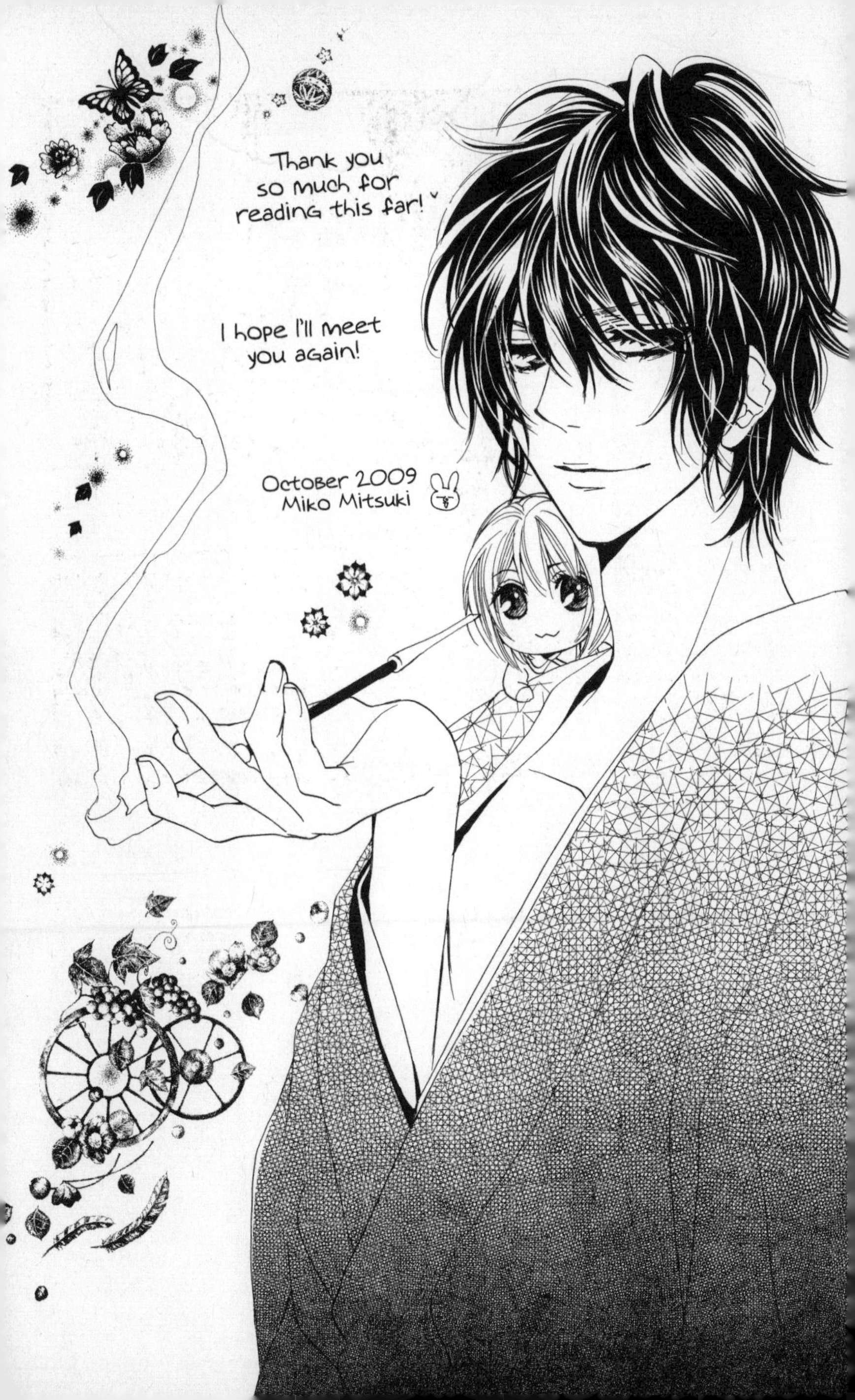
Thank you so much for reading this far!
I hope I'll meet you again!
October 2009
Miko Mitsuki

Special Thanks ♥

· Editor ·
Nakamura

· Assistants ·
Alice Kuon
Hana Mizuki
Aki Momigi

The editorial staff at
Sho-Comi magazine

My family and friends

Everyone who was
involved with the
making of this manga

The
❀ lovely ❀
readers!

Thank you from the
bottom of my heart! ♥

Miko Mitsuki
c/o Honey Blood Editor
Viz Media
P.O. Box 77010
San Francisco, CA 94107

❀ I'd love to hear from you! ♥

Author Bio

Born on October 10, Miko
Mitsuki debuted with *Utakata*
in 2003. She is currently
working on projects for *Sho-Comi* magazine. Mitsuki is
from Kagoshima Prefecture in
Japan, and her blood type is
O. She loves cats the most but
loves dogs as well.

Honey Blood

VOLUME 1
Shojo Beat Edition

**STORY AND ART BY
MIKO MITSUKI**

MITSUAJI BLOOD Vol. 1
by Miko MITSUKI
© 2009 Miko MITSUKI
All rights reserved.
Original Japanese edition published by SHOGAKUKAN.
English translation rights in the United States of America,
Canada, the United Kingdom,
and Ireland arranged with SHOGAKUKAN.

English Adaptation/Ysabet Reinhardt MacFarlane
Translation/pinkie-chan
Touch-up Art & Lettering/Joanna Estep
Design/Izumi Evers
Editor/Amy Yu

Printed in the U.S.A.

Published by VIZ Media, LLC
P.O. Box 77010
San Francisco, CA 94107

10 9 8 7 6 5 4 3 2 1
First printing, October 2014

www.viz.com   www.shojobeat.com